KAILAS MANASAROVAR

KAILAS MANASAROVAR

SWAMI PRANAVANANDA

NANHI
PUBLISHING HOUSE
New Delhi – 110052 (India)

NANHI
PUBLISHING HOUSE

Nanhi Shop Publications
B-195, J.J. Colony,
Wazirpur, Ashok Vihar Phase –IV,
New Delhi-110052 ... Phone: +91-9990860860
www.nanhibooks.com
E-mail: Nanhishop@gmail.com

ISBN: 978-93-7865-914-0 (HB)
978-93-7865-785-6 (PB)

First Published, 1949

Reprinted in 2026

Printed at: M. Enterprises, Delhi.

The Holy Mount Kailas [*See pp.* 6 & 13

The Holy Mount Kailas and Lake Manasa-sarovar
Photo by Courtesy of Mr. Salim Ali (Bombay) [*See p.* 7

KAILĀS - MĀNASARŌVAR

SWAMI PRANAVĀNANDA, F.R.G.S.

(Of the Holy Kailas and Manasarovar)

FOREWORD
BY

The Hon'ble Shree PANDIT JAWAHARLAL NEHRU,
Prime Minister of India

S. P. League, Ltd.,
Calcutta
1949

1. His Holiness Shree 1108 Narayana Swamiji Maharaj. Shree Narayana Ashrama, Himalayas

[See p. 99

DEDICATED

TO

HIS HOLINESS SHREE 1108 NARAYANA SWAMIJI MAHARAJ

OF

Shree Narayana Ashrama (Soosa, Himalayas, District
Almora), as a token of Love and Admiration
for the keen interest he has been taking for
the spiritual uplift of the people of the
Himalayas in general, and for the
particular interest he evinces in
the Author's activities in
KAILAS-MANASAROVAR REGION
OM !

CONTENTS

	Page
Foreword - - - -	xvii
Preface - - - -	xix

FIRST WAVE

A TWELVE-MONTH ON THE HOLY KAILAS AND LAKE MANASA-SAROVAR

Chapter 1

MOUNT KAILAS AND LAKE MANASAROVAR

THE HIMALAYAS - - - -	3
SIGNIFICANCE OF PLACES OF PILGRIMAGE - -	5
MOUNT KAILAS AND LAKE MANASAROVAR - -	6
TIBETAN AND HINDU MYTHOLOGY - - -	8
PARIKRAMA - - - -	10
NEW LIGHT ON THE SOURCES OF THE FOUR GREAT RIVERS OF THE HOLY KAILAS AND MANASAROVAR - -	14
RAKSHAS TAL - - - -	17
GANGA CHHU - - - -	18
ISLANDS IN RAKSHAS TAL - - -	19
DESCRIPTION OF MANASAROVAR - - -	21
LOTUS AND ROYAL SWANS - - -	22
MAHATMAS AND TIBETAN MYSTICS - - -	25

Chapter II

FREEZING OF MANASAROVAR

TEMPERATURE READINGS - - -	27
EARLY PREMONITIONS - - - -	27
ACTUAL FREEZING OF THE LAKE - - -	27
FISSURES AND SOUNDS IN THE LAKE - -	29
LAKE MANAS AND RAKSHAS—A CONTRAST - -	29
PECULIAR SURFACE PHENOMENA - - -	32

Chapter III

MELTING OF MANASAROVAR

EARLY PREMONITIONS - - - -	35
FINAL BREAKING OF THE ICE IN THE LAKE - -	36
EPILOGUE - - - -	37

SECOND WAVE

KAILAS-MANASAROVAR REGION

CHAPTER I

	Page
PHYSIOGRAPHY	
TIBET	41
KAILAS-MANASAROVAR REGION	41
MOUNTAINS	42
RIVERS	42
LAKES	43
CLIMATE	43
FLORA	44
CHAPTER II	
GEOLOGY	
GENERAL	46
FOSSILS	46
THERMAL SPRINGS	47
MINERALS	
GOLD	49
BORAX	49
OTHER MINERALS	50
CHAPTER III	
HUMAN GEOGRAPHY	
PEOPLE AND DWELLINGS	52
FOOD AND DRESS	53
SOCIAL CUSTOMS	53
RELIGION	
ADVENT OF BUDDHISM INTO TIBET	55
DIFFERENT SCHOOLS OF BUDDHISM	55
GOMPA OR MONASTERY	57
LIBRARY	59
CALENDAR	60
MANI-MANTRA	61
SIMBILING GOMPA	62
KHOCHAR GOMPA	64
CHAPTER IV	
AGRICULTURAL AND ECONOMIC GEOGRAPHY	
AGRICULTURE	69
FAUNA	69
DOMESTIC ANIMALS	71

TIBET AND ADJACENT LANDS

Map No. 5

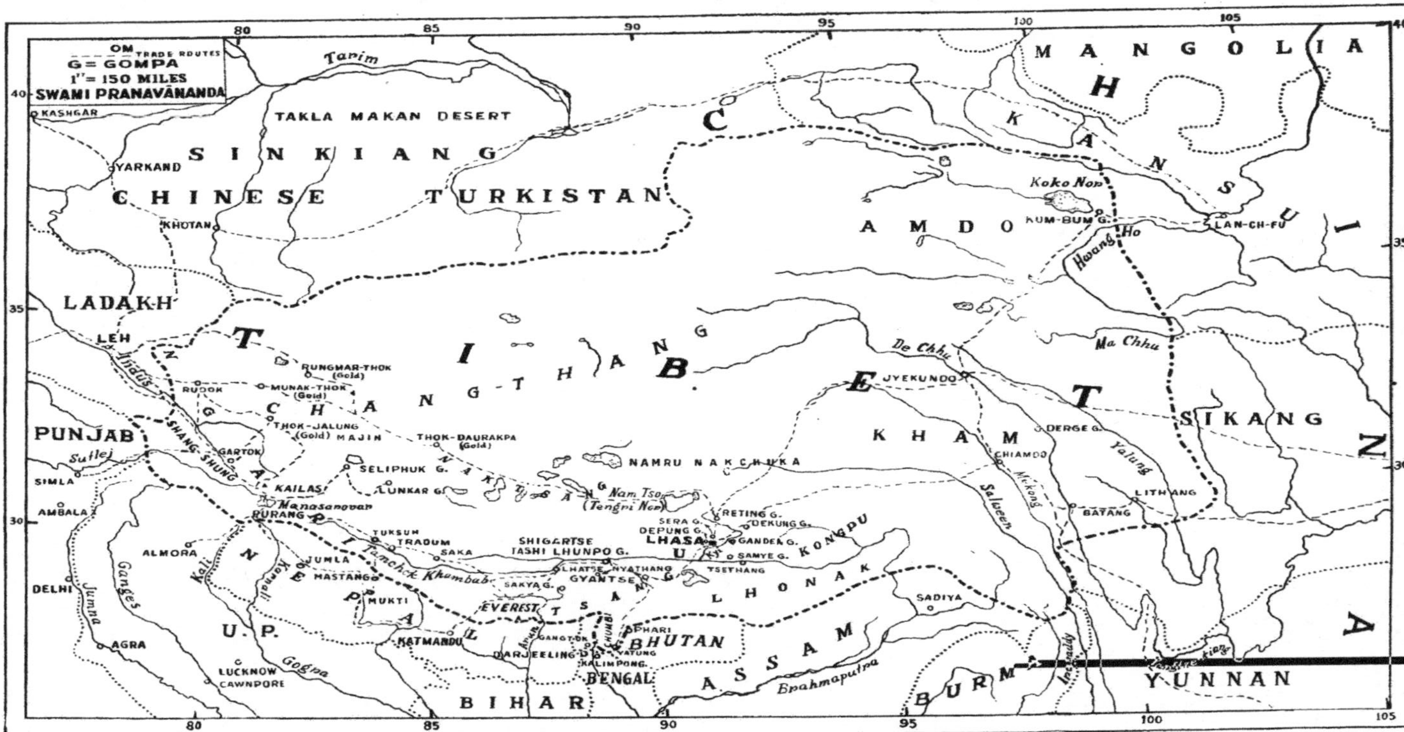

REG. NO. 2489 E'48—6000'48.

PRINTED AT THE SURVEY OF INDIA OFFICES, IP L O

	Page
STOCK-RAISING	71
TRADE AND MARTS	72
CURIOS OF MANASA KHANDA	74

CHAPTER V

ADMINISTRATION

DALAI LAMA	75
GOVERNMENT	75
INDIAN TRADE AGENT	77
CURRENCY	78
KASHMIR AND TIBET	79
GENERAL ZORAVAR SINGH	79
LOPCHAK MISSION	80
RAVAGES OF KAZHAK NOMADS OF RUSSIA	80
NEPAL AND MANASA KHANDA	81
BHUTANESE POSSESSIONS	81
'JANMA-BHOOMI' AND 'JNAN NAUKA' ON THE MANAS	82
SOME REFLECTIONS	82

THIRD WAVE

GENERAL OUTLINE OF THE ROUTE TO KAILAS AND MANASAROVAR VIA LIPU LEKH PASS

VARIOUS ROUTES TO THE HOLY KAILAS AND MANASAROVAR	89
HOW TO REACH ALMORA	90
ALMORA	91
STEEP ASCENTS	92
STEEP DESCENTS	93
THE WHOLE JOURNEY MAY ROUGHLY BE DIVIDED INTO SEVEN STAGES	
FIRST STAGE : JAGESHVAR, GANGOLIHAT, PITHORAGARH, PATALA-BHUVANESHVAR, BERINAG, BHADRAKALI, BAGESHVAR, GORI-UDYAR, BAIJNATH, KAUSANI, AND JAULJIBI	93
SECOND STAGE : CHHIPLAKOT LAKES, DEATH-CAVE, BHOTIAS, DARMA SEVA SANGHA, AND SHREE NARAYANA ASHRAMA	97
THIRD STAGE : LIPU LEKH PASS, TAKLAKOT, SIMBILING GOMPA, GUKUNG, AND KHOCHAR GOMPA	100

FOURTH STAGE : Page
TOYO, GURLA LA, PARKHA OR BARKHA, DULCHU GOMPA, TIRTHAPURI, GURU-GEM, KHYUNGLUNG, AND THE DESERTED CAVE-COLONY OF PANGTHA - - 101
FIFTH STAGE :
KAILAS-PARIKRAMA, TARCHHEN, SERSHUNG, DOLMA LA, GOURI-KUND, SERDUNG-CHUKSUM, AND TSO KAPALA 106
SIXTH STAGE :
MANASAROVAR-PARIKRAMA - - - 107

FOURTH WAVE

ROUTES

TABLE I. FIRST ROUTE TO THE HOLY KAILAS AND MANASAROVAR, FROM ALMORA VIA LIPU LEKH PASS —238 MILES - - - - 111
„ II. KAILAS-PARIKRAMA—32 MILES - - 124
„ III. MANASAROVAR-PARIKRAMA (VISITING ALL THE EIGHT MONASTERIES OF THE LAKE)—64 MILES 130
„ IV. TAKLAKOT TO KHOCHARNATH—12 MILES - 135
„ V. TAKLAKOT TO KAILAS (TARCHHEN) VIA GYANIMA MANDI, TIRTHAPURI, AND DULCHU GOMPA—111 MILES - - - - 136
„ VI. TAKLAKOT TO TIRTHAPURI BY SHORT-CUT AND THENCE DIRECT TO KAILAS (NYANRI)—93 MILES 139
„ VII. KAILAS TO GYANIMA MANDI—38 MILES - 142
„ VIII. ABSTRACT OF THE COMPLETE PILGRIMAGE TO KAILAS AND MANASAROVAR VIA LIPU LEKH PASS AND BACK—580½ MILES - - - 143
„ IX. ABSTRACT OF MILEAGES BETWEEN IMPORTANT PLACES IN KAILASA KHANDA AND KEDAR KHANDA 145
„ X. SECOND ROUTE TO THE HOLY KAILAS AND MANASAROVAR, FROM ALMORA VIA DARMA PASS—227 MILES - - - - 147
„ XI. THIRD ROUTE, FROM ALMORA VIA UNTA-DHURA PASS—210 MILES - - - 148
„ XII. FOURTH ROUTE, FROM JOSHIMATH VIA GUNLA-NITI PASS—200 MILES - - - 152
„ XIII. FIFTH ROUTE, FROM JOSHIMATH VIA DAMJAN-NITI PASS—160 MILES - - - 154
„ XIV. SIXTH ROUTE, FROM JOSHIMATH VIA HOTI-NITI PASS—158 MILES - - - 155

Page

TABLE XV. SEVENTH ROUTE, FROM BADRINATH VIA MANA PASS—238 MILES - - - 155
„ XVI. EIGHTH ROUTE, FROM MUKHUVA (GANGOTRI) VIA JELUKHAGA PASS—243 MILES - - 157
„ XVII. NINTH ROUTE, FROM SIMLA VIA GARTOK—438 MILES - - - - 159
„ XVIII. TENTH ROUTE, FROM SIMLA VIA THHULING—473 MILES - - - - 161
„ XIX. ELEVENTH ROUTE, FROM SRINAGAR (KASHMIR) VIA LADAKH—598 MILES - - 161
„ XX. TWELFTH ROUTE, FROM LHASA, VIA GYANTSE AND SHIGARTSE—800? MILES - - 164
„ XXI. TARCHHEN TO THE SOURCE OF THE INDUS VIA LHE LA AND BACK VIA TOPCHHEN LA—91 MILES - 164
„ XXII. TARCHHEN TO THE SOURCE OF THE BRAHMAPUTRA AND TAG TSANGPO AND BACK TO TAKLAKOT VIA GURLA LA—198 MILES - - 167
„ XXIII. TAKLAKOT TO THE SOURCE OF THE KARNALI, AT MAPCHA-CHUNGO—23 MILES - - 170
„ XXIV. TARCHHEN TO THE SOURCE OF THE SUTLEJ, AT DULCHU GOMPA—21 MILES - - 170
„ XXV. ALMORA TO PINDARI GLACIER—74 MILES - 171
, XXVI. SRINAGAR TO AMARNATH VIA. PAHALGAM—59 $+28\frac{3}{4}=87\frac{3}{4}$ MILES - - - 172
„ XXVII. RAXAUL TO PASHUPATINATH (NEPAL)—77 MILES 176

FIFTH WAVE

TOURIST'S COMPANION

CHAPTER I

GNEERAL INFORMATION FOR PILGRIMS AND TOURISTS

WHO CAN UNDERTAKE THE JOURNEY - - 181
PASSPORT - - - - 181
ARTICLES NEEDED FOR THE JOURNEY
CLOTHES - - - - 181
MEDICINES - - - - 182
MISCELLANEOUS ARTICLES - - - 182
EXPENSES - - - - 184
CONVEYANCE - - - - 185
HELP AND POPULAR PERSONS - - - 189
HIGHWAY ROBBERS, FIREARMS, AND GUIDES - 190
KAILAS TO BADRINATH - - - 191

	Page
LODGING AND TENTS - - - -	191
CLIMATE AND WEATHER CONDITIONS - -	192
BENEFITS OF A MOUNTAIN TRIP - - -	194
WHEN TO START FOR THE JOURNEY - -	194
TIME TAKEN FOR THE JOURNEY - - -	195
MAILS OR DAK - - - -	195
PROVISIONS - - - -	195
FUEL - - - -	197
CURRENCY - - - -	197
GENERAL AILMENTS ON THE WAY AND THEIR TREATMENT	197

CHAPTER II

PRASADS	
KAILAS - - - -	199
MANASAROVAR - - - -	199
REACTIONS OF THE KAILAS-MANAS ON WESTERN MINDS	200
LET US TO THE DIVINE LAKE - - -	201
EPILOGUE - - - - -	202

APPENDICES

I	GLOSSARY OF TIBETAN AND OTHER WORDS -	205
II	SYMBOLISM IN TIBETAN BUDDHISM - -	213
III	DISTINGUISHED VISITORS TO MANASA KHANDA -	218
IV	VILLAGES IN MANASA KHANDA - -	230
V	MONASTERIES OF MANASA KHANDA - -	232
VI	AVIFAUNA OF MANASA KHANDA - -	233
VII	A REPORT ON FOSSILS - -	235
VIII	A SKETCH OF THE AUTHOR'S LIFE AND WORK	237

ILLUSTRATIONS

		Page
	The Holy Mount Kailas	*Frontispiece*
	The Holy Mount Kailas and Lake Manasa-sarovar	"
1.	His Holiness Shree 1108 Narayana Swamiji Maharaj	v
2.	The Hon'ble Shree Pandit Jawaharlal Nehru, Prime Minister of India	xvii
3.	His Highness Maharajashree Sir Krishna Kumar Sinha, K.C.S.I., Maharaja Sahib of Bhavnagar (Kathiawar), His Excellency The Governor of Madras	xxi
4.	The Hon'ble Shree Sampurnanand, Minister of Education and Labour, U. P.	xxi
5.	Shree Amritlal D. Sheth. Editor 'Janma-Bhoomi', Bombay	xxi
6.	Shree Bhupendra Singh Pramar. Raja Sahib of Barwari, and the Author in Dhanaulti Jungle, Tehri	xxi
7.	Shree Nayani Venkata Ranga Rao Bahadur, Zamindar, Munagla Estate	xxi
8.	The Author	xxi
9.	The Himalayas	9
10.	Terrace-Cultivation, near Kosi	9
11.	Group of Temples at Jageshvar	9
12.	Temple at Bageshvar	9
13.	Group of Temples at Baijnath	9
14.	Image of Parvati at Baijnath	9
15.	Pindari Glacier	9
16.	Suspension Bridge on the River Sarayu at Seraghat	9
17.	Hill-Porters from Dharchula	9
18.	Hanging in the Sky, Ro:e bridge on the Kali	9
19.	The Foaming and Jumping Dhauli-Ganga	9
20.	Cosmos or the Wheel of Universe—Brahmanda-Chakra	25
21.	His Holiness Shree 1108 Dr. Swami Jnananandaji Maharaj, the Author's Guru Deva	25
22.	Girls of Chaudans Bhot	41
23.	Bhotia women	41
24.	Shree Narayana Ashrama	41
25.	Circle-dance, Byans Bhot	41
26.	Kalapani, the Spring-Source of the Karnali	41
27.	Lipu Lekh Pass (16,750 feet)	41
28.	Goods-train of the Himalayas entering Tibet	41
29.	Simbiling Gompa	41
30.	Image of Lord Buddha in Simbiling Gompa	41
31.	The Tutelary Deity Demchhog in Yab-Yum Pose, from a Banner Painting in Simbiling	57
32.	Demchhog in Yab-Yum Pose, from the Deserted Cave-Colony	57
33.	Images of Sattu and Butter made on the occasion of a Tantrik Rite performed in connection with the Yidam Demchhog	57
34.	Performing the last Rites in a Tantrik Ceremony called Torma	57
35.	Tulku-Lama Nav-Kushok of Simbiling Gompa with the usual Articles of Worship placed on a Folding-table	57
36.	The Author in Lama's Dress	57
37.	A Page from Kanjur	57
38.	Chhorten—a Stupa or Chaitya	57
39.	His Excellency the Governor (Zongpon) of Taklakot (1942-45)	57
40.	Zongpon's Wife	57
41.	Articles of Punishment kept in the Zong (Fort)	57
42.	Yak with a Pack-saddle	73
43.	Ploughing with a Jhabbu and a Horse	73
44.	Kettle-making at Thugolho	73
45.	Taklakot Mandi with Snow-peaks on the Indian border	73
46.	Tea-churning	73
47.	Double-panniers of Borax and Salt by the side of a Dokpa Tent in Taklakot Mandi	73
48	The Author in Tibetan Costumes	73

		page
49.	Musk-deer in different Postures	73
50.	Musk-pod from Darma	73
51.	Cave-village of Gukung	73
52.	Tent of a Nepalese Merchant in Pururav Chhongra (Market)	73
53.	Tibetan Black Tent	89
54.	A Shepherd Woman from Hor District, Manasarovar	89
55.	This is how she dresses her Hair	89
56.	Wool-shearing at Thugolho, Manasarovar	89
57.	Twisting wool to make into Bales	89
58.	Dhabbus (Bales) of Wool	89
59.	Milking Goats	89
60.	Interior of Khochar Monastery	89
61.	Image of Jambyang (Manju-ghosha) in Khochar Gompa	89
62.	Stucco-image of Prajna-paramita and some Frescos in the background	89
63.	Ruined columns of a Fort at Purbu destroyed by General Zoravar Singh	89
64.	General Zoravar Singh's Samadhi	89
65.	Tasam's (Transport Officer's) Tent in Chhakra Mandi	105
66.	Bales of Gur in a Tasam (Transport Office) awaiting transportation to Lhasa	105
67.	Gyanima Mandi	105
68.	Tirthapuri Gompa	105
69.	Representation of Dolma (Tara) on the back of Tirthapuri Gompa	105
70.	Guru-gem Gompa	105
71.	Khyunglung Gompa and Cave-dwellings situated in the Erosion Terraces and Spries of Volcanic Lava	105
72.	Deposits of Calcium Carbonate near the Thermal springs at Khyunglung	105
73.	The Deserted Cave-Colony of Pangtha	105
74.	Mandhata Peaks from Gurla La	105
75.	View of the Holy Kailas from Zhong Chhu	105
76.	The Holy Mount Kailas (Southern View), Gombo-phang (Ravan Parvat) on the left and Kyangs in the foreground	121
77.	Tarchhen	121
78.	Raising of the Tarbochhe on Lord Buddha's Birthday	121
79.	Tarbochhe and Kailas	121
80.	Nyanri Gompa, the First Monastery of Kailas	121
81.	Western View of Kailas	121
82.	Kailas Peak from the North-West, Pyramidal shape	121
83.	The Holy Kailas between the two Sentinels—Chhagnadorje and Chenresig	121
84.	Dira-phuk Gompa	121
85.	The Holy Kailas between Chenresig and Jambyang	121
86.	Khando-sanglam Glacier	121
87.	Dolma La (18,600 feet)	137
88.	Gouri-kund, Frozen almost all the year round	137
89.	Sounding the Lake Gouri-kund	137
90.	Mount Kailas from Silung Gompa and the Conglomerate Neten-yelak-jung	137
91.	Mount Kailas from its Southern Foot	137
92.	A Glacier at the Eastern Foot of Mount Kailas	137
93.	Kailas-Manasarovar Region from a Tibetan Painting drawn by Lama Nav-Kushok	137
94.	Gossul Gompa, the First Monastery of Manasarovar	137
95.	Sunrise on the Celestial Lake	137
96.	Cygnets in Captivity	137
97.	Thugolho Gompa, the Eighth Monastery of Manasarovar, the Headquarters of the Author in Manasa Khanda	161
98.	'Janma-Bhoomi' on the Holy Manas	161
99.	'Jnan Nauka' on the Holy Lake	161
100.	Shree Kailas-Manas Yajna-Vedi	161
101.	Marble Tablet on the Yajna-Vedi	161
102.	The Sources of the Four Great Rivers as described in Tibetan Scriptures (specially designed)	161

Page

103. Fissures in Frozen Manasarovar - - - - - - - 161
104. Unfissured Ice on Rakshas Tal, as seen from the Island Lachato towards Topserma - - - - - - - 161
105. A Pool of water with a Flock of Brahminy Ducks in the Frozen Manas - - - - - - - - - - - 161
106. Embankments of smaller pieces of Ice, resembling Glass panes - - 185
107. Manasarovar Frozen, with Fissures and Regular Blocks of Ice piled up into Embankments due to Coastal Explosions - - 185
108. Irregular Blocks of Ice - - - - - - - - 185
109. Zebra-like Deposits of Snow on the Southern Shores of Rakshas Tal - 185
110. Lachato with Kailas in the background - - - - - 185
111. The Island Lachato - - - - - - - - 185
112. The Breeding-ground of Nagangba on the Lachato, Mandhata in the background - - - - - - - 185
113. The Island Topserma - - - - - - - - 185
114. Rakshas Tal with Oceanic Waves on one side, Mandhata Massif in the background - - - - - - - 185
115. Rakshas Tal Frozen into Ice on another side, Kailas mirroring in it - - - - - - - - - - 185
116. Sutlej Flowing out of Rakshas Tal - - - - - - 185
117. Ganga Chhu and Chiu Hill - - - - - - - 185
118. Dr. Sven Hedin, the Famous Swedish Explorer - - - - 185
119. Senge Khambab, the Spring-source of the Indus - - - - 209
120. Kanglung Kangri Glaciers - - - - - - - 209
121. Chema-yungdung-pu Kangri, one of the Source-Glaciers of Brahmaputra - - - - - - - - - 209
122. Tamchok Khambab Kangri, the Brahmaputra Glacier - - - 209
123. Mapcha-Chungo, the Spring-Source of the Karnali - - - 209
124. Milam or Gori Glacier - - - - - - - - 209
125. Front of Badrinath Temple - - - - - - - 209
126. Thhuling Gompa - - - - - - - - 209
127. Temple at Kedarnath and the Snow-Peaks behind - - - 209
128. The Majestic Jahnavi Gorge with remnants of a Suspension Bridge hanging at a height of a thousand feet above the level of the River - - - - - - - - - 209
129. Temple at Gangotri - - - - - - - - 209
130. Gangotri - - - - - - - - - 209
131. Snout of the Gaumukh Glacier and the Satopanth Peaks - - - 233
132. Amarnath Cave - - - - - - - - 233
133. Snow-image of Amarnath - - - - - - - 233
134. Lamayuru Gompa - - - - - - - - 233
135. Hemmis Gompa, the Biggest Monastery in Ladakh wherefrom 'The Life of the Unknown Years of Jesus Christ' was discovered - - - - - - - - - 233
136. A Batch of Tibetan Soldiers on the occasion of the Chhongdu Horserace Fair at Gartok - - - - - - - 233
137. Tibetan Ladies in Chhongdu - - - - - - - 233
138. Temple of Pashupatinath, Kathmandu - - - - - 233
139. Carvings on the Temple of Pashupatinath - - - - 233
140. His Exalted Holiness The Dalai Lama, Political and Spiritual Head of Tibet - - - - - - - 233
141. Potla, the Residence of the Dalai Lama - - - - - 233
142. Tashi-Lhunpo, the abode of the Panchhen Lama - - - - 233

SKETCHES IN THE BODY OF THE BOOK

1. Om ma ni pad me hum hri - - - - - - - - 62
2. The Bracket in Khochar Gompa - - - - - - - 66
3. Tanka—Obverse and Reverse - - - - - - - 78
4. Comparative Sizes of the Image of Amarnath in Different Months - - - - - - - - - 174
5. Triangles - - - - - - - - - - - 213

MAPS

			Page
MAP NO.	1.	VARIOUS ROUTES TO THE HOLY KAILAS AND MANASAROVAR (see p. 89) - -	*At the end of the book*
,,	2.	THE HOLY KAILAS AND MANASAROVAR (see p. 120) - - - -	,,
,,	3.	THE HOLY KAILAS (see p. 125) - -	,,
,,	4.	THE HOLY MANASAROVAR AND RAKSHAS TAL (see p. 130) - - -	,,
,,	5.	TIBET AND ADJACENT LANDS - -	41
,,	6.	MOUNTAIN RANGES—THE HIMALAYAS -	3
,,	7.	GOURI-KUND - - - -	11
,,	8.	PANORAMIC SKETCH OF SNOW-PEAKS OF THE HIMALAYAS AS SEEN FROM BINSAR (JHANDI PEAK) AND KAUSANI - -	92
,,	9.	RELIEF OF THE ROUTE TO KAILAS AND MANASAROVAR AT A GLANCE - -	93
,,	10.	KATHMANDU AND ADJACENT TIRTHAS -	178

INSETS IN MAP NO. 1

11. 1. ISLAND LACHATO (see p. 11)
12. 2. ISLAND TOPSERMA (see p. 11)
13. 3. HOW MANASAROVAR FROZE (see p. 27)
14. 4. FISSURES IN MANASAROVAR (see p. 29)
15. 5. HOW MANASAROVAR MELTED (see p. 35)
16. 6. TA-CH'ING MAP AFTER DUTREUIL DE RHINS
17. 7. AUTHOR'S SKETCH OF THE REAL SOURCE OF BRAHMAPUTRA (see p. 16)

Jawaharlal Nehru

FOREWORD

Fifteen years ago, when writing my autobiography, the thought of Manasarovar came to me. That thought had been hovering in my mind for many a year. It was something which filled me with delight and I had worked out many a plan for paying my homage to this wonder Lake of Tibet and snow-covered Kailas nearby. But those plans remained unfulfilled, for my journeys led me elsewhere and I was filled with regret that I would never reach Kailas and Manasarovar. Still the thought of them cheered my mind and I quoted in my book some lines from Walter de la Mare :

"Yea, in my mind these mountains rise,
Their perils dyed with evening's rose ;
And still my ghost sits at my eyes
And thirsts for their untroubled snows."

I wonder still if I shall ever visit Kailas and Manasarovar. But I can atleast read about them and look at pictures of them and thus, to some extent, soothe the longing which has possessed me for so long. And so I welcome this book which tells us so much about these mountains that I have loved and this Lake that I have dreamt about. I hope that it will lead others to undertake this journey across our beloved Himalayas to that roof of the world, where Kailas and Manasarovar are situated.

New Delhi,
17th April 1949.

Jawaharlal Nehru

PREFACE

It is common knowledge that there has been no authoritative book on Kailas and Manasarovar published in English till 1938. The few guides that were available were either haphazard accounts and not systematically done, or compiled by persons who depended for their information on others, or incorporated hearsay material in their guides.

The author had the privilege of travelling in 1928, for the first time, in Western Tibet on a visit to these Holy places. He went from Srinagar (Kashmir) through Ladakh, Gartok, Gyanima Mandi, round Kailas and Manasarovar, to Taklakot, Khocharnath, Chhakra Mandi, again to Gartok, and back to Rishikesh, by the Gunla-Niti pass.

In 1935 he undertook a second journey from Mukhuva (Gangotri) through Nilang by the Jelukhaga pass, Thuling, Mangnang, Dapa, Dongpu, Sibchilim, Gyanima Mandi, Kailas-Manasarovar, Chhakra Mandi, and back to Gangotri by the Damjan-Niti pass. In 1936-37 and again in 1938 he travelled from Almora by the Lipu Lekh pass and returned by the same route. He had the privilege of staying for a full twelve-month in the Thugolho Monastery on the southern shores of Manasarovar for his spiritual *sadhana*. In the course of these travels he had opportunities of tracing the 'Four Great Rivers' of this Region, namely the Brahmapurta, the Indus, the Sutlej, and the Karnali, to their sources, of going over the frozen lake of Rakshas Tal from east to west and north to south, and landing on the two islands in it. He visited these regions again in 1939 by the Unta-dhura, Jayanti, and Kungri-bingri passes.

The author has been visiting these places regularly every year and staying there for periods ranging from two to six months; besides, he had occasion to spend a continuous sixteen-month, a second time in 1943-44 on the shores of the Holy Manasarovar at Thugolho. In all, he completed 23 *parikramas* or circumabulations of the Mount Kailas and 25 of the Lake Manasarovar, of which 7 rounds were done in winter when the surface of the entire Lake was frozen. He collected some fossils from the Ganga Chhu and Thugolho in 1945 and from Bongza range in Central Tibet in 1947. In 1946 he visited the Deserted Cave-City of Pangtha.

He feels confident that with his extensive first-hand knowledge of these regions, he is in a position to render a minute and thoroughgoing account of these places with special emphasis on all important details likely to be of use and interest to pilgrims and tourists. In his first book 'Pilgrim's Companion to the Holy Kailas and Manasarovar', published in 1938, he endeavoured to present the material in some detail. Ever since the publication of the 'Companion' he has been trying to bring out a more comprehensive work on Kailas-Manasarovar Region, useful not only to the tourist but also of general interest to the student of geography. In fact, his book '*Kailas-Manasarovar*'*, written in Hindi, was intended to be a comprehensive and authoritative volume on these two mystic places, held sacred by Hindus and Buddhists alike.

The present publication is just a free English version of the Hindi '*Kailas-Manasarovar*' brought up to date, though, on account of prohibitive cost of printing materials, it has not been possible to bring out as big a volume. In compiling this book he has departed from the usual method ordinarily adopted so far by writers on this subject and has systematized the materials contained in his travel diaries amounting to over 1,500 pages. In his attempt to limit the compass of this book the author has inevitably to omit certain portions which he would have liked to incorporate, viz., 1. An index of reference to all *Puranas* and other Sanskrit works in which Kailas and Manasarovar are described ; 2. A list of authors and books written on Kailas and Manasarovar in English and Indian languages ; 3. A systematic note on the minerals and geological specimens and other articles collected by him from this Region; and 4. A chapter giving an account of his adventures during his sojourn in the Manasa Khanda—which, he hopes, he will be able to include in a future edition. In the attempt to make each Wave self-contained and independent, repetition of certain things has become inevitable, which it is hoped will be appreciated by the reader.

Acknowledgments : The author hereby expresses his deep debt of gratitude and profound respects to his Revered Guru Deva Shree 1108 Dr. Swami Jnananandaji Maharaj, who has always been a source of inspiration and the sole guiding spirit in all his undertakings, both spiritual and scientific.

The author has pleasure in recording his feeling of elation and thankfulness to the Hon'ble Shree Pandit Jawaharlal Nehru, Prime Minister of India, for kindly and readily consenting to go through the book and contribute a foreword, despite his multifarious important activities.

The author's thanks are also due to the Surveyor-General of India for getting the maps printed for him in the Survey of India Office, and to Mr. K. L. Dev, Officer-in-Charge, Photo-Litho Office, and to Mr. P. Sen Gupta, Progressing Officer, for expediting the printing of the maps, in spite of heavy work in the office.

The author expresses his sincere thanks to Dr. S. P. Chatterjee,

* Published by the Hindi Sahitya Sammelan, Allahabad, 440 pp., 117 Illustrations, and 9 maps.

3. His Highness Maharajashree Krishna Kumar Sinha, K.C.S.I., Maharaja Saheb of Bhavnagar (Kathiawar), His Excellency The Governor of Madras

[See preface

4. The Hon'ble Dr. Samparnananda, Minister of Education and Labour, U. P.

5. Amrit Lal D. Sheth

6. Shree Bhupendra Singh Pramar, Raja Sahib of Barwari, and the Author in Dhanaulti Jungle
[*See Preface*

7. Shree Raja Nayani Venkata Ranga Rao Bahadur
[*See Preface*

8. The Author

M.Sc., Ph.D., D.Litt., F.G.S., Head of the Department of Geography, Calcutta University (now in Rangoon University), for the keen interest he has always taken in the author's activities and for having got the sketches of maps Nos. 7-10 fair-copied in his department.

The author is thankful to the Hon'ble Dr. B. V. Keskar, Deputy Minister, External Affairs, Government of India, for the great interest he evinced in these Himalayan tours; and to the Hon'ble Shree Lal Bahadur Shastri, Minister of Police and Transport (U.P.), the Hon'ble Shree Chandra Bhan Gupta, Minister for Health and Civil supplies (U.P.); Mr. A. K. Robertson, M.B.E., J.P., Deputy Commissioner of Police, Calcutta; and to Shree S. C. Das, Deputy Chairman, and Mr. C. F. Kelly, G.C., Deputy River Surveyor of the Port Commissioners, Calcutta, for their co-operation and services rendered in the preparation of the equipment for his expedition to Kailas-Manasarovar in 1948 and 1949.

Shreė Bhupendra Singh Pramar, Raja Sahib of Barwari (Bhagalpur District, Bihar) defrayed the major part of the expenses for his first sojourn on Kailas-Manas for one full year in 1936-37, as a result of which the author has discovered the Sources of the Four Great Rivers and collected a great portion of the material contained in this work.

His Highness Maharajashree Sir Krishna Kumar Sinha, K.C.S.I., Maharaja Sahib of Bhavnagar (Kathiawar), now His Excellency the Governor of Madras, has presented the author with a steel sailing-cum-motor dinghy for exploration work on Manasarovar.

Shree T. N. Krishnaswami of Dalal & Co, Madras has borne the cost of expedition to Rakshas Tal and Tso Kapala in 1942, as a result of which the author made a close study of Rakshas Tal and its islands; and collected some important fossils and some fresh materials regarding the source of the Sutlej and its so-called 'old-bed'.

Shree K. L. Dev, now Chief Manager, Survey of India Office, Dehra Dun, who took great interest in the author's survey and exploration work in the Kailas Region, has borne the major part of the expenses of the author's second sojourn on the Kailas-Manas for a sixteen-month in 1943-44, as a result of which the author could check up the old material and collect a good deal of further information incorporated in this book.

Shree Amritlal D. Sheth, Editor, 'Janma-Bhoomi', Bombay, a distinguished patron of learning lover of ancient culture, a philanthropist, and a widely travelled journalist of repute, has borne the entire cost of the boat-expedition of 1946, as a result of which the author has sounded the Gouri-kund, the highest lake (18,400 feet) ever sounded so far, and collected some fossils and also reached the northern and southern foot of the Kailas Peak and ascertained the nature of the rocks constituting its walls. Shree Amrit Bhai has made another munificent donation to the author in 1947 by which he could transport his full-length non-collapsible metal boat to the Lake Manasarovar which was lying at Almora for five years. The Sheth has also promised to kindly undertake the publication of the Gujarati counterpart of the author's Hindi work *'Kailas-Manasarovar'* and evinces a keen interest in the author's scientific activities on the Manas.

Shree Raja Nayani Venkata Ranga Rao Bahadur, Zamindar, Munagala Estate (Krishna District), who is a great patron of learning, has kindly borne the major part of the expenses of the expedition to Kailas-Manasarovar in 1948, which enabled the author to go round the Mandhata Range and collect fresh material to fix the Nepal-Tibetan boundary adjoining the Manas Region.

The author seeks to convey his grateful thanks to these six gentlemen for the voluntary and generous help they have rendered by which he could fulfil his long-cherished desires.

The author has great pleasure in expressing his sense of appreciation for the help the U. P. Government have been pleased to render him by way of a small grant for his exploration work in Manas Region during the year 1947. The Hon'ble Dr. Sampurnananda, Minister of Education, and Labour, U.P., has been pleased to make a grant from his department in 1948, to defray the cost of an outboard motor for the author's boat and a further grant in 1948-49 to enable the author to complete his exploratory work on Manasarovar. The author cannot be sufficiently thankful to the Hon'ble Dr. Sampurnananda for the keen interest he has taken in the author's exploratory work and for his sustained encouragement. With the aid of this motor-boat the author wants to locate the thermal springs in the bed of the Lake Manas, which would usher in a new chapter in the history of Manasarovar.

The author is equally grateful and thankful to Shree Keshab Mohan Thakur (Zamindar, Shree-Bhavan, Barari, Bhagalpur), Shree Hiralal Amritlal Sheth and Shree Yashvantarai Girija Shankar Pathak (Vasanta Vijaya Mills, Bombay), Shree Chaitmani Sinha and Shree Thakur Prasad Sinha (Zamindars, Sukhpur, Bhagalpur), Shree Rohanlal Chaturvedi, B.A., LL.B. (Zamindar, Etah, U.P.), Pandit Daya Shankar Dube, M.A., LL.B. (Allahabad University), who each bore the expenses of his stay for a season on the shores of the Kailas-Manas.

The author has also to record his hearty thanks to his Guru-Brother Shree 108 Swami Prajnananandaji Maharaj (Chidananda Ashram, Pasivedala, Andhra), Shree M. B. L. Dar, I. A. S. (Secretary to Government, U.P., Local Self-Government Department), Shree D. V. Subba Rao, B.A. (Deputy Commissioner of Police, Prohibition,

Madras), Pandit Jagatram Shankar Prasad Vaidya (Director, Zandu Pharmaceutical, Works, Bombay), Shree C. C. Saha (Calcutta), Shree Nalini Kanta Sarkar (Calcutta), Hari Prasad Vrajaraj Desai (Sholapur), Dr. B. Venkata Narasimham (Nidadavolu), Shree Chunduri Venkata Reddi, B.A., Shree A. Venkata Ramanayya (Andhra Granthalaya Press, Vijayavada), Shree Naresh Mohan Thakur (Zamindar, Barari), Shree K. Ramakrishnamurti, B.A., B.Ed. (Eluru), and several other friends who rendered financial aid for his pilgrimage to Kailas and Manasarovar on various occasions. The author's thanks are also due to Messrs. Laxmilal Anand Brothers, Almora, and to several Bhotia and Tibetan friends who rendered him valuable service in various ways during his several trips to these sacred places.

Last, but not least, it gives the greatest pleasure to the author to take this opportunity of expressing his respectful thanks to His Holiness Shree 108 Swami Kaivalyanandaji Maharaj of the S. P. League, Calcutta, who is mainly responsible for the publication of the book. The author's thanks are also due to Shree A. Jogarao, M.Sc. and Shree S. Raju, M.Sc., Benares Hindu University, who have taken keen interest and pains in going through the manuscript minutely.

SWAMI PRANAVANANDA,
(Of the Holy Kailas and Manasarovar),
Shyam Nivas,
Almora.

Thugolho Gompa,
Manasarovar.

OM

Map No. 2

THE HOLY KAILĀS AND MĀNASARŌVAR

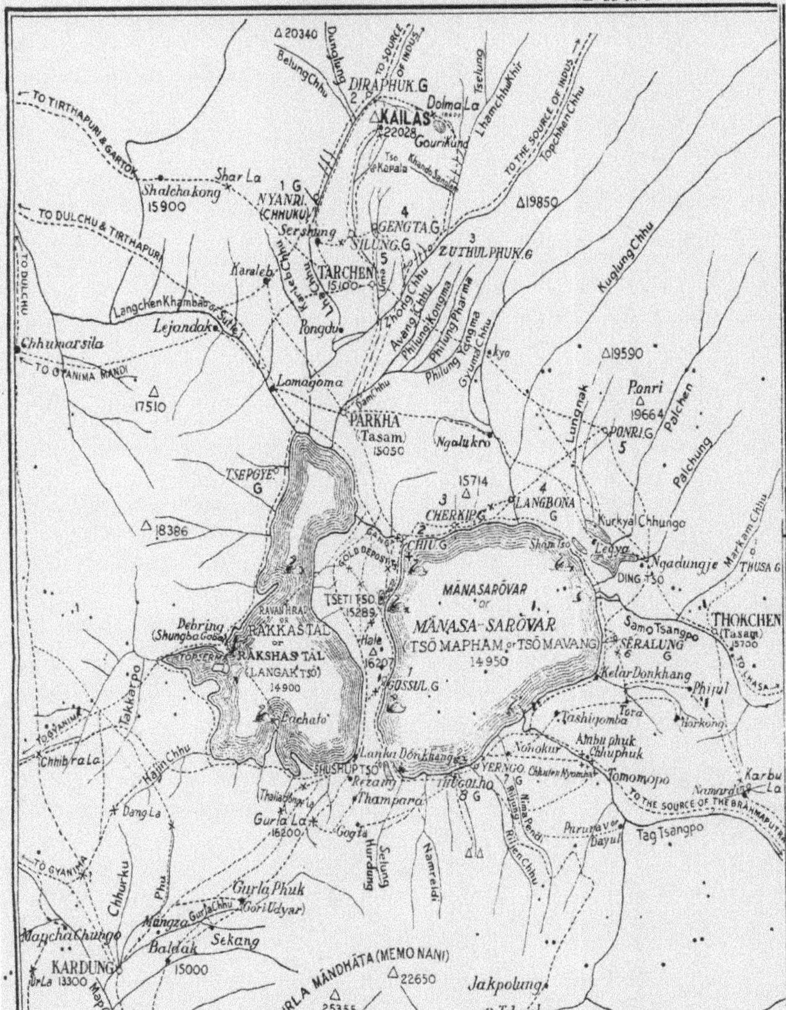

KAILAS - MANASAROVAR

FIRST WAVE

A TWELVE-MONTH ON THE HOLY KAILAS

AND

LAKE MANASA-SAROVAR

CHAPTER I

MOUNT KAILAS AND LAKE MANASAROVAR

THE HIMALAYAS

अस्त्युत्तरस्यां दिशि देवतात्मा हिमालयो नाम नागाधिराजः ।
पूर्वाऽरौ तोयनिधीवगाह्य स्थितः पृथिव्या इव मानदण्डः ॥१॥
यं सर्वशैलाः परिकल्प्य वत्सम् मेरौ स्थिते दोग्धरि दोहदक्षे ।
भास्वन्ति रत्नानि महौषधींश्च पृथूपदिष्टां दुदुहुधरित्रीम् ॥२॥

1. In the northern part there is a mighty mountain by name Himalaya—the abode of perpetual snow—fittingly called the Lord of mountains, animated by Divinity as its soul and internal spirit (or in other words, Divinity Incarnate). Spanning the wide land from the eastern to the western sea, he stands as it were like the measuring rod of earth.

2. At the direction of the King Prithu, the selfsame mountain was used as a calf by all other mountains, while the Mount Meru (Kailas) stood as an expert milker of cows and milched the Mother Earth (as if from a cow) the milk of shining gems and medicinal herbs of wonderful virtues and supreme efficacy (in order to adorn the Himalayas).[1]

Kalidasa's Kumarasambhavam

The Himalayas (snow-abode), also known as *Himavat*, *Himachala*, *Himadri* and *Giri Raja*, are the highest mountains in the world, though the youngest, and extend for 1,600 miles along the whole of the northern boundary of India. Running from Kandhar and Kashmir right up to eastern end of Assam, they cover a tract of land from 200 to 300 miles in breadth. There are picturesque descriptions of the Himalayas in Sanskrit literature and numerous books have been written by the Westerners in praise of these snow-clad mountains. They include several ranges of lofty mountains, one behind another : the Great Himalaya Range, Lesser Himalaya Range, Karakoram Range (Krishna Giri), Hindukush[2], Hindu Raj, Kailas, Ladakh, Zaskar, Mahabharat, Pirpanjal, Dhaol Dhar, Byans, Nagatibba, Siwalik Range (Mainaka Giri), and so on. In these there are several sky-kissing peaks like the Mount Everest[3] (Gouri Shankar, 29,141

1 That is to say that the Himalayas are rich in mineral wealth and flora lavishly bestowed by Nature and extend from the eastern to the western sea. According to Kalidasa's nomenclature, Himalaya Mountains include Namkiu Mountains, Patakai Range, and Arakan Yoma on the east and Hindukush Mountains, Sulaiman, and Kirtar Range on the west.

2 A. Wilson Royle (1875) considers Hindukush to be a part of the Himalayas.

3 Its Tibetan name is Kang-chomo-lungma. People of Arun Kosi area in Majh-Kirat District in Nepal call the Everest by the name of Kumbha-karan Langur (peak).

feet), K2 or Godwin Austen (28,250), Kanchana-jangha[1] (28,146), Makalu (27,790), Dhavalagiri (26,795), Nanga Parvat (26,660), Gosaithan (26,291), Nanda Devi (25,645), Kamet[2] (Ganesh Shikhar 25,447), Gurla Mandhata (25,355), Zongsong (24,472), Chomo-lhari (23,930) ; Dronagiri (23,184), Gouri Shankar (23,440), Trisul (23,406 ; 22,490 ; 22,360), Chaukhamba (Svargarohini, 23,420), Pancha Chulhi (22,650), Nandakot (22,510), Kailas (22,028), and a host of others, besides some hundreds of peaks which are above 20,000 feet high. Stupendous is the scenery of the Himalayas and the most sublime are her snow-peaks. There are some of the deepest and the most beautiful gorges and valleys (like Gilgit and Brahmaputra gorges and Bhagirathi valley near Bhairav-ghati), some of the biggest and finest glaciers (like Pindari and Baltaro glaciers) and some of the highest plateaus. "No Alpine gorge can seriously compare with majestic, almost incredible, transverse gorges of the Himalayas".[3] It is in these mighty mountain ranges that there is habitation even at a height of 17,000 feet above sea-level. In beautiful scenes and exquisite panoramas Himalayas excel the best parts of the Alps of Europe and Rockys of America. Kashmir—the paradise on earth—, Kullu, Lahul, Kumaon, Nepal, Sikkim, and Bhutan—Nature's beauty spots, are all situated in the lap of the Himalayas.

The Himalayas are rich in mineral wealth like coal, borax, lead, iron, lime, gold, etc. ; abound in all kinds of wild animals including the lion, the tiger, the elephant, and the rhinoceros, and the most beautiful birds ; are the abode of the best timber, fruit-trees, plants, medicinal herbs, and beautiful flowerbeds; are full of health-resorts and beauty-spots ; and are the very dwellings of saints and sages. Nowhere else on this globe has Nature been so lavish in the bestowal of her gifts with so much of variety and ideal conditions than in the wilds of these mighty Himalayas.

Sir Francis Younghusband, President of the Royal Geographical Society, London, considered that the Himalayas were responsible for fostering a religious feeling in the people of India, who had discovered a number of places for pilgrimage there. He thought that

1 *Kanchana* in Sanskrit means gold and *jangha* thigh ; so, *Kanchana-jangha* means golden thigh, because this massif appears like gold when the amber rays of the sun fall on it. A few Nepalis indiscriminately call this peak also Kumbhakaran Langur. Its Tibetan name is Kang-chen-chenga which means 'glaciers-big-five' or five big ice-clad peaks. It is also called Kang-chen-zo-nga or 'glaciers-big-treasures-five' or five treasures of great snow, for it is a group of five peaks. The present English pronunciation 'Kinchinjunga' is not liked either by the Indians or the Tibetans.

2 The word Kamet is of Tibetan origin ; *Kang-med*—glacier-fire. This being the highest peak in the region, it would catch the first rays of the rising sun and the last rays of the setting sun, flaring up the ice on the top like a huge mass of fire ; hence the name Kangmed or Kamet.

3 Arnold Heim.

this effect of the Himalayas on the people of the country would be still further increased than in the past, when efforts would be made both in India and England to lead expeditions to the Himalayas to discover the best panoramas of the mountains. Younghusband further says, "Efforts should be made both in India and England to lead expeditions to the Himalayas to find out the best view-points of the mountains and make them known to the outside world. When these best spots would be discovered, they would be turned into and preserved as places of pilgrimage."

SIGNIFICANCE OF PLACES OF PILGRIMAGE[1]

When incense is burnt in a particular place and even after it has been exhausted, its aroma spreads to its surroundings and remains diffused for a shorter or a longer period according to the quality of the incense. If anybody goes into that atmosphere, he is affected by that aroma. Similarly, the atmosphere in those places where *mahatmas*, *rishis*, *yogis* and sages live or have lived in the past is full of subtile vibrations of their *tapas*. Just as a field of the magnetic force is formed around a magnet, similarly there is formed a field of spiritual vibrations in those places where the sages had lived and did *tapas*. And just as every particle of iron that goes into the magnetic field is attracted and affected by it, likewise the mind of every person who goes into the spiritual atmosphere is attracted and affected by it spiritually, knowingly or unknowingly to some extent or other.

Most of the places of pilgrimage of the Hindus are held sacred for the richness of the marvellous spiritual vibrations which pervade those places. In the book called *Shuddha Tattva*, the cause of the sanctity or holiness of *tirthas* or places of pilgrimage has been described thus :

प्रभावाददद्भुताद्भूमेः सलिलस्यच तेजसः ।
परिग्रहान्मुनीनाञ्च तीर्थानां पुण्यता स्मृता ॥

Tirthas are said to be sanctified or considered holy by the great efficacy of earth, water, and fire and by the fact that *munis* or sages have lived there.

It is with the view of elevating and enriching their psychic and spiritual planes by the ennobling vibrations existing in the *tirtha-sthanas* that *jijnasus* or spiritual aspirants visit those places in spite of the various difficulties, dangers, and inconveniences they have to face in the long journey. There are several *tirthas* charged with

1 The subject has been treated in full by the author in his pamphlet 'Spiritual Vibration'.

spiritual vibrations in the Himalayas and on the banks of the Holy Ganges, Yamuna, Narmada, Sindhu, Godavari, Krishna, Kaveri, Tamraparni etc. and elsewhere in this Bharatvarsha. Such were the invaluable treasures of spiritual aura that have been bequeathed to posterity by the Aryan seers, sages, and great teachers of the hoary past. But now-a-days people at large rush with terrific speed to *tirthas*, pay a flying visit and go back in a day or two, without taking proper and full advantage of the spiritual vibrations existing in those places by staying there calmly and quietly for some time and taking to spiritual practices. There are no doubt some aspirants and *mahatmas* who are benefiting themselves consciously by the wonderful effects of the spiritual atmosphere pervading the *tirthas*, by staying there for some time calmly. It is in view of the benefit derived from the spiritual vibrations existing there that there is an injunction in the *shastras* that pilgrims to the *tirthas* should stay there for at least three nights.

So far as our knowledge goes, the Kailas and Manasarovar are the holiest of the several *tirthas* in the Himalayas. In the surroundings of the Holy Kailas and Manasarovar, even the most wandering mind, to whatever religion it may belong—whether to Hinduism or Buddhism, Christianity or Mohammadanism, whether to atheism or agnosticism —becomes concentrated and irresistibly, unknowingly, and unconsciously drawn as if propelled by some one from behind to the Divine Presence, that is hidden behind this apparent vast universe ; while a good *sadhaka* may even enter into sublime ecstasies involuntarily. But, just as a man, the mucus membrane of whose nose has become dull, cannot perceive the sweet odour of a rose, and just as a radio set cannot receive a song from a foreign programme unless it is set to the proper wavelength of that place, even so, it is no wonder that a person devoid of any spiritual tendencies cannot perceive or feel the effect of the spiritual vibrations, existing in a particular place.

MOUNT KAILAS AND LAKE MANASAROVAR

' All that is beautiful is sacred '

Two hundred and forty miles from Almora in U. P. and 800 miles from Lhasa, the capital of Tibet, stand Mount Kailas (कैलास) and Lake Manasarovar constituting one of the grandest of the Himalayan beauty spots. The perpetual snow-clad Peak of the Holy Káilas (styled *Kang Rinpochhe* in the Tibetan language) of hoary antiquity and celebrity, the spotless design of Nature's art, of most bewitching and overpowering beauty, has a vibration of the supreme order from the spiritual point of view. It seems to stand as an immediate revelation of the Almighty in concrete form, which makes man bend his knees and lower his head in reverence. Its gorgeous silvery summit, resplendent with the lustre of spiritual aura, pierces into a heavenly height of 22,028 feet above the level of the even bosom of the sea. The *parikrama* or circumambulation of the *Kailas Parvat* is about 32 miles. There are five Buddhist monasteries (*gompas*) around it singing, year in and year out, the glory of the Buddha, the Enlightened, and his five hundred *Bodhisattvas*, and of the Guardian Deity Demchhog and his consort Dorje-Phangmo (Vajra-Varahi), said to be seated on the top of the Sacred Peak of Kailas. Mount Kailas is reverenced in Sanskrit literature as the abode of the All-blissful Lord Shiva and his divine espouse, Parvati, the All-enchanting *Prakriti* (Nature), which from 20 miles off is overlooking the Holy Manasarovar and the Rakshas Tal on the south, bedecked with graceful swans.

The Holy Manasa-sarovara (मानस-सरोवर) or Manasarovar, the *Tso Mapham* or *Tso Mavang* of the Tibetans, is the holiest, the most fascinating, the most inspiring, the most famous of all the lakes in the world and the most ancient that civilization knows. "Manasarovar was the first lake known to geography. Lake Manasarovar is famous in Hindu mythology; it had in fact become famous many centuries before the lake of Geneva had aroused any feeling of admiration in civilized man. Before the dawn of history Manasarovar had become the sacred lake and such it has remained for four millennium."[1] She is majestically calm and dignified like a huge bluish-green emerald or a pure turquoise set between the two mighty and equally majestic silvery mountains, the Kailas on the north and the Gurla Mandhata on the south and between the sister-lake Rakshas Tal or Ravana Hrada (*Langak Tso* of the Tibetans) on the west and some hills on the east. Its heaving bosom, reflecting the resplendent golden rays of the waning sun and the myriad pleasant hues of the vesper sky, or her smooth surface mirroring the amber columns or silvery beams of the rising sun or moon, adds a mystic charm, all her own, to the already mysteriously charming Lake. From spiritual point of view, she has a most enrapturing vibration of the supreme order that can soothe and lull even the most wandering mind into sublime serenity and can transport it into involuntary ecstasies. Stretching majestically over an extensive cradle of the Tibetan plateau and hanging at a heavenly height of 14,950 feet above the sea-level, the vast expanse of the Lake, with a circumference of about 54 miles and a depth of nearly 300 feet, covers an area of 200 square miles. There stand eight monasteries on the holy shores, wherein Buddhist monks strive

1 S. G. Burrard and H. H. Hayden, 'A sketch of the geography and geology of the Himalaya mountains and Tibet'. Delhi, Survey of India (1934). Part III, p. 228.

all their lives to attain the sublimity of the eternal silence of *Nirvana*.

In order to realize and appreciate the grandeur of the Holy Lake fully, one has actually to spend a twelve-month on her shores. For those who have not paid her even a casual visit, it would be difficult, if not impossible, to imagine the diverse aspects of beauty that she presents round the different seasons of the year to close observers. By far the most magnificent and thrilling of one's experiences would be in winter when the whole Lake freezes hard, and again in spring when she breaks and melts to clear blue waters. It is only the inspired poet or the divine artist with his magic colours that can, for instance, describe and represent adequately the beauty and grandeur of sunrise and sunset on the Lake.

TIBETAN AND HINDU MYTHOLOGY

Two versions of *Kangri Karchhak*, the Tibetan *Kailasa Purana*, have been published in Tibetan, one from Dira-phuk Gompa and the other from Gengta. Also two abstracts of these are printed and they are called *Soldep*. *Kangri Karchhak* says that Kailas is in the centre of the whole universe towering right up into the sky like the handle of a mill-stone, that half-way on its side is *Kalpa-Vriksha* (wish-fulfilling tree), that it has square sides of gold and jewels, that the eastern face is crystal, the southern sapphire, the western ruby, and the northern gold. It also says that the Peak is clothed in fragrant flowers and herbs, and there are four footprints of the Buddha on the four sides, so that the Peak might not be taken away into the sky by the deities of that region and four chains so that the denizens of the lower regions might not take it down.

The presiding deity of Kailas is Demchhok[1] (*Dharmapala*), also called Pavo. He puts on tiger skins and garlands of human skulls and holds *damaru* (vibrant drum) in one hand and *khatam* (trident) in the other. Round Kailas are some more deities sitting in 990 rows with 500 in each. All these also put on tiger skins, etc. as Demchhok. The *Shakti* or the consort of Demchhok is Dorje-Phangmo or *Vajra-Varahi*, who is shown in Tibetan paintings and idols, clinging to him in inextricable embrace interlocked in sexual union. Adjacent to the Kailas Peak is situated on its western side a smaller snow-peak called Tijung, which is said to be the abode of Dorje-Phangmo. Besides these Lord Buddha and his 500 *Bodhisattvas* are said to be residing on the Kailas Peak. At the foot of the sacred Peak is seated Hanumanju, the monkey-god. There are also the abodes of several more deities around Kailas and Manasarovar. All these deities could

1 Also pronounced 'Demchhog', a detailed account of which is given in Appendix II.

9. The Himalayas [See p. 3

10. Terrace Cultivation.

Photo by Courtesy of Dr. Arnold Heim & August Gansser Morgarten-Verlag, Zurich
[See p. 91

11. Group of Temples at Jageshvar
[*See p.* 94

12. Temple at Bageshvar
[*See p.* 95

13. Group of Temples at Baijnath
[*See p.* 95

14. **Image of Parvati at Baijnath**
[*See. p* 95

15. Pindari Glacier.
Photo by Courtesy of Mr. M. B. L. Dar, Lucknow
[*See p.* 171

16. Suspension Bridge on the river Sarayu at Seraghat
[*See p.* 111

17. **Hill-porters from Dharchula**
[*See p.* 97

18. Dangling in the sky (Rope-bridge on the Kali)
[*See p.* 115

19. The Foaming and Jumping Dhauli-Ganga
[*See p.* 116

be seen only by the pious few. Sounds of bells, cymbals, and other musical instruments are heard on the top of Kailas.

There are seven rows of trees round the Holy Manasarovar, and there is a big mansion in it, in which resides the king of *Nags* (serpent-gods) and the surface of the Lake is like an arc with a huge tree in the middle. The fruits of the tree fall into the Lake with the sound *jam*; so the surrounding region of the earth is named 'Jambu-ling', the Jambu-dvipa of Hindu *Puranas*. Some of the fruits that fall into the Lake are eaten by the *Nags* and the rest become gold and sink down to the bottom.

At one place it is written that in the centre of the Jambu is the glorious mountain of Meru of various colours; on the east it is white like a Brahmin; on the south it is yellow like a Vaisya; on the north it is red like a Kshatriya; and on the west it is black like a Sudra. Four mountains form buttresses to Meru and on each of these stand severally a *kadamba* tree, a *jambu* tree, a *pipal* tree, and a fig tree.

Since the advent of Aryan civilization into India, Tibet and especially the Kailas-Manasarovar Region have been glorified in the Hindu mythology as part of the Himalayas. The *Ramayana* and the *Mahabharata*, all the *Puranas* in general, and *Manasa-khanda*[1] of *Skanda Purana* in particular, sing the glory of Manasarovar. It is the creation of the *manas* (mind) of Brahma, the first of the Trinity of the Hindu mythology; and according to some the Maharaja Mandhata discovered the Manasarovar. Mandhata is said to have done penance on the shores of Manasarovar at the foot of the mountains which are now known after his name. Recently the author had read the description of *Achhodasara* in *Kadambari* of Bana Bhatta. He feels that this lake cannot be any other but the celestial Manasa-saras. The description of *Achhodasara* is extremely interesting although it does not fully coincide with facts.

In some Pali and Sanskrit Buddhist works, Manasarovar is described as *Anotatta* or *Anavatapta*, Lake without heat and trouble. In its centre is a tree which bears fruits that are 'omnipotent' in healing all human ailments, physical as well as mental, and as such much sought after by gods and men alike. This *Anavatapta* is described as the only true paradise on earth. It is also said that mighty lotus flowers, as big as the Amitabha Buddha, bloom in the Holy Lake, and the Buddha and the Bodhisattvas often sit on those flowers. Heavenly *Rajahansas* will be singing their celestial melodies as they swim on the Lake. On the surrounding

1 The author has secured a manuscript copy of ***Manasa-khanda*** from Almora District. Though it claims to be a part of *Skanda Purana*, in fact it is not. It is not more than two or three hundred years old and is written by some Pandit of Almora. The author intends publishing it with a translation and foot notes.

mountains of the Lake are found the *shata-mulikas* or hundred herbs.

In Jain literature Kailas is called *Ashtapada*. Adinatha Vrishabhadeva, the first Tirthankar of Jainism, was said to have attained *Nirvana* at Kailas. In *Mahabharata* Manasarovar is also known as *Bindusara* and in Jain works as *Padma Hrada*.

PARIKRAMA

The Kailas Range is running from Kashmir to Bhutan, in which that part of the mountain surrounded by the Lha chhu and Zhong chhu is called *Kailas Parvat*, at the northern edge of which is situated the *Kailas Shikhar* or Mount Kailas. This Peak is tetrahedronal in shape and cannot be isolated for doing a circuit; so pilgrims do the round of the whole of *Kailas Parvat* which is 32 miles in circumference.

Orthodox Tibetans do 3 or 13 rounds of the Kailas and the Manas and some of the more pious pilgrims do the *sashtanga-danda-pradakshina* (prostration-circuit) of Manasarovar in about 28 days and of Kailas in 15 days. Several Tibetans do the *parikrama* of Kailas in a single day which is called *ningkor*. Some rich and sick people who cannot do the *parikrama* themselves engage beggars or coolies to do the circumambulations of Kailas or Manasarovar and pay some remuneration including money and provisions for the laborious undertaking. Well-to-do Tibetans get *parikramas* done for the benefit and peace of the souls of their departed relatives; they pay one sheep or three to six rupees for each *parikrama*. It is believed that one *parikrama* of the Kailas Peak washes away sins of one life, 10 circuits wash away the sins of one *kalpa*, and 108 *parikramas* secure *Nirvana* in this very life.

The five monasteries of Kailas are (1) Nyanri[1] or Chhuku Gompa (west), (2) Dira-phuk Gompa (north), (3) Zuthul-phuk Gompa (east), (4) Gengta Gompa (south), and (5) Silung Gompa (south). There are four *shapjes* or footprints of the Buddha, four *chaktaks* or chains, and four *chhak-chhal-gangs* or *changja-gangs* round Kailas. There is a big flag-staff called Tarbochhe at Sershung on the western side of Kailas. *Dar* or *tar* means flag or *dhvaja* and *chhe* or *chhen* means big; so Darbocche or Tarbochhe means a big flag-staff, or *Mahadhvaja*; it is locally

1 In Tibetan *nyan* means the 'great Tibetan sheep', and *ri* means 'mountain'. According to a certain legend, a *nyan* entered this mountain; so it is called *Nyanri* and the gompa constructed on it, Nyanri Gompa. Indians call it wrongly Nandi but it has no connection whatsoever with the Nandi, Shiva's Bull, or the Katyuri King Nandi Deva. Raja Nandi Deva was a contemporary of the Emperor Asoka, who lived two and a half centuries before the Christian era. Buddhism was introduced into Tibet in the seventh century A.D. and the first monastery in Tibet was constructed in A.D. 835 and none of the monasteries of Western Tibet was constructed before the ninth century. So, the writings of some, like the author of *Kurmachala Kanti*, to connect the name of Nyanri with that of Raja Nandi Deva of the Asokan period, is far from truth and an anachronism.

pronounced Tarbochhe also. To show reverence, it is also called Tarchhen Kushok or Darchhen Kushok. A big fair is held there on *Vaishakha Shukla Chaturdasi* and *Purnima* (full moon day in the month of May), as this full moon day is the day of birth, enlightenment, and death of Lord Buddha. About 600 to 1000 pilgrims from all parts of Tibet (mostly from Purang valley) assemble here for the *mela*. On the *Chaturdasi* day the flag-staff is dug out, old flags are removed, new flags are tied to the pole, special *pujas* are done by the monks of Nyanri or Chhuku Gompa, and half raised by the evening. The flag-staff is fully raised on the full moon day by 9 a.m. and the whole procession moves to Dira-phuk by the evening. The flag-staff is hoisted in honour of Buddha, the Enlightened. The raising of the flag-staff is done by the people of Purang-Taklakot under the direct supervision of the two officers of the Viceroys or *Garpons* of Gartok, specially deputed for the work.

Situated on the eastern side of the Kailas Peak is GOURI-KUND, called Thuki-Zingboo by Tibetans. It is a small beautiful oval-shaped lake about $\frac{3}{4}$ mile long and $\frac{1}{2}$ mile broad, covered with sheets of ice almost all the year round. The descent of avalanches into the lake from the southern heights is rather a frequent occurrence. Pilgrims usually take bath in this lake, for doing which very often, they shall have to break the ice on its surface ; sometimes the ice is so thick that one desperately hurls numbers of stones on it and yet do not reach the water. No Tibetan has ever seen or heard this lake to have been completely free from ice. But in 1946 and 1947 it completely melted away and the author had the unique opportunity of launching his rubber boat '*Janma Bhoomi*' on it on August 28, 1946. He sank his lead in it for the first time and took 51 soundings and the maximum depth recorded was 84 feet. This is the highest lake (18,400 ft above sea-level) ever sounded so far by any explorer or survey party.

SERDUNG-CHUKSUM is a line of 19 *chhortens* distributed in three groups of 8, 9, and 2 (from east to west), situated in a belt, dug out into the horizontal strata of conglomerate of the perpendicular wall of the southern face of the Kailas Peak at its base. As one reaches the base of the Kailas Peak, the grandeur of the view from different points is most imposing and simply sublime. On the southern side beginning from the apex of the Kailas Peak, right up to a few hundred yards above the base, there is a series of bare, rocky horizontal projections. Huge quantities of loose snow come down from the top through the ladder-like groove, to the base of Kailas forming a huge heap mixed with the conglomerate debris by the side of the Serdung-chuksum. After 12 in the noon, long bars of ice are detached from the crags of the walls of Kailas and hurled down with terrific speed and whizzing sounds by the side of the *chhortens*. *Ser* means gold or yellow; *dung* or *tung* means conch or *stupa*; and *chuksum* means thirteen. These *chhortens* were named Serdung-chuksum, perhaps when there were thirteen. These *chhortens* or *chaityas* are the monuments of the abbots of the Dekung Monastery, which is 100 miles north-west of Lhasa. They are looked after by the monks of the Gengta Monastery and are periodically repaired and painted in yellow ochre.

This line of nineteen *chhortens* artistically set in a belt of the perpendicular wall of the Mount Kailas presents a fine view, as if so many sparrows are lining in the chink of a rock. From the Serdung-chuksum the amphitheatre of Barkha plain and Rakshas Tal with the gallery of mountain peaks, extending upto the Indian borders, displays a unique scene extremely superb. Tarchhen is about seven miles from here, the whole distance being almost one continuous steep ascent on sharp stones and moraines. About four and a half miles steep descent from Serdung-chuksum over moraines to the eastern side of Neten-yelak-zung would lead one to the twin lakelets of Tso KAPALA, also pronounced Tso Kapali, Tso Kavala, and Tso Kavali. The first one is called Rukta and its water is black due to the colour of the black stones in its bed, and is 660 feet in circumference. The other is at a distance of a few yards but a 100 feet lower than the former, and is called Durchi. It is about 1,320 feet in circumference; and its water is milky-white. In *Kangri Karchhak* it is said that the water of Rukta is black like *chhang* (Tibetan beer) and of Durchi white like milk. It is further said that the key of Kailas is in the lake Durchi and that of Manasarovar in Langchen-phuk[1]. Though these lakes are situated amidst bare stones with no sign of earth as far the eye could see, at a few places in the bed of the lake Rukta, a soft alluvial soil is thrown up which is carried by pilgrims as the *prasad* of the place. According to Tibetan tradition, only those who had completed thirteen rounds of Kailas can visit these two places. Only the adventurous few can undertake this difficult trip to Serdung-chuksum and Tso Kapala, but the trip would be more than compensatory. The author has visited these two places on four occasions, twice in 1937, once in 1942, and once in 1946. The author is the first non-Tibetan who had ever visited these places. Dr. Sven Hedin did not know of these twin lakes of Tso Kapala, and has wrongly named Thuki-Zingboo or Gouri-kund as Tso Kavala. The author has collected a fourteen-pound marine fossil-bed from Rukta on September 15, 1942.[2]

From Ganga Chhu or Barkha one can easily see the appearance of

1 There are two caves of this name, one below the Nyanri Gompa and the other on the northern shores of Manasarovar.

2 See the heading 'Fossils' and the Route Table II.

a huge swan sitting on the southern face of the Kailas Peak, the steep rock projections forming the neck. The gigantic rock that is situated to the south of the Tijung has got the appearance of a sitting monkey and is called Tyu-punjung or Hanumanju in the *Kangri Karchhak*, Hanuman of the *Puranas*. This is seen from long distances. Situated at the southern foot of Kailas is a mountain called Neten-yelak-jung consisting of horizontal strata of conglomerate and surrounded on either side by streams coming from the southern and the eastern bases of Kailas. It is like a huge bull (*Nandi*) sitting in front of the Nature's Kailas-Temple. The majestic view of the Mount Kailas, the veritable Throne of Gods, soaring high between the peaks of Chenresig and Chhagnadorje on the north, with its stretched out shoulder on the north-east, a little further up with a somewhat conical form shooting up from behind the peak of Jambyang when seen from Charok-donkhang, presenting only a tip from Khando-sanglam chhu on the east, exhibiting two large black spots on its eastern shoulder when seen from Chiu Gompa or the shores of the Lake Manasarovar, with a huge dome-like glacier at its eastern base, with the line-drawing of a big sitting swan on the southern face, with the horizontal conglomerate strata of Neten-yelak-zung mountain squatting at its southern foot like Shiva's bull when seen from Silung Gompa, with a sharp conical form jetting into the pitch blue sky when seen while approaching it from Tirthapuri on the south-west or from the top of Nyanri Gompa, like the inverted crescent a little further on, loaf-like with Saturnian rings on the west, with a collosal Egyptian pyramidal form towering on the north-west, and with the artistic form seen from half a mile before reaching Dira-phuk Gompa, one and all, exhibits a variety of show. As a matter of fact every side of Kailas has a peculiar grace, charm, attraction, and beauty of its own. There is something indescribably fascinating in going round the Peak of Kailas, each hour presenting a fresh scene and each turn revealing new glimpses and beauties of mountain grandeur.

The actual circumference of Manasarovar is about 54 miles at the most and never 200 or 80 miles as the Japanese Buddhist monk Ekai Kawaguchi (who travelled in Tibet for three years) and some other casual visitors, who themselves never undertook the circuit of the Lake, would ask us to believe. Of the 24 circumambulations of the Holy Manas, which the author had undertaken, he did some in four days, some in three days, and one in two days. Skull-like, the Lake is much broader in the north than in the south. The east, south, west, and north coasts of the Lake are roughly 16, 10, 13, and 15 miles in length respectively and it is 14 to 15½ miles across. The *parikrama* of Manasarovar, visiting all the eight monasteries, is about 64 miles.

Tibetans do the *parikrama* (*kora*) of the Holy Lake in winter when the whole Lake and all the rivers and streams flowing into it are frozen, so that they might go throughout along the shores; or in early winter or spring when most of the smaller streams are dry and the bigger contain less water so as to be easily fordable. In the summer and rainy seasons, one cannot go along the shores throughout. On the northern side one shall have to leave the shores and go higher up. Moreover, all the streams and rivers flowing into the Lake will be in high floods in summer due to melting snows and would be flowing very furiously, which oftentimes become unfordable after midday. On such occasions one has to stop for the night and wait till the next morning for low-tide. Moreover, at the time when Indian pilgrims visit Kailas and the Manas, the shores of the Lake are much frequented by nomad robber-tribes going up and down. Those who want to go round the Holy Lake in summer or rainy season, should do so in parties guarded by armed men and they should take good ponies or yaks to cross the rapid rivers.

The eight monasteries round Manasarovar are: (1) Gossul Gompa (west), (2) Chiu Gompa (north-west), (3) Cherkip Gompa (north), (4) Lang-pona Gompa (north), (5) Ponri Gompa (north), (6) Serlung Gompa (east), (7) Yerngo Gompa (south), and (8) Thugolho Gompa or Thokar (south). There are four *lings* or *chhortens* (memorials of some great lamas) and four *chhak-chhal-gangs* (wherefrom *sashtanga-danda-pranamam* or prostration-salute is made) round Manasarovar. The four *chhortens* are at Chiu Gompa, Langpona Gompa, Seralung Gompa, and Thugolho Gompa. The four *chhak-chhal-gangs* are at Momo-dungu (south-west), Sera la (west), Havaseni-madang (east), and Riljung (south-east).

NEW LIGHT ON THE SOURCES OF THE FOUR GREAT RIVERS OF THE HOLY KAILAS AND MANASAROVAR

The Tibetan *Kailas Purana* says that the Ganga had at first descended from Kailas to the spring Chhumik-thungtol; that four rivers emerged out of this spring in copper pipes through the Lake Manas; that (1) the Ganga came out of the elephant-mouth (Langchen Khambab[1], the Elephant-mouthed river, or the Sutlej) near the Dulchu Gompa on the west and went to Chhemo Ganga in *Gyagar* (India); that (2) the Sindu went northwards in the beginning and came out of the peacock-mouth (Mapcha Khambab, the Peacock-mouthed river, or the Karnali) at Mapcha Chungo on the south in Lankapuring and proceeded westwards to Sindu-yul; that (3) the Pakshu or Vakshu went westwards in the beginning and thence came out of the horse-mouth (Tamchok Khambab, Horse-mouthed river, or the Brahmaputra)

[1] The word 'Khambab' means 'coming out of the mouth of'.

THE FOUR GREAT RIVERS

No.	Tibetan Name	English Translation	Indian name according to *Kangri Karchhak*	Present Indian Name	On which side of the Manas it flows	Name and direction according to Buddhaghosha
1	Langchen Khambab	River coming out of the mouth of an elephant	Ganga	Sutlej or Shatadru	West	Elephant-mouthed river on the South
2	Mapcha Khambab	River coming out of the mouth of a peacock	Sindu	Karnali (one of the headstreams of the Saraju)	South	Bull-mouthed river on the north
3	Tamchok Khambab	River coming out of the mouth of a horse	Pakshu or Vakshu	Brahmaputra	East	Horse-mouthed river on the west
4	Senge Khambab	River coming out of the mouth of a lion	Sita	Indus or Sindhu	North	Lion-mouthed river on the east

from a mountain in Chema-yungdung on the east, went to Chang (Tashi-Lhunpo) and thence to Kamarupa in India, where it is called Lohita ; and that (4) the Sita went southwards in the beginning and thence came out of the lion-mouth (Senge Khambab, Lion-mouthed river, or the Indus) from a mountain called Senge, situated on the north of Kailas and went to Baltichen and Changhor ; that the water in the Sutlej is cool, the water in the Karnali warm, the water of the Brahmaputra cold, and the water of the Indus hot ; that there are sands of gold in the Sutlej, sands of silver in the Karnali, sands of cat's-eye in the Brahmaputra, and sands of diamond in the Indus ; and that those who drink the water of the Sutlej would become strong like elephants, those who drink the water of the Karnali would become beautiful like a peacock, those who drink the water of the Brahmaputra would become sturdy like a horse, and those who drink the water of the Indus would become heroic like a lion. It is also said that these four rivers circle seven times round Kailas and Manasarovar and then take their courses towards west, south, east, and north respectively.

According to the Tibetan traditions and scriptures, the source of the Sutlej is in the springs near Dulchu or Dunchu Gompa, about 30 miles west of Manasarovar or in the Rakshas Tal, for all practical purposes from a layman's point of view. The genetic source is in the Kanglung glaciers, about 30 miles east of Manasarovar. The source of the Indus is in the springs of Senge Khambab, north-east of Kailas, about 62 miles from Manasarovar ; the source of the Brahmaputra is in the Chema-yungdung glaciers, about 63 miles south-east of Manasarovar ; and the source of the Karnali is in the spring of Mapcha Chungo, about 30 miles south-east of Manasarovar and the genetic source is in the Lampiya pass. The sources of these four rivers are within a distance of about 45 miles (as the crow flies) from the shores of the Holy Lake. So the description of the Tibetan scriptures that these four rivers take their sources from Kailas and Manasarovar is not far from the truth, also because the author of the *Kangri Karchhak* must certainly have taken Kailas and Manasarovar including the area surrounding them extending up to the sources of these rivers as 'Kailas-Manasarovar Region'.

It may be noted that the combined river of Kali, coming from the Lipu Lekh pass and the Saraju coming from the Nandakot is called Sarada from Tanakpur downwards. The Karnali coming from the Mapcha Chungo, after its mountainous course in Manasa Khanda and Nepal, is called Gogra (Ghagra), which receives the Sarada at

[1] The Pali scholar, Buddhaghosha, makes the *Anotatta*, situated in the enclosure of *Kelasakuta* and other Himalayan peaks with these four rivers flowing out of it—Simha-mukha (the Lion or east face), Hatthi-mukha (the Elephant or south face), Assa-mukha (the Horse or west face), and the Usabha-mukha (the Bull or north face).

OM

THE HOLY KAILĀS

Map No. 3

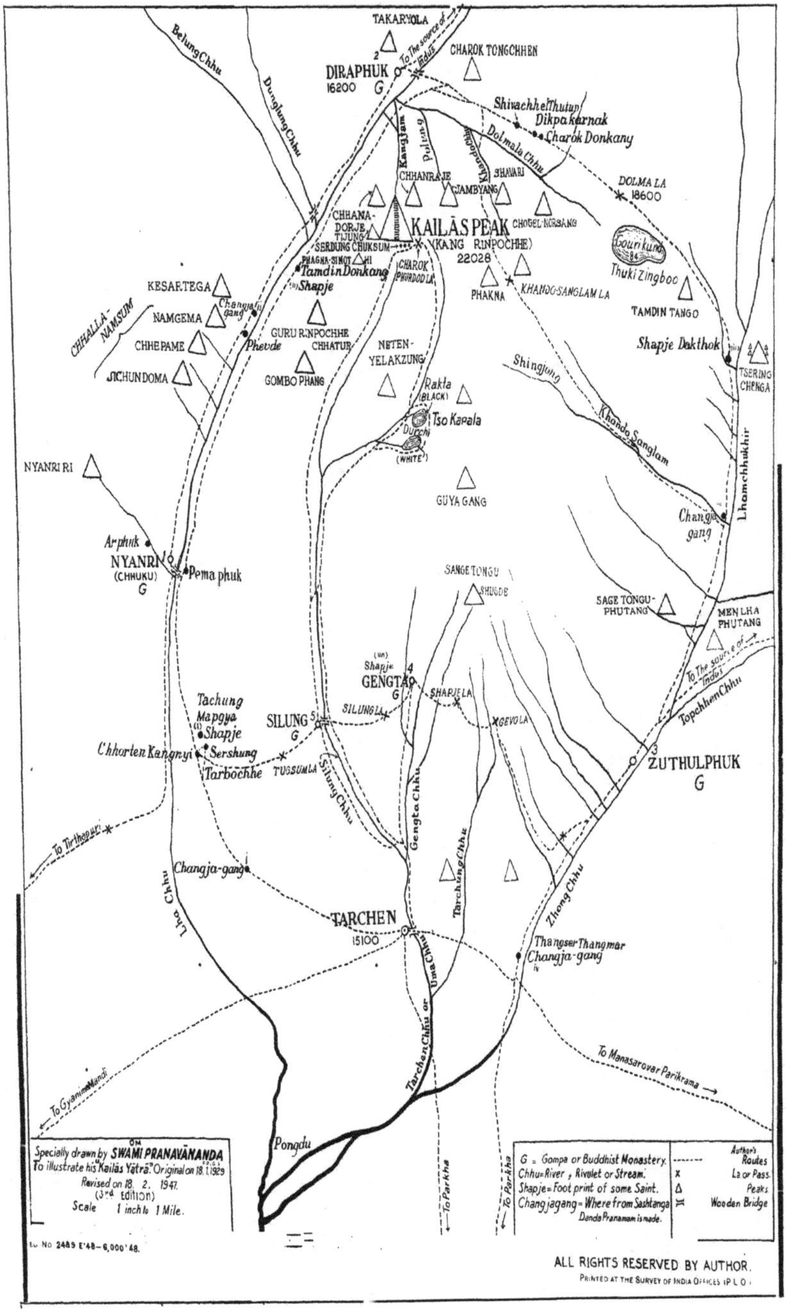

Chouka-ghat. From Chouka-ghat till it falls into the Ganges, down Chapra, the combined river is known by both the names of Gogra and Saraju. Mention of this fact is made here because some people believe that the river Saraju[1] takes its rise from Manasarovar.

RAKSHAS TAL

At a distance of 2 to 5 miles to the west of Manasarovar is the Rakshas Tal, also known as Ravana Hrada, Rakshas Sarovar, or Ravana Sarovar where Ravana of Lanka-fame was said to have done penance to propitiate Lord Shiva, the third of the Hindu Trinity and the dweller of Kailas. It is called Langak Tso in Tibetan. *La* means mountain, *nga* means five, and *tso* lake; so Langak Tso means, a lake in which there are five mountains or in which five mountains are drowned.

After several years of effort the author could procure transport in 1942, for doing the round of Rakshas Tal. He did a full round of the Tal (13th to 16th October) by closely following the highly irregular coast. For want of a guide and due to the unfavourable weather-conditions, he had to do the round in great hurry. Tempestuous winds were blowing and the path was full of sharp stones; night temperature used to be 16° F. below freezing point; and sometimes he had to jump over huge boulders since there was no regular path along the shore at several places; but the changing scenery is most thrilling and romantically beautiful. As a matter of fact, each hour reveals a fresh scene and each bend presents new glimpses of the mountain-grandeur and a variety of show that one is bewildered and becomes dumb-struck. Early in the morning the lake was so rough and raging with high roaring waves that the whole surface was white with foam; after a few minutes he was walking inside a gulf the sides of which fall sheer and the water in it was emerald-green and so perfectly still that the tiniest pebbles in its bed and the swimming fish could be clearly seen and snapped; and perfect stillness reigned supreme.

In one corner one would come across innumerable brahminy ducks warbling in boggy lands; and in another scores of *kiyangs* would be seen fearlessly grazing in grassy plains. From one promontory the Mandhata massif could be seen on the south with its giant heads piercing into the azure, as if watching the raging waves in the lake; and at another place the water in a bay was frozen and the Holy Kailas with all its majesty and sublime serenity was reflecting in it, as if in a mirror. At one place a long narrow embankment jets far into the lake as if going to meet the other shore; and at another point the peninsulas are so peculiarly formed that they had so confounded even Dr. Sven

1 Since it is considered to take its source from the *Saras* or *Manasa-Saras*, it is called Sarayu or Saraju.

Hedin that he saw three islands in the lake, whereas there are only two in reality. From one peninsula, the island in the lake appears to be so near and imposing that one is tempted to jump over it. The author had to undergo great hardships in doing this trip but the pleasure he derived from it and the materials he could collect were more than compensatory.

The Sutlej flows out of the north-west corner of Rakshas Tal, where the river was so deep that he could not cross it on October 15, 1942; and he had to go a mile down to cross it, where it was much shallower. In 1935 also, he had noted the flow of water in the Sutlej from Rakshas Tal up to Lejandak. Just near the place wherefrom the Sutlej starts in the bogs in its left bank, there are several small springs welling out, whose water flows into the Rakshas. So, some people are under the wrong impression that the water in the Rakshas does not flow out through the Sutlej. But he has received definite information from local shepherds who camp in the bogs here that sometimes the lower course of the Sutlej (after a mile from the Tal) is blocked up, but water from the Tal flows out through subterranean passages and reappears at Loma-goma, a few miles further down. Beginning from Rakshas Tal, right up to Guru-gem Gompa, there are boggy lands on both sides of the river, excepting at a few places where the river flows between two narrow rocks.

The circumference of Rakshas Tal is about 77 miles; its east, south, west, and north coasts are roughly 18, 22, 28½, and 8½ miles in length respectively; and it is about 17 miles north to south and 13 miles east to west at the maximum points. About 2½ miles away from the shore, situated on the north-western corner is Chepgey Gompa. It is the only monastery of Rakshas Tal and is a branch of Mashang Gompa. Henry Strachey mentions the gompa 'Chebgia Gumba', but Dr. Sven Hedin makes no mention of it or marks it in his map. About 3 miles from the island Topserma, situated just on the western shore of the Tal, is the only house of the *goba* of Shungba or Jungba. The place is called Debring. See Map No. 4.

GANGA CHHU

There goes a story in Tibetan scriptures about the Rakshas Tal and the Ganga Chhu, the outlet of Manas into the Rakshas. Rakshas Tal was originally the abode of demons; as such nobody drank water out of it. Two golden fishes that were in the Manas fought against each other and one pursued the other into Rakshas Tal. The course which the golden fishes took then is the present course of the Ganga Chhu. When the holy waters of the Manas flowed out of it, through the course of the golden fishes into Rakshas Tal, it became sanctified. From that time onwards people began to drink the water of Rakshas Tal.

The author made 24 rounds of the Holy Manasarovar and found Ganga Chhu to be the only outlet through which the excess water in the Manas flows out into the Rakshas. This outlet is 40 to 100 feet in breadth, six miles long in its winding course and 2 to 4 feet in depth, generally during rainy season. The author had crossed the Ganga Chhu 44 times. Manasarovar and Rakshas Tal might have been one continuous lake once and the range of hills now separating the two lakes might be due to a subsequent upheaval, the Ganga Chhu forming the outlet of Manas into the Rakshas. So the statement and belief of several people who had never made even one full circuit of Manasarovar, that the Brahmaputra and the Indus take their rise on its eastern and northern banks respectively, are absolutely groundless and erroneous like the statements that the Indus has its source at the northern or southern foot of Kailas Peak and flows on its western or southern side, and that the Sutlej takes its rise in Gouri-kund and flows on the eastern side of Kailas.

ISLANDS IN RAKSHAS TAL

There are two islands in Rakshas Tal, one Lachato and the other Topserma (or Dopserma). The author had visited these islands on April 15 and 16, 1937, when the lake was completely frozen. He went over the frozen lake from east to west and from south to north on a yak. LACHATO is a rocky island having the appearance of a tortoise with the neck stretched out towards a peninsula on the southern shore. The distance between the neck of the island and the cape of the peninsula is about half a mile. The circumference of the island is nearly one mile. The island is rocky and hilly and not at all boggy. On the top of the hill is a *laptche*, a heap of white stones, with *mani*-slabs. On the western and eastern sides of the hill there are walled enclosures of egg-gatherers. There were several swans on the gravel-plateau of the north-eastern part of the island. The egg-gatherers of the *goba* (head-man) of the village Kardung were expected there in the last week of April, when the swans begin to lay eggs.

Two accidents that had occurred in Rakshas Tal several years ago were narrated to the author by an old Tibetan. Once, when two egg-gatherers were on the Lachato, Rakshas Tal broke in the night all of a sudden and they were stranded on the island. They had to live on what little provisions they had at that time, on the meat of the few hares that were on the island, and on the eggs of swans; they remained on the island till the lake froze in the next winter to reach the mainland. But they were very much emaciated for want of sufficient food and one of them succumbed to death a few days after; but nobody had the idea of making a small skin boat or a raft to bring the stranded men to the mainland. On another occasion (about the year

1906), in early spring, when a fully loaded yak was crossing the lake, the ice under its feet gave way and it sank down under its own weight.

TOPSERMA, the second island, is completely rocky and hilly like the Lachato but is much bigger. Its southern part is named TONAK. The island is about a mile from east to west and about three-fourths of a mile from north to south. On the eastern projection of the hill there is a *pucca*-walled house in ruins, in which a Khampa Lama was said to have lived for seven years some time ago. He used to come out of the island to the shores in winter after the freezing of the lake to take provisions. The author had picked up a small clay-made image of *Chenresig* (Avalokiteshvara) from the ruins, as a memento of his visit to the island; he is the first non-Tibetan who has ever stood on the tops of the hills on these two islands in Rakshas Tal. Down below the projection there are two or three walled enclosures. Topserma is under the jurisdiction of the *goba* of Shungba. There were no aquatic birds on this island when the author visited it.

In the maps of Dr. Sven Hedin and of the Survey of India office, three islands are shown in Rakshas Tal, although the names of only two of them are given. Further, this third island and Topserma are drawn in broken lines. From a close personal observation and information the author had found ONLY TWO ISLANDS in the RakshasTal. Secondly, the *goba* of the Rakshas Tal area got his house constructed about the year 1930, within three miles from the island Topserma, which is under his jurisdiction. He too says that there are only two islands in the Rakshas Tal. Thirdly, in August 1938, the author had procured a water-colour painting of the Kailas-Manasarovar Region drawn by a monk of the famous Simbiling Monastery of Taklakot, which had, once, Tsepgye Gompa as its branch on the west coast of Rakshas Tal. The monk, therefore, had surely an intimate knowledge of the Rakshas Tal. He has shown only two islands in the Rakshas Tal in his painting. Lastly, when Sven Hedin went round the Rakshas Tal he had with him local Tibetan guides, who doubtless would have given him the name of the third island also, if it had been there. It is therefore evident that both the maps are doubtful about the existence of the third island and about the correct position of the Topserma; yet they show the third island also. That Sven Hedin himself has no definite knowledge about these islands can be seen from the following: " The two islands are easily visible in the south-western corner of the lake, but one can only seldom make out that they are real islands and not parts of promontories. There may possibly be three of them. The greatest is called Dopserma, though other Tibetans called (*sic*) Dotser. "[1]

1 Sven Hedin, 'Southern Tibet', Vol. II, p. 167.

DESCRIPTION OF MANASAROVAR

The water of Manasarovar is as sweet as that of any river or of any glacial lake. The Holy Manas provides fine caves on her shores near Gossul and Cherkip Gompas for hermits, and fine camping grounds and good sites here and there for Tibetans to build monasteries and houses. It is marshy at certain places and rocky or sandy at others. One comes across boulders as smooth and round as pebbles and also slabs as finely cut and shaped as slates. It is warm on the Gossul side and very cold on other sides. In spite of the existence of hot springs the Chiu hillside is very cold. From one monastery the Manas presents a fine view of her northern neighbour, the Kailas, and from another she completely keeps it out of sight, while from a third monastery the Rakshas Tal is presented beautifully. There are some lakelets and lagoons scattered all round the Lake, like Yushup tso on the south-west, Tseti tso on the west, Kurkyal-Chhungo, Sham tso, and Ding tso on the north and north-east. In Tibetan scriptures Kurkyal-Chhungo is described as the head of Manasarovar, set apart for *devatas* or gods to bathe in. In winter, shepherds flock to her shores and in summer they move to the upper parts of valleys. Indians hold a market on one side and the Nepalese on the other. Certain monasteries are owned by Ladakh, others by Bhutan, some by Purang-Taklakot, and still others are affiliated to the Universities or monasteries of Eastern Tibet. Several paths from different parts of the world converge to this holy spot. It would be no exaggeration if this region is styled as the cynosure of the world, for both the Buddhists and the Hindus consisting of nearly 90 crores of souls, look upon Kailas and Manasarovar as the holiest of regions.

One cannot generally escape or get away without noticing a tragic spectacle here and there in the Manasarovar Region. It is, for example, a pathetic sight to see hundreds of fish frozen and crushed in the swimming posture under the transparent ice (as at the mouth of the Gyuma chhu); or a whole flock or a line of ducks with their young ones frozen to death and sandwiched on the surface of the ever-changing mysterious Lake; or scores of new-born lambs and kids frozen to death in a shepherd camp on a single cold night, for winter is the yeaning season of sheep and goats. Sometimes groups of *kiyangs* and wild goats are frozen to death on all fours, in deep snows.

One peculiarity with the Lake is that at times when there are high waves near the shores the middle is calm and clear like a mirror reflecting the silvery dome of the Kailas if seen from the southern side or the Mandhata's giant heads if seen from the north-east. On full moon nights, with the full moon overhead, the scene is simply indescribable. At sunset the whole of the Kailas range on the north becomes a fiery region all of a sudden, throwing an observer into a spell of trance, and by the time he returns to consciousness he sees only the silvery Peak in his front. On another occasion, at the time of sunset, the whole of the Mandhata catches fire and terrible flames with rolling columns of smoke rise in the west, only to be buried very soon into the depths of abysmal darkness; the scene is simply bewitching. Sometimes the morning sun gilds the Kailas and Mandhata Peaks or pours forth molten gold on the Holy Lake; still at other times the last lingering rays of the setting sun gild the snow ranges, the sight of which is very pleasing and soothing, both to the eyes and the mind. On another occasion the whole of the Kailas-Manas Region is completely covered with a thick blanket of snow from head to foot, making it impossible to point out which is which ; one cannot tell a house from a tent, or the Lake from the land ; one cannot distinguish the ground from the pit, or the mound from the bush. A moonlit night with a clear sky beggars description and one becomes simply spellbound. Perhaps moonlight is brightest on the Tibetan plateau. Now you have scorching sun ; the next moment hail and snow begins to fall copiously ; and shortly after, having a nap and coming out of your room, you will see a clear blue sky and bright sun above and a bed of pearl-like hail and white snow on the ground. Hence the oft-quoted Hindi couplet :

मानसरोवर कौन परसे। बिन बादल हिम बरसे।

"Who can approach Manasarovar where snow falls without clouds?" Such phenomena form sufficient material for the ecstatic outbursts of a poet.

Thus the Kailas-Manas Region engages the attention of any person of any calling or profession—whether he be a poet or a painter, a physicist or a chemist, a botanist or a zoologist, a geologist or a climatologist, a geographer or a historian, a hunter or a sportsman, a skater or a skier, a physiologist or a psychologist, an ethnologist or a sociologist, a pilgrim or a tourist, a hermit or a householder, a clergyman or a tradesman, a treasure-hunter or a spirit-hunter, a theist or an atheist, a scholar or a politician, young or old, man or woman.

LOTUS AND ROYAL SWAN

The author has often been asked about the existence of golden lotuses, pearls, and the traditional *Rajahansas* or Royal Swans in Manasarovar, and about the *Mahatmas* and Tibetan mystics round Kailas and Manasarovar. In this connection it may be said without any fear of contradiction that the first two are totally mythological ; but if some one wants to console himself by saying that they might have once existed millions of years back, there is no dispute with them.

It will not be out of place here to mention that since 1940, the author has been making experiments to grow lotus, lily, water-chestnut (*singhara* सिंघाड़ा), and *makhana* (मखाना) in Manasarovar Lakes. Experiments with seeds have not been very successful so far; so he proposes trying now with bulbs brought from Kashmir. It is yet to be seen how far it would be a success. The author would be thankful if anyone interested in the subject could give some useful suggestions.

In connection with swans it may be noted that there are three varieties of aquatic birds in Manas Region. The first is called *ngangba* (ङङ बा) in Tibetan, which to the mind of the author, corresponds to the traditional swan. He had examined three male and two female cygnets, five months old, captured in 1945. Its bill is yellow with a black knob at the tip of it and the legs orange. There are two black horizontal bars on the head, the first being thicker extending from eye to eye. The back of the neck, lower part of the wings, and the tip of the bill are black. The upper part of the body is grey or light-ash in colour and the lower parts and the face are white. The female bird is whiter than the male. It comes to India in October and November and stays up to March and April, but breeds in Tibet and Central Asia. It goes up to Chilka lake on the east and on the west up to Malwa and Surat; very rarely it is seen going up to Mysore. It is about 30 inches in length and is called *savan* (सवन) in the United Provinces. This is the bar-headed goose of Jerdon. The great poet Kalidasa must have seen some stray Siberian mute swan or the whooper swan in Kashmir and combined its description with that of the Tibetan *ngangba* and gave a beautiful poetic description of the Royal Swans or *Raja Hansas* in his celebrated *Kavya*, the *Meghaduta*, as hailing from the *Manasa-saras*. Having known this convention of the modern ornithologist and the Indian ornithologists and poets there should be no objection in calling the *Manas-ngangba*, the swan.

The second variety of bird, called *ngaru-serchung* (ङरु सेरचुङ्) is deep or almond-brown in complexion. Its head and belly are light-brown and white, and the lower part of the wings, tail, legs, and bill are black. This also migrates to India but a few of them stay away in Manas Region near hot springs or some other warmer regions. This is the brahminy duck. The third variety is *chakarma* and is deep grey or like a pigeon in colour. Its head and wings are light grey, neck and belly white, tip of the tail and bill black, and legs and bill pink. The bill is thin like that of a pigeon. By the side of the eyes there are black spots presenting the appearance of another set of eyes. This feeds freely on fish. It is the gull (तित्तिरी). Heron or the black-necked crane (सारस) also is seen in pairs near Ding tso, Kurkyal-Chhungo, so-called 'old bed of the Sutlej', and other places.

There is a black variety of swan in Australia. Swans had been known to attain their second centenary even in captivity. In the beginning of January 1947 a whooper swan was shot near Chilka lake and a mute swan in Baluchistan in December 1946. Since the mute swan, the whooper, the bar-headed goose, the goose, and the wild goose, all belong to the same family, it is only a question of taste as to how to name them, but there is no question as to which is right or which is wrong. For example, the Tibetan *kiyang* is called a wild ass by the Zoologist, whereas Tibetans maintain it to be a wild horse. In fact it has got the physical features of both and looks more like a mule than anything else. Why should a particular rodent be called a guinea-pig when it is not a pig in fact? Why should a particular duck be called brahminy duck? A non-brahmin may as well take objection to it and an over-enthusiastic minister may get the prefix removed forthwith. Though the whooper is considered to be a swan, still many maintain it to be only a Bombay duck. There is no doubt that in ancient days there were in India expert ornithologists[1] who studied avifauna a good deal, long before the modern scientists coined the word ornithology, for we have several references to *Vayasa-vidyika* or *Vayo-vidyika* (वायस–विद्यिक or वायो–विद्यिक) in *Shatapatha Brahmana* XIII. 4. 3. 13, Patanjali IV. 2. 60, and other works.

Tibetans assert the *ngangba* to be a pure vegetarian that lives merely on moss, grass, and water-reeds. It does not touch fish, oysters, or snails. This is considered holy by the Tibetan who does not kill it even for his table although he is not as scrupulous about the eggs, which are freely consumed. This species of the bird exists on the smaller islet Lachato in the Rakshas Tal more abundantly than in the Manas, probably the reason being that except for a short period in winter, neither men or wolves can reach and lay their hands on them or their eggs. These swans daily go to the so-called 'old bed of the Sutlej' in winter to eat grass and moss. The servants of Kardung *goba* go to the island in the first week of April for collecting eggs. They go there and return within two weeks, for after that time the island is cut off from the mainland by the breaking of ice near the shores. It is said that two to four thousand eggs are collected in those two weeks. These eggs are three times the size of normal hen's eggs. Swans are found in large numbers in the Manas near Thugolho, Yushup tso, Gossul, Tseti tso, Chiu Gompa, Ganga Chhu, Kurkyal-Chhungo, Ding tso and at the mouths of the Samo and Tag. The bogs near the lakelets all around the Manas and the Rakshas, Loma-goma, Dulchu, Gyanima-raf, Chhakra, and other places, are the favourite habitat of *ngangba* and the *ngaru*. These swans lay their eggs under small sand-hills. In late

[1] Dr. V. S. Agrawala, 'Ancient Indian Ornithologists', 'Journal of the Indian Museums', December 1945.

21. His Holiness Shree 1108 Dr. Swami Jnanananandaji Maharaj, the Author's Guru-Deva

[*See p.* 25

spring one can see these birds breasting the waves in pairs, keeping a number of young ones in their midst and the chicks could be counted up to ten. They swim in the water producing diverging ripples in the calm Lake.

MAHATMAS AND TIBETAN MYSTICS

Several sensational articles are freely published both in the East and the West about the *Mahatmas* and *Siddhas*[1] in this little seen and less studied part of the world, namely Tibet. Most of the stories gaining currency here are mere exaggerations or misrepresentations and are more of the nature of journalistic stunts than anything else. It may however be mentioned here that the author had visited about 50 monasteries (i.e. almost all the monasteries of Western Tibet and most of them in Ladakh) and met not less than 1,500 monks, both *lamas* and *dabas*; but he did not come across any great *siddha* or a *yogi*, worth mentioning in the whole of Western Tibet. There are no doubt several *lamas* who are learned in their scriptures and well-versed in the external *tantrik* rites and incantation-performances, which are elaborately conducted for days together. People in general are very superstitious, religious-minded, devotional, and mystic in temperament. The author did not meet any really spiritually advanced *lama* or *yogi* nor any monk 90 to 100 years old, though some people claim to have seen sages like Vyasa and Asvatthama and other monks and Christian saints thousands of years old with corporeal bodies. Personally he would neither accept such credulous statements nor would force others to disbelieve them but would prefer to leave the matter to individual judgment and discrimination.

This is not to say, however, that really great *mahatmas* or saints and *yogis* do not exist; nor the above statement be misconstrued to mean that the author is sceptical about the reality of the existence of these advanced souls, as he considers his own Revered Master Dr. Swami Jnanananda to be one such adept, who has been spending his time in maintaining equanimity of mind in order to be in constant communion with the Divine look in static and dynamic forms. In calmness and serenity he dives deep into the Divine Silence of Existence and in his activity, his actions are directed to be in touch with the Divine in manifestation and the Law and its harmony that governs such a manifestation. He had conducted experimental research[2] for their

1 One who has attained high psychic and supernatural powers.

2 Dr. Swami Jnanananda, D.Sc. (Prague), Ph.D. (Liverpool), F.Inst.P. (London), Member Sigma Xi (U. S. A.), M.A.A.A.S., M.M.P.S., F.R S.S., 'New and Precise Methods in the Spectroscopy of X-Radiations', 'Thick Magnetic Electron Lens Beta Ray Spectrometer, its Theory, Construction, and application', 'Radio-active Isotope of Gold 79Au198 and Low Energy Range of its Spectrum', 'B-Radiations of Antimony124, Tantalum182, Tungsten185, Iridium192, and Uranium XI', and 'Higher Vacua', etc.

verification for wellnigh 15 years on the Continent in the Physical Laboratories at Dresden, Berlin, Prague, Liverpool, Ann Arbor (Michigan), and other places and was conferred Doctorate by two Universities, and he is now taking active part as the Senior Scientific Officer, National Physics Laboratory, Delhi. The simple fact remains that really spiritually advanced *yogis* or *lamas* are as rare a phenomenon here as anywhere else.

The author was, however, informed by the Governor of Purang-Taklakot, of monks being immured for some years and in a few cases for life, in Eastern Tibet. But this practice is in the nature of mortification or a miracle rather than a symbol of high spiritual attainment. During his several visits to Tibet he had the good fortune of coming across a *lama* from Lhasa (aged about 50) in the year 1936 and of having the rare privilege of attending some *tantrik* rites (which non-Tibetans are not allowed to attend) he conducted in the Simbiling Monastery of Taklakot continuously for three days. He was a good *sadhaka* and a *tantrik*. The author had also met a young *tulku-lama* (incarnation monk) aged 16, in Ponri Gompa[1] in the year 1928, whom he felt to be an elevated soul. In the Simbiling Gompa of Taklakot there is an incarnation-*lama*, popularly known as Nav Kushok. He is aged about 48 (born in A. D. 1900). He is a highly learned monk, a good painter, and a great *śadhaka*. Pilgrims would do well to pay a visit to him. It is really regrettable to find some people fabricating curious and funny stories which are utterly false to trade upon the credulity of the innocent and religious-minded folk. There is no doubt however that the surroundings of the Holy Kailas and Manasarovar are highly charged with spiritual vibrations of the supreme order, which make one exhilarated and elevated.

1 Fifth monastery of Manasarovar.

CHAPTER II

FREEZING OF MANASAROVAR

TEMPERATURE READINGS

WHEN the author had sojourned on the shores of Manasarovar in 1936-37, winter had already begun to make itself felt from the middle of September. From October 1, onward up to May 14, 1937, the minimum temperature persistently remained below the freezing point. The maximum temperature during that year was 67°F on July 19, in the verandah of the room and the minimum was –18.5°F. On February 18, it was so cold that the sputum of a person standing in the balcony would reach the ground as solid ice. The lowest maximum temperature was 2°F on February 16. The maximum temperature remained below the freezing point for nearly 3½ months; and on several occasions even at 12 in the noon the temperature would be 10°F. Of course the winter of 1936-37 was unusually severe in the Kailas-Manasarovar Region. During the winter of 1943-44, the minimum temperature was –18°F (December–January).

EARLY PREMONITIONS

Occasional snowfalls began from the second week of September, but never more than 1½ feet on the shores of Manasarovar, although there were several feet of heavy snowfall round Kailas. Tempestuous winds began to howl in an ever-increasing manner from the first of November. From the middle of December, water near the edges of the Lake began to freeze to a width of about two feet. From the 21st water towards the middle of the Lake froze here and there to a thickness of 2 to 4 inches and sheets of ice about 50 to 100 yards in edge were drifting towards the shores. Cyclonic gales from the Mandhata peaks were giving rise to huge oceanic waves in the Lake, roaring and thundering aloud. Lamas and other Tibetans were foretelling that the Lake would freeze in her entirety on the full moon day of the month of *Margasirsha* (December-January).

ACTUAL FREEZING OF THE LAKE

It was Monday, December 28, 1936. Somehow that day the author came out of his meditation room at the unusual hour of 7 a.m. and looked around; He could not say why, it was all like the dead of night, absolute silence and perfect calmness prevailing. Curious to know as to what had happened he went to the terrace of the monastery and stood

1 The author had lost all his exploratory diaries from 1937-46 during the Calcutta riots. So he could not give full details of his sojourn on the Manas during 1943-44.

up, and in an instant felt a thrill and lost all physical consciousness for some time—how long he could not exactly tell. As he regained consciousness, he was stunned by the sight of the Holy Kailas on the north-west, piercing into the pitch blue sky and dyed in amber robes of the early morning sun (which had not yet reached other places) and overlooking the Holy Lake in all majesty and dignity, bewitching even the inanimate creation. Not even a single sheep or lamb in the sheep-yard bleated. While he was musing over the splendour and over-powering beauty of the Holy Mount, it rapidly changed several robes of various colours and hues and ultimately decided upon the usual perpetual silver garment, which was reflecting in the clear and calm blue mirror of the mid-Lake. Dazzled at the sight, he lowered his eyes towards the Lake that was just in front of him. The very first sight of the Holy Lake made him forget himself and even the Lake herself for some time, and by the time he could see the Lake again, the sun was sufficiently high on the eastern horizon. For over a mile from the shores, the waters in the Lake were frozen into milk-white ice all around. It was an unforgettable and memorable sight—the middle of the Lake picturesquely with its unfrozen deep blue waters quite calm and serene, reflecting the Kailas and the snowy cap of the Ponri peak and the resplendent rays of the morning sun. Oh! How happy he was! He utterly fails to describe the bliss he enjoyed and the mystic charm of the enchanting Lake. Tears of joy trickled down the cheeks, only to be frozen on the parapet. There was pin-drop silence everywhere. Like the eternal silence of *Nirvana* there was perfect stillness all around. What creature could there be on the face of earth which would not feel and become one with that sublime serenity of silence of the Almighty? He leaned against the parapet of the terrace and stood dumb-struck by the most enrapturing splendour and lustre of the sublime serenity of the spiritual aura of the two holiest places on the face of the earth. How fortunate he felt himself to be under such a wonderful spell! Then he was lost within himself. At about 10 a.m. he was roused by the hailing shouts of the villagers. The whole village was on the house-tops, hoisting coloured flags, burning incense and hailing the gods aloud So! So!! So!!! Lung-ta-ro! Lung-ta-ro!! Lung-ta ro!!! There had descended a thorough change in the whole atmosphere (both physical and mental and spiritual) and he felt as if he was in an altogether new world. By December 30, i.e. in full three days, the entire Lake was frozen like the mythological ocean of curds.[1] But curiously enough Sven Hedin in his 'Trans-Himalaya' reports that the whole of Manasarovar freezes over in an hour![2]

[1] In 1944 the Lake was frozen between January 9-12 (*Paushya Shukla Chaturdasi*).
[2] (1910) Vol. II, p. 180.

FISSURES AND SOUNDS IN THE LAKE

From January 1, occasional sounds and rumblings began to be heard now and then and from the 7th they became more disturbing and terrible for about a month, as if the Lake was reluctant and resisting to put on the white robe. These sounds subsided to a great extent as the severity of winter increased, perhaps indicating her assent for some time, but were heard again intensely in early spring before the breaking of the Lake. About a month after the Lake and her feeders froze (excepting at the mouths of the Ding tso and the Tag, and near Chiu Gompa), the author had recorded that the level of the water in the Lake fell down by over 12 inches below the ice, which consequently, under its own weight, cracked with tremendous sounds and fissures were formed. The level of the water in the Lake must have fallen down still further, later on in winter, which he could not note and record. These fissures or chasms which are 3 to 6 feet broad, partition the entire Lake, so to speak, into a number of divisions or compartments. Within a day the water in the fissures freezes again and breaks, with the result that slabs and blocks of ice pile up to a height of six feet. Sometimes these slabs and blocks pile up loosely over the chasms and sometimes they are cemented to either side of the fissure. Such kind of fissures and eruptions are also formed along the shores just near the edges or a few feet inside the Lake; and these the author names 'coastal eruptions' in contradistinction to the main fissures in the Lake. Later on, when the Lake melts in the month of May, it breaks along these fissures. The disturbance beneath the ice, due to hot springs in the bed, may also be the cause of cracks, sounds, and huge fissures in Manasarovar.

Afraid of the cracks and sounds and also on account of the danger of going down into the Lake due to explosions and fissures (called *mayur* in Tibetan) none dares to go on the frozen Manas even on foot. In spite of the warnings given by the monks the author went into the Lake for over a mile in order to cross it from Chiu to Cherkip Gompa. All of a sudden he was face to face with a big fissure-eruption with blocks of ice loosely piled up to a height of 5 feet. As he was unprepared for the situation he had to cross the fissure at great risk and with utmost difficulty. Before reaching Cherkip he had to cross one more fissure-eruption and one coastal eruption. At that time he was reminded of the line that "The greatest pleasure in life lies in doing what people say you cannot do" (Bagehot). But if one is well equipped, one can cross the frozen Lake in the early hours of the day in midwinter.

LAKES MANAS AND RAKSHAS—A CONTRAST

It is different with the Rakshas Tal. Loaded sheep, yaks, and ponies and even men on horseback cross the frozen Rakshas Tal from east to west and from south to north. The absence of major fissures and eruptions here may be due to the fact that the water that percolates out of it by subterranean paths is being compensated for, by the supply of water into it from its eastern neighbour, the Manas, through underground waterways. There is no appreciable void created beneath the ice between it and the water in the Rakshas Tal and hence, perhaps, there are not many fissures and eruptions in it. There are no doubt a good many coastal explosions and eruptions and a few minor fissures here and there. The author actually crossed two small fissures, one foot broad, while visiting the islands in the lake on April 15 and 16, 1937. He was, however, told by an old Tibetan that rarely once in 8 or 10 years, a good number of fissures make their appearance even on the frozen Rakshas Tal. Both the Manas and the Rakshas freeze into pure white opaque ice in the beginning and within a month or so it becomes transparent greenish blue. The thickness of the frozen ice ranges from 2 to 6 feet near the banks, as far as the observations of the author go.

Unlike Manasarovar, Rakshas Tal freezes 15 to 20 days earlier and melts again 2 to 4 weeks later. It may be mentioned in passing that this is quite the opposite of what Sven Hedin relates, namely that "Langak-tso breaks up half a month before the Tso-mavang."[1] Rakshas Tal froze about 20 days earlier and broke up again nearly a month later. There are many major and minor fissures and coastal eruptions in the frozen Manas, whereas the Rakshas contains only a few fissures and good many coastal eruptions. Another point of difference between the two lakes is that it takes about a week for the Rakshas Tal to freeze completely and a little more than that time to melt again completely. Sheets of ice are seen floating and drifting from side to side in the Rakshas Tal for several days even after the breaking of the Lake, so much so that the Bhotia merchants going early to Tarchhen Mandi (Kailas) oftentimes notice sheets of ice floating in Rakshas Tal, but not in the Manas. The author had noticed and Tibetans too affirm that the Rakshas Tal region is much colder than the Manas area and that there are greater and more massive deposits of snow all round the Rakshas. Also, the zebra-like formations of snow in well-marked stripes in the ups and downs, in the valleys, especially on the south and west in winter, and in the islands and irregular shores with bays, gulfs, promontories, peninsulas, straits, isthmuses, rocky shores etc. lend an additional element to the picturesqueness of the landscape around the Rakshas. Indeed, Rakshas Tal would form a good model for learning geographical terms.

1 'Trans-Himalaya', Vol. II, p, 180.

The Manas is nearly 300 feet[1] in depth, whereas the Rakshas is only half as deep on the northern side; on the southern side it may be deeper but has not been sounded up till now. The Manas has eight monasteries and some houses on its shores and the Rakshas has only one monastery, Tsepgye[2] on the north-west and the only house of the *goba* of Shungba on the west. The area of the Manas is 200 square miles and that of the Rakshas 140 square miles. The coasts of the Manas are more regular than those of her western companion. Rakshas Tal is in no way inferior to Manasarovar in physical beauty; but from the spiritual point of view the Manas is unparalleled. An interesting observation which is a bit difficult to explain, is the temperamental difference between the two lakes though they are next-door neighbours to each other possessing areas almost of the same order of magnitude. Unlike Manasarovar, there are no high mountains on the southern shore of Rakshas Tal to prevent the winds coming from the south. It may be due to this that Rakshas Tal is more stormy and colder than Manasarovar. The comparative shallowness of Rakshas Tal may also be responsible for its shores being colder than those of the Manas and for its freezing earlier and melting later.

Sven Hedin writes, "In winter the surface of the Tso-mavang falls 20 inches beneath the ice, which consequently is cracked and fissured, and dips from the shore; but Langak-tso sinks only one or two-thirds of an inch. This shows that it receives water constantly from the eastern lake, but only parts with a trifling quantity in winter."[3] Sven Hedin was on the lakes during the months of July and August but not when they froze; and so this whole information about winter must be hearsay from some of his Tibetan guides or servants, who certainly gave him wrong information. When the Rakshas receives water continuously from the Manas but parts with only a trifling quantity, what becomes of all the 20 inches of water that filters out of the Manas? If, as Sven Hedin describes, only a trifling quantity of water is filtered out of the Rakshas, the level of the water in it must rise. But in the same breath he says that water in the Rakshas fell down by one or two-thirds of an inch! Could Sven Hedin expect such accurate figures from the ordinary Tibetans who gave the figures of the levels of water in the Manas with discrepancies of several feet? So, contrary to what Sven Hedin writes, the author maintains that it is not a trifling quantity of water that Rakshas Tal parts with, but almost as much quantity as it receives from the Manas either by subterranean passages or otherwise, through the so-called 'old bed of the Sutlej.'

1 The maximum depth recorded by Dr. Sven Hedin in 1907 was 269 feet.
2 Also pronounced 'Chepge' and 'Chepgye'.
3 'Trans-Himalaya', Vol. II, p. 180.

PECULIAR SURFACE PHENOMENA

A series of peculiar phenomena takes place on the frozen Lake of Manasarovar which it is impossible to describe fully. In one corner towards the south of the Naimapendi, the ice on the Lake cracks, and innumerable glassy panes of ice 2 to 4 tenths of an inch in thickness are hurled out into heaps in a minute as if by magic. From Thugolho to Tseti tso, due to coastal explosions huge blocks of ice 20 to 50 cubic feet in volume get hurled and cast ashore to distances ranging up to 60 feet, some of which take nearly a month to melt away, after the breaking of the Lake. Due to coastal explosions blocks of ice 3 to 4 feet thick rise like embankments 10 to 21 feet broad and 6 to 9 feet high, continuously for distances of hundreds of yards, only to collapse suddenly like so many packs of cards, on some evening, due to waves of quakes caused by subterranean disturbances, startling and confounding the *kora*-pilgrims, who might be moving slowly along the shores, unmindfully telling their prayers on the beads of the rosaries. These blocks of ice are irregular in shape from Thugolho to Shushup tso and regular up to Gossul. From Gossul to Tseti tso there are piles of perfectly plane slabs 1 to 2 inches in thickness. From Tseti tso to the volcanic rock-projection of Malla-thak there are irregular heaps of ice mixed with the shore-drifted soft water-reeds. At the Malla-thak, at the mouth of the Gyuma chhu, and at some other places water is frozen into crystal-clear transparent greenish-blue ice, right down to the bottom, exhibiting the pebbles, sands, and water-reeds, and the active live fish in the depths of the Lake, as through the glass cases in an aquarium.

A quarter of a mile beyond the volcanic rock-projection, about 50 yards from the shore, there was an oval patch of water 30 feet in diameter in the frozen Lake, on January 28, when the minimum temperature in the verandah of the room was 2°F, and when the entire Lake was covered with ice 2 to 6 feet thick. Two scores of brahminy ducks were merrily swimming and playing in the pool and on the ice nearby. This makes the author conclusively believe that there must be some hot springs in the bed of the Manasarovar. On the south of this pool of water two scores of birds were frozen alive and sandwiched in the Lake. For about 2½ miles from here the surface of the Lake is almost plain, with some blocks of ice here and there, and then up to Chang-donkhang there are huge blocks of all types. From Chang-donkhang up to the mouth of the Gyuma chhu there are series of parallel banks of white opaque ice, one foot high and three feet apart and running into the Lake for half a mile like the furrows in a potato field. These parallel banks make an angle of about 50° with the shore towards the south-east. At the mouth of the Gyuma chhu hundreds of fish, big and small, are frozen to death in a swimming

THE HOLY MĀNASARŌVAR AND RĀKSHASTĀL

Map No. 4

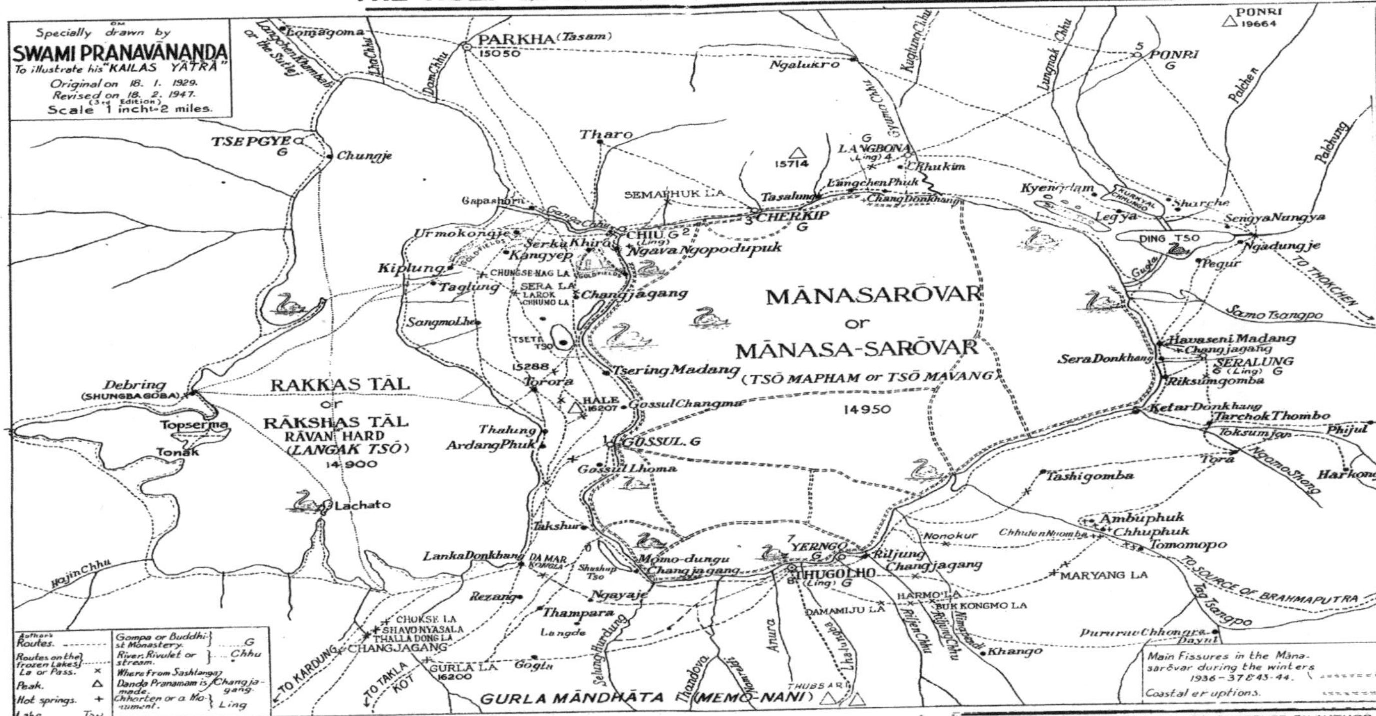

posture, which could be seen clearly through the transparent ice. From the Gyuma chhu to Sham tso there are fine models of regular mountain ranges with peaks, valleys, passes, and tablelands, all of opaque white ice not exceeding eight feet in height. In one of the rounds of the Lake the author mused himself like a schoolboy for full two hours in these ranges to find out the likeness of the various peaks of the Himalayas. He could find in these ranges varieties of peaks—pyramidal, conical, tetrahedronal, trapezoidal, slant, steep, wedge-shaped, hood-like, wall-like, spade-like, club-like and so on—of course not in the same order as in the Himalayas and other ranges. From Sham tso up to the mouth of Gugta, it is a vast field of ice with marks exactly resembling the hoofs of yaks and horses, as in a rice-field made ready for plantation by several bullocks. As a matter of fact, in his first winter *parikrama* of the Holy Lake the author mistook them for the footprints of wild horses and yaks. There is water almost all the year round at the mouth of the Gugta ; for a mile beyond this place, one sees beautiful formations of ice, like coral-reefs. From here up to Thugolho could be seen all varieties of formations and eruptions without any special features at any particular place, excepting at the mouth of the Nimapendi. Mostly between the mouths of the Gyuma and the Tag, all along the edge of the Lake, there is a fine footpath of ice 6 to 10 feet broad where beginners can practise skating and where the author used to slide on merrily.

Besides these, the author would just mention a few more interesting features of the frozen Manas and then proceed to the breaking of the Lake. Now and then the ice on the Lake bursts forth and fountains of water gush out and small pools are formed temporarily on the ice, only to be frozen hard during the night ; but such pools formed in early spring are of bigger dimensions and do not freeze again to welcome the early-coming adventurous pairs of swans. In some corner, thousands of white needles and pins, flowers and creepers of various designs form under and over the transparent greenish-blue ice. Occasionally one sees several regularly-beaten white footpaths and lines on the entire surface of the transparent Lake, which vanish also in a night in an equally mysterious way. These may be termed 'miniature fissures' though there are no chasms. When the Lake breaks, the bigger sheets of ice collide with one another and split up into smaller pieces along these paths and lines. Sometimes it is one white sheet of ice from edge to edge and sometimes the whole Lake becomes turquoise-blue with innumerable geometrical lines, diagrams, and designs. When there is a fresh heavy snowfall, the whole surface becomes pure white. The ice near the coasts bursts sometimes, and huge blocks of ice are pushed on to the shores up to 24 feet with heaps of small pebbles, big stones, sand etc., from the bed of the Lake. Sometimes massive blocks of ice are bodily lifted and hurled from the bed of the Lake on to the shore, carrying with them small pebbles, big stones, mud and sand. These blocks of ice melt away in spring and the pebbles, stones, sand, etc. are left in heaps or spread in beds on the shores, which conspicuously stand out different from those on the banks. When pilgrims go there in summer, they are perplexed to see the materials from the bed of the Lake on the shores at such distances from the edges.

CHAPTER III

MELTING OF MANASAROVAR

EARLY PREMONITIONS

THE breaking of ice and its melting to clear blue waters is even more interesting and awe-inspiring sight than the freezing of the Lake. A month before thawing sets in, along the west and south coasts, at the mouths of the Ding tso and the Tag, ice melts and forms a fine and picturesque blue border, 100 yards to half a mile in breadth, to the milk-white garment of the Lake. Here and there are seen pairs of graceful swans majestically sailing on the perfectly smooth surface of that border setting up small ripples on either side of their course. Especially in the mornings they do not play in the waters or engage themselves in 'belly-filling' but sail calmly towards the sun with half-closed eyes in a meditative mood and at the same time enjoying a good sun-bath. One such sight is a hundred times more effective, impressive, and sufficient to put one into a meditative mood than a series of artificial sermons, meditation classes, or got-up speeches from a pulpit. So it is that our ancestors and *Rishis* used to keep themselves in touch with Mother Nature to have a glimpse of the Grand Architect. Small sheets and pieces of ice are also seen drifting in the blue borders, with a flying couple of swans resting on them now and then.

About 11 days before breaking, the disturbance in the Lake becomes most intense between 6 and 10 a.m. and terrible sounds, rumblings, groanings, crashes resembling the roars of lions and tigers, trumpets of elephants, blowing up of mountains with dynamites, and firing of cannon are heard. One can hear notes of all sorts of musical instruments and cries of all animals. The agitation and the sounds are, in all probability, due to the ice tearing itself off and breaking asunder both in the fissures, and minor lines of cleavage, for, the chasms in the main fissures are seen 50 to 80 feet broad with blue waters. The white ice-garment on the Holy Lake presents a fine and beautiful spectacle of a huge Bengali *sari* with broad blue borders both at the edges and in the middle. Nine days before the breaking of the Lake, the coastwards sheets of ice, ranging in length from a few yards to half a mile, get isolated from the main sheet of ice along the fissures and other lines of cleavage and are drifted by winds mostly to the western, southern, and parts of the eastern shores, to be stranded there in part, depending upon the way and velocity with which they approach the banks. The remaining portions of sheets which still remain floating in the Lake, dash against each other and break to pieces, the smaller of which melt away in a day and the bigger remain for a few days more near the shores, sharing the fate of others. When these sheets of ice drift towards the shores in the evenings, they appear to be moving very slowly but their velocity can very well be perceived when they are partly stranded on the shores to lengths ranging from 6 to 90 feet. It is thrilling to see the lightning rapidity with which these torn pieces of ice get up the shores with great grating noises. These are stranded on the shores either as 1 to 2 feet thick sheets or in heaps 2 to 6 feet high or in smaller heaps of smooth thin glassy sheets. It is rather curious to note that the stranded sheets of ice break up into small and big brick-like pieces, the sides of which resemble the sides of pieces of mercury sulphide.

FINAL BREAKING OF ICE IN THE LAKE

After thus exhibiting a series of interesting and versatile transformations, the whole of the remaining Lake, all of a sudden, one night, breaks into a clear beautiful and charming blue expanse to the surprise and joy of the villagers and pilgrims on the shores, the next morning, who immediately climb up to their house-tops and hail the vast expanse, extending before them even like the very sky overhead; they show the same enthusiasm as they do when they find her frozen in winter, hoisting coloured flags, burning incense, telling prayers and exclaiming words of praise to the gods in heavens. Tibetans believe that the Holy Manasarovar breaks on the full moon or new moon day or on the 10th day of the bright or dark half of the lunar month. But contrary to their traditions the Manas broke on the 12th day of the dark fortnight—*Vaishakha Krishna Dvadasi* according to North Indian almanac and *Chaitra Krishna Dvadasi* according to South Indian calendar, corresponding to May 7, in the year 1937. One forgets himself for hours together gazing at the beauty, charm, and grandeur of the oceanic Lake, teeming with pairs of graceful swans here and there merrily tossing up and down the waves. On account of the high waves dashing against each other, illusory pairs of white foamy swans make their appearance, which it is very difficult to distinguish from the real ones. When the Lake broke finally, some bigger sheets of ice remained unmelted and were drifted to the north coast which also eventually collided against one another on account of severe winds and broke to pieces and melted away within three days in the blue depths.

Two or three weeks before the Lake breaks, a peculiar change occurs in the texture and hardness of the ice. What could not have been struck and broken into smaller pieces even by means of crowbars in winter, now becomes so brittle that a blow with a stick breaks it up

[1] In 1944, the Lake melted on May 1, (*Vaishakha Shukla Navami*).

into small pieces. The sheets of ice that have drifted and piled up on the shores (during the week before the breaking of the Lake), when kicked, crumble down to small crystals like those of saltpetre. When he would go out for a walk in the evenings, the author used to knock down several such heaps of brittle ice and amuse himself as they crumbled down into tiny crystals to melt away in a couple of days. One cannot get a solid piece of hard ice, as big as a cocoanut, from any of these heaps; but some of the huge blocks of ice that are hurled and piled up on the shores by coastal explosions during winter, cannot be moved by half a dozen strong men and exist for as many as 20 to 30 days after the breaking of the Lake.

EPILOGUE

Now with waves rising up to the sky and roaring as in an ocean, and now presenting a perfectly still clear-blue sheet of water mirroring the moon and the stars and the Kailas or the Mandhata; now like a sheet of gold in the morning sun, and now like a mass of molten silver in the full moon light; now rocking the Kailas and the Mandhata on her gentle ripples as in a cradle; now calm, serene, and silent even like the space beyond, and now disturbed and roaring, dashing, and lashing the shores; sometimes raising tempestuous winds flinging even the sheep and goats in the surroundings; now a beautiful blue and now a hard white mass, Lake Manasarovar, with her hundreds of *Avatars* and myriads of changing forms, offers an enigma to the puny self-conceited human being to think, meditate, and perhaps ultimately fail to comprehend all these. All hail, Oh Manas!! Lake of the Royal Sages and Swans!! Victory to Thee!!!

KAILAS - MANASAROVAR

SECOND WAVE

KAILAS – MANASAROVAR REGION

22. Girls of Chaudans Bhot

[*See p.* 98

23. Bhotia women
[*See* p. 98

24. Shree Narayana Ashrama
[*See* p. 99

25. Circle-dance, Byans Bhot
[*See* p. 99

26. Kalapani, the Spring Source of the Karnali
[*See p.* 119

27. Lipu Lekh Pass
See pp. 100 & 12[illegible]

28. Goods Train of the Himalayas entering Tibet
[*See pp.* 72 & 100

29. Simbiling Gompa
[*See p.* 62

30. **Image of Lord Buddha in Simbiling Gompa**

[*See p.* 63

CHAPTER I

PHYSIOGRAPHY

TIBET

TIBET was originally called *Bod-yul*, later on *Both*, *To-both*, *Tuboth*, *Ti-both*, and finally *Tebet*; hence the modern name Tibet. Even now Tibetans call the country *Po*, *Both*, *Bod*, or *Chang-thang* (northern plateau), although there is a separate province called Chang-thang in Tibet.

In Sanskrit literature Tibet is known by the names *Kinnara Khanda*, *Kimpurusha Khanda*, *Trivishtapa*, *Svarga Bhoomi*, or *Svarna Bhoomi*. In ancient times, Tibet on the north, Burma (*Shree Kshetra*), Siam (*Kamboja Rashtra*), and Indo-China (*Malava or Amaravati*) on the east, Malaya, Sumatra (*Svarna Dvipa*), Java (*Yava Dvipa*), Borneo, Vali, and other islands on the south-east, Ceylon (*Lanka*) on the south, and Afghanistan (*Gandhara*) on the west, were a part of Greater India and have been closely connected with it religiously, spiritually, and culturally.

Tibet is the loftiest tableland in the world ranging from 12,000 to 16,000 feet above sea-level, with mountains covered with eternal snows. It has an area of 814,000 square miles with a population of about 3,000,000 to 5,000,000 (?) and with habitation even at a height of 17,000 feet above sea-level. The major part of the country is mountainous, bleak, and barren excepting a few valleys here and there. There are, however, good many forests in the regions adjoining Indian borders, especially the Central and the Eastern Tibet. There are several salt-water lakes like Koko Nor and Lob Nor and fresh water lakes like Tso Mavang and Langak Tso. Koko Nor is the biggest of the Tibetan lakes with an area of about 1,630 square miles. Some of the biggest and the most famous rivers like the Hwang-Ho, Yangtse-Kiang, Brahmaputra, Indus, Sutlej, and Karnali, take their rise here.

The Capital of Tibet is Lhasa (12,890), situated on the right bank of the Kyi chhu and has a population of nearly 50,000, half of which are monks. Shigartse and Gyantse are the next biggest towns with a population of 25,000 each. The population of Tibet is concentrated in the Brahmaputra valley where there is a good cultivable land.

KAILAS - MANASAROVAR REGION

Tibet can roughly be divided into five divisions: (I) Western Tibet or Ngari-Korsum, extending up to Ladakh on the west and up to Tradum Tasam beyond the source of the Brahmaputra,

(2) Central Tibet, comprising of Tsang, Yu (U), Lhonak, and Kongpo, (Lhasa and other biggest towns are situated in this division), (3) Eastern Tibet or Kham (herein is situated the famous Monastery of Derge, noted for its bronzes; most of the parts of this division are under *Gyalpos* or Chiefs, (4) North-Eastern Tibet or Amdo or Koko Nor (herein is situated the famous Monastery of Kum-bum of one lakh images), and (5) Northern Tibet or Chang-thang extending up to the Chinese Turkestan on the north. As a matter of fact a large part of Eastern Tibet and Koko Nor are under China and the boundaries of Tibet are not well demarked. (See Map No. 5).

Ngari-Korsum or Western Tibet originally consisted of three Provinces, namely Ladakh, Shang-Shung or Guge (west of Manasarovar), and Purang; but in the year 1841 Ladakh was annexed to Kashmir. Kailas-Manasarovar Region is situated in the south-eastern part of Ngari, of which Purang is a part.

Based upon the Tibetan and Hindu traditions and certain geographical factors, the author names the region round about Kailas and Manasarovar 'Kailas-Manasarovar Region', 'Kailasa Khanda', 'Kailas Region', 'Manasarovar Region', 'Manasa Khanda' or 'Manas Region'. The extent of Manasa Khanda is up to Tuksum Tasam on the east, Indian borders on the south, Sib chhu on the west, and Gartok and the source of the Indus on the north; though the Greater Manasa Khanda would include the tract up to Chhabrang Zong. This Region is nearly 200 miles long from east to west and 100 miles broad from north to south.

MOUNTAINS

The Kailas, Gurla[1] Mandhata, Surange, and Kanglung, are the chief mountain ranges in the Kailas-Manasa Region. Zaskar Range is on the southern boundary of the Region. The highest peaks are Gurla Mandhata (25,355; 22,650; and 22,160 feet) and Kailas (22,028).

RIVERS

The sources of the Sutlej, Indus, Brahmaputra, and Karnali are situated in this Region. The Sib chhu, Chhunak, Guni-yankti, Darma-yankti, Gyanima chhu, Langchen Tsangpo, Chornak, Missar chhu, Trokpo-nup, Trokpo-shar, Goyak, Chukta, Tsethi, Munjan, Bokhar, Langpoche, Par chhu, Gartong, Angsi, Kubi, Mayum, Kyang, Gurla, Baldak, Ringung, Garu, Dangchen, Gejin, Kangje, Lhalung, Chokro, Thitiphu, and Yangse are the tributaries of the above four rivers. Besides these there are the rivers Dam chhu Topchhen,

1 *Go* means Head and *Lha* means God; So *Go-lha*, *Gorla*, or *Gurla* means the abode of the highest tutelary deity, Sangdul.

Zhong chhu, Tarchhen chhu, Lha chhu, and Karleb chhu, coming from Kailas and falling into the Rakshas Tal; Tag, Nimapendi, Riljung, Riljen, Namreldi, Selung-hurdung, Gyuma, Kuglung, Lungnak, Palchen, Palchung, and Samo falling into the Manasarovar; Tak-karpo and others falling into the Rakshas; and a few others falling into the Kongyu tso. Most of these rivers are dried up in winter and the remaining are frozen.

LAKES

The Manasarovar and the Rakshas are the two biggest freshwater lakes, of which the first is the deepest in Tibet. Kurkyal-Chhungo, Ding tso, Sham tso, Gouri-kund, Nyak tso, and Tamlung, are smaller freshwater lakes. The water of Shushup tso, Tseti, Gyanima, and Chhakra lakes, is slightly brackish. Kongyu (Gunchhu) tso, Arkok tso, and Argu tso are salt-water lakes.

CLIMATE

The climate of Kailas-Manasarovar Region in particular and of Tibet in general is very cold, dry and windy. Monsoon sets in late and rainfall is scanty; but when it rains it does in torrents. In summer all streams and rivers flow very rapidly and sometimes become unfordable in the evenings, due to melting snows. The sun is pretty hot in summer but it becomes very cold as soon as the sky becomes cloudy. During the pilgrim season (July and August), very often the Holy Kailas and the Mandhata Peaks would be enveloped in clouds and be playing hide-and-seek with the visitors. During the cloudy part of day and in nights it would be very cold. There will be tempestuous winds from the beginning of November up to the middle of May. Weather changes like the weathercock. Now you will be perspiring profusely in the hot sun and in a few minutes time cool breeze will start to blow gently, the next moment you will have clouds with terrific thunder and lightning followed by drizzling rain or downpours of water in torrents; sometimes you will see a rainbow; shortly after, you may have a hailstorm followed by showers of snowfall. Here is bright sun; a little further away a shower of rain; and further up lashing rains. Here is perfect calmness; the next moment there break out whizzing tempestuous winds. Now you are on the top of a mountain in the bright sun; below, you see columns of clouds rising like smoke; and further down it is raining. Here on a conical peak the ice is glittering in the sun like a bar of silver; there on a dome-like peak are hanging golden canopies; the far-off mountain ranges are enveloped in thick wreaths of inky-black clouds; there appears a belt of amber clouds or the seven-coloured semicircular rainbow encircles the Dome of Kailas; or the nearby

Mandhata's giant hoods are ablaze in scarlet flames when the sun begins to dip in the west ; or the meagre snow-clad Ponri peak raises its head into the pitch-dark messengers of Indra. Sometimes at sunset, the snow-clad massif of the Mandhata and the Kailas Range, silhoutted against the pitch dark blue sky throws one into raptures. Here in front of you the rising sun pours forth molten gold on the azure expanse of the enchanting Lake, throwing you into a deep spell ; there a far-off valley gives out thick fumes of sulphur under peculiar weather conditions, indicating the presence of big thermal springs. From one side warm winds give you a good welcome and from another valley shivering cold blasts attack you. Sometimes it seems that day and night, morning, noon, and evening, and all the six seasons of the year have their sway simultaneously.

Twilights are unusually long ; that is to say, there would be plenty of light for nearly an hour or even more just before sunrise and after sunset. Due to very high altitude, and the consequent rarified and dust-free air, distant places and objects appear to be nearer. Sometimes, even when there are high waves near the shores of Manasarovar, the middle is smooth like a mirror reflecting the mountains or the midnight moon and stars. Sometimes huge roaring waves are seen dashing against the shores when there are apparently no heavy winds. Oftentimes one can note, from the heights on the shores, path-like bands in the Lake. The occurrence of these phenomena might be due to some hot or cold water currents, set up by the thermal springs situated in the bed of the Lake or due to some kind of tidal waves, though they may not be identical with the ebb and tide of the sea. The dark sapphire-blue of the Tibetan sky is a blue so enchanting, tranquil, and inspiring in itself, that it can lull one into ecstasies.

FLORA

In some villages of the Lake Region the grass is smooth like velvet with a carpet of brilliant tiny flowers in rose, violet, and yellow colours ; at other places it is sharp and cutting like steel blades. In the upper parts of some valleys are countless designs of flowers of various hues, over which botanists could very well devote some time to find out new materials for research. On one side there is a sort of sweet-scented artemisia (*davanam*) used as incense ; on another side a different variety of incense creeper grows in still higher regions like the slopes of Kailas ; here and there are the prickly rugged *dama* bushes (a sort of juniper or furze) 2 to 3 feet high, which provides the people of these parts with firewood, since it burns even when green and freshly cut. In the upper valley of Gurla chhu and in some other places, a variety of red-barked tree called *umbo* or *langma* grows to a height of 6 to 7 feet. *Pema*, a variety of deodar, 8 to

10 feet high, grows in Shar, the last village in Purang valley, the leaves of which are used as incense. A variety of willow called *changma* is specially grown here and there in the Purang valley, but no big trees which would yield timber, although poplars and other trees grow in some places of Eastern Tibet. So it is only the poet's stretch of imagination and the artist's stroke of brush that make Lord Shiva and Parvati sit under a huge tree at the foot of the perpetual snow-clad Peak of Kailas or under a tall deodar tree on the banks of Manasarovar.

A plant called *jinbu* or *jimbu*, the Tibetan onion, grows wildly in abundance near the hot springs of the Tag tsangpo, at Tirthapuri, Nabra, Dapa, Tuling, and at several other places in Western Tibet. *Khampas* (Tibetans domiciled in India) carry hundreds of mule-loads of dried *jinbu* plant to India, where it is used for spicing dishes. *Jeera* is a wild growth in Kardung valley, Khochar, and other places. In the flats formed on either side of streams, in their lowermost course of almost all the beds of streams, a thorny bush, called *taruva* grows in plenty. This bush is a foot high and yields a yellow fruit called *tarchema* which is as big as pepper and is sour in taste. It is called *chook* in hill districts and is used for *chutney*. Tibetan garlic (*gokpa*), *bathuva*, and *bichhoo-ka-booti* grow here and there. Rhubarb and aconite are seen growing in the upper parts of some valleys. Inferior variety of mushroom, both edible and non-edible, grows in the surroundings of Manasarovar.

There are plenty of water-reeds in the Lake under the surface of water. Sometimes the smell of iodine is felt while going on the shores. So it is just probable that the reeds might contain traces of iodine, which should interest a chemist.

Here on the shores of Manasarovar the author had found out a wonderful drug called *thuma*. It is a marvellous specific for spermatorrhoea and an excellent aphrodisiac. *Thuma* is the root of a tiny creeper thriving at a height of 15,000 feet above the sea-level. It is not possible to collect even half a pound of it in a whole day. There is, however, an interesting way of procuring it. When the root is well ripe, wild rats collect and store it in their holes in the month of October for use in winter. The poor folk of these parts deprive the rats of their winter provisions. Just as *vidari-kanda*, a big tuber used in important medical preparations by *Kavirajas* or *Vaids*, is eaten as food by some of the wild tribes, so also this root is eaten by the poor as food for a few days. The well-to-do use it as a delicacy on special occasions like the New Year's Day. The claims of this drug may be verified and put to test by medical men.

CHAPTER II

GEOLOGY

GENERAL

THE walls of Kailas Peak consist of conglomerate (rock composed of pebbles cemented together through the course of age and pressure), which is considered to be not later than the Eocene period, i.e. 55,000,000 years old. The mountains of this Region in general and of Purang valley, those separating the two Lakes, and all those around Kailas in particular, mostly consist of conglomerate. The south and western side of Kailas consist of horizontally stratified conglomerate, but these strata are somewhat inclined on the eastern side. Huge granite boulders and crags border the path from Dira-phuk to Dolma la and down to Lham-chhukhir on the other side of the pass.

FOSSILS

Geology tells us that millions of years back there were no Himalayas and that the area now occupied by them was a huge sea, and that the Himalayas heaved up gradually in course of time and that they are still growing, and that they are the youngest though they are the highest in the world. Shells, snails, and other fauna of the sea, animals, trees, leaves, and other things that remained embedded in the strata of earth have been, in the course of millions of years, petrified, yet maintaining the shape and structure of the originals. These petrified objects are called fossils ; they may be of sea or of land-fauna, of plants, leaves, nuts, fruits, bones, or any other organic substance or even footprints of animals. With the help of these fossils the geologist tries to link up the past with the present.

Shalagrama (शालग्राम), *Shaligram* or *saligram*, is nothing else but the marine fossil ammonite of the Jurassic Tethys. *Shalagrama*, in Sanskrit language means, petrified insect. So Hindus knew of the fossils long before the modern scientist deciphered it. Orthodox Hindus consider *shalagrama* to be the symbol of Vishnu and worship it as such. Several people believe that *shalagrama* contains gold but it is a mere delusion. The cause underlying this wrong notion is that some marine fossils contain iron pyrites which is pale-yellow in colour, having the appearance of gold. This is mistaken by ignorant people both in the West and in the East as gold and hence it is also known as ' fool's gold '. The author had secured some such pyrites fossils from Kuti for the Benares Hindu University and the University of Calcutta, in the year 1940.

Within the knowledge of the author there are many marine fossils at Damodar-kund, Muktinath, Tinker, Lipu Lekh pass, Kuti, Mangshang pass, Darma pass, Kangri-bingri pass, Niti, Puling, and at several other places.

In the year 1942 the author had brought a marine fossil-bed weighing 14 pounds from Tso Kapala, situated at the southern foot of Kailas Peak and sent it to the Geological Survey of India for examination. This is the first find of fossils from the Kailas Range. Here is the report: "The specimens are very hard and tough sandy limestone containing marine fossils belonging to the lamellibranchia, doubtfully referable to the genera Astarte, Ostrea etc. The general look of the specimens and the faunal assemblage indicate a probable Mesozoic age for the beds."[1] Mesozoic period is 190,000,000 years old. In the years 1945 and 1946 the author had brought some more marine and bone fossils and casts of fossils from Manasa Khanda which are awaiting examination. He had also discovered a huge marine fossil-bed on the *parikrama* of Kailas, about a mile before reaching the Dolma la. It may weigh anything between 120 and 160 pounds. In 1947 he has collected 99 fossils from the Bongza Range in Central Tibet. This is the first collection of fossils from Central Tibet and the second find from Tibet. Besides these, he had collected some more fossils from different places in Western Tibet.

The author had also collected a few implements of the stone age from Kailas Region.

A hard substance *dugri,* called *bijli-ka-haddi* by Bhotias, is commonly used by Tibetan medical men. It is believed that it falls on earth through lightning. One of the specimens which the author had examined contained a lot of silica and some alumina and calcium oxide. In 1943 he had procured another specimen which turned out to be a good fossilized joint of a bone; so *dugri* is a bone fossil.

THERMAL SPRINGS

There are three thermal springs on the Ganga Chhu about two furlongs from Manasarovar down the Chiu hill. One spring is on the right bank, and one on the left bank (with a *kund* to take bath), one boiling spring on a small rock in the middle of the Ganga Chhu, having temperatures of 115°, 135°, and 170°F. respectively. There are some in the bed of the Manasarovar, especially ¾ths of a mile south of the beginning of the Ganga Chhu (see p. 18). About 3 or 4 miles from the shores of the Manas, situated on the left bank of the Tag tsangpo, there are several hot springs at Nyomba-chhuten (mad-hot

[1] The author is thankful to Dr. Beni Prasad, Superintendent, Zoological Survey of India and to Mr. P. N. Mukherjee of the Geological Survey of India for having examined the fossil-bed brought from Kailas.

springs), varying in range from lukewarm to boiling temperatures, spread over a large area, out of which a regular stream of hot water flows into the Tag. Opposite these springs on the right bank of the Tag are some caves called Chhu-phuk, where a few monks live in winter. Just near the caves there are some *chhortens* and *mani*-walls and the foundation of an old ruined monastery, said to be of Guru Padmasambhava and pulled down by Zoravar Singh. Some shepherds of Nonokur camp here in early spring and autumn for a couple of months in each season. Near the caves and a mile down at Ambu-phuk there are some more hot springs. About ¾ths of a mile up Nyomba-chhuten, situated on the left bank of the Tag, there are some hot springs and some boiling and bubbling geysers. This place is called Tomo-mopo. About 44 miles north-west of Manasarovar is Tirthapuri where there are some more thermal springs, near which the demon Bhasmasura was said to have been burnt to ashes. There are large deposits of calcium carbonate and other compounds of calcium all around the hot springs, which change their positions now and then and sometimes disappear too. There are several extinct craters near the monastery. There are a few more hot springs on the left bank of the Sutlej at Khyunglung, 14 miles down Tirthapuri. It is interesting to note that like the beads on a string, there is a series of hot springs on the Tag at Tomo-mopo, Nyomba-chhuten, Chhuphuk, and Ambu-phuk, in the bed of Manasarovar, in the Ganga Chhu, at Tirthapuri, and Khyunglung.

There is a thermal spring of luke-warm water on the right bank of the Karnali, midway between Kardung and Taklakot; and some extinct craters on the left bank of the river. There are some hot springs in the upper part of the Yangse valley.

The author feels that these hot springs and geysers, situated at a height ranging from 13,000 to 15,000 feet above the sea-level, have got a great radon content and possess radio-active properties. Patients suffering from rheumatism, lumbago, gout, dropsy, beri-beri, skin diseases, digestive disorders, and incurable diseases, visit these springs and stay there for some days using their water for bath and drink the water. Many are reported to have got good relief from the said ailments. Since the radon content and the radio-active properties of the water are often likely to be lost by the time they are brought to the laboratory in the plains, as it would take more than a month to be brought, those interested in the subject should go and analyse the waters on the spot. Since the Manas Region is full of volcanic and igneous rocks and remnants and extinct craters, the geologist would find a good deal of material for study.

MINERALS

Gold

Almost parallel to the Ganga Chhu at a distance of about a mile on the south there is a vein of gold deposit extending from the shores of the Manas right up to the Rakshas. They were mined about the year 1900, but nothing is being done now-a-days. During the last mining operation it was said that there had been an outbreak of small-pox which was attributed by the Tibetans to the wrath of the presiding deity of the mines and consequently the mining was stopped by the Government. During the last mining operation, it was also said, that one gold nugget as big as a dog (according to another version, a dog-like nugget) was found. At the place where the nugget was found a *chhorten* was constructed, called 'Serka-khiro' (gold-dog). This place is about a mile south of Chiu Gompa.

There are some gold mines in the district of Songkora or Sankora situated at a distance of a week's march on the north-east of Manasarovar. Mining is done here mostly in winter. It is reported that gold is collected at depths ranging from 18 to 24 feet and that one collects 3 to 6 tolas of gold in the course of a season. The gold of this region goes to Gyanima and Chhakra Mandi for sale.

Some 15 days' march northwards from the shores of the Manas leads one to the extensive and richer goldfields at Thok-jalung, Munak-thok, Rungmar-thok, Thok-daurakpa, and to several other places where they are being worked by the most primitive methods, scarcely worth the name of mining. Gold is found in nuggets and spangles in mines and dust in rivers. It is said that once a gold nugget weighing 525 ounces was dug from one of the gold mines. There are hundreds of gold washers in Tibet. In the year 1918, Tibetan gold was sold at the rate of Rs. 10 per tola at Lhasa, according to the account given by the Governor of Taklakot. It is the mining experts and the enterprising capitalist that can ascertain and find ways and means to exploit these vast goldfields on up-to-date scientific methods and on a commercial basis and to explore some more virgin gold and silver mines and other mineral wealth.

Borax

Lake Tseti tso, three miles north of Gossul Gompa, by the side of Manasarovar, has large deposits of borax and soda both on the shores and on the islands in it. The Tibetan Government has now stopped the working of borax at that place due to the superstitious belief that the mining deity became enraged. But some of the white deposits are carried by the people in the surroundings and used for washing hands and clothes. There are very big borax-fields at Langmar (about 140 miles from the Manas) in Western Tibet and at several other places, where, in the year 1928 it was sold at the rate of 30 to 40 pounds per rupee or as much as a big goat could carry.

Other Minerals

There are several lakes in Tibet in which there are large deposits of salt. It is from these deposits that the shepherds bring large quantities of salt to various markets. The salt that comes to the mandis of Manasa Khanda is mostly from Arkok tso and Majin. Thousands of maunds of Tibetan lake-salt are sold every year to a greater part of the Himalayan regions of India.

Trisulphide and bisulphate of arsenic are found near Kungri-bingri pass, round about Chhirchin, and near Mangshang. These two compounds of arsenic are found in other parts of Tibet also. On the eastern shores of the Manas and Rakshas there is a violet-red sand called *chema-nenga* in Tibetan. It contains iron, titanium, and emery. About three miles south of Zuthul-phuk Gompa, in Chhumik-ri, the rocks on both sides of Chhumik-thungtol, and near Kungri-bingri pass, one comes across the *zaharmora* stone (serpentine) of white, red, rose, grey, and mixed colours. This is used by *Hakims* in Unani medicines. It is a soft and smooth stone with a hardness of 2.7. A similar stone of black variety called *thaneri-patthar* is found near Kungri-bingri pass. It is used for ulcers on the breast. Near Gurla-phuk, Lachato, on the south of Zuthul-phuk Gompa, and other places one could see exoteric rocks of peredotite which is in the process of turning into serpentine. Near Tsepgye, Khyunglung and other places, quartz and calcium carbonate are found in crystalline form.

There are vast plains of soda and potash everywhere in Tibet, and near Gyanima, Chhakra, and near hot springs in Manasa Khanda. Limestone is found in Purang valley ; and tons of calcium carbonate deposits at Khyunglung, Tirthapuri, and at other hot springs. The white substance that is brought by pilgrims from the northern foot of Kailas as *vibhuti* contains calcium sulphate, calcium carbonate, and aluminium in small quantities[1]. Yellow and red ochre are found at Tirthapuri, Tag chhu, Purang valley, and at other places with which monasteries and houses are painted. Best pottery clay is found near Riljung chhu, with which pots and tea-kettles are made at Thugolho. At several places beautiful slabs of black and grey and pale greenish-blue alabaster-like slate and other stones are found everywhere on which Tibetans usually engrave their sacred *mantras* and scriptures.

1 The author is grateful to Mr. Susarla Raju, M.Sc., Assistant Professor of Chemistry, and to Dr. Rajnath, Head of the Department of Geology, Benares Hindu University, for the interest they had taken in examining and analysing the minerals and other specimens brought from Kailas-Manasa Region,

Besides gold, silver, copper, lead, iron, coal, limestone, sulphur, mercury, *shilajit*, kerosene oil, and rock-salt are also found in different parts of Tibet. But they are all in virgin state now. At a distance of 3 days' journey from Gartok there are lead mines near Gemuk.

CHAPTER III

HUMAN GEOGRAPHY

PEOPLE AND DWELLINGS

THE population of Manasa Khanda may roughly be computed at 10,000. People, both men and women in general, are strong, sturdy, and hard-working; they have great power of resistance to cold and hardships; they are primitive, cheerful, pleasure-loving, peaceful, religious-minded, very hospitable, contented, but dirty in habits and customs. Lamas and officers are highly cultured and polite. There is no caste system in Tibet. But the smiths are the only second class, with whom the rest of the society does not inter-marry or inter-dine; so every Tibetan is the embodiment of all qualities, beginning from those of a priest to those of a sweeper.

It is only the Purang valley that is fairly well populated with fixed abodes. These abodes are flat-roofed and are often in two storeys, built of big sun-dried bricks and the little timber that they get from the Indian borders. The roofing is made of light timber and bushes, over which mud is spread. The comparative sparseness of houses in the Kailas-Manas Region is due to the fact that transit of timber to their inaccessible regions, encountering difficult passes on yaks and ponies, is highly expensive. Sometimes even two houses go to make a village. Their monasteries are built similarly but on a larger scale.

About half the population of the Region subsists on cattle-breeding especially of the yak, sheep, and goat. They live in black tents made of yak-hair, and wander from valley to valley grazing their cattle.

A part of the population of Purang lives also in caves dug into the conglomerate walls of hills which are made into regular houses by construction of walls and gates in the front side. Some of the caves are even two or three-storeyed high. Such houses are found mostly in Gukung near Taklakot, in the villages Garu, Doh, Ringung, Dungmar, Kardung etc. Gukung is a typical cave-village situated on the right bank of the Karnali about half a mile from Taklakot Mandi. There is a gompa also situated in a three-storeyed cave-dwelling. On the southern side of Manasarovar, situated in the uppermost part of the Namreldi valley, are some caves where the people of southern shores of the Manas took refuge in severe cold, when the Kashmiri General, Zoravar Singh, invaded the Manas Region in the year 1841. There is a deserted Cave-Colony at Pangtha on the Sib chhu, 5 miles down Sibchilim Mandi. The author visited this place in 1946. There are hundreds of caves here which were all once inhabited but now deserted.

In the upper terrace or row of caves there is a monastery belonging to the Sakya Sect of Buddhism, with numerous fresco paintings.

FOOD AND DRESS

The staple food of the people is meat—fresh, dry, cooked, or roasted—, roasted barley powder (*tsampa* or *sattu*, and plenty of dairy products. In the morning and evening they take *thhukpa*, a semi-liquid dish, that is prepared by boiling *tsampa* and meat in water, with salt added to it. The people of the Purang valley eat rice and bread also, for rice and wheat are supplied in large quantities from Nepal and Indian borders. They use Chinese tea in large quantities. Tea is boiled for a long time, salt and butter are added, and churned thoroughly in big wooden cylinders. A small quantity of crude soda called *phuldo* or *seru-tsa* is put in it to emulsify it and not to allow the whole butter to float on the top. They drink 50 to 150 cups of tea throughout the day and in the night till they retire to bed, according to their means. They take *tsampa* made into a thick paste, by mixing with tea. *Chhang*, a light beer prepared from barley, is their national beverage, in which men, women, children, and monks indulge, more often on festive occasions. Tea and *chhang* are taken either in small wooden cups silvered or otherwise, in China cups or China-made stone cups by the rich, which are kept on silver stands with silver lids on.

The whole Region being at a height of 12,000 feet above the sea-level is very cold; and so Tibetans wear long double-breasted woollen gowns with a *kamarband* (waist-band), one foot broad sash. They wear woollen shoes, called *lham*, coming almost up to the knees, which they need not remove even while entering the *sanctum sanctorum* of the temples in the monasteries. In winter they wear coats, trousers, and caps made of sheep or lamb-skins. When it is hot they remove one or both hands off the coat, thereby exposing the shoulders. Women wear almost the same kind of dress as men, with the addition of a horizontally striped woollen piece in the front, from waist down to the toes, and a tanned goat-skin on the back. Men freely use English felt-hats which are brought from Calcutta and other places and sold in their markets. Rich people, officers, and lamas wear costly dresses and silks.

SOCIAL CUSTOMS

Monogamy is common, but polyandry also is in vogue, most probably an economic adjustment to prevent the increase of population, where struggle for existence is very hard. So when the elder brother in a family marries a wife, she automatically becomes the wife to all the other brothers; and all of them live together peacefully without any hitch. The wife is held in common, though the younger brothers form servants to the elder. So much so, the Tibetans to day have only as many houses and families as they had centuries ago. Polygamy and child-marriage are not unknown. Marriage takes place with the mutual consent of the adult bride and bridegroom in consultation with their parents; and the ceremony is officiated by monks. Amongst widow and widower the system of *niyoga* is common, each living in her or his house meeting in the night in the former's house, the woman being the claimant of the offsprings. Such issues have equal legal rights and social status as those of normal marriage. *Niyoga* may be of a temporary character or permanent. Widow-marriage is very common.

Monks and nuns shave their heads and wear a sort of violet-red gowns, whereas householders both men and women plait their hair. Women dress their hair in several plaits. They enjoy full social liberty and equal status with men. As a mark of respect or salutation, Tibetans bend a little and throw out their tongues and say *khamjam-bho* or simply *khamjam* or *joo*. Monks take to all callings in life—Gurus, high-priests, corpse-cutters, officials high and low, traders, shepherds, servants, cooks, coolies, pony-drivers, shoe-makers, cultivators, and what not from the highest to the lowest—from Dalai Lama to an ordinary coolie.

The manner in which the higher order of monks bless varies according to the status and social position of the blessed. The monk brings his head near the head of the other and gently touches it if he is also a high monk, or places both his hands on the heads of those he loves most, or to whom he wants to show a greater favour. In other cases he blesses with one hand, two fingers, or only with one finger. The last mode of blessing is by touching the head with a coloured piece of cloth tied to a short stick. The principle underlying in all the cases is that there should be some contact of the blesser and the blessed in order to pass some power of efficacy to the latter from the former, besides invoking the usual blessings.

Khatak is a loosely woven gauze-like or thin white cloth made of cotton or silk of various sizes, the smallest being a foot long and three inches wide and the largest a yard long and over a foot broad. The presentation of it is a mode of interchanging civilities. When a person writes or visits an officer, a monk, or a friend, he encloses or presents a *khatak*. During marriages and on festive occasions this is presented. The non-observance of this custom is considered a mark of rudeness or lack of etiquette. This ceremonial scarf is given as a reverential offering to the deities in monasteries in place of a garland.

Tibetans have a peculiar way of killing sheep for meat. They suffocate the animal to death by tying the mouth and nostrils tightly with a rope, because it is enjoined in their religious texts that the blood of a living animal should not be spilt. While suffocating the animal they repeat the *mani-mantra,* so that its soul might get a human body in the next incarnation.

The dead bodies of well-to-do monks are cremated while those of poor monks and householders are hacked to pieces and thrown to vultures or thrown in a river if there is one nearby. Both birth and death ceremonies are many and complicated, varying with the individual means and are much akin to those of the Hindus. When the dead body is cremated, the ashes are mixed with clay and moulded into a small pyramid which is kept in a monument known as *chhorten* corresponding to the *stupa* or *chaitya* in India. The *chhorten* is symbolic of the five elements—the lowermost cubical part represents earth, the spherical part over it represents water, the triangular part above it represents fire, the crescent form over it represents air, and the moon over it represents ether.

RELIGION

Advent of Buddhism into Tibet

Buddhism was first introduced into Tibet during the time of King Srongchen Gampo, who reigned from A.D. 630 to 698. It flourished for several years under the royal patronage. Beginning from the ninth century A.D. upto the middle of the seventeenth century, great *Acharyas* like Shantarakshita of Nalanda University, Guru Padmasambhava, Deepankara Shreejnana of Vikramashila University (eleventh century), and a host of other Pandits and Teachers from India, went to Tibet and preached Buddhism, besides translating several Sanskrit, Pali, and other works into Tibetan. The religion of Tibetans is primarily Buddhism with a queer admixture of *Tantrism* or *Saktaism* and the old *Bon Dharma*—pre-Buddhistic devil-worshipping religion of Tibet. Tibet is predominantly a priest-ridden country and as such some Western writers call the religion of Tibet, Lamaism. One or two children from every family are initiated into the order of monks and nuns at the age of two or three. Nearly one third or one fourth of the population are monks and nuns and the standard of morality is low.

Different Schools of Buddhism

Buddhism prevalent in Tibet is of the *Mahayana* School. There are ten different schools or sects now prevalent in Tibet.

(1) *Ngingmapa*[1] of the eighth century was first introduced into Tibet by Chinese monks. This school is prevalent in Bhutan, Western Tibet, and Ladakh. Several books of this school are not present in *Kanjur* and *Tanjur*. (2) *Urgyenpa* of the ninth century. This school is prevalent in those parts that are adjoining Nepal borders. Buddhists of the Himalayan tracts in India are the followers of this sect. Samye in Central Tibet is the chief monastery. They worship *Urgyen* or Padmasambhava. (3) *Kadampa* of the eleventh century. They are the followers of Domten, the principal disciple of Deepankara Shreejnana (*Atisha*). The followers of this school do not strive much for the attainment of higher rungs of spirituality. (4) *Sakyapa* of the thirteenth century. The monks of this and the above three sects put on red caps, as such they are named by lay writers as Red Caps or Red Cap Sect. Their chief monastery is Sakya Gompa[2] and is situated in Central Tibet.

(5) *Gelukpa* (reformed sect) or *Gandenpa* of the fourteenth century. Chonkhapa was the founder of this sect. Ganden is their principal monastery. The followers of this school are the greatest in number. (6) *Kargyudpa*. The followers of this school believe only in *Do* or *Sutra Granthas*. They do not work for higher attainments. (7) *Karmapa*. The followers of this sect believe in the efficacy of *Karma* or action. (8) *Dekungpa*. Dekung is their chief monastery. *Kargyudpa*, *Karmapa*, and *Dekungpa* are only the offshoots of *Gelukpa* ; as such they are the part and parcel of that school. The monks of all these *Gelukpa* Sects put on yellow caps. So they are, by lay foreigners, called Yellow Caps or Yellow Cap Sect. (9) *Dukpa*. The followers of this school worship *Dorje* (*Vajra* or diamond, thunderbolt) which, they believe, has fallen from heavens at Sera Monastery. Sera is their principal monastery. These are the followers of *Tantra Marga*[3]. (10) *Bonpa* or *Penbo*. This is the religion prevailing in Tibet before the advent of Buddhism. But now these have adopted several things from Buddhism and worship the Buddhistic deities. They go to Buddhist monasteries but do anti-clockwise rounds of the holy places. The monks of the Red Cap Sect need not necessarily be celebates and can openly marry if they choose or keep a woman. As a matter of fact one of the two abbots of Sakya Gompa is a married person, but monks of the Yellow Cap Sect are expected to be celebates and if any monk marries openly, he shall have to pay very heavy fines to the monastery to which he belongs. When not in the monastery,

1 *pa* means, one belonging to.

2 The author received an invitation from the abbot of this monastery in 1946, never before accorded to an Indian in recent times. One riding pony, two luggage yaks and two servants were sent to take him, but he could not go due to his other engagements. From this monastery the Buddhist scholar Shree Rahula Sankrityayana brought several Sanskrit manuscripts.

3 See Appendix II.

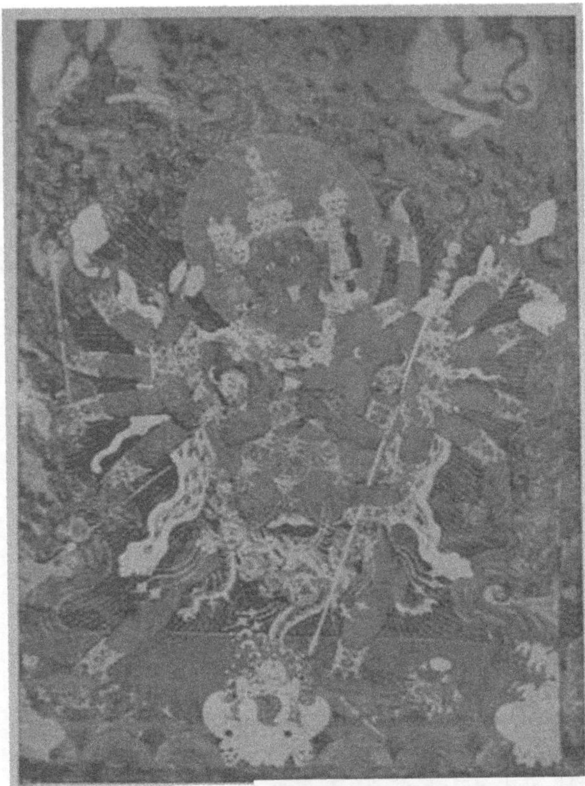

31. The Tutelary Deity Demchhog in *Yab-Yum* Pose from a Banner Painting in Simbiling
[*See* p. 8 & 215

32. Demchhog in *Yab-Yum* Pose from the Deserted Cave-Colony of Pangtha

Photo by Courtesy of Dr. Arnold Heim & August Ganser Morgarten Verlag, Zurich
[*See p.* 8 & 217

33. Images of *Sattu* and Butter made on the occasion of a *Tantrik* Rite performed in connection with the *Yidam* Dem-chhog

[*See* p. 58

34. Performing the last Rites in a *Tantrik* Ceremony called *Torma*

[*See* p. 63

35. *Tulku*-Lama Nav-Kushok of Simbiling Gompa with the usual Articles of Worship placed on a Folding table.

36. The Author in a Lama's Dress
[*See p.* 53

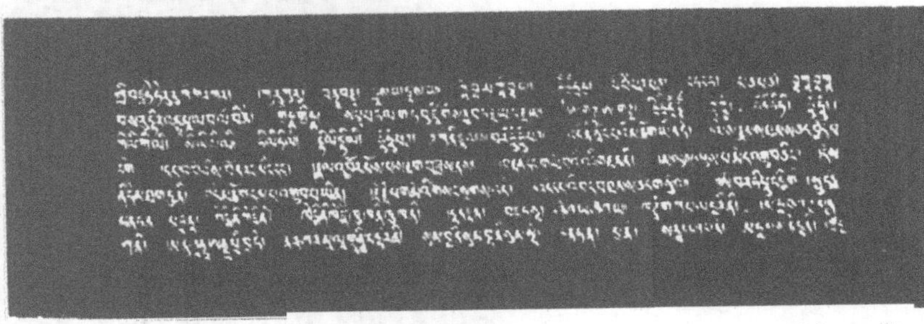

37. A Page from Kanjur. [*See* p. 60

38. ***Chhorten—Stupa*** **or *Chaitya.***
[*See p.* 55

39. His Excellency the Governor (*Zongpon*) of Taklakot (1942-45)

[*See p.* 75

40. *Zongpon's* Wife

[*See p.* 75

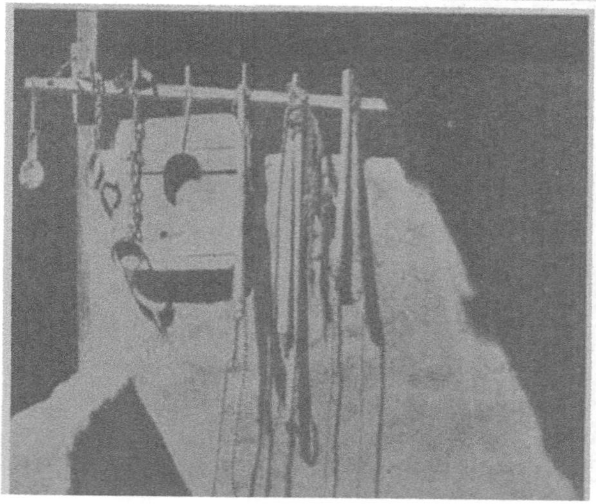

41. Articles of Punishment kept in the *Zong* (Fort)

[*See* p. 76

monks and nuns live freely, but cannot marry openly, though sometimes nuns are seen with babes in their laps. Since monks and nuns are initiated into the order at a tender age, when they have absolutely no idea of the life they are to lead, it is no wonder if they do not have a high standard of morality. It is the system which is at fault rather than the individuals.

Gompa or Monastery

Most of the monks are attached to the monasteries called *gompas*[1] (solitary places). Gompas are a combination of a temple (where the image of the Buddha and other Buddhistic deities are kept and worshipped), a *math* (where monks have their lodging and boarding), and a *dharmashala* (where travellers and pilgrims get a lodging place). The first monastery in Tibet was built between A.D. 823-835 at Samye (about 30 miles south-east of Lhasa) on the model of Udantapuri University at Bihar Shariff, 6 miles from Nalanda or on the model of Nalanda itself. Bigger monasteries also serve the purpose of schools and Universities and are big educational centres.

(1) Depung (rice-heap) Vihara is situated two miles west of Lhasa and was founded by the great reformer Chonkhapa in the year 1416. This was constructed on the model of Shree Dhanyakataka University, situated near the Amaravati Stupa on the bank of the river Krishna. The traditional number of monks in this monastery is 7,700 though there are actually 10,000 monks at present. This is the biggest residential University and monastery in the world. (2) Sera Monastery is two miles north of Lhasa and was founded in 1419. The traditional number of monks in this monastery is 5,500 though there are actually more than 7,000 in it. This is the second biggest monastery in the world. (3) Ganden Monastery is about 35 miles east of Lhasa and was founded by Chonkhapa himself in 1401. These three gompas are said to be the three pillars of Tibet. (4) Tashi-Lhunpo was founded at Shigartse in 1447. The traditional number of monks in Ganden and Tashi-Lhunpo is 3,300 each, though actually over 4,000 monks live in each. (5) Sakya Monastery, founded in 1073, (6) Derge Monastery founded in 1548 in Eastern Tibet, (7) Kum-bum Monastery founded in 1578 near the lake Koko Nor, (8) Dekung Monastery situated 100 miles north-east of Lhasa, (9) Samye Vihar founded in 823-835, south-east of Lhasa, on the left bank of the Brahmaputra, and (10) Nethang founded in 1213, south-west of Shigartse, contain over 3,000 monks each. Besides these, there are several more monasteries, like Reting with more than 1,000 monks in each.

1 Also pronounced '*gonpa*'.

Elementary education is generally imparted to monks in almost all the monasteries of Tibet. One has to go for higher education to some of these big Universities near Lhasa as there are no big educational centres in Western Tibet (*Ngari*). Besides religious education grammar, literature, medicine, image-making, engraving, painting, printing, etc. are also taught. The Nalanda-school of casting bronze images and other bronze casts has been, up to day, faithfully preserved in Tibet. Degre, Lhasa, and Tashi-Lhunpo are the biggest centres of bronzes, though one can get bronze images and bronze models of Buddhistic gods and goddesses, monks, *stupas*, etc. in almost every monastery in Tibet, Nepal, Bhutan, and Rampur Bushahr State. All these Universities and monasteries are residential and are maintained, by big landed properties attached to them, by public charity, and also by the trade and banking business conducted by some of the business-minded monks in them. Out of the total strength of the Universities only half the number are regular students and the rest of the monks are servants, conductors, managers, tradesmen etc. Students from different places like Rampur Bushahr State, Ladakh, Bhutan, Sikkim, Southern Russia and Siberia, and China go to these monastic Universities for study. Almost all of them are monks. There are two Colleges near Lhasa, one for Medicine and the other for Astrology.

Monks are of two orders : *lamas* or superior order of monks and *dabas* or ordinary monks. It is after studying for several years both religious and ritual texts that one is made a lama. There are different orders, high, middle and low amongst lamas also. All monks including lamas indulge in drinking and meat-eating. Tibetans, in general, have no religious bigotry though they are very superstitious and their monasteries can be visited by people of any sect or religion. All the monasteries of Western Tibet[1] were built after the ninth century.

Damarus, conches, drums, cymbals, bells, clarinets, flutes, pipes of human bones, and some other musical instruments, *dorjes* (thunderbolts), human skulls, several cups of water and barley, incense, butter-lamps, *chhang*, *tsampa*, meat, butter, cakes, and many other things are used in the worship of deities in the monasteries. Now and then big *yantras* or *mandalas*[2] are drawn and images of *tsampa* and butter in several colours are made, of different tutelary deities (*yidam*) and elaborate *pujas* are conducted from 3 to 30 days mostly according to *tantrik* rites. On the last day of the worship a big *havan* (fire-oblation) is performed. Several water-colour paintings called

[1] See Appendix V.

[2] A *mandala* or *yantra* is a mystic circle, geometrically divided into circles, squares and chords, in which are painted some symbols, deities, and *Bijaksharas* (letters).

thankas or banner paintings are hung in the image and library halls and other rooms. The paintings represent deities, lamas, scenes, *yantras*, etc. and have silk borders and veils over them to protect them from being damaged. Tibet owes a great deal to India for the development of her culture—religion, civilization, learning, painting, and other arts and crafts. Tibetans possess a good sense of artistic taste; there is no house which does not possess atleast one painting, an artistic folding table, and a few silver-plated cups.

Library

The two great Tibetan works in the shelves of a Tibetan library are *Kanjur* (or *Kangyur*—translations of Lord Buddha's actual utterances) in 108 volumes and *Tanjur* (or *Tagyur*—translation of *shastras*) in about 235 volumes. The latter work comprises of different Schools of Philosophy, *Kavyas*, Grammar, Astrology, Astronomy, *Devata-Sadhana*, *Tantras* and *Mantras*, besides the commentaries on several books of *Kanjur* and Tibetan translations of the Chinese renderings of the original Sanskrit works. *Tanjur* also contains the translations of several other Sanskrit works, whose originals have been for ever lost in the bonfires of the various ruthless Mohammedan invaders and kings. It also contains the lost works of the great astronomer Aryadeva, Dingnaga, Dharmarakshita, Chandrakirti, Shantarakshita, and the lost works of Kamalasila; *Vadanyaya tika* of the great Grammarian Chandragoumi, *Chandra Vyakarana*, *Sutra*, *Dhatu*, *Unadi-path*, *Vritti*, *Tika*, *Panchaka* etc.; *Lokananda Nataka*, several lost works of Ashvaghosha, Matichitra, Haribhadra, Aryasura, and others; Kalidasa's *Meghaduta*; and some works of Dandi, Harshavardhana, Kshemendra, and other great poets. The medical works of *Ashtanga-Hridaya* of Nagarjuna, of Shilihotra, and others with commentaries and glossaries; and the translations of some Hindi books; and also of some of the letters of Matichitra to the Emperor Kanishka, of Yogishavara Jagadratna to Maharaja Chandragupta, and the letters of Dipankar Shreejnana to Raja Nayapala (of Pala Dynasty) are in the volumes of *Tanjur*. Besides these two voluminous collections of works the lives of Nagarjuna, Aryadeva, Asanga, Vasubandhu, Shantarakshita, Chandrakirti, Dharmakirti, Chandragoumi, Kamalashila, Shila, Dipankar Shreejnana and other Indian Buddhist Pandits are also written in Tibetan language.[1]

People speak Tibetan which varies from district to district. When Buddhism was introduced into Tibet during the time of King Srongchen in about the year A.D. 641, at his order, his minister Thonmi

1 The author is grateful to his friend Mahapandit Rahula Sankrityayana for the information given in this paragraph.

invented, for the then spoken language, character on the model of the then Kashmiri Sharada alphabets, in order to translate Pali and Sanskrit, Buddhist and other works into Tibetan. There are five vowels and thirty consonants in Tibetan language. Thonmi wrote the first grammar of the Tibetan language; nearly half the number of letters written are silent, i.e. not pronounced; and necessary modifications have been made so as to include the sounds peculiar to Tibetan and Sanskrit languages. Before the time of Thonmi writing was unknown in Tibet.

In the beginning of the fourteenth century Rinchhen Dub collected all the translations of Buddha's works under the title *Kanjur* and all the *Shastras* under the title *Tanjur*. It was in the year 1728 (?) that the *Kanjur* and *Tanjur* were printed for the first time during the regime of the seventh Dalai Lama, from Nyathang Gompa which was founded in 1213. Later, a second edition of the same works, with an additional volume in *Kanjur*, was published from Derge Gompa. But according to another version it was in the middle of the seventeenth century, the period of the fifth Dalai Lama, that these works were printed. Whole pages of books are engraved on wooden blocks and printed. But the blocks of Derge edition are of bronze, as such the print of this edition is clearer than that of Nyathang since the wooden blocks are subject to greater wear and tear. The author was informed by a Tibetan friend of his that blocks for a new edition of Kanjur had been prepared at Lhasa by the thirteenth Dalai Lama. Books are printed on country-made paper of three qualities: common, superior, and superfine. Books produced in the superfine or de luxe edition have thick strong paper and the letters are printed in gold. If the two works of *Kanjur* and *Tanjur* were to be retranslated into Sanskrit, it would come to about 20 lakhs of *shlokas*.

Calendar

About the year 1027 Pandit Somnath of Kashmir translated the '*Kala Chakra Jyotisha*' into Tibetan and introduced the *Brihaspati* cycle of sixty years called *Prabhava*, etc. (*Rabyung* in Tibetan). This cycle of sixty years is divided into five sub-cycles of twelve years each. In the seventh year (*Ta-lo* or Horse-year) of each of these sub-cycles, i.e. once in twelve years) a big fare is held near Kailas at Sershung. The Kumbha Mela of India, which occurs once in 12 years has nothing to do with this fair, as several people confound. According to Tibetan scriptures, a round made to the Holy Kailas and Manasarovar during the *Ta-lo* is considered as virtuous as thirteen rounds made during other years. *Margasirsha Shukla Pratipada* (December 14 in 1936) is observed as New Year's Day on the southern shores of Manasarovar, as in the days of *Mahabharata*, and this may be of interest to the Indian astronomer. Tibetans of that region say that the sun begins his northward journey from that day. *Paushya Shukla Pratipada* (January 13 in 1937) is observed as New Year's Day on the eastern side of the Manas (Horba) and *Magha Shukla Pratipada* (February 12 in 1937) is the official New Year's Day throughout Tibet. Special *pujas* and services are conducted in the monasteries on the New Year's Day, and feastings and merry-making take place for 10 to 15 days, in which monks and householders, both men and women, freely partake.

The third day of the bright half of a lunar month, dedicated to Padmasambhava or Guru Rinpochhe, the eighth day dedicated to *Devi*, the full moon day dedicated to Lord Buddha, and the new moon day, are the days in each lunar month, on which special *pujas* are performed in the monasteries, besides some other days which differ from place to place. Tibetans know very little of arithmetic excepting counting, so much so, for higher counting and accounting, even high officials use only the beads of a rosary which every one invariably carries with him or her, or use small pebbles, splinters of wood, seeds of apricot and date, and broken pieces of porcelain.

Mani-Mantra

Om ma ni pa dme hum is the most popular and most sacred *mantra*[1] of the Tibetans, which is ever on the lips of men, women, children, monks, householders, and all. They always repeat this *mantra* while sitting, walking, or travelling. Even the ordinary Tibetan repeats this *mantra* for a greater number of times than a most orthodox Brahmin does his *Gayatri Japa* in India. It is said that this *mantra* has been invented by Avalokiteshvara by the grace of his divine father, the effulgent Amitabha Buddha; and as such it is an invocation of the Bodhisattva Avalokiteshvara himself. *Mani* symbolizes *Purusha* or the spiritual element, and *Padma* (lotus) symbolizes *Shakti* or the material. *Om* is the usual prefix of every *mantra* and '*hum*' is the *tantrik* suffix; so the *mantra* means 'Oh! Jewel (of Creation) is in the Lotus!' The letter *hri* is very often added to it; *hri* being the abbreviation of *hridaya* or heart, it implies that this *mantra* is to be meditated upon in the Heart-Lotus. As in *Tantrik* schools, Tibetans assign certain colours to each letter of the *mantra* and they believe that the utterance of this six-syllabled formula extinguishes rebirth in the six worlds of gods, men, titans,

1 A *mantra* is a mystic formula consisting of letters with some symbolic importance attached to them. The repetition of it, in accordance with certain directions attached to it by the teacher, is considered to set up a vibration which gives out a tremendous energy that can be utilised either for physical welfare or for the spiritual benefit of a person.

animals, hells, and infernal hells, and secures *Nirvana*. The colours of the letters are white, blue, yellow, green, red, and black respectively. *Hri* is also said to be white.

Om ma ni pa dme hum hri (ओं म णि प द्मे हुं ह्री)

The *mani-mantra* is inscribed, embossed, or painted on walls, rocks, stones, slabs, caves, monasteries, on horns, bones, flags, and on anything. The *mantra* is engraved on round stones or slabs which are kept on walls at the entrance of villages, on the tops of passes, at camping grounds, on the way to holy places and monasteries, at spots wherefrom some holy place is seen, and at any important place. The *mantra* is written several times on slips of paper which are kept in a small brass, copper, or silver cylinder with a handle. The prayer wheel, cylinder or mill (*korlo*) is turned round and round in the clockwise direction by monks, beggars, men, women, and all. One round of the wheel is believed to be productive of as much virtue as the repetition of the *mantra* as many times as it is written on the slips in the cylinder. Several such *mani*-cylinders of different sizes are set up at the gates and inside the monasteries, and are turned round by pilgrims when they visit them. The author saw some such big *mani*-cylinders in Ladakh, driven by water-power, like *pan-chakkis* (water-mills). They contain slips of paper, on which the *mani-mantra* is written a lakh, a million, or even ten million times.

Simbiling Gompa

Just above the Taklakot Mandi, situated on the top of a hill, overlooking the mandi and the neighbouring villages and the Karnali with its feeders, is the famous Lamasery Simbiling, the biggest monastery of this Region. It has about six branch monasteries at Siddikhar, on Manasarovar, and at other places. Including the branches, it has about 170 monks of whom 6 are lamas and the rest *dabas*. There is a regular school for the junior monks of the monastery. In the main image-hall of the monastery there is a big gilded image of the Buddha about 6 feet high, seated on a high pedestal, with butter-lamps kept burning in the front. Just before entering the image-hall is the general congregational hall, festooned with scroll paintings; and the walls are decorated with fine mural paintings. Once in a year there are held general feasts, merry-making, mystic or symbolic dances by the monks, lasting for a week or two. In the symbolic dance they wear long gowns and a variety of masks of different deities and animals. Street dramatists with a few masks enact some dramas like Treme-Kunden (*Vishvantara Jataka*), Chogel-Norsang, Nyasa-Pomo, etc. both in the monastery compound and villages. The mystic dance of Simbiling Monastery is called *Torgyak* and takes place on the 28th and 29th day of the eleventh month of the Tibetan calendar, that of Khochar Gompa, *Namdong* and takes place on the 15th day of the first month, and of Siddikhar Monastery, *Tsege* and takes place on the 22nd and 23rd of the first month. The author had the chance of witnessing, in 1942, these mystic plays and as well a purely *tantrik* rite called *Chakhar* (iron fort), held every fourth year in Simbiling, in which the blood of a black goat put in a human skull is offered as fire-oblation (*ahuti*); this rite is conducted for about 20 days. When any distinguished person visits a monastery, the monks receive him to the accompaniment of the musical instruments of the gompa.

There are some hundreds of Tibetan books in the shelves of the library rooms of the monastery, including two sets of the voluminous works of *Kanjur* and *Tanjur*. There is a separate image-hall of the *Menlha* (god of medicine) adjacent to the library halls. There are more than 400 excellent *thankas* or banner paintings and four huge silk banners of Buddha and Maitreya each measuring 60 by 30 feet. These are all kept under lock and key by the *Dazang* and are taken out for decorating the monastery on special occasions like the New Year's Day.

Simbiling Gompa is affiliated to the Depung Monastery of Lhasa and as such the *Labrang* or the general managing body including the *Khenpo* or the abbot comes from that monastery appointed for a period of three years. This monastery has three more local managing bodies all elected from amongst the monks of the gompa, the first two being for a period of three years. The first is the *Dazang* or the general managing body which is in charge of the whole property of the gompa; the second is the *Nyarchang* or the kitchen managing body including the *Majin* or the head cook; and the third is the *Chongpon* or the trading body, which is elected annually. The *Geku*, a monk with magisterial powers, who looks to the discipline of the monks, and the *Unje* or the *Pujari* are also elected annually. Adjacent to this gompa, situated on the west, is a branch of the Sakya Monastery.

Khochar Gompa

Situated on the left bank of the river Karnali is the famous Khochar or Khocharnath Gompa, at a distance of about 12 miles south-east of Taklakot Mandi. It is also called *Khechari Tirtha* by some Hindus. Pilgrims visit this place all the year round. Deepankara Shreejnana had spent a rainy season here in the year 1034.

Khochar is one of the most interesting monasteries in Western Tibet. There is an interesting story in the *Khochar Karchhak* regarding Khochar. Seven *Acharyas* from India once took seven loads of silver to Kardung and deposited it with Jambyang Thakpa, the then King of the place and went away saying that they would return in seven years. But they did not turn up even after nine years. So, the King gave the silver to two silver-smiths—one a Nepali by name Ashadharma and the other a Mohammedan by name Vankulla and ordered them to make a divine idol out of it. Accordingly the smiths melted the whole silver to mould it into an idol but suddenly there sprang up a big image of Jambyang out of it on its own accord (*Svayambhu*) out of the molten silver.

A lama and his disciple were staying on the sandy banks of the Karnali where the present Khochar Gompa stands. Every night the disciple used to see a light on the sand, when he would go to fetch water, though he would see nothing in the daytime there. One day the lama asked his disciple to pile up a heap of stones at the place where he saw the light, and the disciple did accordingly. To his great surprise, the heap of stones became a big boulder by next morning. The lama said that that light was the spirit of Jambyang.

Having heard of the *Svayambhu* (self-formed) idol of Jambyang, the King of Kardung ordered that the idol should be brought to Kardung to be installed in a temple. Accordingly the image was put in a two-horsed carriage and was being taken towards Kardung. When the carriage reached the big boulder above described, the spirit of Jambyang entered the idol and it was stuck up on the boulder, and said '*Khor-chhak* — I have come here and stay here only'. This is the first utterance of the idol.

Then a gompa was constructed for the image by the King. When the King was thinking of getting a pedestal made for the idol, it spoke out a second time, 'Let nobody—man, beast, bird, or insect—enter the gompa for seven days'. Accordingly, the monastery gates were

OM

VARIOUS ROUTES TO THE HOLY KAILĀS AND MĀNASARŌVAR

Map No. 1

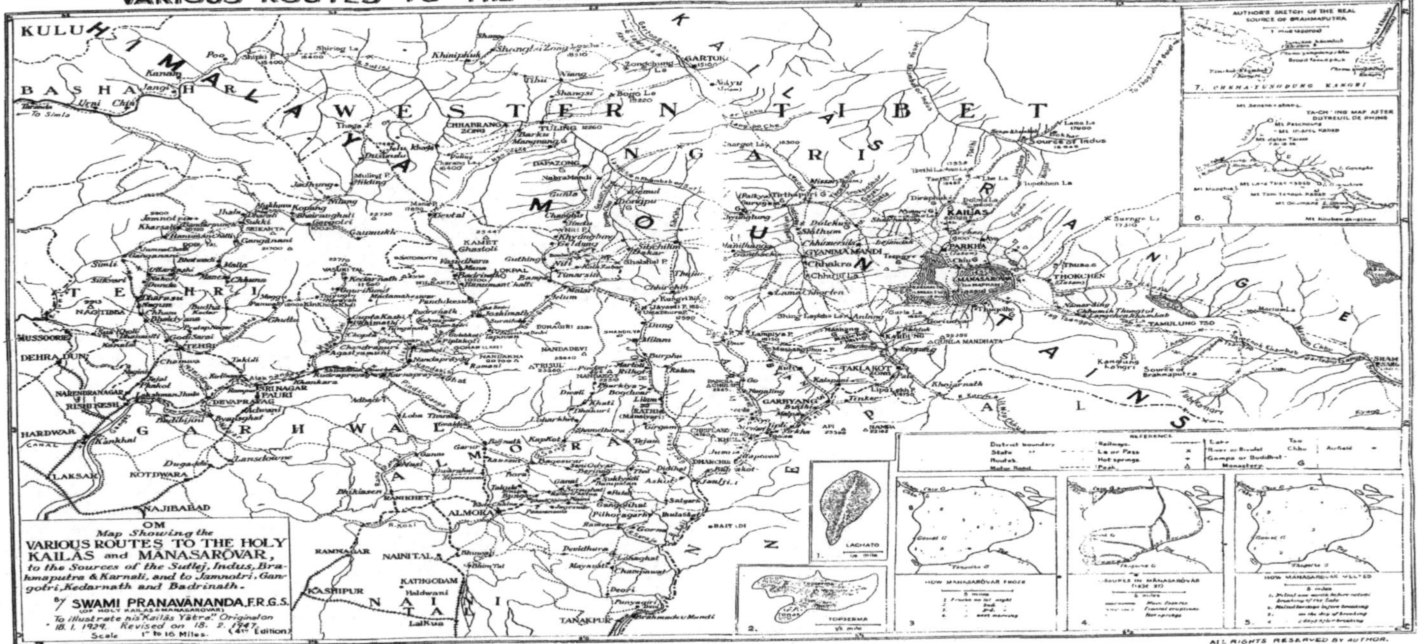

Reg No. 7469 E'48—6,000'48.

ABSTRACT OF MILEAGES BETWEEN IMPORTANT PLACES IN KAILAS KHANDA AND KEDAR KHANDA

	Miles
1. Almora to Kailas via Lipu Lekh pass	238
2. Almora to Kailas via Darma pass	227
3. Almora to Kailas via Unta-dhura pass	219
4. Joshimath to Kailas via Gunla-Niti pass	200
5. Joshimath to Kailas via Damjan-Niti pass	190
6. Joshimath to Kailas via Hoti-Niti pass	138
7. Badrinath to Kailas via Mana pass	238
8. Mukhuva (Gangotri) to Kailas via Jelukhaga pass	243
9. Simla to Kailas via Shipki pass and Gartok	445
10. Simla to Kailas via Shipki pass and Tuling	473
11. Srinagar (Kashmir) to Kailas via Ladakh	605
12. Pashupatinath (Nepal) to Kailas via Muktinath & Khochar	525
13. Lhasa to Kailas via Gyantse & Shigartse	800
14. Kailas Parikrama	32
15. Circumference of Manasarovar	34
16. Manasarovar Parikrama	64
17. Circumference of Rakshas Tal	77
18. Kailas to the Source of Indus via Lhe la or Topchhen la	16
19. Kailas to the Source of Brahmaputra	97
20. Kailas to the Source of Sutlej (at Dulchu Gompa)	21
21. Kailas to the Source of Tag tsangpo	[illegible]
22. Taklakot to the Source of Karnali	[illegible]
23. Kailas to Manasarovar	14
24. Kailas to Tirthapuri	[illegible]
25. Kailas to Dulchu Gompa	21
26. Kailas to Gyanima Mandi	[illegible]
27. Gyanima Mandi to Gartok	76
28. Gyanima Mandi to Tirthapuri	27
29. Gyanima Mandi to Shibchilim Mandi	[illegible]
30. Shibchilim to Nabra Mandi	[illegible]
31. Nabra to Tuling	33½
32. Tuling to Badrinath	109
33. Gyanima Mandi to Taklakot	49
34. Taklakot to Tugolho	41
35. Taklakot to Khocharnath	12
36. Tarchhen to Serdung-chuksum	7
37. Tarchhen to Tso Kapala	[illegible]
38. Tarchhen to Serdung-chuksum & back via Tso Kapala	17½
39. Almora to Lipu Lekh pass	165½
40. Lipu Lekh to Kailas	72½
41. Haldwani to Almora (on foot)	41
42. Haldwani to Almora (by bus)	[illegible]
43. Almora to Pindari Glacier	73
44. Rikhikesh to Jamnotri	[illegible]
45. Rikhikesh to Gangotri	145
46. Rikhikesh to Kedarnath	132½
47. Rikhikesh to Badrinath	167½
48. Rikhikesh to Joshimath	148½
49. Joshimath to Badrinath	19
50. Ramnagar to Badrinath	161
51. Jamnotri to Gangotri	96½
52. Gangotri to Kedarnath	123
53. Kedarnath to Badrinath	101
54. Mussoorie to Jamnotri	86
55. Rikhikesh to Jamnotri, Gangotri, Kedarnath, Badrinath, and back to Rikhikesh	608
56. Rikhikesh to Tehri (motor road)	50
57. Tehri to Gangotri	100
58. [illegible]	[illegible]
59. Badrinath to Chamoli	18
60. Ranikhet to Karnaprayag	60
61. Badrinath to Karnaprayag	67
62. Garur via Baijnath to Nandaprayag	45½
63. Nandaprayag to Badrinath	58½
64. Gangotri to Gaumukh	13
65. Uttarkashi to Dodital	18
66. Kedarnath to Vasukital	2
67. Chamoli to Gohna lake	12
68. Panchkeshwar to Lokpal	12
69. Badrinath to Satopanth	18
70. Milam to Shandilya-kund	6
71. Milam to Surya-kund	13
72. Dharchula to Chhipalekot	25

closed; but on the fifth day, the *Konyer* (keeper of idols or the assistant *Pujari*), in his anxiety to see if the lamps inside were burning or not, opened the doors. He saw the divine smiths that were working out the pedestal or *Simhasana*, had entered the image and the pedestal was left incomplete. The design of the pedestal is given herein. Later on, Vishvakarma, the divine architect, made the silver idols of Chhagna-dorje and Chenresig.

The idol spoke for a third time, 'If the Map chhu rises, it comes near the monastery and I will be taken away by the waters; so keep the image of Jechun Doma (*Tara*) facing the river. If anybody makes an embankment his sins of 500 lives shall be washed away; if any one feeds the workmen, the sins of 10 lives shall be washed away; and if one puts, even a small stone as big as a thumb, on the embankment with a pure heart, the sins of one life will be washed away.'

Once some soldiers entered the gompa and stabbed on the thigh of the idol wherefrom milk came out. The idol spoke a fourth time, 'Oh great sinner!' Whereupon all the soldiers went out of the temple, but the one who had actually stabbed the idol died at the temple gate by vomitting blood.

The King of the southern region had two Queens but no sons. They did all sorts of *pujas* but in vain. The image spoke for the fifth time, 'Come here, Queens, do three prostration-salutes to me, you will have three sons'. The Queens did so and later, they had three sons.

One great lama by name Chang-nyun came here, when, the image spoke out for the sixth time, 'Remove the paper-bird from my back which has been placed by some *Ngakpa* (black magician)'. A *Ngakpa* usually draws the picture of a bird and some other formula on a paper and performs some incantations and rites and puts it in the wall of a house. After a period of 7, 9, or 21 years depending upon the strength of incantations, the bird comes to life and flies away and the person or idol concerned breaks to pieces. Such an incantation paper was kept behind the idol of Jambyang. The lama, Chang-nyun, took out the paper-bird which was just fluttering and threw it in fire with tongs. When Kyangun-Zingba-Nurbu, the lama who has constructed the existing Gossul Gompa, went to Khochar, the idol of Jambyang spoke for the seventh time, 'The flower in my hand has been taken away by a soldier. It will be good if you can replace it'. The gold-silver flower studded with a cat's eye, (*Vaidurya*) in the middle, was replaced by the lama. The gold lamp in front of the image was presented to the gompa by the same lama. It is believed by Tibetans that the image of Jambyang would speak out six times more after which the world would see the day of resurrection.

In the *duvang* or image-hall there are three beautiful images of three of the most important *Bodhisattvas*, made of silver, standing on an artistically designed pedestal or a bracket about 5 feet high. The images are placed on big lotuses. The *Simhasana* including the lotuses are made of *Ashta-dhatus* or eight metals. The middle image *Jambyang* (Manjughosha) is about 8 feet high and its face is yellow. On its right is the idol of *Chenresig* (Avalokiteshvara) 7 feet high and its face is white; and on the left is the idol of *Chhagnadorje* (Vajrapani) 7 feet high and its face is of blue complexion. These three images are erroneously described as and believed by many credulous people to be those of Rama, Lakshmana, and Seeta. It is interesting to note that all the three images are of male deities! On either side of these images are twelve images, each about five feet in height, kept in almirahs, six on either side. Of these, eight are the images of Neve-se-gye, three are the duplicates of Khochar images, and one of Khasarpani.

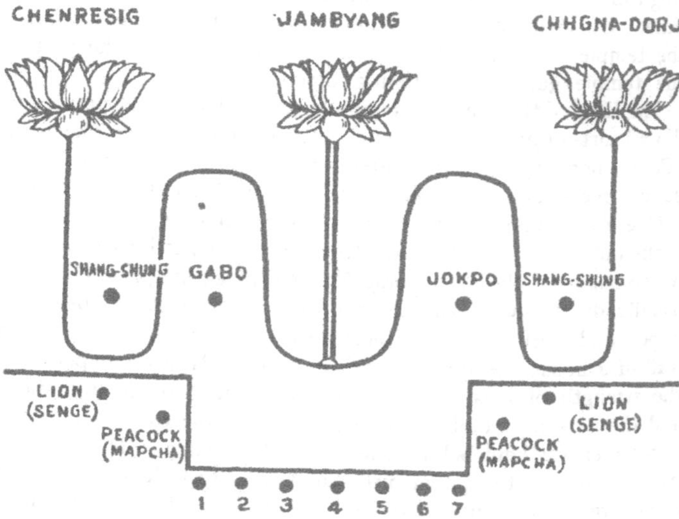

The Bracket in Khochar Gompa

1. Langpochhe (*Iravata* or the cèlestial elephant), 2. Lonpo (*Kubera* or the divine treasurer), 3. Chhunmo (*Rani* or the royal consort), 4. Korlo (*Chakra* orthe wheel of life), 5. Norbu (*Mani* or the precious stone), 6. Magpon (the divine war-general, *Kartikeya*), and 7. Tachhok (*Uchhaishravasa* or the divine horse). These are called *Rinchhen-na-dun* (seven gems or precious things) and are held sacred by Tibetans. Shang-shang are nymphs with the body of a woman and legs of a kite. Gabo and Jokpo are snake-nymphs (*Naga-kanyakas*) with human bodies and snaky lower parts and with seven-hooded snakes over their heads).

Standing on the pedestal there is an arch over the images, on either side of which are carved the images of (i) Langpochhe (elephant), (ii) Senge (lion), (iii) Kataser, (iv) Me (man), (v) Chhu-senge' crocodile), and (vi) Shang-shang; and Chha-chhung on the top, in all 13 images.

The images and the pedestal are of South Indian pattern and were prepared by the Nepalese sculptors. In 1899 a big fire broke out in Khocharnath Gompa and destroyed the two side-images—Avalokiteshvara and Vajrapani. Later they were prepared by Tibetan and Nepalese sculptors. Another tradition says that all the three images along with the pedestal were brought to this monastery from *Lanka* or Ceylon.

There are several cups of water and butter-lamps made of gold and silver and are artistically arranged in front of the images. There are two big and fierce-looking images each about 8 feet high at the entrance gate of the monastery. The image that is on the left hand side is that of *Tamdin,* the fierce form of Avalokiteshvara and that on the right is of *Chhagdor*, the fierce form of Amitabha Buddha. Just after entering the *duvang,* there are four images of the guardian deities of the four quarters six feet high, two on each side. On either side of the image-hall are the shelves containing the volumes of *Kanjur,* kept in perfect order. There are 30 *dabas* and a *Tulku* lama in this monastery. By the side of the main gompa there is a *mani-khang,* a house in which is installed a huge *mani*-cylinder.

There is a big hall in the second building of the monastery where mystic dances called *Namdong* and annual feasts are held. In the hall is hung a stuffed wild yak and an Indian tiger on one side. There are also the images of *Chamba* (Maitreya, the coming Buddha), Mahakala and Mahakali, *Sange-Pavo-Rapdun,* and *Yum-Chhamo-Chhok-Chu-Sange,* placed in different rooms. There is a big *mani*-cylinder 10 feet high and 5 feet in diameter.

The sitting image of Maitreya is about 22 feet in height. Due to its gigantic appearance, Indian pilgrims wrongly identify it with that of Bhimasen of *Mahabharata* fame. *Sange-Pavo-Rapdun* (Buddha-hero-seven) are the images of the seven Buddhas sitting in different *mudras* (postures)—Gautama Buddha, Maitreya Buddha, Kashyapa Buddha, Amitabha Buddha, and others. Ignorant Hindu pilgrims think them to be those of *Sapta Rishis*—Agastya and others. *Yum-Chhamo-Chhok-Chu-Sange* (Mother-great-directions-ten-sages) are eleven images sitting in different postures. The middle one is that of the great Mother *Devi* Prajnaparamita and the five images on either side are those of ten quarters (four quarters, four corners, sky, and netherland), but not of the eleven *Rudras* as is erroneously believed by Hindu pilgrims. There are fine frescos in this image-hall, some of which are getting damaged due to rain-water leaking inside. The room is very dark and so, very few visitors are aware of these valuable paintings. A great service would be done to the cause of art if any visitor could take a series of these paintings under flash-light. In the upper storey of the building there is the image-hall of *Jechun Doma* (White Tara) in which there are the volumes of *Kanjur*. The 21 *Avataras* of *Devi* are depicted on the walls of the hall. Adjacent to this hall is the *Tanjur* Library Hall.

On the back of the gompa, situated in the midst of *mani*-walls on the bank of the Karnali, is the *gaddi* of the great Lochava (translator) Rinchhen-Zangbo, where he delivered sermons for twelve years. There are several houses and *donkhangs* (Tibetan *dharmashalas*) very near the gompa ; and the village itself is a little away from it. Khochar is warmer than Taklakot, though more windy. A little down the monastery there is a bridge on the Karnali, crossing which, Nepal territory begins. About a mile from Khochar is Shar, the last village in the Purang valley where *pema* trees (a sort of stunted deodars) grow.

CHAPTER IV

AGRICULTURAL AND ECONOMIC GEOGRAPHY

AGRICULTURE

THE whole valley consisting of about 50 villages[1] including Taklakot is called Purang valley and is cultivated. Excepting the villages in the Purang valley the whole of Kailas-Manasarovar Region is a barren tract. Barley and pea are grown in sufficient quantities in this valley. The fields are cultivated by water from the hill-streams distributed into small nice channels. The channels are bordered by green grass and present a pleasing appearance in the bleak and barren country. Ploughing is done by *jhabbus* (cross breed of Indian cow and Tibetan bull, the yak) or ponies since yak is not good for ploughing though useful for carrying heavy loads. It is said that agriculture was introduced into Tibet in the beginning of the Christian era during the reign of the king Pude-kur-Gyal. King Srongchen Gampo (630-698) introduced the earthen pot, the water-mill, and the handloom. There are water-mills (*pan-chakkis*) for grinding barley, in some of the villages of the valley wherever there are hill-streams or channels taken out of them. White and red mustard, turnip, and radish are also grown sparsely here and there. Since the year 1940 the cultivation of potato is being experimented at Khocharnath.

FAUNA

Wild yak (*dong*), wild horse or ass (*kyang*), snow-leopard (*chen*) (this kills even horses), leopard (*jik*), lynx (*yi*) (this kills sheep and goat and drinks only blood, its skin varies in colour from pale brown or yellow to silvery white), brown bear (*te*), black bear (*tom*), man-bear (*me-te*) (walks on hind legs like man), the great Tibetan sheep (*nyan*) (Ovis Ammon or Hodgsoni), *bharal* or blue sheep (*na*) (Ovis Nahaura), *ghural* or Tibetan gazelle (*goa*) (Gazelle picticaudeta) (white near the anus, utters '*mya*' like goat), Tibetan antelope (*cho*) (Panthilops Antelope or Hodgsoni) (long horns), *barahsingi* (*shya*), deer (*gya-ra*), wolf (*changu*), fox (*haje*), hare (*regong*), marmot (*phiya*), rat (*sivi*), tail-less rat (*abra*), and lizard are the wild fauna of Manasa Khanda. Lion (*senge*) is said to be seen near Kailas only by the sages; so it is only a mythological creation. Musk-deer (*la*) is very rarely found in Manasa Region near Nepal borders, but it is abundantly found in other parts of Tibet. As a matter of fact musk is one of the chief commodities which Tibet exports to China and India. Fish is found in abundance in Manasarovar and Rakshas Tal

1 See Appendix IV.

and some rivers, but Tibetans do not eat fish and birds. Serpent and scorpion are not seen here. The marmots remain in hybernation in their holes under several feet of snow for 3 to 4 months in winter. It is perhaps by observing these marmots and frogs that *yogis* evolved *Khechari Mudra*, in which they remain for days together in *Samadhi* (trance) without any signs of external growth or decay. The fat and skins of these marmots are considered very effective for rheumatism, which is very common in these cold regions.

Musk-deer[1] (Moschus moschiferus) is chiefly an inhabitant of the Himalayas, Tibet, and Central Asia. It lives at heights ranging between 8,000 and 12,000 feet. It is about two feet high and three feet long. Musk-deer is the only hornless species. Its ears are long, has two upper canine teeth three inches long, hoofs narrow and pointed, lateral hoofs greatly developed so as to rest on the ground, tail rudimentary, colour brownish-grey, varying in shades, and hairs thick, brittle, pith-like and yet soft and springy to the touch. The so-called *Kasturi-ka-nabha* is a gland or pouch of the size of a lemon, situated at the root of the penis, a little behind the umbilical knot and is found only in males. As is generally believed musk-pod, musk-pouch, or *Kasturi-ka-nabha*, is in fact not *nabha* (umbilical knot) or its secretion. The quantity of musk contained in a musk-pod varies from ½ to 2½ tolas. Musk is dark-purplish or brownish in colour and unctuous to touch. It has a remarkable permanence and stability of odour. Its scent is most penetrating and persistent and hence its importance for perfuming purposes. Very often musk is highly adulterated by the sellers taking advantage of this characteristic feature. The price of musk per tola ranges anything from Rs. 35, which a *Shikari* charges, to as much as Rs. 90, which a consumer has to pay in plains.

Swan or bar-headed goose, brahminy duck, gull, fishing eagle, stork or heron, vulture (*thankar*), hawk (*lak*), kite (*chargot*), *koser, konak, singja,* two varieties of owl (*ukpa*), raven (*karok*), red-billed and yellow-legged chough (*kyunka*), yellow billed and yellow legged chough, pigeon (*mugrin*), *chakor* (*takpa*), woodpecker (*phuphu-seli*), lark, house-sparrow (*khang-chil*), rock-sparrow (*ri-chil*), *sari-tak-tak* (red), *pongpo-gyakar* (white and black), *kangaling* (found near Chema-yungdung), *tha* (ash colour, eats sparrows), *phunga* (hunts pigeons), *chhupja*, and butterfly are the avifauna[2]. Besides these, several other migratory birds visit this Region in particular seasons. On the shores of the Manasarovar and Rakshas Tal swarms of harmless and

[1] The author has been conducting interesting researches regarding 'Musk and Musk-deer' for the last twelve years, and he is expected to conclude his work by the end of this year when we hope to publish a full report on the subject—*Publisher.*

[2] Appendix VI.

non-malarial variety of black mosquito are seen. When this mosquito is killed, a sort of deep green substance comes out instead of blood. It does not sting; so it may interest a research student of the Tropical School of Medicine. Like the mythological animal lion, there is a mythological bird, red crow, which, if held in the hand, the person holding it becomes invisible.

DOMESTIC ANIMALS

The chief tame animals are *yak* (Tibetan hairy bull), *demo* (cow), *jhabbu, jemo* (female), Indian cow, and bull, horse, mule, ass, sheep, and goat. There goes a Bhotia saying that 'sheep, goats, and yaks are the chief crop and wealth of Tibetans'. Occasionally once in 7 or 8 years, when the snowfall is heavy, all pasture-lands are buried under snow for days together, and hundreds of animals from the herds have no other alternative but to die of starvation and severe cold, as all domestic animals including dogs, sheep, horses, yaks, etc. are always kept in open compounds without roofs, even in the severest winters. Some people tame the cat (*billa*) as a pet and hen (*chhamu*) for laying eggs; and pig is tamed in Central and Eastern Tibet. Manasa Khanda being a pastoral country, dog plays an important role amongst the domestic animals. There is no household or tent without a dog. It keeps guard over the house and the cattle. The Tibetan dog is very ferocious.

Yak is a great beast of burden and carries heavy loads even on bad roads and higher altitudes, but it cannot withstand the hot climate and dense air of lower altitudes nor can it be used for tilling the land. *Jhabbu*, on the other hand, can withstand hot climate and dense air of the lower altitudes, and the cold climate and the rarified air of higher altitudes. It is useful both for ploughing the land and for carrying loads. So the Bhotias of the mandis in Tibet and the Tibetans of Taklakot keep a good number of *jhabbus*. Some of the yaks and *jhabbus* with nose-strings are also used for riding.

STOCK-RAISING

Tibet is a big wool-producing country. Thousands of maunds of wool are imported to India every year from the Manasarovar Region and other parts of Tibet. All the woollen mills of Northern India and Bombay get the major part of their wool supplies from Tibet. Sometimes there are indents for Tibetan wool from foreign countries. If the wool produce of Tibet is controlled and improved scientifically, Tibet will become one of the finest and biggest wool-supplying countries of the world-market, like Switzerland. Besides supplying wool, the millions of sheep are the chief means of conveyance in and across the Himalayas for carrying enormous quantities of wool, salt and borax from Tibet to India; and grain and miscellaneous goods from India to Tibet. Though Tibet is purely a Buddhist country by religion, half the diet of a Tibetan consists of mutton. There is a Bhotia saying that 'sheep are the goods trains, ponies and mules mail trains'. It is a pleasant sight to watch hundreds of sheep moving slowly with double panniers of salt or grain on their backs, going along the trails up and down the mighty Himalayan ranges, treading their weary way, picking up every now and then hurriedly a blade of grass here and a mouthful there. The approach of these laden sheep is often announced by the rising of clouds of dust and the peculiar whistlings of the Bhotia drivers and by the voice of the little bells tied to the necks of some of the animals, the tinkling of which sounds and resounds along the forest-roads. Generally the Tibetan sheep are not unloaded till they reach the destination, for it is a very tedious business to load these shy and turbulent creatures.

Cheese (called *chhura* in Tibetan), butter, milk, and other dairy products of the Senge Khambab region are considered to be the best in the whole of Tibet. There are thousands of *yaks* and *demos* (Tibetan bulls and cows) and millions of sheep and goats in Tibet. Good dairy farms can be started on up-to-date scientific lines with great profit and advantage, as Tibet is mainly a pastoral country where the chief occupation of the people is cattle-breeding. Crude Tibetan cheese can be had at the rate of four annas per pound and butter at the rate of two rupees per pound. Butter is very badly stored in raw sheep-skins. Thousands of sheep—rather huge masses of sheep—can be seen moving and grazing on the shores and slopes of Manasarovar, spread over miles.

There is an interesting way of milking goats. They are made to stand in pairs facing each other neck to neck and are tied together. Then the milking goes on by drawing out the teat of the animal once or twice and the process goes on a number of times, for they cannot be milked at a stretch since they draw the milk in the udder after taking one or two jets. When they are fully milked, the loosely knotted rope is drawn out and the animals go out leaping and jumping hither and thither.

TRADE AND MARTS

There are several mandis or marts of Bhotia[1] merchants in Western Tibet, most of which are situated in the Kailas-Manas Region. These

[1] Indian borderland of North Almora, North Garhwal, North Tehri etc. is called Bhot. People of Bhot are called Bhotias. Bhot and Bhotias described in this book should not be confused with Bhutan State or the Bhutanese. Tibetans are called *Huniyas* by the Bhotias.

42. Yak with a Pack-saddle
[See p. 71

43. Ploughing with a Jhabbu and a Horse
[See p. 69

44. Kettle-making at Thugolho
[See p. 50

45. Taklakot Mandi with Snow-peaks on the Indian border [*See pp.* 13, 100 & 121

46. Tea-churning [*See p.* 53

47. Double-panniers of Borax and Salt by the side of a *Dokpa* Tent in Taklakot Mandi [*See p.* 72

48. The author in Tibetan Costumes
[*See* p. 53

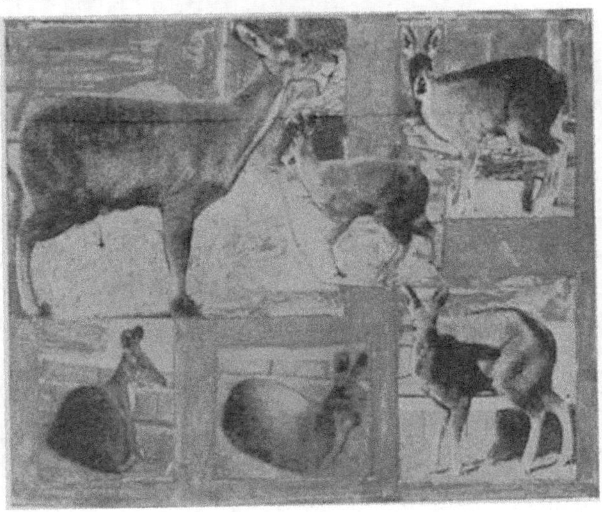

49. Musk-deer in different Postures
[*See* p. 70

50. Musk-pod from Darma
[*See p.* 70

51. Cave-village of Gukung
[*See pp.* 52 & 101

52. Tent of a Nepalese Merchant in Pururav Chhongra (Market)
[*See p.* 73

mandis are held for periods ranging from a fortnight to five months. Gyanima Mandi (also known as Kharko) of Johar Bhotias, Chhakra Mandi (also known as Gyanima Chhakra) of Darma Bhotias, Taklakot Mandi (also known as Pilithanka) of Chaudans and Byans Bhotias, Nabra Mandi of Niti Bhotias, and Gukung Mandi of the Nepalese are the biggest. Tarchhen (Kailas) and Thokar (or Thugolho—Manasarovar), and Gartok Mandis come next in order, of which the first two are big wool-shearing centres. Puling, Tuling, Lama-Chhorten, Silti, and Dayul-Chhongra Mandis are still smaller. Gyanima is the biggest of the mandis in Western Tibet where a brisk transaction of about 25 lakhs of rupees is done annually. In almost all these mandis wool, coarse Tibetan blankets, sheep, ponies, mules, yaks, *jhabbus*, borax, salt, hides, etc. are either sold for cash or exchanged for the commodities of the Indian merchants namely piece-goods, *gur* (jaggery), barley, wheat, rice, utensils, Chinese tea, etc. All the commodities which are available in Indian markets are procurable here. Shepherds from not less than thirty regions[1] come to Taklakot for trade.

Tibetans, both men, women and children, take to spinning at all spare times and weaving is done solely by women. Finer variety of woollens are not produced in the Manas Region, as in other parts of Tibet. Every Tibetan be he a householder or a monk, does some sort of business by way of selling and buying.

Mahatma Gandhi is considered by some monks to be the incarnation of the great *Tantrik* teacher Guru Padmasambhava. He is called Gandhi Maharaja by Tibetans. A coarse type of hand-woven white cloth sold in the mandis is called 'Gandhi-khaddar'.

There are marauders and freebooters of nomadic tribes everywhere in Tibet. They are shepherds wandering from place to place with their sheep, ponies, yaks, kith and kin, and some of them move towards Kailas and Manasarovar also for trade and pilgrimage between the months of May and October. Since no restriction is imposed by the Tibetan Government as regards possessing arms, these nomads carry swords, daggers, old Tibetan matchlock guns, Russian and German pistols, revolvers and rifles with plenty of gunpowder and cartridges. When they come across any unarmed traders or pilgrims they loot them and make good their escape into some ravines or to some distant places. The Tibetan Government make no adequate arrangement to arrest them, nor the Indian Government give any protection against

[1] 1. Hor-Toma, 2. Hor-Taling, 3. Hor-Toshar, 4. Hor-Pangriya, 5. Toshar, 6. Rundra, 7. Bongba, 8. Shungba-Majin, 9. Diji, 10. Songkora, 11. Seli-phuk, 12. Gerke, 13. Chuk-chang, 14. Yagra-ngingba, 15. Yagra-mema, 16. Sokche, 17. Rosra, 18. Tarkop-Lharkep, 19. Baba, 20. Sakya, 21. Nakchang, 22. Ngabri, 23. Boksho, 24. Bokto, 25. Markam, 26. Lhasa-Shigartse (Bodpas), 27. Kham, 28. Amdo, 29. Limi, 30. Rongba, 31. Jumli, 32. Hor-Gyeva, etc.

these freebooters through the Trade Agent. This unhappy menace reached its climax in 1947, when scores of Indian traders and poor pilgrims were looted by Tibetan brigands; and one *sadhu* was shot dead for not surrendering his belongings.

CURIOS OF MANASA KHANDA

The following is a list of articles that could be secured from this Region, and the visitor can make a choice according to his taste. (1) Full-skin of snow-leopard (*chen*). (2) Full-skin of lynx (*yi*), these cost anything between 20 and 50 rupees each. (3) Full-skin of fox (*haje*), costs 2 to 6 rupees and is used for caps. (4) Lamb-skins (*charu*) used for making waistcoats and overcoats, each costs a rupee. (5) *Bungchar* or bigger lamb-skins, used for making *asanas*. (6) Sheep-skin, (7) Goat-skin, (8) Skin of a *goa* (Tibetan wild goat), costs a rupee each. (9) *Chutka*, heavy Tibetan rug, woolly on one side, costs 15 to 45 rupees. (10) *Thulma*, finer type of rug, prepared in Johar, costs 20 to 40 rupees. (11) *Pankhi* or *chadar*. (12) Carpet. (13) Thin or thick rope made of yak-hair, costs up to a rupee and a half. (14) Yak-tail or *chamar-punch*. (15) *Zaharmora*-stone or serpentine. (16) *Thaneri-patthar*, a soft stone, used for boils on the breast. (17) *Himaphuli* (calcite). (18) *Nirbishi*, a variety of aconite, a drug used for scorpion sting etc. (19) *Thuma*, an aphrodisiac drug. (20) *Jimbu*, dried Tibetan onion leaves for seasoning purposes. (21) Silver stand and lid for tea-cup. (22) Wooden tea-cup, silvered inside. (23) Tibetan folding table (*chokse*). (24) Tibetan silver spoon. (25) *Korlo*, Tibetan prayer-wheel. (26) Silver talisman-casket (*gau*). (27) *Mani*-stones. (28) *Pobar*, incense ladle. (29) *Polang*, incensory or incense pot. (30) Tibetan tea. (31) *Lham*, Tibetan full-boot, either for men or women. (32) *Thanka*, Tibetan banner-painting. (33) Phing, Tibetan vermicelli, prepared from specially treated pea-flour. (34) Musk. (35) Tusks of Musk-deer. (36) *Kangri Karchhak*, Tibetan Kailasa *Purana*, can be had either from Dira-phuk Gompa or Gengta Gompa. (37) *Khochar Karchhak* or *Khochar Purana*, can be had from Khochar. (38) *Bhurja-patra* (bark of a birch tree) can be had from any person either in Garbyang or Budi. (39) *Tanka* and other coins. (40) Samples of *thing*, *geta*, *puruk*, *numbu* etc.—superior varieties of woollens. On their onward journey to Kailas, pilgrims should request some merchant at Taklakot to get the articles of their choice ready by the time they expect to return or they may request him to send the goods by post to their homes at his convenience.

CHAPTER VI

ADMINISTRATION

DALAI LAMA

TIBET is a part of Chinese Republic and is ruled by Dalai Lama, and a Council of Ministers acting under the advice of the Chinese Resident. It is said that the first Dalai Lama was born in A.D. 1391, while some say that this system came into existence in 1284. It was the fifth Dalai Lama (1610-1681) who declared himself to be the Divine Incarnation of the *Bodhisattva* Avalokiteshvara. Since then this system is in vogue. The thirteenth Dalai Lama died in December 1933 and the fourteenth Dalai Lama was born on June 1935, in Kum-bum and was installed on the throne in the Potala Palace at Lhasa on February 22, 1940. Dalai Lama is the political head and the Tashi Lama, whose headquarters is at Tashi-Lhunpo at Shigartse is the religious head. Tashi Lama is considered to be the incarnation of Amitabha Buddha. He is more popularly known as Panchhen Lama or Panchhen Rinpochhe.

GOVERNMENT

Western Tibet is governed by two *Garpons* or *Urkos* (Viceroys), one senior (*Urko-Kong*) and one junior (*Urko-Yoḳ*). The summer capital is Gartok and the winter capital Gargunsa. Western Tibet is divided into four Provinces namely, Rudok, Purang-Taklakot, Dapa, and Chhabrang, each in charge of a *Zong* or *Zongpon* (officer of the Fort or Governor). A major part of the Kailas-Manasarovar Region is under the jurisdiction of Purang Zong and the tract west of Chhakra Mandi is under the jurisdiction of Dapa Zong. There are about 55 Zongs in the whole of Tibet.

Besides these, there are *Chhasus*, or Tax Collectors in trade centres, *Yung-Chhongs* or Government Trade Agents or Traders, and *Tasams*, *Tazams* or *Tarzams* (Post-stages or conveyance offices and officers) who are to promptly supply transport-animals to Government officials going up and down. These *Tasams* convey State mails also between Lhasa and Gartok and other Government centres. Out of the 25 *Tasams* stationed along the Lhasa-Gartok high road seven are in the Kailas-Manas Region. Since the year 1935 or so, regular postal stamps have been in use for conveyance of letters and parcels from Lhasa to various Government centres. A special officer called *Shipjo* or *Kashyap* visits Western Tibet once in 30 or 35 years for looking after and settling all affairs of the State up to the petty village-dispute. He tours in the country for nearly a year. He last visited this Region in 1944-45.

All the above mentioned officials are appointed direct from Lhasa for a term of three years, which may be extended by one or two more terms in some cases. The administration of villages and wandering tribal camps is carried on by *Gopas* or *Gobas* (headmen) and *Magpons* (Patwaris) over groups of villages. *Gopa* is appointed every year or every three years and *Magpon* is a hereditary post; and these two posts are held by men of the villages concerned. None of the officials is paid by the Central Government at Lhasa; on the contrary, these officials have to pay certain fixed amounts to the Central Government, and they have to raise this sum as well as their own profit from the civil, criminal, and revenue administration of the regions under their jurisdiction. Besides this income all officials have their own enormous personal trade, for which they get conveyance free of charge from the *Tasams*.

For simple offences the hands of the culprit are tightly tied together with a woollen rope until they start bleeding, he is stripped off his clothes and is awarded 40 to 300 lashes on his buttocks and legs. For serious offences like dacoities the hands of the offender are cut off at the wrists and then dipped into boiling oil in order to prevent the wound from becoming septic; for more serious crimes and for political offences against the State, the accused is brutally killed by red-hot iron rods being thrust into the temples and by the removal of eyes, or by being hurled down from the top of a steep rock or hill. In all these cases flogging precedes and it is so severe that the culprit often succumbs to death. In murder cases the culprit is not only whipped to death, but also tortured by thrusting pins into the finger-nails, by smashing the joints with a hammer, and by many other different ways. One murderer was put to death at Taklakot like this in 1947. One monk by name Serka-Mutup, who organized an agitation to stop *begari* or free-service to the monastery, was whipped to death by the *Labrang* of the Simbiling Gompa in 1943. One turbulent Bhutanese was similarly flogged to death by the Purang Zong in 1947. Oftentimes both the parties in a case are heavily fined and such fines form a great source of income to the officers. After the judgment of a case is given, both parties shall have to pay a court fee of eight *tangas* each. Bilboes, handcuffs, pillory, whips, ropes, and thick leather flaps (tied to a small stick to slap on the cheek), etc. are kept hanging at the gate of the officers.

In Tibet, only a few commodities are taxed. For every six or eight sheep that are sheared and for every six or eight sheep-loads of borax or salt, one *tanga* is collected as tax by the *Chhasu*. There is no land-tax; but it is not to be understood that the government is liberal, as a matter of fact the whole blood of an ordinary peasant or shepherd is sucked out both by the Government officers and by the monks of monasteries by way of extracting free-service for everything and by realizing 25 to 100 per cent interest on tea and other goods which are forced on them by the officers concerned.

Over one-half of the Government posts are held by monks. Women are not debarred from holding high Government positions, including even those of Viceroys and Governors. There is practically no standing army or regular police either at the Viceregal centre at Gartok or the Governors' centres, though of late efforts are being made at Lhasa to maintain a regularly-trained police and military force. Whenever an emergency arises, men are mustered from villages, since all Tibetans know the use of firearms.

Taklakot is the headquarters of Purang Zong and is at a distance of 11 miles from the Lipu Lekh pass, on the Indian border. On the top of a hillock are the quarters of the Governor and the famous Simbiling Monastery. There is a prison-house inside the Zong's building, where whips, handcuffs, etc. are stored. On the narrow plateau called Pilithanka, situated at the foot of the hillock, is held a big mandi from the month of June to October. Indian Bhotia merchants hold the market in walled enclosures made of stones or sun-dried bricks. Tents are set up temporarily over the walls, since according to the treaty of 1904 made between the British and the Tibetan Government, Indians are not allowed to construct roofed houses in Tibet. It is high time that the Indian Government should get this bar annulled.

Trials are being made by the author for the last ten years to secure the permission of the Tibetan Government for the construction of a *dharmashala* on Manasarovar at Thugolho. Though he could not get the necessary permit as yet, he hopes to make some sort of arrangement with the authorities of the monastery to complete the work in an year. He has, however, completed the construction of a spacious *Yajna Vedi* (platform), the foundation of which was laid in 1941. *Havan* is performed there on *Shree Krishna Janmashtami*, *Shravani*, and other festive occasions.

INDIAN TRADE AGENT

Under the orders of Lord Curzon, Colonel Younghusband led an expedition and invaded Tibet in 1903. Thousands of Tibetans were shot down with the British machine guns. The Dalai Lama fled away from the Potala Palace at Lhasa and a treaty was forced on the Tibetans in August 1904. Later on, in 1906, 1907, and 1912 some more treaties were made between the two governments, by which the British had manoeuvred to completely sever the nominal suzerainty of China over Tibet, which China now claims to have regained after the Britishers relinquished their hold on India.

According to the same treaty three British Trade Agents were appointed—two in Central Tibet with headquarters one at Gyantse with a contingent of 500 soldiers, and the other at Yatung, and one in Western Tibet with headquarters at Gartok for six months,—it is said, to look after the interests and grievances of the Indian traders who hold markets in Tibet every year. But nothing has been done for them, since the British Government did not like to put any pressure on the Tibetan Government on the score of the Indian merchants. As a matter of fact, in the year 1943 and 1944, there were three cases in which Indian traders were flogged by the Tibetan officers, contrary to Treaty rules; one Bhotia boy was shot dead by a rowdy servant of the Tibetan Government Trader, in 1947. But no proper action has been taken by the Indian Government so far. Now that the popular government has come to power, the Indian traders expect some redress from the atrocities of the Tibetan officials and highway robbers and marauders. The Indian Government should now have a strong Agent with a small contingent of 25 soldiers to safeguard the interests of the Indian traders in Western Tibet. The British Trade Agent of Western Tibet starts from Gangtok in the month of May, goes to Gartok, visits the important marts, goes again to Gartok, and returns back to India by some convenient pass in the month of November. Since the attainment of the Indian Independence on August 15, 1947, the name of the British Trade Agent has been changed to Indian Trade Agent. A travelling Post Office accompanies him, delivering and despatching mails once a week, during his stay in Western Tibet. Garbyang (30 miles from Taklakot) and Milam (65 miles from Gyanima) are the Indian Post Offices nearest to the Kailas-Manas Region. There are Post and Telegraph Offices and Telephone connections with India, both at Lhasa and Gyantse.

CURRENCY

Tanka—Obverse and Reverse

Tanka or *tanga* is the common silver coin in use throughout Tibet. Half *tanga* called *jav* is also current. The copper coins in use in Tibet are *khagang* ($\frac{1}{6}$ *tanga*), *karmanga* ($\frac{1}{3}$ *tanga*), *chhege* ($\frac{1}{2}$ *tanga*), and *shogang* ($\frac{2}{3}$ *tanga*), which are exchangeable only at Lhasa. Since the year 1934, currency notes and silver rupees have been in use at Lhasa. Indian rupees are freely used everywhere in Tibet in transactions. Tibetans prefer the Indian rupee to their *tanga*. The present rate of exchange is 4 *tangas* per rupee in Western Tibet. The Indian rupee is called *gormo* in Tibetan. For the convenience of transit, Tibetan officials take the Indian currency notes with them when they go to Lhasa, as these are freely exchangeable there. Nepali *mohar* and rupee are also exchangeable in the mandis.

KASHMIR AND TIBET

The King Lalitaditya, who ruled over Kashmir from 699 to 735, invaded Central Asia and Tibet and annexed a major part of Western Tibet including Ladakh. Thus Buddhism was introduced into Tibet from Kashmir also. In fact several *Pandits* from Kashmir went to Tibet to preach Buddhism. Siddha Milarepa's grand guru, the great Tantrik teacher Naropa was a Kashmiri *Pandit*.

GENERAL ZORAVAR SINGH

Maharaja Gulab Singh's Commander-in-Chief, General Zoravar Singh, after annexing the whole of Ladakh to Jammu Raj in 1840, proceeded to Kailas in 1841 ; pillaged all the villages and gompas and destroyed every fort on his way. He first established his headquarters at Tirthapuri and with 1,500 men fought a great battle near Barkha with the Tibetan forces of 10,000 soldiers in which he utterly routed them and advanced to Taklakot. Leaving his army under his subordinate, Captain Basti Ram, Zoravar took a handful of men and went to Gartok to leave his wife there. On his way back he was attacked at Toyo by a big army sent by the Chinese to assist the Tibetans. Zoravar was taken by surprise, but fought so gallantly that the Tibetans believed him to be a *Tantrik* endowed with supernatural powers. Since it was believed that no leaden bullet could penetrate his body, he was shot dead, in the end, with a golden bullet and was afterwards hacked to pieces. A *samadhi* or monument has been erected on his remains, which still stands there in the form of a *chhorten*. Zoravar's testicles and some flesh are still preserved in the Simbiling Gompa and one hand in the Sakya Gompa situated by its side. In some monasteries of Manasa Khanda, Zoravar's armours and shields are to this day preserved as trophies. General Zoravar Singh's Centenary was celebrated by the Darma Seva Sangha at Taklakot, when the author exhibited some of the General's armours and shields brought from Tibetans. This is a unique case in the history of the world where the enemy has built a memorial for the gallantry of a defeated general.

LOPCHAK MISSION

Long before the annexation of Ladakh to Jammu and Kashmir State, the Vassal Chief of Ladakh used to send a trade mission called Lopchak Mission to Lhasa, every third year, in order to encourage trade between Lhasa and Ladakh, a distance of about 1,100 miles. A merchant of Ladakh used to get a financial aid of about Rs. 6,000 to meet the transport expenses for the long journey. In a similar way, the Lhasa Government also used to send a reciprocal Mission to Ladakh. The Chief of Ladakh used to send some curios of Ladakh as presents to the Dalai Lama through this Mission and the Dalai Lama in turn used to send some curios of Lhasa to the Chief of Ladakh. After the annexation of Ladakh to Jammu and Kashmir by the Maharaja in the year 1841, the Maharaja has continued the Mission. After the intervention of the British in the State affairs, the British had begun controlling the Mission, though it was the Maharaja that was actually giving the grant-in-aid to the Mission, in order to wield greater influence on Tibet, in which the British had a marked success. After the withdrawal of the British from India and the subsequent accession of Jammu and Kashmir State to the Indian Dominion, naturally, the interest and responsibility in the said Lopchak Mission (being a subject of External Affairs Department) now devolves on the Indian Dominion.

RAVAGES OF KAZHAKI NOMADS OF RUSSIA

In the year 1941 about 3,000 nomads of Karghiz Kazhak of Russia entered Tibet through Chinese Turkestan and pillaged and plundered the whole of Western Tibet from one end to the other. Kazhakis are Mohammedans by faith. They came with their kith and kin, *namda*-tents, and camels. They had looted all the eight monasteries of the Manas and completely destroyed Tirthapuri Gompa besides several others. Hundreds of Tibetan books were either thrown into fires or flown to winds. The author had picked up some of them. Several yak-loads of cloth costing about a lakh of rupees, belonging to Johar Bhotia merchants, were carried away by these freebooters. When they reached Manasarovar, they were camping on the northern side spread over a distance of 15 miles. The author was at Thugolho Gompa at that time. At Tsepgye Gompa on Rakshas Tal, three inmates gave a tough fight from inside against a contingent of 80 Kazhaki horsemen and shot dead two of the leaders of the party. So they had to turn back. This incident had saved Purang valley from being swept away by these brigands. They used to kill mules and horses for meat instead of sheep and goats.

By the time these plunderers reached Ladakh they were in

possession of over a lakh of sheep and goats, 4,000 yaks, 2,000 ponies and mules, 500 rifles and guns, and thousands of rupees worth of gold and silver images, jewellery, precious stones, gold, silver, and silver coins. On the borders of Ladakh the Kashmir Government, after disarming allowed them passage to go to British India. Due to their alliance with Russia, the British Government had made temporary arrangement for their stay in Hazara district, N.W.F. Province, and had spent 2,38,000 rupees for their maintenance between May 1942 and February 1943. Since then, Bhupal and Nizam States had applied for settling them in their States, but they were finally settled down in Hazara District. These Kazhakis, it is learnt, have been taking active part during the present Kashmir riots, making a good harvest.

NEPAL AND MANASA KHANDA

Srongchen Gampo, the Emperor of Tibet, conquered the whole of Nepal and married Bhrikuti, the daughter of Anshu Varma, the king of Nepal, in the seventh century A.D. Thus began the connection of Nepal with Tibet. Later on, several *pandits* from Nepal went to Tibet for propagating Buddhism ; similarly several Tibetan monks came to India through Nepal. Even today, thousands of Tibetans go to Nepal to visit the three great *Tirthas* of Swayambhu (*Phagva-shingun*), Mahabodhi (*Charung-khashur*), and Namobuddhaya (*Tamo-lujin*). In 1760 the Nepalese invaded Tibet but the Chinese forces pursued them upto Kathmandu and utterly routed them. In 1854 the Nepalese invaded Purang Taklakot and forced a treaty on them by which Tibet had to pay an annual tribute of 10,000 Nepalese *mohars* and receive a permanent Nepalese Resident at Lhasa. Besides this, the Nepalese secured several trade facilities in Tibet. In 1929-30 a severe breach of peace was threatened between the two countries over the right of trial of a particular person but was averted in time. In contravention of some settlement between the Nepalese and the Tibetan Governments, the Zongpon of Taklakot has imposed some trade tax and forced Tibetan tea at cent per cent interest on the people of Limi in the north-western part of Nepal, for non-compliance of which two respectable and well-to-do merchants of Limi were tied and handcuffed and the tax has been realized and the tea was forced on them at cent per cent interest.

BHUTANESE POSSESSIONS

About 300 (?) years back, one famous Bhutanese Lama by name Ngava-Namgyal got the village of Tarchhen from the Tibetan Government for his stay near Kailas. Through his influence he had built Nyanri and other monasteries and gained influence over some other places later on.

Tarchhen, at the foot of Kailas, Nyanri and Zuthul-phuk Monasteries of Kailas, Cherkip Gompa of Manasarovar, the villages of Dungmar, Ringung, Doh, Khochar, Gezon near Gartok, Itse Gompa, Gonphu, Gesur, Sammar, and a few other places in Western Tibet, came to belong to the State of Bhutan. These places are now governed by a Bhutanese monk-officer, whose headquarters is at Tarchhen, where there is a big building owned by the Bhutan State.

'JANMA BHOOMI' AND 'JNANA NAUKA' ON THE MANAS

Before concluding his trips to the Holy Lake, the author wishes to locate definitely the thermal springs situated in the bed of Manasarovar and reach the centre of the Lake, which is considered by the Tibetans to be inaccessible and which has not been reached by any one up till now. To achieve this he took to Almora in 1942 the 'Jnana Nauka'—galvanized steel sailing dinghy-cum-motor boat—presented to him by His Highness Maharajashree Sir Krishna Kumar Sinha, K.C.S.I., Maharaja Saheb of Bhavanagar, which was lying there upto the middle of 1947, for want of official sympathy to secure transport and for want of funds. With the munificent donation of Shree Amritlal D. Sheth of 'Janma Bhoomi', Bombay, and with the co-operation of the Congress ministry of U. P. he could transport the boat to Manasarovar in August 1947. It was at last launched in the Holy Lake on August 17. With the ॐ and Tri-colour flags proudly fluttering side by side on the deck, the Jnana Nauka' rushed into the turquoise-blues of the celebrated celestial Lake amidst deafening cheers of pilgrims, Tibetans, and Bhotia traders. A few soundings were formally taken. As the book is being taken to the press, information is received that the U.P. Government have made a special grant to defray the cost of the outboard motor to complete the exploration work on Manasarovar. After completing the work the boat would be left on Manasarovar under the care of the Darma Seva Sangha for the benefit of future pilgrims and tourists.

In 1946 the author took the 'Janma Bhoomi', a three-seater light rubber boat presented to him by Shree Amritlal D. Sheth of Bombay. He launched it in Manasarovar and sounded the lake Gouri-kund.

SOME REFLECTIONS

Aeroplanes can very easily descend on the plains at Parkha, on the north of Manasarovar, near Gyanima, Chhakra, or as a matter of fact, anywhere in Tibet without spending much for the construction of a runway or an aerodrome. Sea-planes can conveniently descend into the Manas, the Rakshas, or any other lake. Trials are being made to move the Government of India to induce the Tibetan Government to permit the pilgrim planes to go to Kailas-Manas Region. When this is achieved, a sea-plane can very easily be chartered.

An airfield is being constructed at Badrinath, which is an hour's journey from Hardwar. So it is very likely that arrangements for an aerial route to Kailas and Manasarovar also would be made soon for the air-minded. This would be very advantageous to those who cannot afford time and undergo the hardships of the long journey to these places. But this would in no way deter those pilgrims and tourists who love adventure and mountain-trotting, from undertaking the journey by foot or by pony.

We do not wish that the tranquillity and sanctity of this Region should be disturbed in any way, but it would be no wonder if in near future, some enterprising concern starts a 'Kailas-Manasarovar Air Service' and begin taking pilgrims and tourists to this Region in such an amazingly short time that one could return back home the same day after having a dip in the Holy Lake! The author very much wishes that the young men of this Ancient Land take living interest for going to the Himalayas and be benefited both physically and spiritually.

The possibilities of an expedition to reach the top of the Kailas—if and when such a venture be allowed by the conservative, superstitious, and suspicious Tibetans—can be investigated and surveyed from the eastern side only, since on the remaining three sides the Peak rises almost perpendicularly and avalanches slide down headlong.

It is a matter of pity to note that the Indian Universities and the Indian youth of today are not taking any living interest for leading expeditions to the Himalayas, either for mountaineering, exploration, or for trotting, even for a pleasure trip; whereas it has been reserved for the foreigner to reach the top of the Kamet or the Nanda Devi, or to sound the Lake Manas, or to discover the source of the Brahmaputra. This was not the case in the Ancient Aryavarta.

At a time when people of other countries used to dread the mountain and the forest and when they had not learnt to appreciate and enjoy the beauty of nature and mountain grandeur, thousands of years back our ancestors had explored the most inaccessible mountains, forests, and regions in the Himalayas; they had gone to every nook and corner of these snow ranges and used to hold unspoken talks with Nature; they had discovered the best view-points and panoramas and enjoyed their beauty in all nakedness and bequeathed them to us as legacy by way of places of pilgrimage. The very fact that the most inaccessible mountains, rivers, streams, brooks, springs, passes, and places have been stamped with names is a proof of this statement. In one word, their very life-blood—their best writings, both spiritual and secular, Vedas, Upanishads, Epics, Poetry, Art, Astronomy, Medicine, etc.—was all inspired by these hoary mountains. Even in the later period of Indian history, the Great Shankaracharya had established one of his monasteries at Joshimath near Badrinath in the heart of the Himalayas. In the eighth and tenth centuries Acharya Shantarakshita and Deepankara Shreejnana crossed the invulnerable Himalayas from one side to the other, went to Tibet, and travelled from one end of the country to the other to preach the gospel of Buddha even at the ripe age of one hundred years.

The author cannot resist the temptation of repeating once again the lines of Burrard and Hayden, "Manasarowar was the first lake known to geography. Lake Manasarowar is famous in Hindu mythology; it had in fact become famous many centuries before the lake of Geneva had aroused any feeling of admiration in civilized man. Before the dawn of history Manasarowar had become the sacred lake and such it has remained for four millennium."

What is the state of affairs now in this very country where our ancestors showed so much of interest and enthusiasm, in the past, in the Himalayas? What a deplorable condition! Modern India is not wanting in men or money; there are thousands of educated youths with finer tastes and scientific attitude, but unfortunately they always complain of political bondage; whereas in foreign lands people have not stopped exploration work even when the whole world was engaged in dreadful wars. In Switzerland and other countries there are regular schools and seasonal training courses in mountaineering, skating, ski-ing and allied subjects. Even the general public, men, women, young and old, and children, undergo training in these subjects, and go on a holiday trip for mountain-excursions even during winters. Readers need not be surprised in this, the author's side-trekking from the main subject; one often enjoys a side-trekking in the Himalayan travels.

In the opinion of the author our young men are wanting in enthusiasm for mountaineering and adventure, for which the modern Universities are mainly responsible. So the Universities should now encourage and inspire students and finance them by sending batches of them to the Himalayas in the beginning, on educational and health tours. When once it is started, in the course of a decade, the author is sure, that wonderful progress will be made in this direction. "The Himalayan germ, once caught, works inside like a relapsing fever; it is ever biding its time before breaking out again with increased virulence ".[1] " Once a man has found the road in the Himalayas, he can never keep away for long ".[2] The Geography Departments of Universities should evince special interest in this regard and invite foreign mountaineering experts for training their students. This work is long overdue and should be immediately taken up both by the Indian Universities and the Government in right earnest.

1 Marco Pallis, 'Peaks and Lamas'.
2 Dr. T. G. Longstaff.

KAILAS - MANASAROVAR

THIRD WAVE

TOURIST'S COMPANION

53. Tibetan Black Tent [*See p. 52*

54. A Shepherd Woman from Hor District, Manasarovar [*See p. 54*

55. This is how she dresses her hair [*See p. 54*

56. Wool-shearing at Thugolho, Manasarovar
[*See* p. 71

57. Twisting wool to make into Bales
[*See* p. 71

58. *Dhabbus* (bales) of Wool
[*See* p. 71

59. Milking Goats [*See* p. 72

60. Interior of Khochar Monastery
[*See* p. 66

61. Image of Jambyang (Manju-ghosha) in Khochar Gompa
[*See* p. 66

62. Stucco-image of Prajna-paramita and some Frescos in the background
[*See p.* 67

63. Ruined columns of a Fort at Purbu destroyed by General Zoravar Singh
[*See pp.* 79 & 122

64. General Zoravar Singh's Samadhi
[*See p.* 79

GENERAL OUTLINE OF THE ROUTE TO KAILAS

AND

MANASAROVAR VIA LIPU LEKH PASS

VARIOUS ROUTES TO THE HOLY KAILAS AND MANASAROVAR

THERE are several routes to the Holy Kailas and Manasarovar from different places, of which the following are important.

(i) From Almora via Askot, Khela, Garbyang, LIPU LEKH PASS (16,750 ft.), and Taklakot to Kailas (Tarchhen)—238 miles.

(ii) From Almora via Askot, Khela, DARMA PASS (18,510), and Gyanima Mandi—227 miles.

(iii) From Almora via Bageshvar, Milam, UNTA-DHURA PASS (17,590), JAYANTI PASS (18,500), KUNGRI-BINGRI PASS (18,300), and Gyanima Mandi—210 miles.

(iv) From Joshimath via GUNLA-NITI PASS (16,600), Nabra Mandi, Sibchilim Mandi, and Gyanima Mandi—200 miles.

(v) From Joshimath via DAMJAN-NITI PASS (16,200), Tonjan La (16,350), Sibchilim Mandi, and Gyanima Mandi—160 miles.

(vi) From Joshimath via HOTI-NITI PASS (16,390), Sibchilim Mandi, and Gyanima Mandi—158 miles.

(vii) From Badrinath via MANA PASS (18,400), Thuling Math, Dapa, Nabra, Sibchilim, and Gyanima Mandi—238 miles.

(viii) From Mukhuva-Gangotri, via Nilang, JELUKHAGA PASS (17,490), Puling Mandi, Thuling, Dapa, Sibchilim, and Gyanima Mandi—243 miles.

(ix) From Simla via Rampur, SHIPKI PASS (15,400), Shiring La (16,400), Loache La (18,510), GARTOK (15,100), Chargot La (16,200), and Tirthapuri—445 miles.

(x) From Simla via Rampur, SHIPKI PASS, Shiring La, THULING, Dapa, Sibchilim, and Gyanima Mandi—473 miles.

(xi) From Srinagar (Kashmir) via ZOZI LA (11,578), Nammik (13,000), Fotu La (13,446), LEH (LADAKH), TAGLANG LA (17,500), Demchok, Gargunsa, GARTOK, Chargot La (16,200), and Tirthapuri—605 miles.

(xii) From Kathmandu (Nepal-Pashupatinath) via MUKTINATH, KHOCHARNATH, and Taklakot—about 525 miles.

(xiii) From Lhasa via TASHI-LHUNPO—about 800 miles.

(xiv) From Kullu in Kangra District through Rampur Bashahr State via THULING.

The first route, i.e. from Almora via Lipu Lekh pass is the easiest and safest for people going from the plains, hence, it is described in full; and brief outlines of other routes are also given for the benefit of pilgrims and tourists who may select any of the other routes.

HOW TO REACH ALMORA

The last railway station on the way to Almora is Kathgodam (O. T. Railway). For all those who start from the plains it is advisable to get down at Haldwani station (5 miles before reaching Kathgodam) as it is a big mandi and because better and cheaper arrangements can be made for boarding and lodging, for buses, lorries, cars, coolies, etc. from here than from Kathgodam. There is a Post Office, a Telegraph Office, a Dak Bungalow, a Hospital, a Motor Agency, Hotels, etc. besides a big mandi. The usual fare for a seat in the bus from Haldwani to Almora (about 88 miles by motor) is Rs. 4-6 plus a toll of as. 8 at Almora. The Motor Transport Agency is at a distance of fifty yards from the station, and the Arya Samaj *dharmashala* is by its side.

Kathgodam is 64 miles to the north of Bareilly junction. There is a Post Office, a Telegraph Office, a Dak Bungalow, a Motor Transport Agency, Hotels, etc. Kathgodam being the starting station, pilgrims will be well advised to entrain here on their return journey.

It is about seven hours' motor journey from Haldwani to Almora. After the twelfth mile from Kathgodam[1], motor road to Naini Tal branches off; Naini Tal is 15 miles from here; at the fifteenth mile is the popular Hill Crest Sanatorium, for tuberculosis, started in 1936; at the sixteenth mile, down below the road is the Government Apiary or Bee-culture Farm; from the seventeenth mile (Gethia) one footpath branches off to Naini Tal (6,400), which is 3 miles from here; at the twentysecond mile is Bhowali (5,700), the well known Government Sanatorium for T.B. patients; apples, pears, apricots, peaches, etc. can be had here, (Bhim Tal is only 5 miles from here); after the thirty-fifth mile is a place called Garampani, where there are hotels, water-*dhara*, etc. and where buses stop for half an hour, so that passengers might take their tiffin or meals; and between the forty-ninth and fifty-third mile is the Cantonment of Ranikhet (5,980); also a big bazaar; if the sky is clear, one can have a beautiful view of the snows; (Karna-Prayag on the route to Badrinath is 60 miles from here and Badrinath is 67 miles from Karna-Prayag); about 8 miles before Almora, one motor road splints to Garur and Baijnath which are 43 miles from here; $6\frac{3}{4}$ miles before reaching Almora one crosses the Kosi-bridge; (from Garampani up to Almora, one

1 The numbering of mile-stones is from Kathgodam.

sees, as far as the eye could travel, extensive terrace-cultivation; the whole country being mountainous, plots of land, big and small, are cut into terraces or just like so many steps; it is a pleasant sight to look at these revolving terraces, both above and below and on both the sides, while the bus speeds on the road); and 2½ miles before Almora is the toll-bar, where each passenger is required to pay a toll of eight annas. From Kathgodam up to Bhowali it is a steep ascent, descent up to Garampani, steep ascent up to Ranikhet, steep descent up to Kosi, and steep ascent up to Almora.

From Haldwani to Almora it is about 41 miles by footpath and it is 16 miles to Naini Tal.

Haldwani to Bhim Tal	..	12 miles	There are ascents and descents throughout; but the scenery is charming.
Bhim Tal to Ramgarh	..	9½ ,,	
Ramgarh to Phyuda	..	10 ,,	
Phyuda to Almora	..	9½ ,,	
	Total	41 ,,	

ALMORA

Almora is the headquarters of Almora District, the *Pauranic* name of which is Kurmachala. The town of Almora is situated at a height of 5,494 feet above the sea-level and is one of the healthiest and most beautiful hill-stations in India with a population of about twenty thousand. There are two Second-Grade Colleges, High Schools for boys and girls, Post and Telegraph Offices, Banks, Hospital, District Court, District Jail, Forest Office, District and Municipal Boards, Cantonment, decent bazaars, Hotels, Motor Transport Agency, O. T. Railway Out-Agency, Government Woollen Stores, health-resorts, old fort of the Kings of Chand Dynasty, temple of Nanda Devi, Narasingabadi, Badrishvar, Baleshvar, Patal Devi, Kasar Devi, Syahi Devi, and some other holy places, Ramakrishna Mission, Christian Mission, and all other amenities which go to make up a decent town. Living is much simpler and cheaper here than in many other hill-stations.

Royal, Capital, and Himalaya are fairly good hotels. Those who want to stay in a high class hotel, can put up in Deodar Hotel, where the charges are Rs. 10 to 15 per day. The long-felt want of a *dharmashala* here has been removed by the opening of Anandamayi *dharmashala* in 1944, very near the Railway Out-Agency, just by the side of the road, a furlong before reaching the Motor Station.

One can have a fine view of the snows from Almora when the sky is clear. Far away to the north stands out the wonderful line of snow-peaks, towering up to the sky to a height of 25,000 feet and showing their well-defined peaks, the Nanda Ghunti (Nandakna 20,700 feet), Trisul—the Trident of Shiva (23,406 ; 22,320 ; 21,850), the sharp wedge of Nanda Devi (25,645) and Nandakot (22,510) ; Kedarnath (22,770), the square mass of Chukhamba (Badrinath 23,420), Nilakanta (21,650), Kamet (25,447), Gouri Parvat (22,027), and the Hathi Parvat (22,370) on the west ; and Naulphu (21,446), Pancha Chulhi—the fire stalls of Gods (22,650), and the Nepal peaks of Api (23,399), Nampa (22,162) and others towards the eastern extremity, the whole stretch of arc measuring over 250 miles. Best snow-view can be had also from Binsar, Kausani, Berinag, and Sandev (see Map No. 8).

Some Western *Sadhakas* like Shree Earl E. H. Brewester (America), Mr. Alfred Sorenson (Denmark), and others have made their abodes here. Four miles west of Almora, situated on the hill of Kasar Devi, Dr. Evans Wentz of America has built a small *Ashram* in the middle of a pine forest of 10 acres. This place commands a grand view of the valleys and hills below and the snow-ranges beyond. The famous Indian dancer Uday Shankar's Culture Centre also worked here till 1943.

About 13 miles north-east of Almora is the health-resort of Binsar. There are some apple, pear, and other fruit-gardens and some bungalows for visitors to stay in. From the top of the Jhanda peak here, one can have a grand view of the snow-ranges. Fifty miles south-east of Almora is Mayavati Vedanta Ashram situated in the middle of a thick jungle, within a short distance from the townships of Lohaghat and Champavat. On the south, at a distance of 14 miles is the famous Veterinary Research Institute at Mukhteshvar, situated on the top of a hill 7,702 feet high. It was started in 1895 and is one of the biggest Veterinary Institutes in the world.

The whole route to Kailas and Manasarovar being in mountains the journey consists of a series of ascents and descents, excepting the *parikrama* of Manasarovar, which will be described later in the route table (see Map No. 9).

STEEP ASCENTS

			Miles
(i)	From Supai	..	1
(ii)	To Dhaul-chhina	..	2
(iii)	Seraghat to Naruaka-ghol	..	2¾
(iv)	To Berinag	..	2
(v)	From Thal	..	3
(vi)	To Chholiokhi-dhar	..	1
(vii)	Rounti-gad to Khela	..	2

(viii)	Dhauli-Ganga to Thani-dhar	..	3
(ix)	Jungti-gad to Soosa	..	$1\frac{3}{4}$
(x)	To Sumaria-dhar	..	3
(xi)	Nijang to Bola	..	$\frac{3}{4}$
(xii)	From Malpa	..	$\frac{1}{2}$
(xiii)	Pelsipi to Kothla	..	$4\frac{1}{2}$
(xiv)	From Budi	..	$2\frac{1}{2}$
(xv)	To Kirong-kong	..	1
(xvi)	Ngavidang to Lipu Lekh pass	..	5
(xvii)	From Garu	..	$\frac{3}{4}$
(xviii)	Gori-udyar to Gurla la	..	4
(xix)	Dira-phuk to Dolm la	..	4
		Total	$44\frac{1}{2}$

STEEP DESCENTS

(i)	Chitai to Chaukhutiya	..	$1\frac{1}{4}$
(ii)	Dhaul-chhina to Bhoura-gadhera	..	$4\frac{1}{2}$
(iii)	From Dungarlekh-chhina	..	1
(iv)	From Naruaka-ghol	..	$\frac{1}{2}$
(v)	Berinag to Gurghatia-bridge (with reliefs here and there)	..	6
(vi)	To Askot	..	$3\frac{1}{2}$
(vii)	Askot to Garjiya-bridge	..	3
(viii)	To Kalika	..	1
(ix)	Khela to Dhauli-Ganga	..	$1\frac{1}{2}$
(x)	From Tithlakot to Sirkha	..	$1\frac{1}{4}$
(xi)	Sumaria-dhar to Sinkhola-gad	..	$3\frac{1}{4}$
(xii)	Bindakot to Jumli-udyar	..	$2\frac{1}{2}$
(xiii)	From Bola	..	$1\frac{1}{4}$
(xiv)	From Kothla	..	$\frac{3}{4}$
(xv)	From Kheto (Budi-top)	..	1
(xvi)	Lipu Lekh to Pala	..	6
(xvii)	From Gurla la towards Manasarovar	..	5
(xviii)	From Dolm la	..	3
		Total	$46\frac{1}{4}$

The first 18 ascents and the 17 descents on the outward journey become descents and ascents respectively on the return journey.

The whole journey may roughly be divided into seven stages.

FIRST STAGE

ALMORA to DHARCHULA—90 miles. It is 7 days' journey; ponies mules, coolies, and *dandies* can be had for conveyance.

JAGESHVAR is situated in a beautiful narrow valley under deodar trees. It is about 18 miles from Almora via Bade-chhina and Panwanaula. Some believe this to be one of the twelve *Jyotir-lingas*. Here are the temples of Bala Jageshvar, Mrityunjaya, Pushti Devi, Navagrahas, Sun, besides a host of smaller temples, and broken idols which received rude shocks from the hands of the Mohammedan invaders. There are some fine specimens of sculpture here. A small stream flows nearby and there are a few houses and several *dharmashalas*. It is an ancient place and has a good spiritual vibration. Fairs are held on *Shivaratri* and on the full moon day of the month of *Vaishakha*. Vriddha Jageshvar is at a distance of about 1½ miles situated on the top of a ridge. Those who want to visit Jageshvar may do so and come to the main road again at Dhaul-chhina.

GANGOLIHAT (5,580) is a big village, 18 miles from Jageshvar. Here are a number of temples in the bazaar; and two furlongs beyond the bazaar, situated in the middle of the thick grove of deodars is the temple of Maha Kali, where a big *mela* is held on *Durgashtami* day during the *Dasahra*. From here one road goes to Pithoragarh (17½m.).

PITHORAGARH is a small township situated in the valley of Sor. There is a High School, a Post Office, a Telegraph Office, a Hospital, Tehsil, and the Deputy Collector's Court. There is also an old Fort, Dak Bungalow, remnants of an old fortification, hotels, and bazaars. Sor is the most beautiful valley in the whole of Almora District, resembling Kashmir valley on a miniature scale, and is a big rice-producing valley. A motor road is under construction from Tanakpur Railway Terminas to Pithoragarh and thence to Askot. See Table I. When this road is ready, it would be more convenient for pilgrims to Kailas to get down from the train at Tanakpur and go to Pithoragarh by bus, which is 25 miles from Askot. Askot is 69 miles from Almora. By taking this new route the pilgrims would save about 45 miles or three days' journey.

PATALA-BHUVANESHVAR is 6½ miles from Gangolighat. Here are three ancient temples. At a distance of one furlong from the temple is an interesting cave, the entrance to which is very narrow. While traversing it one shall have to go sometimes sitting and crawling. Several images are engraved on the walls to the cave inside, which are believed to depict the anecdotes of Mahabharata. The cave is cold and damp and at places there are sialagmites and stalactites with water tickling down from the roof. One should take a torch-light while going in. Archaeologists would find interesting materials here. The *Pujari* of the temple, a Kshatriya would guide the visitors to the cave.

BERINAG or VENINAG is 11 miles from Patala-Bhuvaneshvar and is said to be the abode of Veni Nags. In the neighbourhood are the abodes of Pingal Nag, Mul Nag, Phani Nag, Dhaul Nag, Vasuki Nag, and Kal Nag, also known as Ramanika Dwipa, which is 5 miles from Berinag proper. Those who want to visit Jageshvar, Gangolihat, and Patal-Bhuvaneshvar may do so and come to the main road at Berinag; and those who want to visit Bageshvar should go there from Berinag on their return journey.

Four miles from Berinag is the village Nargoli situated on the road to Bageshvar. A mile away from this village, situated on the top of a hill is the temple of BHADRA-KALI, where the river Bhadra-Kali or Bhadravati flows through a tunnel under the hill and the view is grand. Ten miles from Berinag is Sani-udyar, where the Rishi Shandilya was said to have done penance.

BAGESHVAR is situated at the confluence of the two rivers Sarayu and Gomati, 26 miles from Almora. Situated at the confluence are the temples of Baghnath, Dattatreya, Bhairavanath, and Gangaji. Bazaars are located on either side of the river Sarayu. In the middle of the river Sarayu near the suspension bridge is a big boulder called Markandeya Shila, where the Rishi Markandeya was said to have done penance and written the *Durga Saptashati* and Lord Shiva was married to the daughter of Himavan. A big fair is held here on the occasion of *Makara Sankranti* (14th January), when the Bhotias sell thousands of rupees worth of all sorts of Tibetan goods. In the surroundings of Bageshvar, there are mines of soapstone, iron, copper, graphite, and quartz in crystalline form.

GORI-UDYAR is a big cave situated six miles north of Bageshvar. This is an interesting cave full of big stalagmites, stalactites, and stalactitic coloumns. A brook flows nearby forming a number of cataracts.

BAIJNATH is situated on the left bank of the river Gomati, 13 miles north-west of Bageshvar. It is also called Vaidyanath. During the ninth or tenth century A.D. Katyuri Kings from Joshimath came and settled down here. The temples of this place belong to the twelfth or the thirteenth century which are all now in ruins, the more important of which are Bamani Deval, Baijnath temple, and Kedarnath temple. Besides these there are several other temples and idols. Amongst the sculptures the idol of Parvati, which is kept outside the temple of Baijnath, is a fine specimen. Quarter of a mile from here is the village Talihat, where there are a number of images and temples of the same period as those of Baijnath. There is the *gaddi* of the Katyuri kings, temple of Lakshminarayana, Rakshas Deval, and the temple of Satyanarayana. The idol of Satyanarayana and other images near it are all very excellent specimens. About a mile and a half from here, situated on the top of a hill is the fort of Ranchulkot and the temple of Bhramari Devi. Half a mile from here is the temple of Naguath. The Katyuri

Many Europeans and several District Magistrates of Almora visited this cave, but nobody entered the cave so far. Two *Patwaris* of Chaudans experimented by sending two goats inside, tied to a rope. One goat died instantaneously as it entered the cave, and the other was dragged out immediately it fell down and brought to consciousness by splashing water on the face. The author entered the cave again on October 18, 1939 with nostrils closed and with ropes tied to the waist, held by two men outside. There was some suffocating gas up to a height of 3 feet but it could not be tested, but burning splinters of pine were put out in that gas. On November 12, 1940 the author entered the cave for the third time with nostrils closed and brought out a test-tube full of gas and tested it by adding barium-peroxide solution. The suffocating gas was found to be carbon-dioxide. This time the gas was spread to a height of 4 feet above the ground. During the rainy season when water enters the cave, carbon-dioxide is given out very profusely filling the whole cave; hence a flying bird as soon as it enters the cave is suffocated and falls down dead. Those who are interested in the cave may go there on their return journey from Kailas. One can start early in the morning from Khela and return back by evening.

BHOTIAS: From Dhauli-Ganga ($11\frac{1}{2}$ miles beyond Dharchula) upwards it is inhabited by Bhotias. Bhotias are the inhabitants of the Indian borderland lying in the Himalayas. The people of Darma (from Khela up the Dhauli-Ganga), of Chaudans (from Dhauli-Ganga up to Bindakot), and Byans (from Bindakot up to the Lipu Lekh and Lampiya pass), of Chhangru and Tinker (on Nepal borders), and of Johar (from Tejam up to Kungri-bingri pass) in North Almora, the people of Niti and Mana side in North Garhwal District, and the people of Nilang on the northern extremity of Tehri-Garhwal State are called Bhotias (भोटिया). The Bhotias of Mana are also called Marchhas and of Nilang, Jads. That part of the country which they inhabit is called Bhot (भोट). The Tibetans are called Huniyas (हुणिया). These Bhotias are Hindus by religion and Kshatriyas by caste; all their names end in 'Singh'. Many of them wear sacred thread (*yajnopavita*) and speak a mixture of Hindi and Tibetan languages. In summer they go to the various mandis or marts in Western Tibet by various passes for trade and come down in winter to the plains with wool, borax, and other Tibetan commodities and take back piece-goods etc. to Tibet during the next season. Bhotias are very sturdy and industrious people. As they have to deal with the Tibetans every year, they eat and drink freely with them. So the orthodox people of the plains generally do not interdine with the Bhotias.

Womenfolk also are very hard-working. They do all work in the fields the abodes of Pingal Nag, Mul Nag, Phani Nag, Dhaul Nag, Vasuki Nag, and Kal Nag, also known as Ramanika Dwipa, which is 5 miles from Berinag proper. Those who want to visit Jageshvar, Gangolihat, and Patal-Bhuvaneshvar may do so and come to the main road at Berinag; and those who want to visit Bageshvar should go there from Berinag on their return journey.

Four miles from Berinag is the village Nargoli situated on the road to Bageshvar. A mile away from this village, situated on the top of a hill is the temple of BHADRA-KALI, where the river Bhadra-Kali or Bhadravati flows through a tunnel under the hill and the view is grand. Ten miles from Berinag is Sani-udyar, where the Rishi Shandilya was said to have done penance.

BAGESHVAR is situated at the confluence of the two rivers Sarayu and Gomati, 26 miles from Almora. Situated at the confluence are the temples of Baghnath, Dattatreya, Bhairavanath, and Gangaji. Bazaars are located on either side of the river Sarayu. In the middle of the river Sarayu near the suspension bridge is a big boulder called Markandeya Shila, where the Rishi Markandeya was said to have done penance and written the *Durga Saptashati* and Lord Shiva was married to the daughter of Himavan. A big fair is held here on the occasion of *Makara Sankranti* (14th January), when the Bhotias sell thousands of rupees worth of all sorts of Tibetan goods. In the surroundings of Bageshvar, there are mines of soapstone, iron, copper, graphite, and quartz in crystalline form.

GORI-UDYAR is a big cave situated six miles north of Bageshvar. This is an interesting cave full of big stalagmites, stalactites, and stalactitic coloumns. A brook flows nearby forming a number of cataracts.

BAIJNATH is situated on the left bank of the river Gomati, 13 miles north-west of Bageshvar. It is also called Vaidyanath. During the ninth or tenth century A.D. Katyuri Kings from Joshimath came and settled down here. The temples of this place belong to the twelfth or the thirteenth century which are all now in ruins, the more important of which are Bamani Deval, Baijnath temple, and Kedarnath temple. Besides these there are several other temples and idols. Amongst the sculptures the idol of Parvati, which is kept outside the temple of Baijnath, is a fine specimen. Quarter of a mile from here is the village Talihat, where there are a number of images and temples of the same period as those of Baijnath. There is the *gaddi* of the Katyuri kings, temple of Lakshminarayana, Rakshas Deval, and the temple of Satyanarayana. The idol of Satyanarayana and other images near it are all very excellent specimens. About a mile and a half from here, situated on the top of a hill is the fort of Ranchulkot and the temple of Bhramari Devi. Half a mile from here is the temple of Naguath. The Katyuri valley is the second most beautiful valley in the whole of Almora District like the Lolab valley of Kashmir. Both Katyur and Bageshvar are big rice-growing valleys.

One mile south of Baijnath is the village Garur. The distance between Garur and Nanda-Prayag is 45½ miles and between Nanda-Prayag and Badrinath it is 54½ miles. Some people go to Badrinath by this route, visiting the famous Gohna lake on the way. Buses from Almora (42 miles) and Haldwani (116 miles) come up to this place. Five miles (by foot) south of Baijnath is the place called KAUSANI (6,060). This place is a good health-resort and the view of the snow-peaks from here is simply superb. It is here that the world's greatest man Mahatma Gandhi has written his book *Anasakti Yoga*. Down below Kausani, at Someshvar and Dvarahat also, there are several old temples and ruins. Near Someshvar there is a big centre of the All India Spinners' Association managed by Shree Shantilal Trivedi.

JAULJIBI is situated at the confluence or *sangam* of the Gouri or Gori Ganga coming from Milam and Kali-Ganga coming from Lipu Lekh pass. *Jaul* means confluence and *jib* means a narrow strip of land like the tongue between two rivers. A little above the confluence stands a small temple of Mahadev, situated in a thick grove of mangoes and other trees. Just opposite the temple is a *dharmashala* constructed by the Rani of Askot in 1944. One can command a fine view of the *sangam* from here, which presents a fine spectacle. The Kali is almost throughout a tearing, ranging, and foaming torrent and hence unfordable. Down below the temple, situated along the Gori is the village, the inhabitants of which are Musaliyas or Mohammedans, male members being converts mostly from Hindu weaver-class and all the womenfolk being converts from Harijan Shilpikars. At the western end of the village are the winter residences and camping places of Bhotias.

A big fair is held here on *Vrishchika Sankranti*, the 14th of November, when the Bhotia merchants of both Johar and Darma Parganas gather here in great numbers with Tibetan goods—woollen blankets, skins, wool, salt, etc.; and a brisk trade of about 4 lakhs of rupees is done annually. Nepalis and the down-country people numbering about 10,000 gather here for the *mela*, which lasts for three or four days. Woollen goods from Bhot and Tibet (such as *thulmas*, *chutkas*, *pankhis*, and carpets), skins of snow-leopard, lynx, snow-martin, Tibetan goat, musk-deer, and lambs, ponies, mules, ghee, honey, *gur* of *chura* flowers, *chura*-ghee and musk are the specialities, besides all other commodities usually found in *melas*. A few days before the *mela* temporary bridges are constructed on both rivers Gori and Kali, a little up the confluence, when the level of the water in them falls down, which serve for about six months in the year.

About $2\frac{1}{2}$ miles down the confluence, situated on the right bank of the Kali, is the place called Hanseshvar, where there is a small temple of Hanseshvar Mahadev. There lived a Swami here who was considered to be over 130 years of age. He died in 1945.

SECOND STAGE

DHARCHULA TO GARBYANG—55 miles. It is five days' journey and only coolies and *dandies* can be had for conveyance in this stage.

CHHIPLAKOT LAKES: Five miles beyond Dharchula, leaving the main road, one footpath goes through the village of Jumma to the famous Chhiplakot lakes which are at a distance of about 21 miles, situated at a height of 14,000 feet, wherefrom one can have the best panoramic views of the Panch Chulhi group. This trip may be undertaken on the return journey from Kailas, only by the very adventurous. Beginning from the road, right up to the lakes it is almost one continuous and very steep ascent and oftentimes very dangerous; but the trip is worth the trouble. The lakes are also called Chhipla-Kedar or Najuri-Mund, they are the pilgrim places of about 15 villages. The bigger lake called Kakrola-kid, about 1,020 feet in circumference, is a place of pilgrimage for the people of Gorichhal; and the smaller lake, about 840 feet in circumference is a place of pilgrimage for the villagers on the side of Dharchula; the bigger lake is several feet deep and the smaller one is very shallow and becomes dry in early winter. The author visited these lakes on October 22 and 23, 1937; several coins are offered to the deities of the lake, but nobody would remove them for fear that something untoward might happen to him. During the rainy season thousands of *Brahma Kamal* are seen blossoming, giving out a sweet fragrance all around.

DEATH-CAVE: Nine and a half miles up Khela on the Darma road is a hamlet of three houses called Nyo, very near the village Sovla. Some 80 yards behind the houses is a cave called 'Khar-udyar' or 'Death-Cave'. The cave is 24 feet long, 6 feet broad inside and 9 feet at the mouth, and 6 feet high inside and 12 feet at the mouth. It is said that whatever creature enters it dies instantaneously. The author entered the cave with certain precautions for the first time on October 5, 1937 in the presence of some villagers, but there was no gas in the cave on that occasion. Inside the cave he found about 40 *kalchuna* birds, some crows, several big wild spiders, rats, and a few other birds, besides the old skeletons of two boa-constrictors said to have entered the cave a few years back and died instantaneously. The cave was damp and the dead bodies of some of the birds were fresh.

13

Many Europeans and several District Magistrates of Almora visited this cave, but nobody entered the cave so far. Two *Patwaris* of Chaudans experimented by sending two goats inside, tied to a rope. One goat died instantaneously as it entered the cave, and the other was dragged out immediately it fell down and brought to consciousness by splashing water on the face. The author entered the cave again on October 18, 1939 with nostrils closed and with ropes tied to the waist, held by two men outside. There was some suffocating gas up to a height of 3 feet but it could not be tested, but burning splinters of pine were put out in that gas. On November 12, 1940 the author entered the cave for the third time with nostrils closed and brought out a test-tube full of gas and tested it by adding barium-peroxide solution. The suffocating gas was found to be carbon-dioxide. This time the gas was spread to a height of 4 feet above the ground. During the rainy season when water enters the cave, carbon-dioxide is given out very profusely filling the whole cave; hence a flying bird as soon as it enters the cave is suffocated and falls down dead. Those who are interested in the cave may go there on their return journey from Kailas. One can start early in the morning from Khela and return back by evening.

BHOTIAS: From Dhauli-Ganga (11½ miles beyond Dharchula) upwards it is inhabited by Bhotias. Bhotias are the inhabitants of the Indian borderland lying in the Himalayas. The people of Darma (from Khela up the Dhauli-Ganga), of Chaudans (from Dhauli-Ganga up to Bindakot), and Byans (from Bindakot up to the Lipu Lekh and Lampiya pass), of Chhangru and Tinker (on Nepal borders), and of Johar (from Tejam up to Kungri-bingri pass) in North Almora, the people of Niti and Mana side in North Garhwal District, and the people of Nilang on the northern extremity of Tehri-Garhwal State are called Bhotias (भोटिया). The Bhotias of Mana are also called Marchhas and of Nilang, Jads. That part of the country which they inhabit is called Bhot (भोट). The Tibetans are called Huniyas (हुणिया). These Bhotias are Hindus by religion and Kshatriyas by caste; all their names end in 'Singh'. Many of them wear sacred thread (*yajnopavita*) and speak a mixture of Hindi and Tibetan languages. In summer they go to the various mandis or marts in Western Tibet by various passes for trade and come down in winter to the plains with wool, borax, and other Tibetan commodities and take back piece-goods etc. to Tibet during the next season. Bhotias are very sturdy and industrious people. As they have to deal with the Tibetans every year, they eat and drink freely with them. So the orthodox people of the plains generally do not interdine with the Bhotias.

Womenfolk also are very hard-working. They do all work in the fields except ploughing, and take to weaving during leisure hours. They enjoy full social liberty and wear very heavy silver jewellery. Bhotias, like all other people of the hill districts, are very fond of dancing, which is called *gol-nach* (circle-dance). The people of Chaudans Bhot celebrate a festival called *Kangdali-ka-ladai* (fight of the *kangdali*), once in twelve years. This is a very interesting festival observed when a particular plant called *kangdali* blooms once in twelve years. Last time they celebrated this festival in autumn 1939.

Most of the inhabitants of Bhutan, Sikkim, and northern outskirts of Nepal are Tibetans. They are called Bhotias by many people, most probably because they are the followers of Buddhism or Bodh. The Indian Buddhists of Rampur Bushahr and Kangra are also called Bhotias by many. But the term 'Bhotia' as applied to these people is not to be confounded with the Bhotias[1] described in this book.

DARMA SEVA SANGHA was started by the late Thakur Moti Singh of Chaudans for uplifting and socially reforming the Bhotia community. Its chief objects are: (1) to render service to the pilgrims to Holy Kailas and Manasarovar, (2) to disseminate education, (3) to encourage cottage industries, (4) to construct *dharmashalas*, to open libraries, and render medical aid, and (5) to purge out the evil customs in the Bhotia society and in its religious rites. Though the Society is still in its infancy, much more work is expected of it. The Sangha has its *dharmashalas* at Almora, Khela, Thani-dhar, Pangu, Jungti-gad, Soosa, Sirdang, Malpa, and Garbyang and a tent-*dharmashala* at Taklakot. The society is trying to construct more *dharmashalas* at Dharchula, Khela, Malpa, Kalapani, and Manasarovar. Anybody interested in the construction of *dharmashalas* at any of these places or want to contribute anything towards the cost, should correspond with its President or Secretary. Thakur Mohan Singh Garbyal is the President and Thakur Jaman Singh Garbyal and Thakur Param Singh Hyankey, Chaudansi are the Secretaries.

SHREE NARAYANA ASHRAMA was started in the year 1936 by Shree 108 Narayana Swamiji Maharaj, on the spur of a mountain nearly 9,000 feet high, overlooking the serpent-like torrential River Kali, flowing at the bottom of a gorge about 5,000 feet deep. The terrace-cultivation on the foot-hills all round right up to the River Kali and the snow-clad range of mountains on the east on Nepal borders add to the picturesqueness and charm of the *Ashrama*. A spacious two-storeyed building consisting of an artistically decorated

1 The author has given a full account of the 'Bhotias' in his Hindi work *Kailas-Manasarovar*.

Sankirtan-Hall, Library, and several rooms, a guest-house, and a big kitchen consisting of several rooms and halls, some *kutiyas* for hermits to stay in for silent contemplation, and the Celestial Cottage of the Swami himself, spacious lawns, flower-beds, and vegetable and fruit-gardens have already been constructed. Pilgrims should not fail to pay a visit to this beautiful *Ashrama* and be benefited by the impressive *Sankirtan* of the Swami either on their outward or return journey.

Shree Swamiji Maharaj lives here with some *sadhakas* and is helping a good deal for the spiritual and social upliftment of the Bhotias and other people of the hills by his thrilling *Kirtans* and *Bhajans*, and by his philanthrophy. He has made huge donations to various institutions like schools, *pathshalas*, hospitals, *dharmashalas*, bridges, etc. We heartily wish him a long life and good health to serve humanity, both spiritually and materially.

THIRD STAGE

Garbyang to Taklakot—31½ miles. It is two or three days' march; and *jhabbus*, yaks, mules, and ponies can be had for conveyance. One shall have to arrange for the guide and servant and provisions for the whole journey and back, though ponies shall have to be changed at Taklakot. At Garbyang there is a Post Office which functions from May 5 to November 30.

Lipu Lekh pass (16,750) is to be crossed in this stage, which is 20½ miles from Garbyang. From the other side of the Lipu Lekh pass begins the Tibetan territory, which the Indians call Hun Desh (हुण देश). Before starting for the pass one should take out some lozenges and *gur-papari* for ready use on the way. If there is no wind at that time one should stop on the pass for a short while and enjoy the grand view of the scenery on both sides.

Taklakot is at a distance of 11 miles from Lipu Lekh pass and is the first Tibetan village on this route, where there is plenty of barley and pea-cultivation. The whole valley consisting of several villages including Taklakot is called Purang. A big mandi is held at Taklakot every year from the month of June to the middle of November, where Bhotia merchants of Darma Pargana (Darma, Chaudans, and Byans *pattis*) sell their piece goods, *gur*, and other commodities and buy in exchange or for cash enormous quantities of Tibetan wool, salt, and borax. Walled enclosures are constructed with gates and tents are set up temporarily on these walls but there are no roofed houses. There are about 200 such tents in the mandi. When the merchants wind up the mandi, they keep the gates, tents, and unsold commodities in the cave-houses of some known Tibetan customers and leave the place.

Barley and pea-*sattu* (for distributing alms to beggars), *dal*, etc. may be supplemented from this place for further journey and firearms and fresh transport shall have to be engaged. While in Tibet, one should not leave any article outside one's tent, for the children, who often flock round the pilgrims, pilfer them. One should also be very careful about the Tibetan dogs, especially when approaching Tibetan shepherd-camps and tents, as they are very ferocious and at times tear men to pieces, if they are not alert.

SIMBILING GOMPA is situated on the top of a hill just above the Taklakot Mandi, overlooking the mandi and the neighbouring villages and the Karnali with its feeders. Adjacent to the monastery is the *Zong's* (Governor's) fort or building (see p. 62).

GUKUNG is a village situated in caves on the right bank of the Map chuu or Karnali, about half a mile from Taklakot Mandi. There is also a gompa in a three-storied cave. A big market is held by the Nepalis on the left bank of the Karnali, where large quantities of wheat, wheat-flour, rice, and barley are exchanged for wool, salt, borax, and sheep.

KHOCHARNATH Gompa is at a distance of about 12 miles south-east of Taklakot Mandi, situated on the left bank of the River Karnali. The village of Khochar belongs to Bhutan State and is under the jurisdiction of Tarchhen Labrang. Pilgrims may visit this place either on their onward journey to Kailas or on their return journey. If one takes a pony and starts early in the morning from Taklakot, one can return back the same evening (see p. 64).

FOURTH STAGE

TAKLAKOT TO TARCHHEN via Manasarovar—62 miles. It is 4 or 5 days' journey. If one wishes to visit Tirthapuri one may go via Gyanima Mandi (49 miles), then to Tarchhen (28 miles), Kailas-*parikrama*, Manas-*parikrama*, and then to Taklakot direct; or one can go from Taklakot to Tirthapuri direct (65 miles) via Chhipra la and Dulchu Gompa.

While engaging ponies at Taklakot one should fix up the following conditions with the pony and yak-men: (1) If one has to go to Kailas direct, the ponies shall have to go via Manasarovar and not via Rakshas Tal.[1] (2) If one is to go via Tirthapuri, the ponies shall have to be taken direct to Tarchhen, but not to Nyanri Gompa, for in that way one is deprived of seeing Tarchhen, the flag-staff, and the Chhorten-kangni. (3) Kailas-*parikrama* should begin from Tarchhen and end there again, for usually pony-men get down to

1 Since the route via Rakshas Tal is about 4 miles shorter, pony-men take the uninformed pilgrims by that route, depriving them of the opportunity of their staying on the shores of the Holy Lake for three days.

Barkha direct from Zuthul-phuk Gompa, and one should be shown all the roadside monasteries.

TOYO is about 3 miles from Taklakot where there is the *samadhi* of General Zoravar Singh called 'Singba-ka-chhorten' (see p. 79).

GURLA LA : After going for 24¾ miles from Taklakot, one reaches the top of Gurla pass (16,200). Here are several big heaps of stones called *laptche*, flags, and festoons. Gurla la is a pass in the Mandhata Range. Mandhata was said to have done penance at the foot of these mountains, on the shores of Manasarovar. From the top of the Gurla pass one can command a grand and glorious panoramic view of the Holy Manasarovar with its crystal clear water of emerald-green on the right, the Rakshas Tal on the left and the majestic ice-clad silvery dome of Mount Kailas (*Rajitachala*) far beyond on the north, and the Mandhata massif on the south, overlooking the two lakes.

MANASAROVAR : See First Wave.

RAKSHAS TAL : See First Wave.

GANGA CHHU is the only outlet of Manasarovar and it flows into Rakshas Tal : See p. 8.

PARKHA OR BARKHA : The village Parkha (15,050) is midway between Kailas and Manasarovar. There are two houses here, one belonging to the *Tasam* or *Tarzam* (Staging Officer or Transport Agent) and the other Government Officers' Staging Place. All round Parkha there are extensive plains and pasture-lands, and a good number of black tents are pitched by shepherds, where thousands of sheep, goats, yak, and ponies graze in summer. Hundreds of wild horses (*kyangas*) are seen marching on this *maidan* in perfect military order. Aeroplanes can very easily land anywhere on this plain, where the land is firm. It would be more convenient for the pilgrims to camp at Gapudosa two miles further than at Parkha.

" The river which falls out in the middle of the northern shore of the lake (Rakshas) is formed from the brooks of the valley on both sides of Kailas, one of its branches passes Parkha. When I crossed the river on July 28, 1908, *it flowed in two branches*, one having two or three cub. m., the other 15 "[1]. In fact the three rivers of Kailas—the Lha chhu, the Tarchhen chhu, and the Zhong chhu, along with the Karleb form one river, and the Avang chhu, Philung-kongma, Philung-pharma, and Philung-yongma form the Dam chhu, the bed of which is very marshy and is altogether a different river. Sven Hedin shows only one river in his map, though these are two different rivers falling into the Rakshas Tal, at two different places 1½ miles apart. Sometimes, a small brook branches off from the Zhong chhu and joins the Dam chhu.

[1] Sven Hedin, 'Southern Tibet', Vol. II, p. 170.

DULCHU GOMPA is 14 miles fown Tirthapuri and 21 miles from Tarchhen. Tibetans say that the mountain on which the monastery is situated has the appearance of an elephant. The traditional source of the Sutlej is in the springs situated in the marshes, at a distance of about 250 yards from the gompa. As such, Sutlej is called Langchen Khambab, river coming out of the mouth of an elephant. The Sutlej is a mere brook here. There is one *tulku*-lama and 23 *dabas* in the gompa. There is only one image-hall and Sakya-Thubha is the principal deity. There are all the volumes of *Kanjur* and the *chhorten* of Lobsang-dechhung, the founder of the monastery. According to some, this was founded in the last quarter of the 17th century and according to others in the middle of the 19th century. There is a flag-staff and some *mani*-walls in front of the gompa; there are three houses and some black tents also, and a freshwater spring very near the monastery.

TIRTHAPURI, called Tetapuri in Tibetan, is 76 miles from Taklakot, via Gyanima and 65 miles by the direct route via Chhipra la, which is 5 to 6 days' march. Tarchhen is 28 miles from here and is two days' march; and Gartok is at a distance of 49 miles from here. Tirthapuri is situated on the right bank of the river Sutlej, which is here called Tirthapuri tsangpo. Tirthapuri Gompa, originally belonged to the Hemmis Gompa of Ladakh and was completely destroyed by the Kazhakis in 1941; but in 1945-46 the *Shipjo* got it rebuilt and handed it over to the Simbiling Gompa of Taklakot from which three officers, the *Nerba* (secretary), the *Unje* (*pujari*), and the *Majin* (cook) are sent for a period of three years. There are 15 monks in this monastery. Sakya-Thubha (*Sakya-Muni*) is the principal deity in it. There are several big *mani*-walls outside the gompa. Tirthapuri region was once a huge volcanic area and there are several extinct craters near the monastery. There is the image of Dorje-Phangmo (*Vajra-Varahi*, the divine consort of Demchhog, the presiding deity of Kailas) in a cave-room and there is a third building of the monastery on the Sindura hill. The yellow ochre from this hill, called *sindura* is taken as the *prasad* of Devi by pilgrims. Just behind the gompa, situated on its *parikrama*, there is a heap of horns and *tarchok* (flags) representing Dolma (*Tara*). About 300 yards from the gompa there are some hot springs and geysers just by the side of the river, which change their places from time to time and sometimes disappear. There are some more hot springs near Dorje-Phangmo's cave. Round about the hot springs there are huge mounds of tons of calcium carbonate and sulphate. This white substance called *chugan* by Tibetans, is taken as *vibhuti* by pilgrims. This place is believed by Hindus to be the place where the demon Bhasmasura was said to have done penance to propitiate Lord Shiva and where he had been burnt down to ashes by his own villainy, by virtue of the very boon he got from the Lord of Kailas. It is believed both by Indians as well as Tibetans that the pilgrimage to Kailas is incomplete or does not bear full fruit unless one visits Tirthapuri also.

GURU-GEM : Nearly $5\frac{3}{4}$ miles down Tirthapuri, situated at the confluence of the Langchen Tsangpo or Langchen Khambab (Sutlej) and Chornak (or Sumnak) is the site of the ruined village of Palkya, destroyed by Zoravar Singh in 1841. The foundations of the monastery and some Ladakhi type of *chhortens*, and a water-mill still stand there to remind one of the past glory of the place. There are some ruined columns of buildings on the surrounding mountains, said to be the royal mansions of the Kings of Kardung.

One Khampa lama of *Pembo* Sect came here in 1930 and began to live under the projection of a rock (*kem*). He became famous very soon and had built a well-planned monastery in the vast plains at the foot of his mountain-abode. So this place came to be known as Guru-kem or Guru-gem. The monastery was almost ready in 1934 though finishing touches were given later. The lama spent thousands of rupees over this gompa and made it the 'Cynosure of the neighbouring eye'. The monastery itself is called Donga-thagya-ling. The monastery proper is about 110 feet square and is two-storeyed with an open space of 140 feet square in front of the gompa bounded by several rooms, the whole having the appearance of a big fort. The *duvang* or the general image-hall is well decorated with beautiful frescos and banner-paintings and the special image-hall behind it is furnished with seven highly artistic stucco images of (1) Thousand-headed Chenresig, (2) Jambyang, (3) Nambar-jekhar, (4) Lhasa-chho, (Buddha), (5) Dolma, (6) Chamba, and (7) Demchhog in *Yab-Yum* pose, each 9 feet high. There are *Kanjur* and *Tanjur* library halls on either side before entering the image-hall. Mystic plays are enacted at the end of the ninth month of the Tibetan year. There are 20 monks here including the founder-lama.

In the mountain behind the gompa are the abodes of the lama and senior monks and a furlong down the place is a convent or nunnery, attached to this gompa ; and there are 30 nuns in it. Adjacent to the monastery there are a few plots of land in which turnip and radish are grown. Due to the over-confidence of the lama in the efficacy of his *mantra-tantra*, Kazhakis besieged this gompa for two days in 1941 and completely peeled off everything costly in the monastery and carried away thousands of rupees worth of cloth belonging to Johari merchants. During the engagement, two monks of the monastery and seven Kazhakis died and the lama was let off completely naked.

63. *Tasam's* (Transport Officer's) Tent in Chhakra Mandi
[*See p.* 28

66. Bales of *Gur* in a *Tasam* (Transport Office) awaiting transportation to Lhasa
[*See p.* 75

67. Gyanima Mandi
[*See pp.* 73 & 138

68. Tirthapuri Gompa
[See p. 103

69. Representation of Dolma (*Tara*) on the back of Tirthapuri Gompa
[See p. 103

70. Guru-gem Gompa
[See p. 104

71. Khyunglung Gompa and Cave-dwellings situated in the erosion Terraces and Spries of Volcanic Lava [*See pp.* 43 & 105

72. Deposits of Calcium Carbonate near the Thermal springs at Khyunglung [*See pp.* 48 & 105

73. The Deserted Cave-Colony of Pangtha [*See pp.* 52 & 106

74. Mandhata Peaks from Gurla La
[See pp. 102 & 123

75. View of the Holy Kailas from Zhong Chhu—*Photo by Courtesy of Mr. Salim Ali Bombay*
[See pp. 102 & 126

This is an interesting place from the view-point of an explorer and a geographer. Hardly 300 yards from the confluence of the Sutlej and the Chornak is the confluence of the Langchen Tsangpo coming from the Indian borders, flowing northwards and the Tirthapuri tsangpo coming from Rakshas Tal via Dulchu and Tirthapuri Gompa flowing in a south-westerly direction. The bed of the Langchen Tsangpo is broad and majestic and carries under normal conditions nearly twice as much water as Tirthapuri tsangpo, which is like a brook. When asked why the Langchen Tsangpo was so named, the guide said that at their confluence Tirthapuri appears like a child entering into the lap of the mother Langchen Tsangpo, that it carries much less water than the Langchen, that the Langchen is the biggest head-stream of the Sutlej though the traditional source is at Dulchu, which is meant for religious purposes, and that the river is called Langchen Tsangpo or Langchen Khambab, only after its confluence with the Tirthapuri branch.

The four rivers, Chhu-nak, Guni-yankti, Darma-yankti, and the Gyanima chhu, join together to form Langchen Tsangpo. The Chhu-nak and the Gyanima branch carry much less water than the other two. The Guni-yankti (called Chhu-Minjung—small river, in Tibetan) and the Darma-yankti (Chhu-Minjen—big river) taken individually also, very often, carry more water than either the Tag tsangpo where it falls into Manasarovar, or the Tirthapuri tsangpo where it falls into the Langchen Tsangpo.

Of the two rivers the Darma-yankti and the Guni-yankti, the former carries more water than the latter. So, should the quantity of water be taken into account, the source of Darma-yankti should be the source of the Sutlej, which is in the Zaskar Range near the Darma pass. Also because of the fact that the Darma-yankti coming from the Indian borders is called Langchen Tsangpo by Tibetans after it receives the Chhu-nak, the Guni-yankti, and the Gyanima chhu, and of the fact that the name Langchen Tsangpo is applied to the river even after the meeting of the Tirthapuri tsangpo but not to the Tirthapuri tsangpo, it is quite evident that the Tibetans believe that the Darma-yankti (or the Langchen Tsangpo) to be the main river Langchen Tsangpo (Sutlej). From the view point of quantity of water, the Tirthapuri tsangpo is a mere tributary, though held sacred from the religious point of view.

Khyunglung (14,000 feet): Nine and a half miles down Guru-gem, situated on the left bank of the Sutlej, is the village Khyunglung. The whole of Khyunglung was once a huge volcanic area and is an interesting subject for study from the geological point of view. There are a few houses situated in caves, dug out in a huge mound of thousands of tons of calcium deposits. There is a hot spring near the bridge, where a beautiful dome of stalagmites and stalactites is formed. Crossing the bridge to the right bank, there is a vast area of volcanic lava formed into huge columns like the ruins of a fort. Several caves were dug into these spires, most of which are now desolate. On the top one of the mounds is the monastery of Khyunglung and on the topmost column is the old fort. There are 10 *dabas* in this monastery. Here are the images of Gombo and Jigje in *chenkhang,* and in *duvang* those of Chhuku Rimpochhe, Sangę, and Chenresig. Two armours, two iron shields, and two skin shields of Zoravar Singh are preserved here.

THE DESERTED CAVE-COLONY OF PANGTHA (13,100): Five miles down Sibchilim Mandi, situated opposite the confluence of the Sib chhu and Tisum chhu is a huge wall of conglomerate. In it were dug out a few hundred caves, situated about 400 feet above the level of the river. They are all now empty and are encrusted with soot. Roughly speaking, the caves are in two terraces. On the upper terrace there is a big monastery belonging to the Sakya Sect (Red Cap Section). The author visited this cave-colony on July 26 and 27, 1946, but was withheld by a huge landslip within a distance of 20 yards from the gompa. Inside the gompa there are numerous fresco paintings ; so when he would visit it next time he proposes to bring some photos of these frescos and collect some historical data. When Khyunglung was in a flourishing condition all these caves were occupied both by monks and householders. Even now-a-days a few shepherds come here for stay in winter and in early spring. The author was given to understand that the monastery was in a flourishing condition between the 13th and 14th century. Khyunglung is at a distance of about 12 miles from here.

FIFTH STAGE

KAILAS PARIKRAMA—32 miles. The *parikrama* of Kailas can easily be done in three days and hurriedly in two days. Several Tibetans do the round in a single day, which is called *ningkor* (see First Wave).

TARCHHEN OR DARCHHEN is on the southern side of the Kailas Peak wherefrom Kailas-*parikrama* begins. *Dar* means *dhvaja* or flag and *chhen* means big ; so Darchhen means a big flag-staff or *Mahadhvaja,* named after the flag-staff on the western side of Kailas, which is 3½ miles from here. It is also pronounced Tarchhen. There are 3 or 4 houses here. A small mandi is held here in summer and there would be about 60 to 80 tents in all. And it is a big wool-shearing centre. Tarchhen belongs to the State of Bhutan and a monk-officer called *Labrang* lives here to look after the Bhutanese possessions in Tibet. Here is a big building of the *Labrang* in which there is his private chapel, but not a gompa. Pilgrims may leave all their luggage, not needed for the *parikrama* with some merchant here and collect it again on their return journey; by doing so they would be able to spare a few animals for their servants to ride on the ascent to Dolma la. There are three monasteries directly on the *parikrama*-route and two more in the interior, on the southern slopes, two miles above Tarchhen.

From the hills situated just on the northern side of Tarchhen, one can enjoy the grand view of the great amphitheatre of the huge Barkha plain, stretching east to west as far as the eye could travel, intercepted by a network of winding streams and the hills gradually mounting up to the Mandhata and Nepal peaks with the Rakshas Tal-blue picturesquely set in it.

SERSHUNG is at a distance of 3½ miles from Tarchhen where there is a big flag-staff called *Tarbochhe* or *Darbochhe* (see p. 10). Within 200 yards from this place is Chhorten-kangni (two-legged). Men and animals pass through the arch of this monument which is considered an auspicious act.

DOLMA LA or *Devi's* pass is the greatest height which one has to negotiate in this pilgrimage, and it is 18,600 feet above sea-level.

GOURI-KUND: About 200 yards down the Dolma pass is Gouri-kund (see p. 11).

SERDUNG-CHUKSUM and TSO KAPALA: See p. 11 and 12 and Route Table II.

SIXTH STAGE

MANASAROVAR-PARIKRAMA—The actual circumference of Manasarovar is 54 miles and the *parikrama* can be done in four days. Those who want to do the *parikrama* of Manasarovar also can do so direct from Zuthul-phuk Gompa and finish the combined circuit of Kailas and Manas both, either at Gurla la or at Taklakot (see First Wave and Route Table III).

KAILAS - MANASAROVAR

FOURTH WAVE

ROUTES

KEY TO THE USE OF ROUTE TABLES

In these Route Tables the very first numeral indicates the number of the stage and after that the name of the actual staging place of some important place is given. Then the distance between two places and the total distance are given in two sets of small brackets; and the height of a place in feet above sea-level, if any, is given in large brackets. The mileages, given without brackets at the beginning of a sentence in the description of the routes, or in the middle of a sentence after semi-colon, represent the distance between two consecutive places. Fuller details are given in footnotes. For economy of space lines in the Route Tables had to be omitted.

ABBREVIATIONS

P.	Post Office.	*D.*	*Dharmashala.*
T.	Telegraph Office.	C.	Camping ground.
H.	Hospital.	*le*	Camping ground with camping parapets or walled enclosures.
D.B.	Dak Bungalow.	tea	Tea shop.
F.	Forest Rest House.	m.	mile or miles.
R.	Rest House.	(?)	Information doubtful.
S.	School Building.		

GRADATION IN ASCENTS AND DESCENTS

Gentle up.	Mild descent.
Mild ascent.	Descent.
Ascent.	Steep descent.
Steep ascent.	Very steep descent.
Very steep ascent.	Falling descent.
Almost perpendicular ascent.	

All the Tibetan names are given as they are actually pronounced but not as they are written, for nearly half the letters written are silent. Every effort is made to give as correct a pronunciation as possible of all the Tibetan words. The pronunciation varies from district to district.

Very often ch or y is pronounced as j (Chiu as Jiu and Yogi as Jogi), k as g (Kangri as Gangri), p as b (Parkha as Barkha), and t as d (Tarchhen as Darchhen). Ts is almost equivalent to a sound midway between ch and chh, as Tsepgye or Chhepgye.

TABLE I

FIRST ROUTE TO HOLY KAILAS AND MANASAROVAR

FROM ALMORA VIA LIPU LEKH PASS—238 MILES

Almora (0) (0) [5,414], District Headquarters, P., T., H., D.B., F., Anandamayi *dharmashala*, hotels, bazaars, Motor Agencies, Railway Out Agency, etc., Haldwani Railway station is 41 miles by foot and 88 miles by motor,

1m. Dunga-dhara Toll-bar, shops, tea,

$\frac{1}{2}$m. Baldhoti, pony-halting place,

1m. Christian Mission Sanatorium,

1$\frac{3}{4}$m. Chitai, shops, tea, *dhara* (water-tap), temple, snow-view,

1$\frac{1}{4}$m. steep descent to Chaukhutiya or Petsal, shops, cross the bridge on a stream, temple, tea, from here gentle ascent up to Bade-chhina,

$\frac{1}{2}$m. shop, tea, *dhara*,

$\frac{3}{4}$m. cross a narrow suspension bridge,

$\frac{3}{4}$m. Seel, shop, tea,

Bade-chhina[1] (8$\frac{1}{2}$) (8$\frac{1}{2}$) [4,000] 1m. P., F., S., bazaar, tea, mangoes can be had from here up to Dharchula in season,

1m. Supai, shop,

1m. steep ascent through pine forest,

1m. mild descent,

1. Dhaul-chhina[2] (5) (13$\frac{1}{2}$) [6,000] 2m. steep ascent to Dhaul-chhina, P., D.B., shops, tea, cool place; from here continuous steep descent of 5m. up to Bhaura-ka-gadhera,

Bunga (2$\frac{1}{2}$) (16) 2$\frac{1}{2}$m. descent through a thick forest to Bunga, shops, tea, halting place of pony-men, good staging place,

2m. further descent through pines to Bhaura-ka-gadhera,

Kanari-chhina (2$\frac{3}{4}$) (18$\frac{3}{4}$) $\frac{3}{4}$m. P. F., shop; $\frac{1}{4}$m. steep descent; 1$\frac{3}{4}$m. Jalikhet, shop, mango groves,

$\frac{1}{2}$m. ascent to Dungralekh-chhina, plenty of mangoes in the neighbourhood; 1m. steep descent,

1$\frac{3}{4}$m. mild descent up to the suspension bridge on the Sarayu, cross the river by bridge[3] to

1 From here one path goes to Mirtola (5$\frac{1}{2}$m. by footpath and 7m. by bridlepath) where Shree Krishna Premji (Mr. Nixon) and Shree Anandapriyaji (Major Alexander) and some other western *sadhakas* had started an *ashram* by name Uttar Brindavan, where they had built a small temple of Lord Krishna. It is a beautiful spot worth visiting. Jageshvar is 2m. from here.

2 From here one path goes towards east to Mirtola 5m., and one path goes towards west to Binsar 6m. which is a good health-resort, situated at a height of 7,913 feet. Five furlongs before reaching Dhaul-chhina is a place called Kalun with two shops and a *dhara*.

3 There is a big mango grove, 2 furlongs before reaching the bridge, wherefrom one can get good graft mangoes.

Seraghat-malla ($5\frac{1}{4}$) (24) Seraghat, situated on the left bank of the Sarayu, shops, tea, hot place, plenty of plantains and mangoes, (from here one road goes to Pithoragarh and Tankapur Railway Station via Gangolihat); a little down the shops is a small Shiva temple, opposite which the stream Jaigan joins the Sarayu; the confluence is beautiful,

2. Shalya ($2\frac{1}{2}$) ($26\frac{1}{2}$) $2\frac{1}{2}$m. steep ascent to Shalya, shop, tea, *dhara*,

$\frac{1}{4}$m. further ascent to Naruva-ka-ghol, shop, tea,

$\frac{1}{2}$m. steep descent, cross the bridge on Padyali,

Ganai ($3\frac{1}{2}$) (30) $2\frac{3}{4}$m. mild descent to Ganai, P., S., shop, tea, *dhara*, half a mile away from the road is the F., hot place,

$\frac{3}{4}$m. Tapovan, shop, tea, neat halting place,

$1\frac{3}{4}$m. Simalta, shop: 1m. Sata, shop.

1m. cross the Bistardyo suspension bridge on the Kulru-gad ($\frac{1}{4}$m. before reaching the bridge there is a small temple of Vishvanath Mahadev, situated in a grove),

Banspatan (6) (36) $1\frac{1}{2}$m. Banspatan, one of the beautiful spots on the route; several valleys meet, terrace-cultivation, steep gorges, narrow valleys, variety of cultivation, shop, tea,

$1\frac{1}{2}$m. Godi-gad, shop, tea, pony-men's halting place,

$\frac{1}{2}$m. Shyali, shop, tea,

Suklyadi (3) (39) 1m. shop, tea, halting place of pony-men,

1m. even road,

2m. steep ascent through pines to Berinag-top (Bageshvar is 23m. from here); from here up to the bridge of Gurghatiya ($6\frac{3}{4}$m.) it is one continuous steep descent, very slippery during rains,

3. BERINAG[1] ($3\frac{1}{4}$m.) ($42\frac{1}{4}$) [7,000] $\frac{1}{4}$m. Berinag or Verinag, P., H., F., S., shops, tea, last place to get sweets, Vijay *dharmashala*, Tea Estate, Nag temple is $\frac{1}{2}$ a mile away from the bazaar, cool place, from here fine view of the snow-peaks of Badrinath, Nandadevi, Nandakot, Trisul, Panchachulhi, etc., and Chhiplakot, beautiful scenery

1 Intending pilgrims to Jageshvar, Gangolihat and Patala-Bhuvaneshvar, should leave Bade-chhina for these places and come back to the main road again here. Almora to Bade-chhina $8\frac{1}{2}$m., to Panwanaula $5\frac{1}{2}$m., Jageshvar 3m., Naini 8m., Harara $2\frac{1}{4}$m., Talla-Seraghat $1\frac{3}{4}$m., Gangolihat $6\frac{1}{2}$m., Patala-Bhuvaneshvar $6\frac{1}{2}$m., and Berinag 11m. (total 53m.).

Those who wish to visit Bageshvar on the return journey should go there from Berinag and return to Almora direct. Berinag to Sani-odyar 10m., Bageshvar 13m., Takula 12 m., and Almora 15m. (total 50m.). Someshvar is 14m. from Bageshvar by footpath wherefrom Almora is 25m. by bridle-path. Baijnath is 13m. from Bageshvar by bridle-path, from where Someshvar is 18m. (via Kausani) by motor road, and thence Almora is 42m. Buses regularly run from Baijnath (Garur) to Almora and Kathgodam.

up to the end of the descent (from here one path goes to Patala-Bhuvaneshvar and Gangolihat),

1½m. descent to Mund-katta-Ganesh, shop, plantains,

Mangroli (1¾) (44) ¼m. descent to Mangroli, shop, milk, plantains, good *dhara*, nice halting place,

Gartir (¾) (44¾) ¾m. descent to Gartir, shops, tea, plenty of plantains and milk, good halting place,

½m. descent to Baghora, shop,

¾m. descent to Danuthal or Chaubat, shop; 1m. Balgari, shop, tea,

1½m. descent to Liktad, shop, guava gardens; ¼m. descent to Gurghatia-bridge, cross the bridge on the stream,

1m. ascent; ¾m. Amtad, big village,

4. Thal (7) (51¾) [3,000] 1¾m. Thal, shops, tea, hot place, plenty of plantains and mangoes, at the end of the bazaar, a little beyond the bridge is the beautiful stream of Bard-gad, (there is a F., on the top of a mountain [3,400], situated in the midst of a pine reserve); Thal is situated on both sides of the river Rama-Ganga, cross the suspension bridge on the Rama-Ganga to its left bank, here is an old temple of Baleshvar Mahadev, a big fair is held on *Vaishakha Purnima* which lasts for a week; nearby is a small hill-stream (one road goes to Pithoragarh, which is 28m. from this place),

¼m. ascent to S., shop[1], (from here one road goes to Milam via Tejam, 12+47¾=59¾m.),

3m. steep ascent (ascents up to Sandev with reliefs at intervals),

2¼m. Sata, one Missionary building, Berinag is seen from here,

1¼m. Mapani, a hill stream falling down from above,

Sandev (7¾) (59½) [6,400] 1m. F. 200 yards above the road, fine view of the snows,

½m. shop, tea, *dhara*,

5. Didihat (2½) (62) [6,000] 2m. steep descent to Didihat, P., Middle School, shops, tea; this place is called Diktad; the village Didihat itself is situated in the beautiful valley of the river Charma one mile below the road,

3½m. ascent with reliefs up to Kana-dhar, shops, tea, from here begins the state of Askot; ½m. *dhara*[2]; 1m. Chorpani,

[1] About ¾m. beyond this place, situated at a distance of 200 yards on the right side of the main road there is a temple called Ek-hatiya deval (or temple carved out of a rock by a one-handed architect). Between the deval and the pilgrim route, flow two streams with two pretty-looking small waterfalls. The temple is carved out of one single boulder 30′ long, 17′ broad, and 17′ high, and the temple itself is 7½′ long, 3½′ broad, and 10′ high.

[2] About 200 yards up the road, at the place called Dharmagarh, a High School is being started by Shree Narayana Swamiji in an extensive plot of about 25 acres of land. An agricultural research institute also is under contemplation.

ASKOT[1] (7) (69) [5,000] 2m. steep descent to Askot, H., P., F., S., *D.*, bazaar, temple, Rajbar or Zamindar of Askot lives here,

3¼m. steep descent to Garjiya suspension bridge through a pine-forest, very slippery during rains, there is a beautiful waterfall sliding down from the top of a mountain over the rocky wall in several ramifications; cross the bridge on the Gori-Ganga to its left bank, here is a small shop, (from here one road leads up the Gori-Ganga to Johar), a few yards beyond the bridge at two or three places, stones often fall on the road when the weather is dry, since the wall of the mountain is highly sandy,

1m. plain road (from here up to Dudigaon it is a steep ascent of ¾m. by the main road),

6. Jauljibi (5) (74) [2,100] ¾m. leaving the main road to the left, down along the bank of the river Gori to Jauljibi, the confluence or *sangam* of Gori and Kali (see p. 96), P., S., from here up to the Lipu Lekh pass the route goes almost along the River Kali, the boundary line of India and Nepal,

½m. ascent to Dudigam, winter quarters of Darma Bhotias; 2½m. ascent with reliefs here and there to Khinkhola; 1m. ups and downs; ¾m. steep descent to the village Tola, the village proper is situated a little above the road, the view of Nepal side is very beautiful; ¼m. descent to Band; ¼m. a stream; ¼m. steep ascent to Venda,

Balvakot (6½) (80½) [3,000] ¾m. descent to Balvakot, the village is situated above the road, S., *D.*, shop, hot place, winter residences of Darma Bhotias, from here up to Pangu one comes across poisonous serpents; a furlong beyond cross the bridge on a big stream,

1m. Kuchiya, Government C., D.B., shop, hamlet, two furlongs before reaching Kuchiya there is a beautiful freshwater spring flowing out as a small brook, on the left bank of which there is a small temple, a *dharmashala*, and a shop,

1m. Nantadi, hamlet; 1¼m. Chharsam; ¾m. mild ascent,

[1] *Assi-kot* means 80 forts; it is said that 80 kings ruled here once; hence it is called Askot. H., P., and F. are situated at the junction of the Pithoragarh and Almora roads, which is ½m. from Askot proper. Tanakpur is 90m. from here and a motor road is under construction from Tanakpur to Pithoragarh. The route is as follows: Tanakpur to Sukhidang camp or Malijhari 9m. (Punyagiri Devi is 7m. from here and as well from Tanakpur), to Deori 8m., Champavat 15m. (Mayavati Ashram is 2m. up this place), Lohaghat 6m., Chhira 9m., Gurna 10m., Pithoragarh 8m., Kanali-chhina 10m., Singalikhan 9m., and Askot 6m. (total 90m.).

1m. steep ascent to Chholioki-dhar, just opposite this place, on the other side of the Kali, there is a big village with extensive terrace cultivation with huge plots of sugar-cane plantations beginning from the edge of the river to the top of the mountain which presents a grand spectacle,

Kalika (6) (86½) 1m. steep descent to the village Kalika, while descending to Kalika one can have a fine view of the fields below and the winding and descending Kali, cross the Kali stream here; ¼m. beautiful spring of Kali under the shade of a huge tree, the village Kalika is situated on either side of the stream Kali; ¾m. Gothi, winter houses of Darma Bhotias; ¾m. Nigalpani, cross the stream, winter houses of Darma Bhotias; ½m. Phultadi, village; ¼m. cross the Galati-gad, ¼m. winter houses of Bhotias on both sides of the stream,

7. **Dharchula**[1] (10) (90½) [3,000] 1¾m. Dharchula, P., D.B., *D.*, S., shops.

Tapovan[2] (2) (92½) 2m. Tapovan, shop,

½m. Ranthi or Tanthra-gad, flowing in two or three branches, (about 2 miles up above on the top of a mountain is the big village of Ranthi),

3m. Kula-gad, which presents a beautiful view by its coming very precipitously through and over huge boulders forming a series of cascades with every now and then a deep rocky pool, cross the stream by bridge,

1m. from here one path goes to the village Jumma and thence to Chhiplakot (see p. 97),

¼m. steep descent to Yela-gad or Rel-gad, which comes from Chhiplakot mountains, this is the boundary line of the State of Rajbar of Askot, cross the bridge on the stream,

1 Rai Sahib Pt. Prem Vallabh or Pt. Haridatta may be consulted for help; horse conveyance ends here; coolies to be engaged from here up to Garbyang or to Khela if through coolies are not available; plenty of plantains and mangoes are available, and guavas on return journey; here are winter residences of Byans Bhotias; down below, on the Kali is a rope bridge connecting Dharchula with Nepal State, where there is posted a Nepali Lieutenant with 50 policemen; hundreds of tins of ghee is exported from the Nepal side to Almora; good ghee is sold at the rate of Rs. 3 per seer. There is a great need of a good *dharmashala* at Dharchula, though the Darma Seva Sangha has hired a house for a temporary *dharmashala*.

2 Up to 1932 or so, there used to be a centre of Ramkrishna Mission here, which was started through the strenuous efforts of Shrimati Ruma Devi of Byans, but it was all wound up. Now the *Ashram* is controlled and repaired at a great cost by Shree Narayana Swamiji Maharaj. The Darma Seva Sangha is trying to take charge of the *Ashram* from the court of Wards, Rajbar of Askot and expand it into a big centre for pilgrims to Kailas. Attached to the *Ashram* is a small *Shivalaya* and a *dharmashala*; 200 yards from here are some thermal springs situated on the bank of the River Kali, which will be under water when the river is in floods.

$\frac{1}{4}$m. shop,

$\frac{1}{2}$m. Yela, shop, tea, *D.*, (the village Sakuri is on the mountain a mile from here) ; $\frac{1}{2}$m. Rounti-gad,

8. KHELA[1] (8) (100$\frac{1}{2}$) [5,500] 2m. steep ascent to Khela, shop, *D.* ; P. and S. are situated in the village which is $\frac{1}{2}$m. from here,

1$\frac{1}{2}$m. steep and winding descent to Tova-ghat [3,600] ; cross the roaring, foaming, and jumping Dhauli-Ganga to its left bank by a wooden bridge ; the Dhauli or Dhaul comes from Darma pass and falls into the Kali-Ganga $\frac{3}{4}$m. down the bridge ; grand view of the Dhauli from the bridge ; from here begins the Chaudans Patti of the Bhotias,

3m. very steep ascent to Thani-dhar [9,000 ?], from here very fine view of Khela and the surroundings ; here is seen the first heap of stones, with flags placed on the pass, a hundred yards further *D.*, *dhara*,

Pangu (6) (106$\frac{1}{2}$) [6,900] 1$\frac{1}{2}$m. gradual ascent to the first Bhotia village of Pangu on this route, Middle School, many walnut trees ; from here upwards provisions can be procured from any of the villagers, as they are all merchants; there are some sort of *dharmashalas* in every village,

1$\frac{1}{4}$m. descent to Jungti-gad stream [6,698], *D.*,

9. Soosa[2] (3) (109$\frac{1}{2}$) [8,400 ?] 1$\frac{3}{4}$m. steep ascent to Soosa, S., *D.*, provisions can be had from the village, plenty of potatoes, cold place,

Tithlakot (1$\frac{1}{2}$) (111) [9,068] 1$\frac{1}{2}$m. ascent to Tithlakot ; Dharma Dvara, a bell dedicated to a goddess, piles of stones and flags, good camping place, no village or shop ; but midway between Soosa and Tithlakot there is a small *D.*,

Sirdang ($\frac{3}{4}$) (111$\frac{3}{4}$) $\frac{3}{4}$m. steep descent to the village Sirdang, S., *D.* by the road side, good halting place,

Sirkha ($\frac{1}{2}$) (112$\frac{1}{4}$) $\frac{1}{2}$m. further descent to Sirkha, which is a furlong below the road, P., S., *D.*, shop, one furlong above the road is the garden of a Missionary where peaches, apples,

1 This is a good health-resort; and the peculiar setting of the mountains all round adds a special charm to the place ; visitors would do well to stay here for a couple of days. A kind of spice called *bhangeri* is available here, which is used for preparing *chutney* ; best cow ghee can be had from here for further journey. Kunwar Pratap Singh, shopkeeper, would look to all sorts of comforts for the pilgrims. *Pranava Vishramashala*, a temple, and a *Vedi* (platform) are under project here. If the District Board takes a little interest it can make the road from Dharchula to Khela negotiable for ponies, by constructing three iron girder bridges on the way, when Khela will become a centre for Kailas pilgrims, for picking up coolies. From here one road goes to Kailas via Gyanima (see Second Route to Kailas). Khar-odyar or Death-Cave is 9$\frac{1}{2}$m. from here (see p. 97).

2 Three miles east of this village situated on a beautiful spot is the Shree Narayana Ashrama of Shree Narayana Swamiji Maharaj of South India (see p. 99).

and pears can be had either on the outward journey or on the return journey ; big walnut trees (a little down below the place is the village Rung, wherefrom one can get fresh vegetables),

1¾m. descent to Sumariya or Samre, sometimes a shop,

2¾m. very steep ascent through thick forest to Rungling or Sumariya-dhar [9,840], a heap of stones with flags, temple,

3¼m. very steep descent through a thick forest to the stream Sinkhola-gad, (midway there is a spring), cross the two branches of the stream by wooden bridges,

1½m. gentle up, to the village Galla [7,000], walnut trees and oaks,

10. Jipti (11¾) (123¼) [8,000 ?] 1¾m. gentle up, to Jipti, one shop with a neat *dharmashala* attached to it, *dhara*, Kali which is missing from Khela, appears here again flowing several hundred feet down below in a gorge, provisions for Malpa should be taken from here,

1m. descent to a place called Bindakot or Binju-kuti, *dhara*, Byans Patti begins, from here up to the Najang falls it is called Nirpani; from Bindakot up to Garbyang it is the worst part of the whole journey,

2½m. very steep and often steppy descent to Jumli-odyar also called Najang-talla or Lagorphu, hill-stream nearby, Kali also is very near, (crossing a wooden bridge on the Kali to its left bank, the road used to be on Nepal side for about a mile, but now the road is on this side of the river), caves, Bhotia camping place,

½m. (on Nepal side Tampaku-gad or Thing waterfalls, about 50 feet high, falling into the Kali-Ganga below ; 3/8m. very steep and steppy ascent ; 3/8m. very steep and steppy descent ; ½m. plain road, 3/8m. steep ascent.

Najang falls (5¾) (129) ⅛m. steep descent to the beautiful Najang-gad waterfall about 70 feet high, the stream also is coming down precipitously foaming and jumping, forming cascades, cross the wooden bridge on the stream,

¾m. steep ascent to Bola pass[1] [8,000], here Kali is flowing like a reptile, 1,500 feet to 2,000 feet down below through a steep-walled rocky gorge ; and it takes a sharp hair-pin bend,

1 From here, going over the Najang falls there used to be the old Nirpania route direct to Galla-gam without touching Jipti. There used to be scarcity of water on that route, hence the name Nirpania (waterless place). Now it has fallen out of use.

¾m. steep descent to Lung-tiyar, caves, (100 yards below the road is a luke-warm water spring, the water of which is sweet and does not smell of sulphur or any other substance); ½m. steep descent; ½m. Bhotia *padav* of Malpa, cross the Malpa-gad by bridge,

11. Malpa (2½) (131½) (7,200) 200 yards ascent to Malpa, *D.*, mail-runners' hut, no shop, but firewood and wheat-flour may be had from the mail-runner, cold place; from Malpa to Garbyang the road is very dangerous and full of hopeless landslips during rainy season,

2½m. steep ascent with reliefs here and there to Pelsiti, C., caves, a little before this place there are two big fans of waterfalls falling like shower-baths on to the road from a height of over 300 feet; path is very slippery here; 2m. ascent to Lamari [8,000], fields of Budi, no village; 2½m. steep ascent to Kothla, fields of Budi (¼m. before reaching the end of the ascent a *D.*); ¾m. steep descent to Pala-gad or Budi-gad, cross the stream by bridge,

Budi (8¾) (140¼) [8,500] 1m. gentle up to the village Budi, situated a furlong away from the road, S., a big Bhotia village, provisions can be had from the village, fine view of the snow-slopes of Namjung on Nepal side just opposite the village; two crops are grown in this village; from this village upwards all people get down to Dharchula and to other warmer places in winter, only a few people live in the villages to guard them,

2½m. very steep ascent to a very narrow pass [10,500], flags, a little further is a small temple with several flags, there are three houses of Budyals here, where several years back Tibetans used to come in the beginning of winter to exchange their salt for grain,

3/8m. C., on a plateau called Chheto-thanga, extending for about 3 furlongs, one of the most beautiful spots full of flower-beds,

½m. very steep and slippery descent through pines to a small stream; ⅛m. to Chhongphu chhu stream, C; ¾m. gentle ascent to the village-bell, on the way there are beautiful grassy plains bedecked with flowers of various hues and kinds, on plants hardly rising above the ground; these flower-beds are simply charming;

12. **Garbyang**[1] (5) (145¼) [10,320] ¾m. descent very slippery and muddy if rainy, to Garbyang, last Indian village on this route, last P., D.B., S., *D.*, Surmadevi *dharmashala*, Dalip Singh *dharmashala*, biggest Bhotia village of about 200 houses,

¾m. very steep and slippery descent to the bank of the Kali,

½m. confluence of the milky Tinker River and the ovaltine-coloured Kali[2]; cross the wooden bridge of Sita-pul on the Kali to its left bank to Nepal side, here is the Nepali Police Chauki[3]; ½m. up along the Kali,

1¼m. ascent with reliefs, cross the Jhakti-nala; ¼m. steep ascent, from here fields, campings, and huts of Kauva-Talla begin,

1¾m. confluence of the Kali and the Kuti rivers; the confluence is at a distance of 2 or 3 furlongs down below the road. Though the River Kuti is almost twice or thrice as big as Kali, the Kali is taken to be the main river; from here begin the fields, huts, and halting sheds of Kauva-Malla; Kauva is the temporary habitation of the villagers of Gunji during cultivation season; 1¼m. fields of Kauya;

½m. cross the Shangduma bridge on the Kali to its right bank to Indian side; 1¼m. Larela camps; 1¼m. Singdudup-gad; 2m. further cross the bridge to the left bank of the Kali.

13. Kalapani[4] (11) (156¼) [12,000] a few yards further up is a big spring or springs gushing out of huge boulders situated

1 The guide, Patvari, School Master, or Post Master may be consulted for further preparations; coolies should be discharged and ponies or *jhabbus* should be engaged up to Takla-kot; tents and woollen blankets can be got on hire; all provisions available; wheat, barley, *papar* (buck-wheat) are grown here; potatoes, cabbage, mustard, turnip, and a few other vegetables can be had on the return journey; very cold; there are fresh water *dharas* but water is scanty, and the Kali is at a distance of about ¾m. down below. The people of Garbyang are called Garbyals, of Budi Budyals, of Kuti Kutyals, of Chhangru Chhangryals, and so on. A little before reaching Garbyang and for three miles onwards one comes across gigantic, stratified walls of earth and sand, in all probability, the bed of the river once millions of years ago. They would be an interesting study to the geologist.

2 From here one road goes to the village Kuti which is 18½m. from Garbyang. In the neighbourhood of the village are found varieties of marine fossils including pyrited ones. 7m. beyond Kuti there is a place called Jolinkong, where a small mandi is held; 13m. beyond this place is Lampiya pass; midway between Jolinkong and Lampiya pass are Chhota Kailas and Manasarovar, which are worth visiting.

3 ¾m. up the bridge situated on the tableland is the village Chhangru (9,990) of the Bhotias. There is a big cave about ½m. above the village, considered to be the abode of evil spirits, where there are several human skeletons. When there broke out an epidemic of smallpox, the villagers fled away to the cave with all their belongings, where all perished due to the same disease. But several weird stories are woven round the cave. 12 miles from Chhangru up the Tinker river is the village Tinker. The inhabitants of both these villages are Bhotias, of the same stock as of Darma Bhot.

4 The spring is said to be the **Traditional Source of the Kali**, though the main river is coming from the Lipu Lekh pass. The spring is dedicated to Kali, so it is called Kalipani, which is corrupted into Kalapani (blackwater). The stones over which the water of the spring

at the foot of a mountain. The water of the spring is flowing out as a small brook into the foaming river below after a few yards' course; the spring is called Kalapani, and the brook, Kali River; as such Nepal Territory ends here.

¾m. cross the stream of Pankha-gad by a wooden bridge,[1]

½m. confluence of the Gariphu and the Yirkha-gad (Kali); a little further cross the Kali by the bridge to its right bank, a little cultivation, (2 furlongs up this place, situated on the left bank of the Gariphu-gad, are the ruins of two big buildings),

1m. steep ascent to Kirmo-kong, shop, two *dharmashalas*, a *dhara*, *jhabbu-chaukidar* lives here, fine view from here,

1m. Ngyur, camping parapets, *D.*, cross the Ngyur-gad,

1/8m. Talla Tara, 2 *dharmashalas*,

3/8m. ascent to Malla Tara, 2 *D.*,

Nga-vidang (4¼) (160½) ½m. ascent to Nga-vidang, 2 *D.*, *pema* shrub for fuel, Lilingti flowing in a broad valley meets the Kali on its left bank, scarcity of fuel, good pasture for ponies; from here up to Lipu Lekh pass it is a steep ascent,

¾m. ascent to Chil, C., cross stream,

Shangcham (1¾) (162¼) [15,000] 1m. ascent to Shangcham, *D.*, with 2 rooms, damp, very cold,

1¼m. ascent to Chinku, foot of the Lipu Lekh pass,

LIPU LEKH PASS[2] (3¼) (165½) [16,750] 2m. steep ascent to the Lipu Lekh pass, called Chang-labochhe la by the Tibetans, festoons, flags and heaps of stones,

2m. very steep descent into Tibet to Namashen, travellers usually stop here to take their tiffin after crossing the pass,

is flowing are also black, so some think that the spring is called Kalapani (black water). There are camping places on either side of the spring. From here for over a mile are the fields of Garbyals. Pony-men often make a halt at Shangcham which is a very cold place. So, as far as possible, pilgrims should start early from Kalapani and try to cross the Lipu Lekh the same day and reach Taklakot, instead of halting at Shangcham or at Pala. Keep some sour articles in the pocket for use on the way and start from Kalapani at 4 or 5 a.m. in the morning and cross the Lipu Lekh pass before the sun gets hot so that you might not feel much exhaustion while ascending to the pass.

1 This place is called Pankha by Bhotias, but the whole area from Kalapani spring up to this place is called Kalapani, by down country people; here are four or five huts of the farmers, often used by pilgrims for night halt, if vacant. Here is seen the first heap of *mani*-stones.

2 In June one may have to go on snow for a furlong before reaching the pass but very little ice in July. This is the boundary line of India and Tibet. Rest a while on the pass if it is not windy, enjoy the grand view of both the sides of the pass, take a little tiffin and move on. From the pass right up to Pala it is one continuous descent, the first half being very steep. One can have a good view of Mandhata from here.

Mileages given in Tibetan are subject to slight corrections.

76. The Holy Mount Kailas (Southern View) Gombo-phang (Ravan *Parvat*) on the left and Kyangs in the foreground
Photo by Courtesy of Mr. Salim Ali, Bombay [*See pp.* 102 & 126

77. Tarchhen
[*See p.* 106

78. Raising of the *Tarbochhe* on Lord Buddha's Birthday
[*See pp.* 10 & 60

79. *Tarbochhe* and Kailas
[*See pp.* 10 & 60

80. Nyanri Gompa, the first Monastery of Kailas
[*See pp.* 10 & 25

81. Western View of Kailas, Pyramidal Shape
[*See pp.* 13 & 125

82. Kailas Peak from the North-West [*See pp.* 13 & 126

83. The Holy Kailas between the two Sentinels—Chhagnadorje and Chenresig [*See pp.* 13 & 126

84. Dirá-phuk Gompa
[See p. 126

85. The Holy Kailas between Chenresig and Jambyang
[See pp. 13 & 126

86. Khando-Sanglam Glacier
[See p. 127

$1\frac{3}{4}$m. further very steep descent to Komba-chhumi, cross the Lipu Lekh stream to its right bank,

2m. descent to Pala-kong, *D.* with four rooms,

Pala (6) ($171\frac{1}{2}$) [14,000] $\frac{1}{4}$m. further descent to Pala, 2 *D.* with four rooms in each, extensive campings, if one is exhausted he can stop here and go to Taklakot next day early in the morning,

$\frac{1}{4}$m. further on is the confluence of the stream Tisum or Chhumi-guldum coming from the Lipu Lekh and Jungjin chhu coming from Tinker Lipu Lekh [18,300]; cross the Jungjin chhu by bridge, the animals have to wade the stream; this stream swells in the afternoon and sometimes becomes unfordable, in which case one has to stop that day there and cross the river next morning,

$1\frac{1}{4}$m. down along the river; water from this river is diverted into small canals and taken to several villages of Taklakot for cultivation,

$1\frac{3}{4}$m. further on is the village Tashigong with two houses, then through barley and pea fields,

$1\frac{1}{4}$m. to the village Magrum, several houses, one is reminded of the plains with vast fields and canals, there are *panchakkis* or *gharats* (flour mills run by water-power), cross the river by bridge to its left bank and proceed to,

14. **Taklakot**[1] (5) ($176\frac{1}{2}$) (13,100) $\frac{1}{2}$m. Taklakot Mandi.

1/8m. ascent; 3/8m. steep descent to Gukung, village in caves, gompa, Tibetan Government Rest House very near the bridge, cross the bridge on the Karnali or Map chhu to its left bank; here is the mandi of the Nepalis where rice, wheat, and barley are sold and exchanged, Zongpons Trade House,

1m. to the village Chhemo-chhorten, here are two big *chhortens* by the roadside, said to be the memorials of Guru Rimpochhe according to some; and according to some others, they are of the Lieutenants of Zoravar Singh; barley and pea cultivation up to Garu,

1 It is also called Pilithanka, situated on a narrow plateau at the foot of hill 300 feet high, on which stand the famous Simbiling Gompa, and the Zongpan's (Governor's) residence. There are 300 to 500 tents of Byans, Chaudans, and Darma Bhotias in the Mandi: all provisions and other requirements can be had from the mandi; there is scarcity of fuel here. Conveyance arrangements should be made here for further journey to Kailas and back to this place and provisions bought; blankets (*chutka*) can be bought; tents and firearms may be hired and guides engaged. Here is a tent-dharmashala of the Darma Seva Sangha, and a *sadavarta* for *sadhus*, started by Shree Narayana Swamiji Maharaj in 1945. If one wants a quiet place, one can camp by the side of the river or the canal just below the mandi. There are some water-mills nearby. From here the famous Khochar monastery is at a distance of about 12m. which may be visited before going to Kailas or on the return journey.

Toyo (2½) (179) 1m. Toyo, big village, here is the *samadhi* or *chhorten* of the brave General Zoravar Singh (see p. 79),

½m. Garu chhu, cross the river by bridge,

¼m. ascent to the village Garu,

1¼m. mild and steep ascent to Hara la, a big *laptche*, Simbiling Gompa is seen from here; ½m. ascent,

¾m. descent to a beautiful brook, Khirok chhu, called Lee chhu in its lower course,

2m. mild ascent to Shiktha, big *laptche*,

1¾m. plateau,

Ringung (8¼) (187¼) [14,400] ¼m. steep descent to Ringung chhu, cross it to its right bank (the village Ringung is about half a mile down the river, away from the road), *mani*-walls,

1/8m. cross the channel (taken from the Ringung gorge to village Ringung); 1/8m. a branch from Ringung Chhu which falls into Barfu chhu, cross it; 2¼m. gentle ascents and descents to Laje-kep,[1] C., bogs,

15. Baldak[2] (4½) (191¾) (15,000) 2m. Baldak chhu, cross it to its right bank, vast campings,

1½m. mild ascent, 3 *laptches* within 50 yards, if the sky is clear, one can have the first glimpse of the top of the Holy Kailas peak from here,

1¼m. *laptche*, top of Kailas peak seen again from here,

¼m. Sekang, camping parapets in the midst of marshes,

1½m. Gurla chhu, cross it to its left bank,

Gurla-phuk or Gori-Udyar (4½) (196¼) Gurla-phuk is called Gori-udyar by Bhotias, here are several camping places and some caves, said to be the birth-place of Ganesh; from

[1] The village Parbu or Burfu is at a distance of about 1m. from here, with only one house and some barley cultivation. On the left bank of the stream which flows by the side of the house, situated on the edge of a plateau, are the ruined columns of a fort about 22 feet high destroyed by Zoravar Singh in 1841. The brook of Leje-kep flows into the stream, which in turn debouches into Karnali down the village Dungmar. Dungmar is one mile from here and most of the houses are situated in caves.

[2] From here one road goes via Rakshas Tal, touching the Manas at Tseti tso or direct to Barkha without touching the Manas. This route is 2 or 3 miles shorter than the route described above; but by following the route given above, pilgrims would enjoy the march along the west coast of the Manas in its close proximity and at the same time have the opportunity of taking bath in the Lake for three days. So pilgrims should fix up with the pony-men at the beginning of the journey to take this route. If, however, they are doing the round of the Manas also, they may, if they choose, visit Rakshas on the onward journey, for it is also an interesting lake.

The village Kardung is 3 or 4 m. from Bladak; Barkha Tasam lives here in winter. Once a king ruled over this area; there are eight houses here mostly situated in caves and plenty of cultivation. Situated on the top of a hillock is a gompa, said to have been built in about the year 1932 in the present form, which is a branch of Mangshang Gompa. In the *chenkhang* there is the image of Dolma and in the *ducang* there are big images of chhopame, Sankhya Thubha and Chenresig. In the second building there are four big *mani*-cylindoe. Zoravar Singh destroyed the fort here.

here up to the Gurla pass it is a steep ascent on sharp stones,

3½m. steep ascent, big *laptche*; 1/8m. another big *laptche*; 3/8m. descent to Chhang chhu coming from the Mandhata peaks and falling into the Rakshas Tal,

Gurla La[1] (4) (200¼) [16,200] about 200 yards steep ascent to Gurla la' or Gurla pass, big *laptche*, flags, festoons and cairns; ¼m. descent, big *laptche*; ½m. descent to Lang chhu coming from the Mandhata and flowing into the Rakshas Tal, here are some camping parapets; ¾m. descent to stone piles or cairns, footprints of a lama; 2½m. steep descent to the camp Thampara, spring in marshes, C.,

16. **Manasarovar** (9) (209¼) [14,950] 3m. further descent to the **Holy Manasarovar**, just near the Shushup tso, a semicircular lakelet on the north-western corner of the Holy Lake, almost parallel to it; several swans, brahminy ducks, and gulls are found in large numbers here,

Gossul Gompa[2] (4) (213¼) [15,100] 4m. along the western shore of the Lake to Gossul gompa,

1¼m. along the margin of the lake to Gossul-changma, C.; ¾m. further to Tsering-manithang, a *mani*-wall, C; ½m. from here leave the shore of the Lake to the right and proceed towards the left,

¼m. a few yards to the left of the path is Tseti tso[3] and on the right parallel to the shore of the Lake is a narrow

1 From here one can command a grand panoramic view of the surrounding regions. On the back is the long range of snow peaks beginning from Kamet, Lipu Lekh to Nepal; on to the right are the massive giant heads of Mandhata [25,355; 22,650; 22,160] and in the front are the crystal emerald-watered Holy Manas Lake and Rakshas Tal on the right and left respectively and in the background stands aloof in the Kailas range, conspicuously and picturesquely the majestic and silvery Kailas Dome with awe-inspiring solemnity and weird grandeur, facing the proud Mandhata and overlooking the twin lakes bedecked with graceful families of *Rajahansas*. From here one path goes towards N.E. to Thugalho-Gompa or Thokar (9¾m.), the eighth monastery of the Holy Lake situated on its southern shores.

2 About 150 feet above the level of the beach, Gossul Gompa is hanging like a swallow's nest from the rock over the Lake. This is the first monastery of the Lake. One can have a grand view of the Holy Lake from the top of the gompa and can spend hours together in silent contemplation. This is the warmest of all the places on the Manas. But to have a view of the Kailas one has either to go for a furlong over a steep ascent up the gompa or go along the shores of the Lake for over 3 furlongs northwards. Near the gompa and down below, just by the side of the Lake are some caves. Ascending to the top of the mountain on the back of the gompa for nearly 2½m. one of the finest panoramic views can be had of Rakshas Tal with its islands on the west, Mandhata on the south, the entire expanse of the Lake Manas on the east and the Kailas range on the north.

3 Tseti tso is nearly half a mile from the Manas. There are some small islands in it. It is about 1m. long and half a mile broad (see p. 49). The route that branches off from Baldak and comes via Rakshas Tal meets here. The details of the route are as follows:

and shallow crescent shaped lakelet; $1\frac{1}{4}$m. between the two lakes,

$\frac{1}{2}$m. mild ascent to *chhak-chhal-gang* (wherefrom *sashtanga-danda-pranam* is made), *laptche*, *mani*-wall,

$\frac{1}{2}$m. Sera la; $\frac{3}{4}$m. descent, from here up to Serka-khiro are seen, old diggings of gold mines,

$1\frac{1}{4}$m. Serka-khiro red *chhorten* on the left (see p. 49),

1m. mild up,

17. **Ganga Chhu**[1] (near Chiu Gompa) ($8\frac{1}{4}$) ($221\frac{1}{2}$) $\frac{1}{4}$m. descent to thermal springs situated on the left bank of Ganga Chhu, C.; cross it to its right bank, caves,

PARKHA or BARKHA[2] (9) ($230\frac{1}{2}$) [15,050] 9m. on a sandy plain to Parkha or Barkha, *Tasam* or *Tarzam* (Tibetan Transport Agent or Staging Officer) lives here, fine view of the southern aspect of the holy Kailas (see p. 102); cross the Dam chhu to its left bank,

2m. through marshy lands to Gapu-dosa[3],

18. **Tarchhen** or **Darchhen** ($7\frac{1}{2}$) (238) [15,100] $5\frac{1}{2}$m. through marshes crossing several ramifications of the Zhong chhu and Tarchhen chuh to Tarchhen or Darchhen (see p. 103),

Baldak to Gurla chhu $3\frac{3}{4}$m.; cross the Gurla chhu; on plain 1m.; steep and very steep ascent with intervals to Thalla-thong la $5\frac{1}{2}$m.; descent to Rezang chhu $1\frac{1}{4}$m.; to Lanka-donkhang $\frac{1}{2}$m.; (total 12m., first day's march): along the shores of Rakshas Tal 2m.; leaving Rakshas Tal very steep ascent of $1\frac{1}{2}$m.; Tarko la 2m.: descent from Tarko la to Tseti tso 4m. (total $9\frac{1}{2}$m. for the second day). So from Baldak to Tseti tso via Rakshas Tal it is $21\frac{1}{2}$m. and via Manas it is $24\frac{1}{4}$m. i.e., there is a difference of nearly 3m. between the two routes.

1 Here a *donkang* (Tibetan *dharmashala*), some caves and a hot water *kund*, Ganga Chhu is the only outlet of Manasarovar and flows into the Rakshas Tal. There is a boiling hot water spring on a rock situated in the middle of the Ganga Chhu and another hot spring on the right bank. The channel Ganga Chhu is 40 to 80 feet in breadth, 2 to $4\frac{1}{2}$ feet in depth and about 6m. in length in its winding course from Manasarovar to Rakshas Tal. It is nearly 2 furlongs steep ascent to the Chiu or Jiu Gompa, situated on a pyramidal hill, roosting like a bird. There are 5 *dabas* in this gompa and is attached to Dira-phuk Gompa of Kailas. This monastery is situated on the N. W. corner of the Holy Manas and is the second Monastery of the lake. It is better to camp either on the shores of the Manas near Malathak or at the hot springs on the Ganga Chhu than in the gompa.

2 There are two houses here, of which one belongs to the *Tasam* and the other is the Government Rest House. There are some black tents of the shepherds wherefrom milk, curds, cheese, butter, and other dairy products are available. Parkha is the third Tasam on the highroad from Gartok to Lhasa. If one wants to camp here, one should take a big stone from Ganga Chhu for driving tent pegs, since there are no stones in the neighbourhood. When one is not halting here, one need not go to this place but cross the Dam chhu two or three furlongs up this place. On both sides of this river there are *dam* or marshes; so it is called Dam or Dam chhu.

3 If one wants to make a halt before reaching Tarchhen, one should stop here, for there are some Johari merchants; and dairy products are easily available from Tibetan shepherds. From here one can either go direct via Pongdu to the *parikrama*-route, a mile beyond Tarchhen, or via Tarchhen and reach Dira-phuk Gompa in the evening.

KAILAS-PARIKRAMA—32 MILES

Tarchhen or **Darchhen** (0) (0) [15,100] Kailas-*Parikrama* begins, from the surrounding mountains one can have a grand view of the Parkha plain and Mandhata, (see p. 107),

$2\frac{1}{4}$m. with slight ups and downs to *changja-gang*, several *mani*-walls, view of Kailas,

Sershung ($3\frac{3}{4}$) ($3\frac{3}{4}$) $1\frac{1}{2}$m. descent to Sershung, here is a big flag-staff called Tarbochhe, dedicated to Buddha, a big fair is held here every year on *Vaishakha Purnima* (see p. p. 10, 60 and 106) ; a few yards further is Chhorten-kangnyi (see p. 107),

1m. up along the Lha chhu, *mani*-walls and *chhortens* ; in the mountain on the right side there is a cave of Naropen-chhung called Pema-phuk ; wade one branch of the river and cross the main river by bridge,

Nyanri or **Chhuku Gompa**[1] ($1\frac{1}{4}$) (5) $\frac{1}{4}$m. steep ascent over sharp stones to Nyanri or Chhuku Gompa, *mani*-walls, cross the river, back to its left bank after visiting the gompa,

$2\frac{1}{2}$m. further up to Gombophang or Ravan Parvat, a black hood-like peak standing just to the west of Kailas peak ; there are some big and beautiful fans of streams falling from the Nyanri mountain on the right bank of the Lha chhu, one of which is about 700 feet high ; inverted crescent view of Kailas,

2m. Tamdin-donkhang, here is a *shapje* or footprint of Buddha (one mile before reaching this place one can have the western view of Kailas, which has got a peculiar shape of its own something like the rings of Saturn),

1 The gompa is perching like a bird's nest in the mighty fort of Nyanri mountain. This is the first monastery of the Holy Kailas with five *dabas*. The chief image in the *duvang* is of Chhuku Rimpochhe, made of white marble, in all probability taken from India. On either side of this image there are two big elephant tusks which are each 20 inches in circumference at their thicker ends and 54 inches long. There is an image of the Bhutanese Lama, Ngava-Nangyal (who founded this monastery about 300 years back), which has got a white beard and a hat resembling that of Guru Nanak: so some people are under the wrong notion that this is the image of Guru Nanak. Here are the volumes of *Kanjur*. In the *chenkhang* that is on the top of the monastery, there are the images of Kangri-Lhabchen, Mahakali, and Mahakala. Nearby are two more smaller tusks of an elephant. In the *chenkhang* proper and the outer rooms are some armours, helmets, and swords of Zoravar Singh. One can enjoy a fine view of the Kailas Peak from the top of the monastery. Just below the monastery there is a cave called Langchen-phuk. One can continue the journey either on the right bank of the Lha chhu or cross the river again to its left bank and continue on that side which is a bit shorter than the route by the right bank.

½m. further on are the two streams of Belung and Dunglung chhu, falling into the Lha chhu on its right bank, which are to be crossed by those going on the other side of the river; there is a small bridge on the Dunglung chhu[1]; 2¼m. cross the Kangjam chhu, pyramidal view of Kailas,

¼m. cross the main branch of Kangjam chhu[2], C.,

1. **Dira-phuk Gompa**[3] (7¼) (12¼) [16,400], cross the Lha chhu to (ii) its right bank and reach the Dira-phuk Gompa, also called Dithin-phuk, *mani*-walls, *donkhang*,

¼m. descent from the monastery to the bridge on the Lha chhu, cross it to its left bank; from here up to the Dolma la it is a steep and tiring ascent, huge granite boulders border the path,

1 In the upper valley of this stream there are *dong* or wild yaks. Up along this stream one road goes to the source of Indus.

2 Usually big parties camp here, but if it is not a very big one, not exceeding 30 members, they would do well to send a man in advance to the monastery and book the topmost hall or some other room in it. Though one would be put to a little inconvenience due to smoke, the stay in the monastery would save a good deal of time and great trouble in pitching and unpitching the tents, this being the coldest place in the journey. If they could lodge in the monastery they could start early for the Dolma la the next morning.

3 Dira-phuk Gompa is the second monastery of the Holy Kailas with one lama and five *dabas*. Sakya-pendo is the chief deity. Situated in the cave of the image-hall is the image of Geva-gozangba, who is said to have discovered the *parikrama*-route to Kailas. There is a flag-staff in front of the monastery. One version of *Kangri Karchhak* and *Kangri Soldep* are printed in this monastery. Mount Kailas displays itself to the pilgrim in its full, magnificence here and one can have the best view of the Kailas from the top of the monastery. It is like a huge silver dome placed on a pedestal with two guards on either side, Vajrapani and Avalokiteshvara. Facing the Kailas the names of the peaks from west to east are as follows: *Chhagnadorje*, (Vajrapani), the **Holy Kailas Peak** (*Kang Rinpochhe*), *Chenresig* (Avalokiteshvara), *Jambyang* (Manjughosha), *Chhogel-norsang*, and *Shivari*. One can spend days and nights like minutes without being tired, watching the splendour of the Sacred Kailas Peak, sitting in front of one of the small windows or on the top of the monastery. The grandeur and sublimity of the view and the spiritual atmosphere pervading there is simply indescribable. On a moonlit night the view is all the more grand. From here one path goes up the Lha chhu to the source of the Indus which is at a distance of about 34m. via Lhe La. The Indus does not take its source from the foot of Kailas as some wrongly believe and describe.

One should make a halt for a day here and go to the southern foot of Kailas Peak. The route is as follows ¼ m. descent from the gompa to the Lha chhu, cross it to the left bank; ½ m. steep ascent, *chhortens*; ½ m. green ice; ½ m. steep ascent over ice or by the side of Kangjam chhu over huge boulders; *guggul*, herbal incense of Kailas, and varieties of flowers grow here; here is the snout of the Kangjam glacier, black in colour due to the earth in it; it is dome-like in shape; over it there are innumerable icicles like *Shiva-lingas*; Kangjam chhu is gushing out between two sections of the glacier; get up a 100 yards over loose debris by the side of a small stream on the right side, and climb up to the spine of the glacier and proceed upwards for 1 m. on the glacier over moraines; one could pick up stones of various colours that have fallen from the Kailas conglomerate; here is an open ice-field free from pebbles; ¼ m. on this ice, small pebbles regularly shoot down from the wall of Kailas Peak; then a 100 yards steep ascent over very slippery ice and snow. Now you are face to face with the perpendicular wall of the Mount with bottomless crevasses separating the head of the Kangjam glacier from the Kailas-wall. The scenery of the surroundings is so serene, sublime, and grand, that one forgets all about the difficulty one might have to face in reaching the place. It often snows here. From Dira-phuk to this place, it is about two miles in all.

1m. steep ascent to Tangyu, C.,[1]

1m. Ascent to Shivachhal-tuthup, Tibteans offer their hair here and a drop of blood by scratching their gums and lie down there once as if dead, for dying here is considered meritorious,

½m. steep ascent to Dikpa-karnak[2] or sinners' test stone, a few yards further is another small Dikpa-karnak, a little up the road is the ruined Charok-donkhang, C., walled enclosures; shooting up from behind the peak of Jambyang, the Peak of Kailas presents a fine view here,

¼m. plain road but full of boulders, a stream flows through boulders, about a quarter of a mile beyond this place is the big fossil bed referred to on page 47.

DOLMA LA[3] (4) [16¼] [18,600] 1m. very steep and hard ascent to Dolma la,

1 ¼ m. from Kangjam chhu cross the Polung chhu (*po* means incense and *lung* means valley); in this valley Kailas incense grows in large quantities; 1 m. steep ascent to Tangyu; from here Kailas presents a new view between Chenrezig and Jambyang peaks stretching its glacial arm up to Jambyang, just like a huge silver *Siva-linga* placed on a pedestal. Dolma la is 2¾ m. from Tangyu. According to Tibetan traditions those only who have completed 12 rounds of Kailas would be entitled to do the 13th round via Khando-sanglam la, leaving the regular *parikrama* route from here to the left, the details of which are as follows:

⅜ m. steep descent to the Dolma la chhu, cross it to its left bank; (300 to 400 yards down the stream there is a cave situated under a huge boulder. The cave is sheltered from wind by stones piled up into walls. Several years back one famous lama lived here after whose name it is called Lama Kyangun-Kangri-Phukpa); ¼ m. further cross the Khando-sanglam chhu to its left bank; ¾ m. steep ascent over scree and moraines (on the left side there is a beautiful turquoise blue glacial lake at the head of the Khando-sanglam chhu); 1m. further ascent across the Khando-sanglam glacier which is full of crevasses (sometimes deceitful, being covered with fresh snow) to **Khando-sanglam la**. On the right hand side is the peak Phakna-ri and on the left Khando-sanglam peak; the scenery is very grand here; a few yards further is the *lapche* of the pass. (This place is 2 m. from Tangyu and 3¼ m. from Dira-phuk). 1¾ m. almost perpendicular descent on scree to the confluence of Khando-sanglam chhu coming from the left and Shingjong coming from the right; cross the stream here; ¾ m. steep descent through huge boulders to the confluence of Khando-sanglam and Lham-chhu-khir; one comes here again to the *parikrama* high road (this place is 2½ m. from Khando-sanglam la and 5¾ m. from Dira-phuk); no animals can negotiate this path; Khando-sanglam la seems to be lower than the Dolma la and this route is shorter than the main road by about 3 m. The adventurous few who wish to go by this route should take a monk-guide and a rope from Dira-phuk and the journey should be done only when the day is sunny, for it snows very heavily if it is cloudy. The author crossed this pass once on July 11, 1941 with the aid of a guide and a second time on September 13, 1942, all alone. No non-Tibetan has ever crossed this pass before or heard of it.

2 Here is a big boulder under which there is a narrow marmot-hole passage, through which a lean person can crawl out on the belly with difficulty, fully stretched. The entire passage is not more than 12 or 15 feet long, but the roof not being even, one may get stuck up in it, if he is confused while in it, in which case one shall have to be dragged out either by legs to the back or by the hands to the front. One who could pass through it is considered sinless. It may even be impossible for a stout person to do this feat.

3 On the pass there is a big boulder called Domla (*Devi*) block and flags, festoons, streamers, and cairns are set up all around it. Fallen teeth are stuck by the Tibetans into the chinks of the Dolma block, forming rosaries of teeth. Pilgrims smear butter on the boulder, hoist flags, and do the rounds of it. It is alleged that Devi disappeared under this block in the form of 21 wolves; it may be noted that there are 21 forms or *Avataras* of *Devi* according to Tibetan scriptures. From here Gouri-kund is seen down below in all its glory. For about 3 m. from here the path is lined up by heavy granite boulders and crags.

GOURI-KUND ($\frac{1}{4}$) ($16\frac{1}{2}$) [18,400], $\frac{1}{4}$m. very steep descent to the Gouri-kund called Thuki-Zingboo by the Tibetans. This lake is covered with sheets of ice almost all the year round, which is often broken for taking a bath in it. (see p. 11.) (It is a very steep and falling descent from here to Lham-chhukhir and descent up to Zuthul-phuk gompa).

$2\frac{1}{2}$m. very steep descent through stones to Shapje-dak-thok; there is a footprint of Buddha on a big boulder, camps, cave,

$\frac{1}{4}$m. descent to the bank of the Lham-chhukhir chhu,

$1\frac{3}{4}$m. descent through marshy lands down the Lham-chhukhir to the Khando-sanglam chhu, cross it to its right bank, from here one can have a glimpse of the tip of the Kailas peak from eastern side.

$3\frac{1}{2}$m. descent to the confluence of the Lham-chhukhir and the Topchhen chhu, which joins the Lham-chhukhir on its left bank; from this place downwards the river is called Zhong chhu, (those who go to the source of Indus from Dira-phuk via Lhe La return via Topchhen La down along the Topchhen chhu to this place),

2. **Zuthul-phuk Gompa**[1] ($9\frac{1}{4}$) ($25\frac{3}{4}$) $1\frac{1}{4}$m. further down is Zuthul-
(iii) phuk Gompa, several *mani*-walls both on the way to and near the gompa,

1m. cross 3 or 4 streams during the course of a mile[2],

3m. further is *Changja-gang*[3], *mani*-walls; from here the Zhong chhu leaves the gorge and enters the Parkha *maidan* and the route takes a westward turn; this place is also called Zhong-chhu-go, (crossing the Zhong-chhu here to its left bank, one route goes to the Manas *parikrama*),

1 This is the third monastery of Kailas with three *dabas* and it belongs to Tarchhen Labrang. In the cave of the monastery there are the images of the great Tibetan mystic (*siddha*). Milarepa and other deities and two elephant tusks, which are smaller than those in Nyanri gompa. Situated just outside the cave on the right side of the *duvang*, there is the idol of Ngava Nangyal and on the left side a seven foot four-sided stone beam, said to be the stick of Milarepa. Pilgrims test their strength at it by lifting it up. Kailas is not seen from here. Since the cave over which the monastery was later constructed, being the outcome of the miracle of Milarepa, it is called Zuthul-phuk. *Zuthul* means miracle, and *phuk* means a cave.

2 From here one path goes to Gengta Gompa, which is at a distance of 6 m. Since the path is full of ascents and descents, very few non-Tibetans would like to take this route, though the author had been several times by this route which has got a charm of its own. Crossing the Zhong chhu to its left bank here, one route goes for the round of the Manas.

3 From here one can command a beautiful view of the Barkha plain in the front and the Rakshas and Mandhata beyond; and one path goes direct to Chiu Gompa, which is at a distance of 13 m. (Dam chhu $4\frac{1}{2}$ m., Chiu Gompa $8\frac{1}{2}$m. = 13 m.). On the way one shall have to pass over a very boggy land for a distance of half a mile on either side of the Dam chhu. Quarter of a mile before reaching this *changja-gang*, on the mountains that are to the right side of the road, *Zahar-mora* (serpentine) stone is found and also on the left bank of the Zhong chhu.

1m. further Tarchhen is seen,
½m. further cross the Tarchung chhu,
¾m. further are long *mani*-walls,

3. **Tarchhen**[1] (6¼) (32) cross the Tarchhen chhu or Uma chhu to its right bank to Tarchhen. The *parikrama* of the Holy Kailas is completed here. Neither the river Sutlej nor the Indus falls on the circuit to the Holy Kailas as has been wrongly described by many people.

1 Tibetans compare the Holy Kailas with the *sahasrara chakra* (the thousand petalled Psychic centre in the head) and the three rivers—Lha chhu, Zhong chhu, and the Tarchhen chhu—to the *Kengma*, the *Rengma*, and *the Uma*, which are the *Ida*, *Pingala*, and the *Sushumna* respectively of the *yoga shastra*. Tarchhen chhu joins the Zhong chhu; the Kerleb chhu joins the Lha chhu; further on the Zhong chhu debouches into the Lha chhu, which in turn debouches into Rakshas Tal; Dam chhu separately debouches into the Rakshas Tal. So all the rivers of Kailas fall into the Rakshas.

From Tarchhen also there is one path that goes northwards to the **Gengta Gompa (iv)** (2¼m. very steep ascent), situated on a hillock like a big fort. This is the fourth and the biggest monastery of Kailas with one lama and five *dabas*. The chief deity in *duvang* is Chholokeshvari, and in *chenkhang* Khando. In one of the rooms of the monastery, there are preserved, as trophies, two steel armours, a helmet, a sword, and a battle axe of Zoravar Singh. There is a flag-staff outside the monastery and Kailas is not seen from here. The fourth *shapje* of Kailas which used to be midway between Gengta and Zuthul-phuk has been brought here in 1931. From here one can have the view of the whole scene up to the Indian borders. Near the gompa are two or three houses and some *mani*-walls and some *chhortens* of Ladakh-type. A second version of *Kangri Karchhak* and *Kangri Soldep* is printed in Gengta Gompa.

Silung Gompa (v) is within two miles from here (½m. descent; ¾m. ascent; 1m. very steep descent; ½m. crossing the Silung chhu to its right bank is the gompa). This is the fifth and the smallest gompa of Kailas, with two *dabas*. In the *duvang* there are the idols of Dorje-chhang, and Ngojun-duptho and in *chenkhang* that of Apchi. Gengta and Silung are both branches of Dekung Monastery. The southern view of Kailas from here is very picturesque. From here one path goes to Tarbochhe which is 2m. sheer on scree. One lama who is not officially connected with this monastery, has been living here since 1939 and has rebuilt the whole monastery in 1946. From here one road goes to Serdung-chukshum, the details of which are as follows:

Silung Gompa is at a distance of 2½m. ascent from Tarchhen along the Tarchhen chhu; 1¼ m. steep ascent through stones, on the left hand side there are some caves in the horizontal strata of conglomerate; ¾m. steep ascent on stones, *mandal*, *changja-gang* (down below the mountain is the confluence of Serdung-chukshum chhu and Kailas-east chhu; situated at the confluence of these two rivers and encircled by them is the mountain called Neten-yelak-jung which has got the appearance of a bull seated in front of the Kailas-temple); ½m. descent on moraines, here is the footprint of a horse called Ling-singjen; ½m. in the stony bed of the Serdung-chhuksum chhu; 1 m. steep ascent on huge mounds of moraines; 1 m. across the lower base of the heap of ice lodged down from the top of Kailas; ½m. very steep ascent into the belt of the Kailas peak to **Serdang-chuksum**.

So, Tarchhen is about 7 m. from Serdung-chuksum, ½ m. along the belt of the Kailas peak to CHAROK-PHURDOD LA; 1m. descent sheer on scree; on the left hand side situated at the eastern base of the Kailas peak is a magnificent dome-like glacier. As a matter of fact each of the four sides of Kailas has got a peculiar beauty of its own and it would be very difficult for one to say which side is more beautiful. To whichever side one goes, one feels that that side is the most beautiful. 2 m. steep descent to the river side; ¾m. descent, cross the river to its left bank; ½m. steep ascent over hopeless debris to **Tso Kapala**. Tso Kapala, called Kapali, Kavala, or Kavali are two twin lakelets called **Rukta** and **Durchi**; (see p. 12.); 1½m. very steep descent over debris to the Silung chhu; cross it to its right bank 2¼m. further descent to Silung Gompa: 2½ m. descent to Tarchhen. In this way Tarchhen to Serdung-chhuksum it is 7 m.; and Serdung-chhuksum to Tso Kapali 4½ m.; Silung is 3¼ m. and Tarchhen is 2½ m.; total 17¼ m. from Tarchhen to Serdung-chhuksum and back via Tso Kapala. On the way to Serdung-chhuksum and to Tso Kapali large quantities of herbal incense of Kailas can be picked up. The best way of doing this journey is to go to the Silung Monastery in the night, start early next morning for Serdung-chhuksum and come back via Tso Kapala to Silung or Tarchhen by evening.

TABLE III

MANASAROVAR-PARIKRAMA—64 MILES

(Visiting all the eight Monasteries of the Lake)

Gossul Gompa[1] (0) (0) First monastery of the Holy Manasarovar, (i) 3 *dabas*, (see p. 123),

$1\frac{1}{4}$m. along the shore to Gossul-changma, C; $\frac{3}{4}$m. Tsering *mani*-thang, C., *mani*-wall; $1\frac{1}{2}$m. beginning of Tseti lagoon;

$1\frac{1}{4}$m. along the shore on the thirty-foot broad shingle bank between the Lake and the lagoon to Red Rock Spur (from here one path goes to Sera *chagaja-gang*),

$1\frac{1}{4}$m. Serka-khitong, *mani*-wall, C., (from here up to Rakshas Tal there are gold mines, which were worked for some time in the year 1900),

$1\frac{1}{4}$m. further along the shore to Malläthak Volcanic rock projection into the Lake, which is almost perpendicular here,[2]

$\frac{1}{4}$m. leaving the shore very steep ascent, (from here one path goes to due north direct to Ganga Chhu, crossing which to Chiu Gompa),

1m. descent to the hot springs on Ganga Chhu (midway one can see the Serka-khiro *chhorten* on the left), (see p. 49), cross the Ganga Chhu to its right bank,

Chiu or **Jiu Gompa**[3] ($8\frac{1}{2}$) ($8\frac{1}{2}$) $\frac{1}{4}$m. steep ascent to Chiu Gompa, (ii) second monastery of the Lake, 5 *dabas*, (see p. 124),

1 In the *chenkhang* of the gompa there is the idol of Gombo-setup and in *duvang* there are the idols of Thuji-chhimbo, of Chanresig with 11 heads and 1,000 hands, of Kyangun-jimba-Nurbu-Kangri-lama-shakbar, the founder of the gompa, and some other images. There used to be the 108 volumes of *Kanjur* but were taken away to Thogolho Gompa in the autumn of 1946. There is a big cave down below the monastery, just on the shore of the Lake in which Deepankar Shreejnan stayed for a week.

2 Beyond this point one cannot proceed along the shore of the Lake, for, the rock is very steep and the water deep, but when the Lake is frozen in winter, one can walk over it. After going for about 200 yards on ice, one can proceed along the shores. One or two furlongs further situated in the wall of a steep rock is the cave called Ngava-ngopo-duphuk, named after a great lama who lived there several years back. Sometimes, some monks live here in winter for *chham*. Two furlongs beyond this place, there are some *mani*-walls and walled enclosures situated at the foot of the Santokpari hill, where the shepherds of Chiu Gompa camp in winter and spring. There are some hot springs situated in the bed of the Lake about 50 yards from the shore. Pilgrims usually pick up some pebbles of their liking from the west coast, since they pass by this side. As a matter of fact, pebbles can be picked up from any shore of the Lake.

3 The chief image in the *chenkhang* is of Padmasambhava, situated in a cave. Here is the first ling or *chhorten* of the Manas. This is under Dira-phuk Monastery of Kailas which is itself a branch of Dadingbochhe Gompa, 30 m. north of Lhasa. This monastery is like a bird sitting on the top of a hill; *chiu* means a bird; hence the name Chiu Gompa. From here one can have a grand view of the Rakshas, Manas, Kailas, and Mandhata. On the back of the monastery there is a big pen-yard.

$\frac{1}{2}$m. descent to the north-west corner of the Lake,
$\frac{3}{4}$m. steep ascent to Semo-phuk la, *laptche*, grand view of Kailas, Manas, and Mandhata; 2m. mild descent,

Cherkip Gompa[1] (iii) ($4\frac{1}{2}$) ($12\frac{1}{2}$) $\frac{3}{4}$m. steep descent to Cherkip Gompa, third monastery of the Lake, 1 *daba*,
1m. along the shore of the Lake to Tasaulung, *mani*-wall at the mouth of the valley; leaving the Lake to the right 1m. ascent,

Langpona Gompa[2] (iv) ($4\frac{1}{2}$) (17) $2\frac{1}{2}$m. descent to Langpona Gompa, fourth monastery of the Lake with 1 lama and 5 *dabas*; $\frac{1}{8}$ mile to the Gyuma chhu, cross the three-foot deep river to its left bank and proceed across the vast *maidan*; hundreds of wild horses called *kiyangs* roam in herds,
$4\frac{5}{8}$m. cross the Lungnak chhu; $1\frac{1}{4}$m. further cross another stream,

Ponri Gompa[3] (v) (8) (25) 2m. mild and steep ascent to Ponri Gompa, fifth monastery of the Lake with 1 lama and 5 *dabas*,
$1\frac{3}{4}$m. steep descent to Kojin-chungo camps, *le*,
$2\frac{1}{4}$m. mild descent on the *maidan* to Palchen chhu, 2-3 feet deep, cross to its left bank,
$1\frac{1}{2}$m. to Palchung chhu, big *laptche*, *mani*-stones, cross the three branches of the river to its left bank which are

1 This monastery is situated just within a few yards from the shore of the Lake at the mouth of a dry stream. There is only one image-hall in which there is the image of Guru Rinpochhe. This is the smallest of the Lake-monasteries and belongs to Tarchhen. Kailas is seen from here. Not far from the gompa, situated in the walls of the mountain on the shore of the Lake, there are several caves, where some monks live in winter to spend their time in meditation and solitude. The caves are facing south and so they get sunshine the whole day and are comparatively warmer. Very near the gompa are some camping parapets, where some shepherds live in winter.

2 This gompa is situated on the right bank of the Gyuma chhu and is $1\frac{1}{2}$m. away from the Lake. Kailas is seen from the flag-staff that is outside the gompa. This belongs to Hemmis Gompa of Ladakh. In the *chenkhang* there are the images of Lhabsen, Lhamo, and others; and in the *duvang* that of Sakya-muni. There is a flag-staff in the courtyard of the gompa. About fifty yards to the south of the gompa there is a projection of the hill resembling the trunk of an elephant, on which a small hut is constructed called Langpona. There are vast pasture lands all round, as at Barkha; so shepherds from Hor and Purang come here in winter to graze their yaks, sheep, and goats.

3 This gompa is situated in a high valley at the foot of the meagerly snow-capped peak of Ponri which is 19,554 feet high. The chief deity in *chenkhang* is Lhabsen, and Gombochamba in *duvang*. Here is the second *ling* of the Lake. This monastery is a branch of the Sera University. The monastery itself is about 1,000 feet above the level of the Manas and commands a grand view of the whole of the Mandhata Range reflecting on the Holy Manas and of the lakes Kurkyal-chhungo, Sham tso, and Ding tso situated between the Manas and Ponri. Kurkyal-chhungo is described in the Tibetan scriptures as the head of Manas where *devatas* (angels) take their bath and that the *parikrama* of the Manas is not complete without doing the round of this lake.

2-3 feet deep[1], in almost all the beds of the streams the one-foot *taruva* bush grows in abundance,

¼m. Nga-dungje, camping parapets, *mani*-wall, shepherd camps in winter,

1½m. Pegur, C., spring, *mani*-wall ;

1m. Samo tsangpo, *mani*-walls, cross the two-foot deep river to its left bank, *mani*-wall,

1m. to the shore of the Lake,

1m. along the shore of the Lake to Havaseni-madang (*mani-thang*), *mani*-wall, second *chhak-chhal-gang* of the Manas;

½m. leave the Lake to the right and get up the valley, *lapt-che* ;

½m. on the plateau,

Seralung Gompa[2] (11¾) (36¾) ½m. descent to Seralung Gompa,
(vi) sixth monastery of the Lake, 1 *tulku* lama and 19 *dabas*,

¼m. descent down the Seralung valley to the shore of the holy Lake, a ruined *dharmashala*, called Sera-donkhang[3] C., *mani*-wall,

1m. along the shore of the Lake to Riksum-gombo—three mounds of Chhagnadorje, Chenresig, and Jambyang; one path coming from Seralung meets here which is 1½m. long, half of which is a very steep descent over loose sand,

2m. along the shore of the Lake, to the dry bed of Ngomo-

1 The direct route coming from Tarchhen meets here ; the stages are as follows : Tarchhen to Zhong chhu 3m. ; cross the three-foot deep river to its left bank ; Avang chhu 3m. ; Philung-kongma chhu 2m. ; Philung-pharma chhu ¾m. : Philung-yongma chhu 2¾m. ; Gyuma chhu 3m. : cross two or three ramifications 2½ feet deep : Kyo ½m. ; *le, mani*-wall ; Kuglung chhu 2½m. ; (Total 17¼m. to be done on the first day) ; Lungnak chhu 3¾m. ; beginning of Kurkyal-chhungo 2½m. (Kurkyal chhungo itself is about 2¾m. long) ; Palchen chhu 2½m. ; Palchung chhu 1½m. ; Seralung Gompa 6¼m. (total 16 m. to be done on the second day). Those pilgrims who do the combined *parikrama* of Kailas and Manasarovar, usually leave Zuthul-phuk Gompa late in the morning and halt at Kyo for the night, since it is a good camping place with plenty of grass for their animals. The next day they go direct to Sera-donkhang for camping.

2 Just before reaching the gompa there is a line of beautiful *mani*-walls and *chhortens*. The gompa is situated on the right edge of the valley and a small brook flows nearby and there is a fresh water spring for drinking water. In the *chenkhang* there is the image of Apchi, in *duvang*, of Loben Rinpochhe (Padmasambhava), Sakya Thubha, and others. The third *ling* of Manas is here. There are three or four houses, a *donkhang* and five black tents. This monastery and Gengta and Silung Gompas of Kailas, belong to the Dekung Monastery. Kailas is not seen from the roof of the monastery itself but if one comes out of the monastery to the middle of the valley, a few yards in front of it, one can command one of the grandest and most beautiful views of the Holy Lake, the setting sun, and the Kailas Peak. The Lake is 1½m. from here.

3 This place is about a mile from Havaseni-madang, where one leaves the Lake of Seralung Gompa. Beginning from Havaseni-madang for about 3m. along the shores of the Holy Lake, thin layers of a sort of violet-red sand called *chemanenga* (see pp. 50 and under heading Prasads) is found.

shang chhu, on the left bank of which is Ketar-donkhang[1],

$\frac{3}{4}$m. to the winding Dungak-chemdong chhu,

$4\frac{1}{4}$m. leaving the Lake about half a mile to the right, over ups and downs of sandy mounds to Tag tsangpo[2], cross it to its left bank,

2m. ascent and descent to Nimapendi chhu[3], cross the $1\frac{1}{2}$ feet deep river to its left bank,

$\frac{1}{2}$m. across the Nimapendi valley,

2m. along the shores of the Lake to a small brook called Riljung chhu, cross it to its left bank, *mani*-walls, *chhortens*, third *changja-gang* of the Lake,

Yerngo Gompa[4] ($14\frac{3}{4}$) ($51\frac{1}{2}$) 1m. Yerngo Gompa, seventh mona-
(vii) stery, of the Lake, with 1 lama and 5 *dabas*; cross the Riljen-chhu to its left bank,

3. **Thugolho Gompa**[5] or **Thokar Mandi** ($2\frac{1}{4}$) ($53\frac{3}{4}$) $2\frac{1}{4}$m.
(viii) almost along the coast to Thugolho Gompa, eighth and

1 About 120 years back the founder of the Gossul Gompa had constructed Ketar-donkhang, Momodungu-donkhangLanka-donkhang, Chang-donkhang, Sera-donkhong, and Baldak-donkhang. As they turned out to be shelters for robbers, all except ketar have been pulled down by the Tibetan Government; but this was completely destroyed by the Kazhakis in 1941. Hundreds of Tibetan pilgrims used to take shelter here while during the *parikrama* of the Holy Lake; so the author had it rebuilt in 1947.

2 This is fordable about half a mile from the Lake. During the rainy season the water in the river rises to five feet and becomes unfordable. Three or 4m. from Manasarovar there are hot springs on both sides of the river (see p. 47). Large quantities of *jimbu* grows in the surroundings. During rainy season *Khampas* come and camp here) for a fortnight to collect it (see p. 45). Two or 3m. beyond this place a mandi is held on the left bank of the river at a place called Puraray in the first fortnight of September. The mandi lasts for a week when merchants from Limi (north-western corner of Nepal) bring rice, barley, wheat flour, and wooden articles to be bartered with Tibetan salt, yaks and wool brought by the *Dokpas*. The mandi is held on alternate years at Jakpolung on Nepal borders. Some Bhotia merchants also go to this mandi. One road goes to the source of the Brahmaputra up this river via Tag la, which is 63m. from Manas. Some have erroneously written and several still believe that the Brahmaputra takes its rise from the Manas on its eastern shore: but it is far from truth. The source of the Tag tsangpo which is in the Kanglung-Kangri glaciers, is considered the genetic source of the Sutlej, inasmuch as this is the biggest of the rivers that fall into the Holy Lake and the Holy Lake has no other outlet but the Ganga Chhu, which flows into the Rakshas Tal, from which in turn the Sutlej or the Langchen Khambab flows out.

3 The valley is very broad, deep and grand. There is a big shepherd camp called Nonokur of about 25 black tents, a mile off the shore of the Lake. The tents are spread into nine groups, situated on either side of the river, extending over 1m. In summer these camps move to the upper part of the valley called Taling. The drug *thuma* is grown in abundance here and the surrounding regions (see p. 45).

4 There is only one image-hall in this monastery and the principal deity is Guru Rinpochhe. There are two or three houses adjacent to the gompa. This is a branch of the Sakya Gompa. The gompa is situated very near the Lake; and the river Riljen flows nearby. There are innumerable smooth stones in the upper course of this river, a sort of dirty dark-red in colour; and they are used for inscribing and embossing *mani-mantras* on them. Midway between this place and Thugolho there are several *mani*-walls and *mani*-piles.

5 *Thu* means bath, *go* means head, and *lho* means south. Tibetans take their bath here or at least wash their heads. Even the sheep and yaks are sprinkled with the holy water of the Lake. This gompa is situated within a few yards from the shores of the Lake and is facing east. This is the most imporant of all the lake-monasteries. There is the image

the last monastery of the Holy Lake with 1 lama and 7 *dabas*; from here up to Gossul the path goes along the shores of the Lake,

½m. Anura chhu, swan-colony,

1¼m. through marshes to Namreldi chhu[1]; cross the 1½ feet deep river to its left bank,

¼m. Thandova chhu, a tributary of the above.

1¼m. Selung-hurdung chhu, cross the 2 feet deep river to its left bank; this river often wanders and changes its course and sometimes joins the Namreldi chhu in its lower course,

1m. Momodungu[2], foundations of a ruined *donkhang*,

¼m. Shushup tso or Yushup tso,

2m. over shingle bank to the other extremity of Shushup tso[3], C.,

1m. Takshur, *mani*-wall, a little up the road are the walled enclosures of shepherds who camp here in winter,

of Kangri-Lhabsen in *chenkhang* and Dorjechhang in *duvang*. Here is the fourth *ling* of the Lake. The 108 volumes of *Kanjur*, the image of Thuji Chhimbo (?) studded with precious stones, and some other idols, and some valuable banners were brought here from Gossul Gompa in the autumn of 1946 for safe custody and better use. Through a window in the northern side of the gompa one can enjoy a fine view of Kailas over the Holy Lake. There are two flag-staffs, one inside the courtyard and the other just outside the gompa. Thugolho and Gossul Gompa are the branches of Simbiling Monastery of Taklakot, from where monks are deputed here for a period of three years.

The author had sojourned here for his *sadhana* for a twelve-month in 1936-37 and a sixteen-month in 1943-44 and spends the rainy season every year here. *Bhajans* and *Havans* are conducted here on the occasion of *Janmashtami* and *Shravani* every year since 1936. At his suggestion Sri Kanakadandi Narayana Sastri, Gopal Krishna Sastri, and Shankara Sastri of Yenugumahal, Godavari District (Andhra) have got a beautiful *Yajna Vedi* constructed here in memory of their father Shree Visvapati Sastri. A two-storeyed *Manasa Vishramashala* is under construction.

There are eight houses and a small *donkhang* near the monastery, but the villagers mostly live in shepherd camps and come here occasionally. A mandi is held here for about a month in July-August where about 15 Bhotia merchants of Chaudans and Byans gather. This is a big wool-shearing centre and is popularly known as Thokar Mandi by Indians; but it has no connection whatsoever with the word *Thakur*. On the south of the gompa there are two peaks over 17,000 feet high in the Mandhata Range. The western peak is called Thubba-ri and is at a distance of about 5½m. from here. From the top of this peak one can command one of the grandest panoramic views of the whole of Manas, Rakshas with its islands, Kailas, and the whole stretch from Tirthapuri to Thokchen. One can also have a peep into the Namreldi gorge on the south.

From Thugolho one road goes to Gurla la, the details of which are as follows: Thugolho to Namreldi chhu 2m.; Selung-hurdung chhu 1¼m. (from here upto Gurla la it is a gentle ascent); Gogta 2½m., C.; C., *le*, 3½m.: Gurla la 1½m.; total 9¾m.

1 In the upper parts of the valley of this river there are varieties of flower-beds, some caves, and two beautiful emerald-green lakes almost at the head of the valley. Going a little further up, one path goes to Purang, but it is a very difficult journey.

2 There are seven cairns set up in a row, each cairn containing stones like the *bhelis* of *gur*, brick-tea, *thhu* etc. It is believed by the Tibetans that seven maidens from Bharatavarsha brought and placed them here. Here is the fourth *changja-gang* of the Manas.

3 *Shushup* means bow and *tso* means lake. This lakelet Shushup tso is bow-like in shape and runs almost parallel to the Manas, a shingle bank of about 60 feet broad separating the both. The lake is about 400-500 yards broad and is the breeding place of *ngangba*, *ngaru*, and *chakarma*. At the western end of the lake there is another small lakelet. Beginning from the middle of Shushup tso up to ½m. beyond Gossul Gompa, Kailas is not visible from the pilgrim route.

$2\frac{1}{4}$m. Gossul-lhoma, a little above the road is a *chhorten* (a little higher up this place is the camping place of shepherds), one path goes to Gossul Gompa via this *chhorten*; one may either go along the shore or via this *chhorten*,

4. **Gossul Gompa** ($10\frac{1}{2}$) (64) $\frac{3}{4}$m. further along the shores and then very steep ascent of about 100 yards to the gompa. The *parikrama* of the Holy Manasarovar[1] is completed here.

TABLE IV

TAKLAKOT TO KHOCHARNATH—12 MILES

Taklakot (0) (0) (see pp. 100, 121); $\frac{1}{8}$m. ascent to the new *chhorten*;

Gukung ($\frac{1}{2}$) ($\frac{1}{2}$) $\frac{3}{8}$m. steep descent, cave-dwellings, gompa, cross the bridge on the Map chhu or Karnali to its left bank,

Dangechhen chhu ($\frac{1}{4}$) ($\frac{3}{4}$) cross the river by bridge, and the ponies shall have to wade the river, the village Dangechhen is about a mile up the bridge, from here up to Gejin there are villages and cultivation on both sides of the road, long *mani*-walls and *chhortens*,

Kirong ($1\frac{1}{4}$) (2) just on the left side of the road is the *dama*[2],

Gejin chhu (1) (3) cross the river to its left bank,

Gejin[3] ($\frac{1}{4}$) ($3\frac{1}{4}$) the village is situated on both sides of the road,

Dup-chhu (1) ($4\frac{1}{4}$) on the left side of the road there is a small spring

1 Manasarovar is 54 miles in actual circumference and is much broader in the north than in the south and it has regular coasts; and the Rakshas is 77m. in circumference and has most irregular coasts. The former is 200 sq. miles in area and the latter 140 sq. miles. During the rainy season one cannot go along the coast of Manas between Mallathak and Cherkip and Tasalung to Samo tsangpo; but when the Lake is frozen in winter one can go throughout along the shores. (see First Wave).

2 *Dama* or *trama* is a sort of gompa for temporary stay of the monks during the harvest season. The monks of Simbiling Gompa belonging to the Kirang group of villages come and stay here for a fortnight to do *pujas* for a good crop and for five or six weeks in the harvest season to collect the annual donations of grains from the villagers. Lama Nov-Kushok has got this constructed. It is kept very neat and clean and the deities in the image-hall are those of Chamba, Jambyang, Lobsangdava, and Dolma.

3 Very near the village 100 yards up the road are the footprints of Atisha or Shreejnana; Just opposite this place on the left bank of the river Karnali, situated on the top of a mountain, is the gompa of Siddi-kar, a branch of Simbiling. From the top of the monastery one can have the beautiful view of the Karnali valley from Simbiling to Khochar. There used to be a big fort here, which was destroyed by the Gurkhas in 1854; six feet thick and 25 feet high ruined columns are still seen. There are some villages nearby with plenty of cultivation. Those who want to visit this gompa shall have to do so from Taklakot direct along the right bank of Karnali, for it is dangerous to cross the river during pilgrim season.

of this name, said to have been dug by Deepankar Shreejnan, from here no fields up to Kangje,

Kangje chhu (3¾) (8) cross the river to its left bank[1]; 1m. steep ascent, *laptche*, from here up to Khochar it appears to be volcanic area once; 2m. descent, ruined *chhortens*, *mani*-walls, *laptche*, cairns; Khochar is first seen from here,

Lalung chhu (3¼) (11¼) ¼m. from here fields begin again, cross the river to its left bank,

1. **Khocharnath** (¾) (12) Tibetans call it simply Khochar, G., *mani*-walls (see pp. 64, 101).

TABLE V

TAKLAKOT TO KAILAS (TARCHHEN)

via GYANIMA MANDI, TIRTHAPURI, AND DULCHU—III MILES

Taklakot (0) (0) (see pp. 101, 121),

3m. Toyo, village, plenty of cultivation,

¼m. cross the Garu chhu to its right bank by bridge, Delaling village, *mani*-walls, two big *chhortens* above the village,

2m. cross the Lee chhu to its right bank, Lee or Toyoling, 7 houses of the villagers of Toyo, cultivation,

1¼m. Chhurkuti, extinct craters (on the other bank of the Karnali there is a luke-warm water spring),

1½m. Salung camp, C., (the village Salung is on the right bank of the Karnali with four houses and cultivation, a little further up is the village Doh with plenty of cultivation),

1½m. Ronam, two furlongs up the road is the village of Ronam, with three houses, cultivation,

1m. Ringung chhu, cross the river to its right bank, the village Ringung is about a mile up this place,

Siddi-khar is 5m. from Taklakot and the village Lukpu is 9m. from there, and Khitur-phuk is 9m. beyond that place. There is a cave here about which it is said that a dog once entered it and disappeared (*khi*-dog, and *tur*-fled away or disappeared). It is believed that lepers are cured of their disease by visiting this cave. From here one path goes to Khocharnath which is at a distance of 10m.

1 On other side of the river there are *pan-chakis* or water-power driven mills for grinding barley and pea. There is big grove of *changma* trees in the bed of the river a little up this place. On the left bank of the river the village of Kangje is situated on both sides of the road with plenty of cultivation. There is a monastery in the village that is on the left side of the road and it is a branch of Chang-sug-ling Monastery.

87. Dolma La (18,600 feet)
[See p. 12

88. Gouri-kund. Frozen almost all the year round
[See pp. 11 & 128

89. Sounding the Lake Gouri-kund
[See pp. 11 & 128

90. Mount Kailas from Silung Gomp and the Conglomerate Neten-yalak jung
[*See pp.* 13 & 129

91. Mount Kailas from its southern foot
[*See p.* 11

92. A Glacier at the Eastern foot of Mount Kailas
[*See pp.* 11 & 129

93. Kailas-Manasarovar Region from a Tibetan Painting, *drawn by Lama Nav-Kushok*
(*See pp.* 10, 14, 123

1. Holy Mount Kailas
2. Tijung
3. Tsering-Chenga
4. Nyanri Peak
5. Ponri Peak
6. Gurla Mandhata
7. Thuki-Zingboo
8. Tso Kapala
9. Kurkyal-Chhungo
10. Holy Lake Manasarovar
11. Rakshas Tal or Ravan Hrad
12. Lachato
13. Topserma
14. Lha Chhu
15. Tarchhen Chhu
16. Zhong Chhu
17. Ganga Chhu
18. Samo Tsangpo
19. Tag Tsangpo
20. Nimapendi
21. Tarehhen
22. Parkha
23. Nyanri Gompa
24. Zuthul-phuk Gompa
25. Gengta Gompa
26. Silung Gompa
27. Gossul Gompa
28. Chiu Gompa
29. Cherkip Gompa
30. Langpona Gompa
31. Ponri Gompa
32. Seralung Gompa
33. Yerngo Gompa
34. Thugolho Gompa (Thokar
35. Tsepgye Gompa
36. Tarchhen Chhak-chhal-gang
37. Tarbohchhe (flag-staff)
38. Chhorten Kangnyi
39. Shapji (footprint)
40. Hanumanjoo
41. Serdung-Chuksum
42. Dolma La
43. Shapje-dakthok
44. Tarko La or Sera La, Chak-chhal-gang

94. Gossul Gompa, the First Monastery of Manasarovar
[*See pp.* 123 & 130

95. Sunrise on the Celestial Lake
[*See p.* 123

96. Cygnets in Captivity
[*See p.* 23

$\frac{1}{4}$m. Map chhu or Karnali, cross the 3-4 feet deep Karnali to its right bank,

$1\frac{1}{4}$m. Harkong chhu, on the right side of the road *le*, a few plots of cultivation, (a little below this is the confluence of Harkong chhu and the Karnali, on the other side of the Harkong chhu are some caves or *Kem*),

1. Harkong ($14\frac{1}{4}$) ($14\frac{1}{4}$) $2\frac{1}{4}$m. up the Harkong valley, 1 house, black tents, a little cultivation, caves, on the top of the mountain on the right are the ruined columns of a fort destroyed by Zoravar,

$6\frac{3}{4}$m. [17,000 ?] Ur la, the last $\frac{3}{4}$m. steep ascent, *laptche*, Mandhata is seen from here,

1m. very steep descent to Tarachen, C.,

Mapcha-Chungo[1] ($8\frac{3}{4}$) (23) [14,300] 1m. **Traditional Source of the Karnali,**

$1\frac{3}{4}$m. Rapka chhu, C., cross it to its left bank,

$\frac{1}{4}$m. Map chhu, cross the 3-4 feet deep and rapid torrent of Karnali to its left bank, C.,

1m. ascent, *laptche*,

2. Aulang ($14\frac{1}{2}$) ($28\frac{3}{4}$) $2\frac{3}{4}$m. descent to Anlang or Amlang, *le*, much infested by robbers,

$1\frac{1}{2}$m. Shing-laptche la, last one mile steep ascent, *laptche*,

1m. very steep descent to a stream, cross to its right bank, C.,

4m. Phangma-digir, *laptche*, the road takes a sharp turn towards the left.

2m. Chhuju or Chhuja, several black tents, *le*,

$2\frac{3}{4}$m. Chhuju la, last. two miles steep ascent, *laptche*,

Chhakra Mandi[2] (15) (44) 4m. the first two miles very steep descent,

1 On the right side of the road situated on the edge of the right bank of Map chhu there is a big *mani*-wall with several *mani*-slabs and streamers. Getting down a few yards towards the river is the big spring of Mapcha-Chungo (peacock-head) gushing out from the perpendicular wall of the steep bank of the river. There are some *mani*-stones and streamers near the spring. The water gushing out of the spring flows down into the Karnali below over a beautiful green velvet mossy dome-like mound. The moss over which the spring flows down has some resemblance to the colour of the neck of the peacock, hence the name Mapcha-Chungo. The glacial sources of the Karnali is in the Lampiya pass which is at a distance of two short days' march from here.

At a distance of about 4m. from here is the famous Mangshang Gompa situated on a mountain on the left but it is not seen from the road. It belongs to the Red Cap Section of monks. It was constructed about the year 1919 and a six-year old *tulku* lama has been installed on the *gaddi* in August 1940. This is the second abbot to sit on the *gaddi* of the gompa.

2 This is called Chhakra or Gyanima-Chhakra. This is a big mandi chiefly of the Darma Bhotias, but some Johari merchants also come here after the mandi of Gyanima-Kharko is wound up. The mandi is held in August and the first half of September. There is a small fresh water spring near the mandi and a lake all around which there are white deposits of soda. A stream from this lake flows into the Gyanima lake. Chhakra is under the jurisdiction of Parkha Tasam. From the top of the hill at the foot of which the mandi is held, one can enjoy the beautiful view of the Kailas Peak.

3. **Gyanima Mandi**[1] (5) (49) [15,000] 5m. on bogland to Gyanima, also called Kharko,

$4\frac{1}{2}$m. Gyanima-rap on marshy ground, cross the 3-4 feet deep Gyanima chhu to its right bank, from here the source of the Darma-yankti is at a distance of two days' journey ;

$3\frac{1}{4}$m. low pass, last $\frac{3}{4}$m. steep ascent,

5m. Chhurulba la, first $\frac{1}{2}$m. steep descent and the last $2\frac{1}{4}$m. very steep ascent,

4. **Shithum** ($15\frac{3}{4}$) ($64\frac{3}{4}$) 3m. to Shithum, first $\frac{1}{2}$m. steep descent and the rest descent, C., four valleys meet here, a narrow place, a small brook,

3m. ascent up to Tara la, *laptche*,

5m. continuous and very steep descent to the dry bed of a stream,

3m. down the bed of a stream to the Tirthapuri tsangpo or Sutlej,

$\frac{1}{4}$m. down the Sutlej, cross the river to its right bank,

5. **Tirthapuri Gompa** ($11\frac{1}{4}$) (76) [14,600] called Tretapuri in Tibetan, (see p. 103),

$5\frac{1}{4}$m. Trokpo-nup chhu, cross 2-3 feet deep swift river to its left bank, *le* on either side,

$\frac{3}{4}$m. Trokpo-shar chhu, cross the 3 feet deep ferocious river to its left bank,

2m. Sutlej, cross the 2-3 feet deep Sutlej to its left bank, (river Goyak flows into the Sutlej on its right bank opposite this place),

4m. Chukta, (this river also flows into the Sutlej on its right bank), from here the river Sutlej becomes a mere brook like a small channel used for watering fields ;

1m. further cross the Sutlej to its right bank.

6. **Dulchu Gompa** (16) (90) [14,820] 1m. further is the Dulchu Gompa situated on the right bank of the Sutlej. At a distance of 250 yards from the gompa is the **Traditional Source of the Sutlej** (see p. 103, 105, and Table VI),

[1] Gyanima is the biggest mandi in western Tibet mostly of Johar Bhotias held from the middle of July to the end of August, but merchants from Niti, Mana, Nilang, Rampur, Rudok, Kullu, Ladakh, Limi, Nepal, Lhasa, and Purang and other parts come here. About 500-600 tents are pitched here. Two or three feet high parapets are erected with clods of earth brought from nearby marshes and tents are set up over them. Stones are spread on the ground since it is very damp. Excepting vegetables every other articles that could be had from any bazaar in India can be had here. There is no *pucca* house here so far : but a *kutcha* hut has been built for the Yung-chhong (Tibetan Trade Officer) in 1945. There are freshwater springs for drinking water and a small stream rising out of the marshes flows by the side of the mandi and falls into the lake called Gyanima-rap. There are the ruins of an old fort destroyed by Zoravar Singh, situated on the northern extremity of the hill, that is to the east of the mandi. Hence this place is called Gyanima-kharko (fort). Kailas is seen both from this place and from the top of the hillock in the mandi. Gyanima is under the jurisdiction of Dapa Zong.

8¼m. Changje-changju, *le*,
7½m. Kerleb chhu cross the 2 to 2½ feet deep river to its left bank,
3m. Lha chhu, cross the 2-3 feet deep swift river to its left bank,
7. **Tarchhen** (21) (111) 2¼m. to Tarchhen (see p. 106 and Table II).

TABLE VI

TAKLAKOT TO TIRTHAPURI

BY SHORT CUT AND THENCE DIRECT TO KAILAS (NYANRI GOMPA)—93m.

Taklakot (0) (0) (see p. 121 and Table V),
10½m. Ringung chhu (see Table V),
1. Map chhu (11¼) (11¼) ¾m. on the left bank of the Karnali,
½m. Dungmar chhu[1]
½m. just opposite this place on the other side of Karnali is the confluence of Harkong chhu and the Karnali,
¾m. Baldak chhu, from here up to Gurla chhu marshes, riding pilgrims should be careful, it would be better if they could walk this distance,.
1m. Gurla chhu[2], cross the 1½ to 2 feet deep river to its right bank (a little down this place the Gurla chhu falls into the Karnali),
1¾m. up along the Karnali; leaving the route to the left proceed 200 yards towards the right to a *laptche*,
¾m. on a plateau,
¼m. descent to a place called Ro, a little cultivation,
2m. Gyungdi, springs in marshy lands,
¾m. Chhami, fields of Kardung; (¾m. further leave the Karnali to the left and go up along the Chhibra chhu),
2. Chhipra camp (12¾) (24) 4½m. Chhipra or Chhibra camp on the Chhipra chhu,
2m. Chhipra la steep ascent, *laptche*, *tarchok*, from here Mandhata and Dhauli peaks of Nepal are seen,
2m. very steep descent up to Chhipra-do; the left side valley leads to Anlang and the right one to Rakshas Tal,

1 The village Dungmar is at a distance of ½m. from here; Dungmar to Purbu 1m. and thence to Baldak it is 4m.
2 1½m. up this place situated on the left bank of Gurla chhu is the village Kardung (*Kar*—white and *tung*—conch); named after the hill which is like a white conch.

$\frac{3}{4}$m. ascent to a *la* or pass, *laptche*, Kailas is seen from here,
2m. very steep and steep descent to Gyekung[1],
$\frac{1}{4}$m. ascent, *laptche*,
$\frac{3}{4}$m. descent, *laptche*, Mandhata is seen,
1m. on an extensive *maidan*, crossing of Gyanima-Rakshas road,
$\frac{1}{2}$m. mild descent,
$\frac{1}{4}$m. mild ascent to the spur of a hill, *le*,
1m. along the foot of a mountain at the edge of a *maidan*,

3. Yupcha[2] ($11\frac{1}{4}$) ($35\frac{1}{4}$) small springs, extensive plain,
$2\frac{1}{2}$m. mild ascent to a *la*, Rakshas Tal, Mandhata, Nanda Devi (?), and Trisul (?) are seen,
$\frac{1}{2}$m. very steep ascent,
$2\frac{1}{4}$m. plain (water from this *maidan* flows towards Rakshas),
1m. mild ascent to Chhalam la, also called Thalam la, fine view of Kailas, cairns, *laptche*, crossing of Gyanima-Kailas route, (Chhumikshala is about 3m. from here);
2m. mild, steep, and mild descent, *le*,
$\frac{1}{2}$m. steep and mild descent to the dry bed of a stream which meets the Chhumikshala which in turn falls into the Sutlej,
3m. on plain to Domar, *mani*-wall at the foot of the spur of a red mountain,

Sutlej ($14\frac{1}{4}$) ($49\frac{1}{2}$) $2\frac{1}{2}$m. along the foot of a mountain to the bank of the Sutlej,
1m. along the winding course of the Sutlej on marshes, Sutlej is 6 feet broad and 2 feet deep; cross it to its left bank,

Langchen Khambab ($1\frac{1}{4}$) ($50\frac{3}{4}$) $\frac{1}{4}$m. on marshes to the Langchen Khambab springs situated in a 50 yard square of marshes. This is the source of the Sutlej according to Tibetan traditions and mythology; from here up to Rakshas Tal the river is called Tso-lungba,

4. **Dulchu Gompa** ($\frac{1}{4}$) (51) $\frac{1}{4}$m. gompa *mani*-walls, (see p. 103),
$\frac{1}{2}$m. cross the Sutlej to its left bank,
$\frac{1}{4}$m. good camping ground,
$\frac{1}{2}$m. Sutlej broadens into a lake,

[1] Here is a valley in the midst of mountains with a small brook flowing in the middle. During summer months *dokpas* of Hor-gyeva camp here. One road goes to the left to Anlang and the other to the right to Tak-karpo.

[2] About $\frac{3}{4}$m. from here, situated in the middle of a *maidan*, there is a hillock which has the colour of a *yu* or turquoise, which is in all probability an exoteric rock of peridotite turning into serpentine, so this place is called Yupcha.

¾m. Chukta chhu[1] is flowing into the Sutlej on its right bank,
½m. the Sutlej flows through a narrow passage between two mountains,
1½m. *laptche,*
1½m. dry bed of a stream,
½m. Sutlej, cross the 3 feet deep swift Sutlej to its right bank; (for 2 miles up the Sutlej several shepherds camp in rainy season, for there is good pasture here; this place is called Shekarije),
2m. Trokpo-shar chhu[2], cross it to its right bank, route is marshy (see Table V),
¼m. steep ascent, *laptche,*
¼m. ups and downs,
¼m. steep descent to Trokpo-nup, this river is also very ferocious, 3 feet deep, cross it to its right bank,
¾m. steep ascent, *laptche,*
2½m. on plateau, to a circle of *mandals* called Khandoma,
1½m. on a plateau to the bed of a dry stream,
½m. dry stream,

5. **Tirthapuri** (14) (65) ¼m. Tirthapuri Gompa (see p. 103),
6½m. Trokpo-nup chhu, cross the 3 feet deep swift river to its left bank, *le* on either side of the river,
1m. Trokpo-shar, cross the 3 feet deep river to its left bank, *laptche,*

1 The Chukta chhu comes from the Kailas Range and falls into the Sutlej on its right bank opposite this place. The mouth of the river is about ½m. broad, and flows into the Sutlej in several ramifications and brings down about ten times as much water as the tiny brook of Sutlej brings. During the rainy season sometimes it swells to 50 times that of the Sutlej. Up till here the Sutlej has got the appearance and size of a small watering channel or a brook; but after receiving the Chukta it attains the grandeur and dignity of a Himalayan river. The flow also becomes more rapid. For ½m. from here it flows in a narrow valley through steep and high mountains. The scene here is at once grand and sublime and one feels a sort of exhilaration while passing through this valley.

2 It is also called Tokpo-shar. Trokpo-shar and Trokpo-nup are both ferocious and deep torrents. So some pilgrims camp here, go to Tirthapuri, and come back by the evening to save the trouble of making all the luggage animals cross these two rivers twice over. The confluence of this river with the Sutlej is very near and is situated in the middle of a steep and narrow gorge. The details of the road from Trokpo-shar here to Tarchhen is as follows: Tirthapuri to Trokpo-nup chhu 5¼m., Trokpo-shar ¾m., Goyak chhu 2m., Chukta chhu 7½m., cross the 3 feet deep river to its left bank, (total 15½m.) for the first day; Chukta to Sharlachakang 2½m., Shar la ¾m., *laptche*, it is only a pass in name but not a pass at all, (here is a mountain on which falls the shadow of the Holy Kailas Peak on *Vaishakha Purnima*; red ochre from this mountain is taken as *prasad* which is considered efficacious in curing certain cattle diseases); ¾m. Karleb chhu, *laptche*; 1/16m. *laptche*, 3/16m. *laptche*, row of cairns, cross 1½ feet deep Karleb; 1¼m. one branch of Karleb; ¼m. on marshes: 1m. main river of Karleb chhu, cross the 2-2½ feet deep river to its left bank: 1¼m. *le*; 1¼m. a chhu; ¼m. another small brook: ¼m. one more small brook; 1/8m. steep ascent, *laptche*, grand view of Kailas and the Lha chhu; 1/8m. on the pass; ½m. very steep descent to the bank of the Lha chhu; 1½m. up along the Lha chhu to Nyanri Gompa, Lha chhu bridge (total 12m. for the second day). So Tirthapuri is 27½m. from Nyanri and Tarchhen is almost equidistant from Tirthapuri.

$2\frac{3}{4}$m. Tasam-lam crossing,
$1\frac{5}{8}$m. a branch of Goyak,
$\frac{3}{8}$m. Goyak chhu, *le*,

6\. Chukta chhu (15) (80) $2\frac{3}{4}$m. camping ground of Korpons,
1m. Sakchung chhu, a small brook,
$\frac{3}{4}$m. Shalachakong (1m. up this place are the black tents of Korpons, the subjects of Tarchhen Labrang),
2m. Tak-chung chhu,
2m. Jalung-kha-mar.

Karlep chhu ($7\frac{3}{4}$) ($87\frac{3}{4}$) 2m. also called Karleb chhu, *le*, after mid-day the river becomes very turbulent and unfordable, since huge stones are incessantly washed down by the heavy floods of melted ice, cross the 2 feet deep river to its left bank, *le*,
$2\frac{1}{2}$m. Jamarmo chhu (from here one route goes direct to Tarchhen),
$\frac{1}{4}$m. a brook, big *le*, *mani*-walls,
$\frac{1}{2}$m. steep ascent to a pass, *laptche*, grand view of Kailas and the Lha chhu branching into a network of several sparkling streamlets,
$\frac{1}{2}$m. very steep descent through boulders to the right bank of Lha chhu,

7\. **Kailas (Nyanri Gompa)** ($5\frac{1}{4}$) (93) $1\frac{1}{2}$m. along the Lha chhu to the bridge on the river below Nyanri Gompa (see Table II).

TABLE VII

KAILAS (TARCHHEN TO GYANIMA MANDI--38 MILES

Kailas (Tarchhen) (0) (0)
$2\frac{1}{4}$m. Lha chhu, cross the 3 feet deep river to its right bank,
3m. Karleb chhu, cross the $2\frac{1}{2}$ feet deep river to its right bank,
$8\frac{3}{4}$m. on a sandy plain to Sutlej, cross the one-foot deep brook of Sutlej to its left bank,
$\frac{1}{2}$m. Lejendak or Lalungtak, *le*, leaving the Sutlej to the right, situated in the wall of the mountain to the right side of the road, here are several big caves which are often infested by robbers,
$\frac{3}{4}$m. ascent to Lalingtak la, *laptche*,

1\. Chhumikshala ($21\frac{3}{4}$) ($21\frac{3}{4}$) $6\frac{1}{2}$ miles also called Chhumarshala and Chhumishala, *le*, cave, small brook, Dulchu Gompa is seen at a distance on the right hand side,

3m. Chalam la, *laptche*, cairns, Kailas is seen up till here, from here one road goes to Dulchu Gompa which is at a distance of 9½m.
4m. mild descent to Randak chhu, C.,
1m. Pasalung la, *laptche*,
3m. Pasalung, first ¾m. steep descent, C.,
4m. Rap, cross the 2 to 3 feet deep Rap of the Gyanima chhu to its left bank, the ground is marshy here; (*rap* means fording place),

2. **Gyanima Mandi** (16¼) (38) 1¼m. get up the Gyanima-khar hill, then get down to the other side, cross the stream to Gyanima Mandi, (see Table V).

TABLE VIII

AN ABSTRACT OF THE WHOLE ROUTE FROM ALMORA TO THE HOLY KAILAS VIA LIPU LEKH PASS, TAKLAKOT, DULCHU GOMPA AND TIRTHAPURI, KAILAS-PARIKRAMA, MANASAROVAR-PARIKRAMA, AND BACK TO ALMORA VIA GURLA PASS, TAKLAKOT, KHOCHARNATH, AND GARBYANG—580½ MILES

			Distance between two places	Total mileage
1.	**Almora**	..	0	
	Bade-chhina	..	8½	
	Dhaul-chhina	..	5	13½
	Bunga	..	2½	
	Kanari-chhina	..	2¾	
2.	Seraghat	..	5¼	24
	Ganai	..	6	
	Banspatan	..	6	
	Suklyadi	..	3	
3.	BERINAG	..	3¼	42¼
	Gartir	..	2½	
4.	Thal	..	7	51¾
	Sandev	..	7¾	
5.	Didihat	..	2½	62
	ASKOT	..	7	
6.	Jauljibi	..	5	74
	Balvakot	..	6½	
7.	**Dharchula**	..	10	90½
	Tapovan	..	2	
8.	KHELA	..	8	100½
	Pangu	..	6	

9.	Soosa	..	3	109½
	Sirdang	..	2¼	
	Sirkha	..	½	
10.	Jipti	..	11	123¼
	Najang falls	..	5¾	
11.	Malpa	..	2½	131½
	Budhi	..	8¾	
12.	**Garbyang**	..	5	145¼
13.	Kalapani	..	11	156¼
	LIPU LEKH PASS	..	9¼	165½
	Pala	..	6	
14.	**Taklakot**	..	5	176½
	Ringung chhu	..	10½	
15.	Map chhu or Karnali	..	¾	187¾
16.	Chippra camp	..	12¾	200½
	Chhipra la	..	2	
17.	Yupcha	..	9¼	211¼
	Thalam la	..	6¼	
	Sutlej	..	8	
	Langchen Khambab	..	1¼	
18.	**Dulchu Gompa**	..	¼	227
	Trokpo-shar chhu	..	8	
19.	**Tirthapuri**	..	6	241
	Takpo-shar chhu	..	7½	
20.	Chukta chhu	..	7½	256
	Karlep chhu	..	7¾	
21.	**Kailas (Tarchhen)**	..	5¼	269
	Nyanri Gompa	..	5	
22.	Dira-phuk Gompa	..	7¼	281¼
	DOLMA LA	..	4	
	Gouri-kund	..	¼	
	Zuthul-phuk Gompa	..	9¼	
23.	Zhong chhu go	..	4	298¾
	Gyuma chhu	..	11½	
24.	Kuglung Chhu	..	2¾	313
	Palchen	..	8½	
	Palchung	..	1¼	
	Samo tsangpo	..	2¾	
25.	Seralung Gompa	..	3½	329
	Tag tsangpo	..	9¼	
	Yerngo Gompa	..	5½	
26.	**Thugolho Gompa (Manasarovar)**	..	2¼	346
	Gurla la	..	9¾	
	Gurla-phuk (Gori-udyar)	..	4	

27.	Baldak	..	4½	363¾
28.	**Taklakot**	..	15¼	379¾
29.	**Khocharnath**	..	12	391¾
	Taklakot	..	12	
30.	Pala	..	5	409
	LIPU LEKH PASS	..	6	
31.	Kalapani	..	9½	424¼
32.	**Garbyang**	..	11	435¼
33.	Malpa	..	13¾	449
34.	Jipti	..	8¼	457¼
35.	Soosa	..	13¾	471
36.	KHELA	..	9	480
37.	**Dharchula**	..	10	490
38.	JAULJIBI	..	16½	506½
39.	Didihat	..	12	518½
40.	Thal	..	10¼	528¾
41.	BERINAG	..	9½	538¼
42.	Seraghat	..	18¼	556½
43.	Bade-chhina	..	15½	572
44.	**Almora**[1]	..	8½	580½

TABLE IX

ABSTRACT OF MILEAGES BETWEEN IMPORTANT PLACES IN KAILAS KHANDA AND KEDAR KHANDA

		Miles
1.	Almora to Lipu Lekh pass (Indo-Tibetan Border)	165½
2.	Lipu Lekh to Kailas ..	72½
3.	Almora to Kailas via Lipu Lekh pass	238
4.	Almora to Kailas via Darma pass ..	227
5.	Almora to Kailas via Unta-dhura pass ..	210
6.	Joshimath to Kailas via Gula-Niti pass ..	200

1 Leaving a margin of 16 days more for halts and making arrangements for conveyance, one can finish the whole journey in two months, including the *parikramas* of the Holy Kailas and Manasarovar and a visit to the Gyanima Mandi, Tirthapuri, and Khocharnath. Those who cannot spare so much time and cannot undergo privations for such a long time may chalk out the itinerary for themselves to suit their convenience, from the tables given herein.

7.	Joshimath to Kailas via Danjan-Niti pass ..	160
8.	Joshimath to Kailas via Hoti-Niti pass ..	158
9.	Badrinath to Kailas via Mana pass ..	238
10.	Mukhuva (Gangotri) to Kailas via Jelukhaga pass	243
11.	Simla to Kailas via Shipki pass and Gartok ..	445
12.	Simla to Kailas via Shipki pass and Tuling ..	473
13.	Srinagar (Kashmir) to Kailas via Ladakh ..	605
14.	Pashupatinath (Nepal) to Kailas via Muktinath & Khochar	525
15.	Lhasa to Kailas via Gyantse & Shigartse ..	800
16.	Kailas-Parikrama	32
17.	Circumference of Manasarovar	54
18.	Manasarovar-Parikrama	64
19.	Circumference of Rakshas Tal	77
20.	Kailas to the Source of Indus via Lhe la or Topchhen la	46
21.	Kailas to the Source of Brahmaputra ..	97
22.	Kailas to the Source of Sutlej (at Dulchu Gompa)	21
23.	Kailas to the Source of Tag tsangpo	69
24.	Taklakot to the Source of Karnali ..	23
25.	Kailas to Manasarovar	16
26.	Kailas to Tirthapuri	28
27.	Kailas to Dulchu Gompa	21
28.	Kailas to Gyanima Mandi	38
29.	Gyanima Mandi to Gartok	76
30.	Gyanima Mandi to Tirthapuri	27
31.	Gyanima Mandi to Sibchilim Mandi	28
32.	Gyanima Mandi to Taklakot	49
33.	Taklakot to Tugolho	34
34.	Taklakot to Khocharnath	12
35.	Sibchilim to Nabra Mandi	38½
36.	Nabra to Tuling	33½
37.	Tuling to Badrinath	100
38.	Tarchhen to Serdung-chuksum	7
39.	Tarchhen to Tso Kapala	6
40.	Tarchhen to Serdung-chuksum & back via Tso Kapala	17½
41.	Haldwani to Almora (on foot)	41
42.	Haldwani to Almora (by bus)	88
43.	Almora to Pindari Glacier	73
44.	Rishikesh to Jamnotri	118½
45.	Rishikesh to Gangotri	145
46.	Rishikesh to Kedarnath	133½
47.	Rishikesh to Badrinath	167½
48.	Rishikesh to Joshimath	148½
49.	Joshimath to Badrinath	19

50.	Ramnagar to Badrinath	164
51.	Jamnotri to Gangotri	98½
52.	Gangotri to Kedarnath	123
53.	Kedarnath to Badrinath	101
54.	Mussoorie to Jamnotri	86
55.	Rishikesh to Jamnotri, Gangotri, Kedarnath, Badrinath, and back to Rishikesh	608
56.	Rishikesh to Tehri (motor road)	50
57.	Tehri to Gangotri	101
58.	Rishikesh to Chamoli (motor)	121
59.	Chamoli to Badrinath	48
60.	Ranikhet to Karna-prayag	60
61.	Karna-prayag to Badrinath	67
62.	Garur or Baijnath to Nanda-prayag	45½
63.	Nanda-prayag to Badrinath	54½
64.	Gangotri to Gaumukh	13
65.	Uttarkashi to Dodhital	18
66.	Kedarnath to Vasukital	2
67.	Chamoli to Gohna lake	12
68.	Pandukeshvar to Lokpal	12
69.	Badrinath to Satopanth	18
70.	Milam to Shandilya-kund	6
71.	Milam to Surya-kund	13
72.	Dharchula to Chiplakot	25

TABLE X

SECOND ROUTE TO HOLY KAILAS AND MANASAROVAR

FROM ALMORA via DARMA PARA—227 Miles

Almora (0) (0)

1—7...............

8. KHELA (100½) (100½) (see Table I) last P. on this route, up along the Dhauli-Ganga,

$9\frac{1}{2}$m. Nyo, hamlet of 3 houses, Death-Cave (see p. 97),
$\frac{1}{2}$m. Sovla, Darma-Bhot begins, sotre houses of Darma Bhotias,

9. Dar (12) ($112\frac{1}{2}$) 2m., hot springs; 3m. Boling, 5m.; Udthing, caves; 1m. Sela,
10. Nagaling (14) ($126\frac{1}{2}$) 5m.; in the neighbourhood of this village the drug called Ephedra Vulgaris (*soma* or *soma-kalpa*) grows abundantly; it is nowadays used as a specific for asthma, both in allopathic and Ayurvedic therapy; 4m. Baling, 4m. Dugtu or Dugling and Saun; 2m. Dantu,
11. Go (12) ($138\frac{1}{2}$) 2m. last village,
    6m. Bidang, a mandi is held here in August, when people from Darma, Niti, and Nepal and Khampas and Dokpas gather here; wool, salt, and grains are bartered,
12. Dave (17) ($155\frac{1}{2}$) 11m. *D.*, ascent to the pass begins,
    DARMA PASS ($5\frac{1}{2}$) (111) [18,510] last half a mile is a very steep ascent, Indian borderland, pass is crossable from June to the end of September, there are deceitful crevasses both on the pass and on either side of it,
13. Mangval or Mangul[1] (4) (165) descent up to this place, C.; $5\frac{1}{2}$ m. Silti, since 1930 a small mandi is held here for 10 or 15
14. Lama-chhorten (10) (175) $4\frac{1}{2}$m. several *mani*-walls and *chhortens*, a mandi is held here,
15. CHAKRA MANDI (12) (187) mandi of Darma Bhotias (see Table V),
16. Chhumik-shala ($18\frac{1}{4}$) ($205\frac{1}{4}$) via Chhalam la to Chhumik-shala (see Table VII),
17. **Kailas (Tarchhen)** ($21\frac{3}{4}$) (227) (see Tables I and II),

TABLE XI

THIRD ROUTE TO HOLY KAILAS AND MANASAROVAR

FROM ALMORA via UNTA-DHURA PASS—**210** MILES

Almora (0) (0) (see Table I),
$6\frac{1}{2}$m. Dinapani, F., shops, tea,

[1] One mile before reaching this place a road goes to Lampiya pass. Mangval to Lampiya pass [18,150] $5\frac{1}{2}$m.; to Jolinkong 13m.; Kuti $6\frac{1}{2}$m. and Garbyang $18\frac{1}{2}$m. total $43\frac{1}{2}$m.

1m. Kapadkhan, shop, motor road up to this place, one road goes to the sanatorium Binsar which is 5m. from here,

$2\frac{3}{4}$m. Bhaisodi-chhina, pass,

$1\frac{1}{2}$m. steep descent to Basauli, village, shop,

1. Takula ($14\frac{3}{4}$) ($14\frac{3}{4}$) 3m. P., shops, tea, $\frac{1}{2}$ a mile further is D.B.,

$5\frac{1}{4}$m. Devaldhar Estate, last $1\frac{1}{2}$m. steep ascent,

$4\frac{1}{2}$m. steep descent to Bilonsera,

2. **Bageshvar** ($12\frac{1}{4}$) (27) [3,200] $2\frac{1}{2}$m. cross the bridge on the Gomati to Bageshvar, P., T., H., D.B., S.D., bazaars (see p. 95),

3m. Lahur-gad, from here one path goes to Gori-udyar which is 3m. (see p. 95),

3. Kapkot (14) (41) 11m. P., D.B., S., shops,

$3\frac{1}{4}$m. Bhani-gaon, from Bageshvar up to this place the route is along the Saraju,

Shyama-dhura ($11\frac{1}{2}$) (52) [6,900] $7\frac{3}{4}$ m. last two miles steep ascent, P., shops,

$\frac{3}{4}$m. steep ascent up to the pass,

2m. steep descent,

$1\frac{1}{2}$m. very steep descent up to Rama-Ganga,

$2\frac{1}{2}$m. further cross the rope bridge on the Rama-Ganga to its right bank,

4. Tejam[1] (7) (59) [3,280] $\frac{1}{4}$m. to Tejam, P., S., Ayurvedic Dispensary, cross the bridge on the Jakul,

4m. Baman-gaon is up the road, just opposite this place on the other side of the river, there is a beautiful waterfall,

$2\frac{1}{4}$m. La, from Tejam up to this place along the river Jakul, cross the river by bridge,

2m. steep ascent to Girgaon, small D.B., village is far away from here,

$2\frac{3}{4}$m. ascent upto the Kalamuni pass,

$5\frac{1}{4}$m. steep descent with reliefs to Tiksen,

5. RATHI (MANSIYARI) ($18\frac{1}{4}$) ($77\frac{1}{4}$) 2m. steep descent to Rathi, P., D.B., the surrounding region is called Mansiyari (at the place called Dandadhar, 'Shri Gita Satsang Ashram' has been started in 1946 by Shree 108 Swami Vidyananda Saraswatiji Maharaj, for the propagation of the *Gita Dharma*); Bhotias of Malla Johar come down here in winter; there are sulphur and sulphide of arsenic mines in this *paragana*,

2m. descent to Suring-ghat, from here up to Milam the road runs along the Gori-Ganga,

[1] It is difficult to cross the rope bridge on the Rama-Ganga, so very few pilgrims take to this route. Talla Johar begins from Tejam and Bhotias of Malla-Johar get down to this place in winter. Thal is 12m. from here.

2¼m. Lilam, the village is a little away from the road,
2½m. on the other side of the river Palti-gad falls into the Gori from a great height like a big water fall,
1¼m. Ralam-gad, this river also falls into the Gori on its left bank,
1¾m. Rar-gadi,
2m. Poting-gad, cross by bridge,

6. Bag-udyar (12) (89¼) [8,600] ¼m. caves, *le*,
2m. Tibu-nahar, shed of the road *jamadar*,
2¾m. Mapang, *le*, between Tibu and this place there are two huge ice slides or miniature glaciers, like a drop-scene the mountain scenery changes suddenly from here,
1m. Laspa-gadi, cave, village is far from the road,
2m. Rilkot, [12,200], cross one stream and reach the village, six houses, *D.*, a little cultivation, ½m. further are the ruins of old Rilkot,
2¼m. Martoli [11,070], big village, S., temple of Nanda-Mayi, Thakur Divan Singh, the famous guide to Trail pass hails from this village, birch forest nearby,
½m. very steep descent to Lovan river, cross it,
½m. cross the Gori by bridge to its left bank,
1m. Burfu, big village, S., *D.*,
2½m. Bilju, S., a little beyond the village grand view of the Nanda Devi east peak,
2¼m. cross the bridge on Khopang or Gonkha river, which comes from Unta-dhura and falls into Gori a little down this place,

7. **Milam**[1] (17½) (106¾) [11,232] ¾m. further to Milam, P., S., *D.*,
5¾m. Shilang-talla, *le*,

1 This is the last Indian village on this route, and the biggest in Johar and there are about 500 houses here. In the month of July most of the male members go to Tibetan markets for trading. So, 90% of the cultivable land is left barren. Pandit Nain Singh and Pandit Krishan Singh, the famous Himalayan explorers hail from this place. All arrangements up to Gyanima have to be made from here.

Gori-Ganga is about 250 yards from the village. Milam glacier is at a distance of 3m. from here. The snout of the glacier is 24 feet high and 16 feet broad. It has a grand and beautiful view from here. Huge blocks of ice are lying in front of the snout and stones are often pelted from the top of the glacier by the melting ice. 3m. up the glacier, situated at the foot of a mountain on an open ground is the lakelet called Shandilya-kund or Shangas-kund which is about 450 feet long and 225 feet broad. Shepherds come here in summer to graze their sheep. There is plenty of firewood here. Opposite the Shandilya-kund a small glacier by name Sikdam comes and meets the Milam glacier on its right side. A *mela* is held here on *Shravana Purnima*, when people from Milam and other villages gather to have a dip in the holy lake, the water of which is not ice-cold. Seven miles up this glacier situated at its head is a glacial lake called Surya-kund. A party of explorers from Poland came here in July 1939 to climb the Trisuli peaks situated at the head of the Milam glacier. While on the climb two of the members of the party perished under an avalanche while bivouacing in the third camp.

1m. Shilang-malla, *le*, *D.*,

1m. Chhotpani or Shuntpani, on the right side is the black glacier (having been mixed up with black earth the glacier looks black),

½m. Palthang, *D.* on the top of a hill, *laptche*,

8. Dung or Dhunga (9) (115¾) [13,720] ¾ m. very near the river Gonkha, three or four big caves, *le*, scarcity of fuel, ascent to the pass begins from here,

2¼m. [15,010] Bomlas-malla, *le*, on the left hand side a beautiful glacier,

1m. Kala-matiya, the earth is black here, probably graphite, *le*,

1m. Saphed-gal or white glacier,

½m. Unta-ka-jam, *le*, foot of the pass,

UNTA-DHURA PASS (6¾) (122½) [17,950] 2m. very steep ascent,

¼m. very steep descent to Gang-pani, *le*, this stream flows into Girthi,

JAYANTI PASS or Janti-dhura (3¼) (125¾) [18,500] very steep ascent,

2¼m. Nhaz-gam, very steep descent, *le*, this stream flows into Girthi, no fuel,

KUNGRI-BINGRI PASS (3¾) (129½) [18,300] 1½m. very steep ascent, Indian border, about 200 yards further *laptche*, Kailas is seen from here, pass is crossable from July to October,

9. Chhirchin[1] (5) (134½) 5m. steep descent with reliefs, *le*, caves,

¼m. further cross 1½ feet deep branch of Chhirchin,

3m. Sumnag or Sumnath, *le*,

½m. in the bed of the river, cross another branch of the river, *le*,

¾m. Tokpu, *le*,

2¼m. Survey of India boundary line.[2]

1½m. Chhilim-pani, this river goes to Sibchilim, *le*,

1m. Latuva, *le*, caves a little further,

10. Thajang[3] (12) (146½) 3m. *le*,

2¼m. *le*,

2½m. Chhunak or Chhinaku, (*chhu* means water and *nak* means

[1] Usually one should start from Dung early in the morning, cross the three passes and reach here in the evening to camp; otherwise if one stops on the way after crossing two passes, there would be a great difficulty for fuel; and the camping place between two passes is very cold. Three streams meet here to form Chhirchin, the bed of which is about ¾m. broad and full of pebbles and looks like a long lake though the actual course of the river itself is not very broad. Between Chhirchin and Sumnag both in the bed of the river and on the mountains on either bank, fossils, *thaneri* stone, *zaharmora*, calcite in crystalline form, and trisulphide of arsenic are found. From Chhirchin one road goes to Sibchilim.

[2] The Survey of India Office has set up long wall of stones here (11¾m. from Kungri-bingri pass) 3 feet broad and 2 feet high in 1938 to show the Indian boundary.

[3] On the left side of the camping place, situated on the top of a hill, are a *laptche* and *tarchoks*, where Tibetans and Bhotias both offer their old guns and other arms.

black) the water of this river is black and muddy, cross the verandah of 2 feet deep river to its right bank,

3m. last ½m. ascent to Thampa, *le*, spring,

¼m. ascent to *lapche*, Kailas seen from here,

½m. descent,

11. Guni-yankti[1] (11½) (158) 3m. on plains to the river Guni-yankti or Chhu Minchung, cross the 2 to 2½ feet deep river to its right bank, *le* on both sides of the river,

2¼m. Darma-yankti or Chhu Minjen, cross the 2 to 3 feet deep rapid river, Mandhata is seen from here,

12. **Gyanima Mandi** (14) (172) 11¾m. (see Table V),
13. **Chhumikshala** (16¼) (188¼) (see Table VII),
14. **Kailas** (Tarchhen) (21¾) (210) (see Table VII),

TABLE XII

FOURTH ROUTE TO HOLY KAILAS AND MANASAROVAR

FROM JOSHIMATH via GUNLA-NITI PASS—**200** MILES

Joshimath[2] (0) (0) [6,200] P., T., H., D.B., *D.*, temple bazaar, Police Chouki, *dharas*,

6m. Tapovan, hot springs, (from here Bhavishya Badri is 3m. away for the main road),

4m. cross the bridge on the Dhauli to its right bank, Niti-Bhot begins from here,

[1] Five or 6m. from here on either side of a river Guni-yankti, and Darma-yankti, there are camping parapets and camping places everywhere. Merchants camp and ford these rivers at any place that suits them. So the distance between Thampa and Gyanima varies according to the place where one fords these rivers. Some people wrongly call these rivers Gunavanti and Damayanti. *Yankti* means river in Bhotia language. The Tibetan names of these rivers are Chhu-Minchung (small river) and Chhu-Minjen (big river).

[2] Joshimath or Jyotirmath is one of the four great *Mathas* or Monasteries established by the great Acharya Adi Shankaracharya. For 350 years it remained without an abbot but in the *Kumbha Mela* (Allahabad) of 1942, an *Acharya* has been appointed. Here are the temples of Vasudeva and Narasingh. Badrinath is 19m. from here, Rishikesh 148½m., and Ramnagar 164m. There is bus service now-a-days up to Chamoli, which is 29m. from here. That is to say that Badrinath is at a distance of 48m. from the bus service station. From Joshimath up to Niti pass the road goes up along the Dhauli-Ganga.

1. Suraitota (16) (16) 6m. *le*, *D.*, no village,
7m. Tamak *le*, *D.*,
2m. Jumma, *le*, *D.*, village is away from the road,
3m. Jilam, village is away from the road,
2. Malari (18) (34) 6m. to Malari, big village, S., *D.*,
5m. Bampa, P., S., *D.*,
1½m. [10,317] Gamshali, *D.*,
3. **Niti** (9½) (43½) 3m. last village, S., *D.*,
4. Guthing (8¼) (51¾) two steep ascents and one steep descent on the way, *le*,
3½m. Shephuk, *le*,
2¾m. Nakula ice bridge, cross it to its right bank,
4½m. Patal-pani, *le* on either side of the river,
¾m. Geldung, *le*,
5. Khyunglung (15¾) (67½) [14,703] 4¼m. *le*, from here up to the pass very steep ascents,
NITI PASS (4½) (72) [16,600] last 1½m. is almost a perpendicular ascent, Indian boundary, the pass is crossable from June to November, Kailas is seen from here,
2m. on the pass, *laptche*,
1¼m. very steep descent to Jindu, *le*,
6. Changlus (12) (84) 8¾m. *le*,
5m. Hartha, C., *le*, Gunla camp is not far from this place,
7. **Nabra Mandi**[1] (11½) (95½) 6½m. big mandi of the Niti Bhotias,
5¾m. Gemul chhu, also called Geyul or Gyung-yul, two houses, a few plots of cultivation, *le* on either bank of the river, cross the three feet deep river to its right bank,
7½m. Dongpu chhu, *le*, cross the three feet deep rapid river to its right bank,
8. Dongpu Gompa (14) (109½) ¾m. steep ascent to the village, 20 houses, gompa, good cultivation,
9. Dongu chhu (5½) (115) *le*,
2½m. Dongu, C., no water,
1¼m. Tisum chhu, *le* on either side of the river, cross the river to its right bank,

1 This mandi is held from July to September and 250 tents are pitched. Dapa is about 6½m. from here; as a protest against the oppression of the Zongpon of Dapa, the Bhotias of Niti had shifted the site of their mandi in 1939, from Dapa to Nabra, situated in a broad valley which is on the Gartok-Niti high road. Three or four *pakka* houses also have been built here by the Niti merchants. This is under the jurisdiction of Dapa Zong. Large quantities of *jimbu* are collected from the neighbourhood. Sutlej-bridge is 3m. from here.

10. **Sibchilim Mandi**[1] (19) (134) 2½m. mandi on the left bank of the Sib chhu, *le*, cross the 3 feet deep Sib chhu to its right bank,

7¼m. Mani-thanga, *mani*-walls, *le*, several black tents of Khyunglung, extensive pastures, one road goes to Khyunglung,

3½m. Gombachen, extensive *le*; once a big mandi used to be held here, one road goes to Khyunglung; between Mani-thang and Gombachen one shall have to cross several ramifications of the Chhu-nak chhu, in their winding course,

11. Guni-yankti (15) (149) 4¼m. cross the 2 to 2½ feet deep river to its right bank, *le*, on either side of the river,

3¾m. Darma-yankti, cross the 3 feet deep swift river to its right bank, *le*, on either bank of the river (see Table XI);

12. **Gyanima Mandi** (13) (162) 9½m. (see Table V),

13. Chhumikshala (16¼) (178¼) *le*,

14. **Kailas** (Tarchhen) (21¾) (200) (see Table VI).

TABLE XIII

FIFTH ROUTE TO HOLY KAILAS AND MANASAROVAR

FROM JOSHIMATH via DAMJAN NITI PASS—160 MILES

Joshimath (0) (0) (see Table XII),

3. **Niti** (43½) (43½),

7m. very steep and almost perpendicular ascent to Bomlas pass, *laptche*, *tarchok*,

4. Damjan (10½) (53¾) 3¼m. steep descent, *le*,

5. DAMJAN-NITI PASS (5¾) (59½) [16,200 ?] very steep ascent to the pass, *laptche*, *tarchok*, Indian boundary, pass crossable from June to October, Kailas is seen from here,

5. Hoti camp (5½) (65) very steep descent, *le*, route from Hoti pass meets here,

3½m. [16,350] Tonjen la, *laptche*,

1 Between July and August seven or eight Niti merchants hold a mandi here, sometimes a few Joharis also come here. Sib chhu flows here in two or three ramifications. The Cave-Colony of Pangtha is about 5m. down this place (see p. 106). From here one road goes to Khyunglung, a day's march and Tirthapuri 2 days' march.

4m. descent down a stream to Sag, *le*,
3m. ascent,
6. Chhalampa (13½) (78½) 3m. descent, *le*,
3m. ascent,
3m. descent to Dakar, *le*,
6½m. Tisum, *le*,
7. **Sibchilim** (15¾) (94¼) 3¼m. (see Table XII),
8. Guni-yankti (15) (109¼), *le*,
9. **Gyanima Mandi** (12¾) (132),
10. Chhumikshala (16¼) (138¼) *le*,
11. **Kailas** (Tarchhen) (21¾) (160).

TABLE XIV

SIXTH ROUTE TO HOLY KAILAS AND MANASAROVAR

FROM JOSHIMATH via HOTI-NITI PASS—158 MILES

Joshimath (0) (0),
1-2 ....(see Table XII),
3. Timarsim (42½) (42½) a small hamlet one mile before reaching the village Niti, steep ascent right up to the pass,
3m. Kasai, *le*,
4. Kalazabar (6) (48½) 3m. *le*,
HOTI-NITI PASS (7) (55½) [16,390] Hoti, also called Chor-Hoti or Hoti-dhura, *laptche*, Indian boundary, pass used mostly during rainy season, very steep descent right up to Rimkhim,
2½m. Banjar-malla, *le*.
1½m. Banjar-talla, *le*,
1½m. [14,250] Rimkhim, *le*,
5. Hoti camp (7½) (63) 2m. up the Hoti river to Hoti camp, *le*, route from Damjan pass meets here,
6-10 ....(see Table XIII),
11. **Kailas** (Tarchhen) (95) (158).

TABLE XV

SEVENTH ROUTE TO HOLY KAILAS AND MANASAROVAR

FROM BADRINATH via MANA PASS—238 MILES

Badrinath (0) (0) [10,159], P., T., H., D.B., *D.*, airfield, temple of Sri Badri Narayana one of the four *Dhamas* or Great *Tirthas* of

India, Rikhikesh is 168m. from here and Kedarnath [11,000] 101m.,

2m. Mana or Mani-bhadrapuri, last village on this route, the only Bhotia village on this side ; the Bhotias of Mana are called Marchhas,

3m. Balvan, cave, *le*,

2m. Musapani, *le*,

1½m. Shakpadunga, 4 good caves, *le*,

½m. Bujkuli, 4 good caves, *le*,

1. Ghastoli (11½) (11½) 1½m. cave, *le*,

3m. Budchaun, *le*,

½m. Khorjavkot, *le*,

2. Sarasvati (8½) (20) 5m. *le*, ascent to the pass begins from here,

2½m. Rattakona, *le*,

1m. Tarai, *le*,

3m. Rakshas Tal, glacial lake,

½m. Devtal, glacial lake 400 yards long,

MANA PASS or Chirbitiya (8½) (28½) [18,400] 1½m. Indian boundary, crossable from July to September.

3. Poti (9) (37½) *le*, descent up to this place,

4. Jogorav (8) (45½) *le*,

3m. Shiphuk *Maidan*, *le*,

3m. [16,400] ascent to Charang la, *laptche*,

5. Ramurav (16) (61½) 10m. *le*, first three miles ascent,

6. Shankara (10) (71½) *le*,

7. Sattu-khana (21½ ?) (93) *le*,

8. **Thhuling Gompa**[1] (7 ?) (100) [12,200] also called Thhuling Math, Thhuling, Tuling, and Totling, one mile beyond Tuling 2m. steep ascent [13,176], and then descent in gradations to

1 Thhuling Gompa, classically known as Thunding, is situated on the left bank of the river Sutlej at a distance of about a mile from the edge of the water. This was founded in A.D. 1030 and is the most famous monastery in Western Tibet. Turks had pillaged this monastery on more than one occasion and set fire to it when, several hundreds of valuable Sanskrit and Tibetan manuscripts were reduced to ashes. The great Acharya Deepankara Shreejnana of Nalanda University fame came here in 1042 to preach Buddhism. He sojourned here for nine months and wrote many books including translations. Several other Indian *pandits* and Buddhist preachers had translated several Pali works into Tibetan here. There are about 108 image-halls with thousands of images of Buddhistic deities, lamas, and *Acharyas* of various sizes made of earth, bronze, silver, and gold. Here are the volumes of *Kanjur* and *Tanjur* and several other printed and unprinted books well-arranged in big shelves. The chief idol in the main image-hall is of Sakya-Thubbha (*Sakya-Muni* or *Buddha*) in *Padmasana* (lotus pose) guilded and seated on a high pedestal. It is over 6 feet high and is wrongly believed by the Hindu pilgrims to be that of Adi Badrinarayana ; and often cows, sheep, and goats are offered to burn lamps with their ghee, but these animals are sold away every three years and the money distributed amongst the monks. In one of the image-halls there is an eight-foot image of Chamba or Maitreya, the coming Buddha. A *dakshinavarta shankha* (right handed conch), a grain of barley as big as a swan's egg, and a few other things are the specialities of this monastery, which are kept under lock and seal by the Labrang and

9. **Mangang** (11) (113) village, cultivation, a very interesting gompa, affiliated to Depung Vihara, cross the 4 feet deep, very furious, and broad Mangang tsangpo to its right bank,

10. DAPA or DABA (14) (127) [14,000] village, cultivation. Zong, gompa with one lama and 15 dabas, mandi of this place was shifted to Nabra in 1929; Gyanima Mandi, Nabra Mandi, and Missar Tasam are under the jurisdiction of Dapa Zong,

11. NABRA MANDI ($6\frac{1}{2}$) ($133\frac{1}{2}$) (see Table XII),

12-17.

18. **Kailas** (Tarchhen) ($104\frac{1}{2}$) (238).

TABLE XVI

EIGHTH ROUTE TO HOLY KAILAS AND MANASAROVAR

FROM MUKHUVA (GONGOTRI) via JELUKHAGA PASS—243 MILES

Mukhuva (Gangotri) (0) (0) village of the *Pandas* of Gangotri, Rikhikesh is 145m. via Narendranagar and Tehri; Mussoorie is 110m. and Gangotri is 13m.,

4m. Jangla, F., shop,

1m. Kopang, *le*, camping place of Harsil Jads or Bhotias,

$\frac{3}{4}$m. From here one road splits to Gongotri[1] which is $7\frac{1}{4}$m.; (confluence of Jahnavi and Bhagirathi is $\frac{1}{2}$m. down this place); from here up to Jelukhaga pass the road goes

are shown only by giving good presents. The monastery has got 150 yds. square compound wall. There are two lamas and 70 dabas in this monastery and it is a branch of the Sera Gompa. The abbot of the monastery comes from Sera for a period of three years. Before the Mana pass is blocked up with snow, the abbot sends every year some offerings to Badrinath temple and in return gets some *prasad* from the *pujari* or *Raval* of Badrinath. It is not known how and when this custom has come into vogue. There are several *chhortens* in the neighbourhood of the monastery reminding one of the past glory.

On the southern side of the gompa there are about 15 houses of the village and plenty of cultivation, extending for a couple of miles up to the bank of the Sutlej. Thhuling is a sufficiently warm place and as such some trees grow near the shores of the river up to a height of 12 feet. There is a garden of *peepal* trees grown by the gompa in the valley of a small brook nearby. During the months of July and August a small mandi is held here by a few Khampas coming from Gangotri side and a few Bhotias coming from Niti. *Jimbu* grows in abundance in the neighbourhood. Eight miles down the river situated on the left bank of the Sutlej is Chhabrang Zong, which was once a flourishing principality with good cultivation. 2m. up Thhuling there is a bridge on the Sutlej. From here one road goes to Gartok and one to Tirthapuri without touching Dapa and Sibchilim, one to Simla, one to Kullu, and one to Dapa and Gyanima.

[1] There is a temple of Gangaji and Bhagiratha Shila at Gangotri [10,070]. Gaumukh [13,570] the actual and glacial source of the Ganges, is at a distance of 13m. beyond Gangotri. The snout of the Gaumukh glacier is conceived, by the Hindus, as the mouth of a cow, the front of the glacier as the face, and two of the prominent snow peaks of Satopanth [23,240] on the north of the glacier as the horns, hence the name Gau-mukh (Cow-mouth) to the source of the Ganges. About 4m. up the glacier, situated on the left bank there are some hot springs

up along the River Jahnavi or Jad Ganga; a little up the majestic Jahnavi gorge, there is an iron rope, the remnant of a suspension bridge, hanging at a height of a thousand feet above the level of the river,

$2\frac{3}{4}$m. Dang, *le*, *padam* trees from here,

1. Lamathang ($13\frac{1}{2}$) ($13\frac{1}{2}$) $2\frac{1}{4}$m. *le*,

$\frac{3}{4}$m. first *laptche*,

$1\frac{3}{4}$m. Kadoli,

$2\frac{1}{2}$m. *le*,

Nilang ($7\frac{1}{2}$) (21) [11,181] 5m. cross the Rishi Ganga to the village Nilang, last village on the route, Jads or Bhotias of Gangotri, plenty of cultivation, cold place.

$1\frac{1}{2}$m. Mani-ringuva, *le*,

$3\frac{3}{4}$m. Magru, *le*,

$\frac{3}{4}$m. confluence of Jahnavi and Muling (one path goes to Badrinath up the Muling river),

$\frac{1}{4}$m. Nagatoru, *le*,

Do-sundu or Du-sundu ($8\frac{1}{2}$) ($29\frac{1}{2}$) $2\frac{1}{2}$m. confluence of the Jahnavi and Jad Ganga, *le*, (*sundu* means confluence, 2m. up the confluence situated on the Jad Ganga is the village Jadhung),

$2\frac{1}{2}$m. Hilding, *le*,

$1\frac{1}{2}$m. Sunama or Sonam, *le*,

$1\frac{3}{4}$m. Chhamreyasa, *le*, *laptche*, *tarchok*, *mani*-wall,

3m. Changma-garia, *le*,

$\frac{1}{2}$m. Yangra, C.,

3. Tipani ($11\frac{1}{4}$) ($40\frac{3}{4}$) 2m. confluence of three rivers, *le*,

$1\frac{3}{4}$m. Guggul-sundu, *le*,

1m. [12,984] Puling-sundu, *le*, extensive *maidan*,

$1\frac{1}{2}$m. Du-sundu, *le*,

1m. Tingtya, or Tingta, *le*, ascent to the pass begins,

$1\frac{3}{4}$m. Kaidvas, *le*,

4. Mandi ($9\frac{1}{4}$) (50) $2\frac{1}{4}$m. Mandi or Khage-ka-niche (foot of the pass),

JELUKHAGA PASS ($3\frac{1}{4}$) ($53\frac{1}{4}$) [17,490] $3\frac{1}{4}$m. (?) very steep ascent to Jelukhaga pass called Tsagchhok la by Tibetans, Indian boundary, pass crossable from the middle of June to the middle of October, from here up to the river it is a very steep and falling descent.

1m. Pangde, *le*,

and a small hot water lakelet, formed out of the hot water from the springs. Both the Satopanth and Kedar peaks were scaled from Gaumukh side and the shortcut to Badrinath via Arwa valley and Ghastoli was also negotiated. The scenery of Gaumukh, surrounded by beautiful snow peaks on all three sides is simply superb. The length of the main glacier of Gaumukh is about 15m. and of the Chaturangi, the sub-glacier on to its north is about 10m.

2¼m. Pilpila, foot of the pass on the Tibetan side,

5. River Op (4¼) (57½) 1m. cross the 2½ feet deep Op to its right bank, (½m. down this place is a bridge on the river),

4m. Dak, *le*,

4m. Phula la camp, *le*,

1¼m. Phula la, *laptche, tarchok*,

2¼m. Guru-ka-pani, *le*,

1m. Jara, *le*,

6. Puling Mandi[1] (16¼) (73¾) 3¾m. last 1¼m. steep descent, *le*,

1¼m. a river, cross the 2 feet deep river to is right bank, *le*,

4½m. Babra, *le*.

7. Sharvarao (9¼) (83) 3½m. cross the 2 feet deep river to its right bank, *le* on either side of the river ; it is also called Shabrak ; from here one road goes to Mana pass and one direct to Mangnang without going to Thhuling ; from here Dupang is 10m. and Mangnang is 10m. further,

1½m. steep ascent,

½m. steep descent,

½m. steep ascent,

5¾m. on the Kanchen-thanga, *laptche, tarchok*,

2m. steep descent through beautiful erosion terraces and spires,

1¼m. across the dry bed of a stream to Thusi la, *le*, Mana-Chhabrang road crosses here (Chhabrang Zong is about 3m. south of this place),

1½m. Barkhu, 16 caves, Tibetans live here in winter.

8. **Thuling** (22) (105) 9m. (see Table XV).

9-17 ....

18. **Kailas** (Tarchhen) (138) (243).

TABLE XVII

NINTH ROUTE TO HOLY KAILAS AND MANASAROVAR

FROM SIMLA via GARTOK—438 MILES

Simla (0) (0) [7,043] Viceregal Headquarters during summer, City, Hill station, Simla to Poo it is P. W. D. road and is called Hindustan-Tibet Road,

1 There are three houses and several walled enclosures here. A mandi is held here from the middle of July to the end of August, when merchants from Nilang and Rampur Bashahr State come here with barley and *phapar*-flour to be bartered with Tibetan salt, wool, and borax.

1. Phagoo (12) (12) Rest House,
2. Matiana (17) (29) R.,
3. Narkanda (11) (40) R.,
4. Thanadhar (11) (51) R., *sarai*, Rampur, Bashahr State, along the left bank of the Sutlej,
5. Nerth (11) (62) State *sarai*,
6. **Rampur** (9) (71) [3,063] town on the left bank of the Sutlej,
7. Gaura (7) (78) R.,
8. Sarhan or Sarahan (13) (91) R., from here up to Chini excellent scenery on both sides of the Sutlej,
9. Taranda (14) (105) R.,
10. Nichar (10) (115) [7,900] Forest Headquarters, right bank of the Sutlej,
11. Urni (13) (128) P. W. D. R.,
12. Chini (15) (143) state Bungalows and Tahsil, from Chini to Kanam good scenery,

Pangi (5) (148) P. W. D. R.,

13. Jangi (10) (158) P. W. D. R.,
14. Kanam (14) (172) P. W. D. R.,

• Chaisoo (10) (182) P. W. D. R.,

15. **Poo** (6) (188) Town, last Post Office, all provisions are to be taken from here for further journey, P. W. D. road ends, after 3m. cross the Sutlej by bridge to the left bank,
16. Mamgia (10) (198) village, monastery, ascent to the pass begins from here,

SHIPKI PASS (4) (202) [15,400] Indian boundary, pass is crossable from May to November,

17. Shipki camp (8) (210) [10,600] *le*.
18. Kuke (5) (215) village,
19. Tiag (15) (230) village, cross the Sutlej bridge to the right bank,
20. Miyang (12) (242) village,
21. Foot of Shiring la (8) (250) *le*, very cold, ascent to pass begins, Shiring la [16,400],
22. Nooh (15) (265) village,
23. Hulle (12) (277) *le*,
24. Khini-phuk (13) (290) village (2m. further one route splits to the right to Thhuling),
25. SHANGTSI ZONG (15) (305) [13,760] Chhabrang Zong's summer Headquarters,
26. Shang (6) (311) village,
27. Debring (14) (325) *le*, very cold, Loache la [18,510],
28. Daglag (14) (339) *le* ; Avilaptcha, Zongchhung la [17,400],

97. Thugholho Gompa, the Eighth Monastery of Manasarovar, the Headquarters of the Author in Manasa Khanda [*See p.* 133

98. "Janma Bhoomi" on the Holy Manas [*See p.* 82

99. 'Jnan Nauka' on the Holy Lake [See p. 82

100. Shree Kailas-manas Yajna-Vedi [See p. 134

101. **Marble Tablet on the Yajna-Vedi**

[*See p. 134*

102. **The Sources of the Four Great Rivers, as Described in Tibetan Scriptures (specially designed).**

Oil-painting by Earl E. H. Brewster, Almora [See p. 14

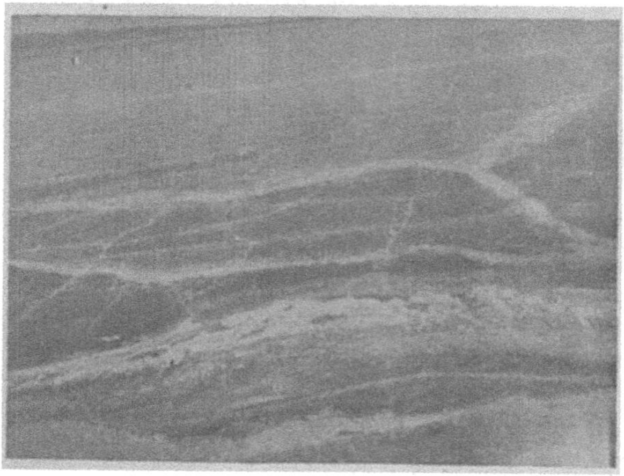

103. Fissures in Frozen Manasarovar
[See pp. 29 & 30

104. Unfissured Ice on Raksha Tal, as seen from th Island Lachato towards Topserma
[See pp. 29 & 30

105. A Pool of water with a Flock of Brahminy Ducks in the Frozen Manas
[See p. 32

29. Jingjum (12) (351) *le*,
30. **Gartok**[1] (9) (360) [15,100], summer capital of Western Tibet,
31. NOKYU TASAM (6) (366) 3 houses, first Tasam on Gartok-Lhasa caravan route,
8m. Dokyu, *le*,
5m., Par chhu *le*, on either bank of the river, two feet deep,
3m., Langpoche chhu *le*, on either bank of the river, 3 feet deep.
32. Chhopta (21) (387) 5m. *le*, ascent to Chargot la begins,
2m., Chargot la [16,200' *lapiche*.
2m., Ningri, C.,
33. MISSAR TASAM (18) (405) [14,300] 14m. second Tasam on the way to Lhasa, 3 houses,
34. **Tirthapuri** (4) (409) gompa (see p. 103 and Table VI).
35. Chukta chhu (15) (424) *le*,
36. **Kailas** (Tarchhen) (14) (438).

TABLE XVIII

TENTH ROUTE TO HOLY KAILAS AND MANASAROVAR

FROM SIMLA via THHULING—473 MILES.

Simla (0) (0) (see Table XVII).
1-23 ....
24. Khini-phuk (290) (290) village, 2m. further leave Gartok Route to the left,
25. Tibu (20) (310) *le*,
26. Niang (9) (319) *le*; Shangsi, *le*,
27. **Thhuling** (16) (335) (see Tables XV and XII).
28-36 ....
37. **Kailas** (Tarchhen) (138) (473).

TABLE XIX

ELEVENTH ROUTE TO HOLY KAILAS AND MANASAROVAR

FROM SRINAGAR (KASHMIR) via LADAKH AND GARTOK—598 MILES

Srinagar (0) (0) [5,260] Summer Capital of Jammu and Kashmir

[1] The two Garpons or Viceroys of Western Tibet (Urko-kong and Urko-yok) live here in summer and go to Gargunsa in winter months. Here are the two buildings of the two Viceroys, 8 houses, a *donkhang*, a monastery, and some black tents. A big horse-race fair called *Chhongtu* is held here on *Bhadrapada Purnima*, when the representatives of all the four Zongs (Governors) of Western Tibet assemble. The fair lasts for 4 or 5 days. A small mandi is held by the Bhotias, mostly of Johar and Niti, from the middle of August to the middle of Sept., though a few merchants go there earlier. It is also the Headquarters of the Indian Trade Agent, Western Tibet in summer. Rudok Zong is about 160m. from here.

State, the Paradise on Earth, P., T., College, House-boats, Banks, Hospitals, Clubs, Aerodrome, Fort, gardens, health-resorts, etc.,

1. Gandarbal (13) (13) P., T., R., health resort.
2. Kangan (11) (24) [5,795], P.R., Passports checked,
3. Gund (13) (37) [6,500] P.,
4. Sonmarg (14½) (51½) [8,750], P., T., R., health resort,
5. Baltal (9) (60½) [9,450] no village, R., (Amarnath cave is 12m. from here),

ZOZI LA (2½) (63) [11,578] Ladakh Province begins,

Machoi (6) (69) T., R., no village,

6. Matayan (7) (76) R.,
7. Drass (12½) (88½) [10,636] P., T., R., *sarai*, Buddhistic images on the road-side,
8. Samsa-kharbu (22½) (111) R.,
9. **Kargil** (16¼) (127¼) [8,790], P., T., H., R., Tahsil, etc.,
10. Mulbek (22½) (149¾) [10,350] R., first gompa on the way,

Nammik Top (6) (155¾) [13,000] about 1½m. steep ascent to pass; 1½m. steep descent from the pass,

11. Bodh-kharbu (8½) (164¼) R., *sarai*,

Fotu la (10) (174¼) [13,446] 1m. steep ascent to the pass; 1m. steep descent from the pass,

12. Lamyuru (5) (179¼) [11,400] one of the biggest monasteries in Ladakh,

Khalsi (10¼) (189½) P., T., (from here for nearly 270m. the route goes up along the Indus, leaving the river here and there),

13. Nurla (8½) (198) R.,
14. Saspul (14¾) (212¾) P., R.; 7½m. Bazgo, gompa,
15. Nyimoo (11½) (224¼)4m. gompa, R.; 13¾m. Pitak, gompa,
16. **Leh (Ladakh)** (17¾) (242) [11,503]4m. P., T., R., gompa, Wazir-I-Wazarat, Kashmir Joint Commissioner, Indian Joint Commissioner, Big mandi, trade centre of Yarkand, Kashgarh, Tibet, and India; last Post Office, take provisions for further journey, palace of old Raja of Stok of Ladakh,
17. Chushot (12) (254) village,

Hemmis garden (11) (265) Hemmis Gompa,[1] the biggest and the most famous monastery in Ladakh, is 1m. up the road,

[1] Hemmis or Himi is one of the oldest Buddhist monasteries. Jesus Christ spent some of his 'unknown years' here, studying Buddhism. The author was informed by one of the old monks of the monastery that one Russian traveller by name Notwitch visited this monastery and took away the *Namthar* or the biography of Jesus. It was written in that book that Jesus had some household quarrel with his parents and ran away from his home and came to *Gya-kar* (India). He had sojourned at *Chargot-ri* (Gridhrakuta or Rajagriha), *Varanasi* (Sarnath), and at several other places in India for some years and had learnt Pali and studied Buddhistic scriptures and had embraced Buddhism in the later days of his stay here. Jesus later on returned to his native land after several years and started a new religion

18. Marchalang (2) (267) village ; 5m. Ugu bridge,
19. Upshi (10) (277) 5m. village ; 7m. Miroo village,
20. Gya (17) (294) [13,500] 10m. village ; 5m. Shagrot, *le*, ascent up to the pass,

TAGLANG LA (12)(306)[17,500] 7m, last 3m. very steep ascent, *laptche*,

21. Debriug (4) (310) [15,780] very steep descent, *le*: 12m. Pongonagu, *le*,
22. Thugje (15) (325) 3m. *le*, gompa and some houses in caves; Pologonka la [16,400 ?],
23. Puga (16) (341) [14,300] hot springs, sulphur deposits, custom house,
24. Langsham (18) (359) custom shed, (on the other side of the river are the two big villages of Nyima and Moth ; the bed of the Indus is ¾m. broad here),
25. Dungti (18) (377) *le*,
26. Niguche (13) (390) *le*,
27. Phugche (14) (404) *le*,
28. Lagankhel (12) (416) *le* ; 7½m. Tetor-yongma, *le* ; 1½m. Tetor-kongma, *le*,
29. DEMCHHOK (12) (428) 3m. also called Demchhog, village, a few barley fields, Kashmir-Tibet boundary, hot springs up the village ; 7m. Tama-kolak, a little cultivation,
30. TASHIGONG (19) (447) [13,900] 12m. village with 25 houses, the gompa is situated on a mound in the middle of the Indus valley, originally it belonged to Ladakh, but it was later given to Sera Gompa and, in return Kashmir Government had obtained certain rights in Missar,

Confluence (4) (451) confluence of the Indus and Gartong chhu, from here five days' march up along the Gartong chhu,

31. Langmar (12) (463) village, a few plots of cultivation, 1m. further are the extensive Borax fields, situated on the right bank of the Gartong chhu,
32. **Gargunsa** (18) (481) [14,065] Winter Headquarters of the Viceroys of Western Tibet, gompa, a little cultivation, several black tents,
33. Namru (24) (505) village, a little cultivation, hot springs up the village situated in a valley,
34. **Gartok** (15) (520) (see Table XVII).

35-39 ....

40. **Kailas** (Tarchhen) (78) (598).

incorporating the principles of Buddhism in it. So it is that many of the sayings and teachings of Jesus Christ, including the 'Sermon on the Mount', appear to be verbatim translations of the teachings of Buddhism and Hinduism. The lama further informed that he had received a translation of the above mentioned *Namthar* which was in Roman characters but he could not tell whether the language was Russian or English. Later, when some white traveller visited this monastery, he took away that book, by paying a good present to the monk.

TABLE XX

TWELFTH ROUTE TO HOLY KAILAS AND MANASAROVAR

FROM LHASA via GYANTSE AND SHIGARTSE—**800** ? MILES

Lhasa [12,890].

1. Nethang.
2. Chhushul.
3. •Kamba-pachik.
4. Peteo.
5. Nak-karchhe Zong.
6. Ralung [14,700].
7. Kopshe.
8. **Gyantse** [13,120].
9. Tokri.
10. Panang Zong.
11. **Shigartse.** (Tashi Lhunpo) [12,850].
12. • Nathang Gompa.
13. Kangchhen Gompa.
14. Shipkiding.
15. Tashigong.
16. Pungchhok-ling.
17. Chakdhong.
18. Mohri.
19. Sang-ling.
20. Ngavring.
21. Ralung.
22. Kondun.
23. Korgep.
24. Sang-sang.
25. Sheru.
26. Kheto-rung.
27. Kheto.
28. Ruchen.
29. Rapka.
30. Samku.
31. Ukshu.
32. **Saka Zong.**
33. Lalung.
34. Nyukku.
35. Bank of a river.
36. Lukchang.
37. Tamsakrang.
38. TRADUM.
39. Lung-pharma.
40. Tootoo.
41. TUKSUM.
42. Ngakchaksung.
43. TAMSANG.
44. Sundo.
45. Lholung.
46. Tak-karpo.
47. Thokchen.
48. Ngalukro.
49. PARKHA.
50. **Kailas** (Tarchhen).

TABLE XXI

TARCHHEN TO THE SOURCE OF THE INDUS

via LHE LA AND BACK via TOPCHHEN LA—**91** MILES

Tarchhen (0) (0) Kailas-*parikrama* begins here (see Table II), 5m. Nyanri Gompa,

1 Based on the information obtained from a lay trader.

$4\frac{3}{4}$m. Dunglung chhu, up this valley one road goes to the source of the Indus,

Dira-phuk Gompa[1] ($12\frac{1}{4}$) ($12\frac{1}{4}$) $2\frac{1}{2}$m. second monastery of Kailas, most imposing view of Mount Kailas, leave the *pari-krama*-route to the right and proceed northwards up the Lha chhu.

$3\frac{1}{4}$m. Se-lungma, *le*,

$2\frac{1}{8}$m. on the left hand side is chhu-lungma, *le*,

$1\frac{1}{8}$m. Ke-lungma, *le*, from here steep ascent begins.

1. Do-lungma[2] ($7\frac{1}{4}$) ($19\frac{1}{2}$) $\frac{3}{4}$m. also called Do-lungva, *le*, very cold, from here very steep ascent over scree up to the pass,

LHE LA ($3\frac{1}{2}$) (23) also called Laptche-chipa la, *laptche*, cairns,

$5\frac{1}{4}$m. steep descent to Sharshumi, *le*,

6m. descent along the stream coming from Lhe la to its confluence with Lungdhep chhu (opposite this place Nyima-lung chhu falls into the Lungdhep on its right bank),

2. Lungdhep camp ($13\frac{1}{2}$) ($36\frac{1}{2}$) $2\frac{1}{4}$m. along the left bank of the Lung-dhep chhu to Lungdhep camp, *le* on either bank of the river, black tents, (about 1m. down this place, situated on the right bank of the river, is the hill Lungdhep-ngingri at the foot of which the river broadens into a lake called Lungdhep-ngingri tso) cross the 2 to 3 feet deep river to its right bank,

$7\frac{1}{2}$m. over ups and downs to Rungmagem camp,[3] *le*, black tents, cross the stream to its right bank,

$\frac{3}{4}$m. very steep ascent to the top of Senge-chava, *laptche*,

$\frac{3}{4}$m. very steep descent to the Bokhar chhu, cross the 2 feet deep river to its left bank,

3. **Senge Khambab**[4] ($9\frac{1}{2}$) (46) [16,956] nearly $\frac{1}{2}$m. to Senge

1 There are three Routes from Dira-phuk to go to the Senge-Khambab : (1) up the Dunglung chhu via Dunglung la, (2) up the Lha chhu via Tsethi and Tsethi-lachen la, and (3) up the Lha chhu via Lhe la, which is the shortest of the three routes ; the second route is very bad and a long one ; and the first one is the longest of the three. For returning to Tarchhen from Senge Khambab the route by the Topchhen la is the nearest. Tibetan pilgrims to the Senge Khambab follow the route given in this table because in so doing they can also complete the circuit of the Holy Kailas by avoiding the steep ascent and descent of Dolma la.

2 *Lung, lungma, lungba*, and *lungva*, all mean a valley.

3 The upper course of the river is called Munjan chhu and the lower course Rungmagem chhu till it joins the Senge or the Indus. Besides the local people, shepherds from the eastern and north-eastern parts of Lhasa especially Amdo, come here with hundreds of yaks and thousands of sheep and goats to graze their cattle and at the same time do a number of rounds of Kailas and Manas ; as such they stay in the Senge area for four or five years continuously and then return to their homes. There are extensive pasture lands here and the dairy products of this region are considered the best in the whole of Tibet. One may start good dairy farms here with great advantage.

4 Here are four big fresh water springs and several small ones welling up out of the ground. Nearby is a quadrangular *mani*-wall with several *mani*-slabs. There are some stones over $1\frac{1}{2}$ feet high, each containing a single letter of the *mani-mantra*. On another stone the wheel of life (*jeevana chakra* containing the letters of the *mani-mantra*) is inscribed,

Khambab or the **Source of the Indus**, *le*, black tents in the surroundings,

2m. back to Rungmagem camp, *le*,

3m. steep ascent,

1¼m. very steep ascent to Lungdhep-ngingri, *le*,

2m. Lungdhep chhu, *le* (from here up along the Lungdhep chhu), it is all marshy bog-land up to the foot of Topchhen la,

4½m. Nyimalung chhu, cross it to its left bank (this falls into the Lengdhep, about 250 yards down below, almost opposite the Lhe la chhu),

4m. further up cross the 1½ to 2 feet Lungdhep to its left bank,

1¼m. further, one big stream falls into Lungdhep on its right bank,

4. Foot of Topchhen la (20) (66) 2m. further up, camp at the foot of the pass, *le*, very cold,

TOPCHHEN LA[1] (5) (71) 5m. very steep ascent through huge boulders to Topchhen la, about 200 yards on the pass, the whole pass was under snow when the author crossed it,

6¾m. very steep descent over huge boulders,

5m. descent down the Topchhen valley, Kailas is seen from here, *laptche*, cairns,

¾m. further down is the confluence of Topchhen chhu and Lham-chhukhir chhu, there are big *le* everywhere along the Topchhen valley, cross the 3 feet deep Lham-chhukir to its right bank a little up the confluence and then proceed,

Zuthul-phuk Gompa (13¾) (84¾) 1¼m. mild descent to the gompa (see Table II),

5. **Tarchhen** (6¼) (91).

The temperature of the combined waters of the springs was 48.5°F. The water coming out of the springs forms into weedy ponds and flows out into the Bokhar chhu as a small brook ½m. down below. Just by the side of the springs, situated on the edge of a huge slab of white rock are three pillar-like cairns or *lha-do* or *lha-to* (gods'-stones), *laptches*, and some *mani*-slabs. On one of these there are some coloured rags of cloth—*tarchok*, offered by some Tibetan pilgrims. The rugged hill on the north of the spring is called Senge-yura and to the south situated on the left bank of the Bokhar chhu is Senge-chava, crossing which one gets down to Rungmagem camp. To the north-east of the Senge Khambab is the Lama la [17,800]. The author visited the Source of the Indus on July 4, 1937, and stayed in the surroundings for three days. Senge is also pronounced as Sengi or Singi, and Khambab is pronounced as Khamba or Kabab in Central and Eastern Tibet.

[1] Topchhen la is the water-shed between the Lungdhep chhu (the highest of the head-streams of Senge in this area) and the Topchhen chhu (which meets the Lham-chhukhir chhu a little up Zuthul-phuk Gompa to form Zhong chhu). These two rivers are just on either side of the Topchhen la but Dr. Sven Hedin placed them nearly 20m. apart as the crow flies. This is due to the fact that he did not negotiate this pass. Anyway, this is given here as a piece of information for the guidance of future explorers. The author is the first non-Tibetan who had crossed the Lhe la and the Topchhen la.

TABLE XXII

TARCHHEN TO THE SOURCES OF THE BRAHMAPUTRA AND THE TAG

AND BACK TO TAKLAKOT via GURLA LA 198 MILES

Tarchhen (0) (0) (see Table II),
3m. Zhong chhu, *le* (for details up to Seralung see Table, III),
5m. Philung-kongma chhu,
$6\frac{1}{4}$m. Gyuma chhu,
1. Kuglung (17) (17) $2\frac{3}{4}$m. Kuglung, *le*,
$8\frac{1}{2}$m. Palchen chhu,
$1\frac{1}{4}$m. Palchung chhu,
2. Seralung Gompa (16) (33) $6\frac{1}{4}$m. sixth monastery of the Holy Manas,
$3\frac{1}{2}$m. ascent and descent to Harkong, black tents, *le*,
4m. Chhomokur, black tents, *le*,
3. Namarding (15) (48) $7\frac{1}{2}$m. cross the Namarding chhu, Manas is seen from here,
2m. up the valley,
$1\frac{1}{2}$m. ordinary ascent,
$1\frac{1}{4}$m. very steep ascent to Changsha la,
$1\frac{1}{2}$m. very steep descent, *le*,
CHHUMIK-THUNGTOL[1] ($7\frac{1}{2}$) ($55\frac{1}{2}$) $1\frac{1}{2}$m. through big boulders and stones to the sacred spring Chhumik-thungtol, named Chakko in Sven Hedin's maps, from here up to Tagramochhe path goes along the Tag,
LANGCHEN KHAMBAB ($\frac{3}{4}$) ($56\frac{1}{4}$) spring gushing out of black boulders and flowing into the Tag that is nearby; this is also a sacred spring and is marked by several cairns and a big *lapche*, in which is fixed a small pole bedecked with pieces of coloured rags like a scare-crow,

1 *Chhu* means water, *mik* means eye, *thung* means see, and *tol* means slavation or *Nirvana*, i.e. whosoever even sees this spring obtains salvation, or whosoever sees this eye-like spring obtains salvation. The spring Chhumik-thungtol is situated in a narrow valley of the Tag with high volcanic mountains on either side of the river. It is surrounded by a big quadrangular *mani*-wall 16 yds. long and 10 yds. broad, and the flags and festoons on it are overhanging the spring, which is 3-4 feet deep and 3 feet in diameter. Through the crystal clear charming turquoise-blue water could be clearly seen the blue and red beads, four inferior turquoises, two bangles, some shells and some other petty articles thrown in as offerings by devout pilgrims. The water in the spring flows out from the bottom in the form of a small brook, into the Tag on its left bank a few yards below. Sven Hedin has wrongly named it Chakko. It is written in *Kangri Karchhak* that Ganga or Langchen Khambab take its rise from Kailas but it appears here; and then re-appears at Dulchu Gompa. The names of the three volcanic mountains between which the spring is situated are Chenresig (white), Chhagnadorje (blue), and Jambyang (yellow). There are several cairns set up by pilgrims all round and in the neighbourhood of the spring.

$2\frac{1}{4}$m. further there are white sands for 2m. on either bank and in the bed of the river,

4. Tag-ramochhe ($2\frac{3}{4}$) (59) $\frac{1}{2}$m. Tagramochhe, big camps, *le*, black tents (from here one path goes up along Tag tsangpo for about 10m. to the **Kanglung Kangri** glaciers, the **Source of the Tag Tsangpo**),

1m. on marshes to Tag-ramochhe chhu,

1m. steep ascent to Tak-karbu la, *le*, *laptche*,

$5\frac{1}{4}$m. proceed on beds of sharp gravel, stones, and big boulders, over ups and downs to Chamar, *le*, a hill on the left side of the road, there are some *laptche* and *tarchoks* and *mani*-stones on the top of the hill; Kanglung glaciers are just opposite this hill and present a beautiful view; there are several small lakelets between Tak-karbu la and Chamar,

TAG LA (8) (67) [17,382] $\frac{3}{4}$m. *laptche*, *tarchok*, cairns,

$3\frac{1}{2}$m. Tamlung tso, extensive camps on the shores of the lake, there are also several other small lakelets connected with one another,

$2\frac{1}{2}$m. along the banks of the lake on marshes, (a stream starts from this lake and flows into the Angsi chhu),

$2\frac{1}{2}$m. further on one path goes to Kongyu tso, Bongba, etc.,

$2\frac{1}{4}$m. over gentle up towards the south (Kongyu tso is seen from here on the north),

5. Angsi chhu (13) (80) $2\frac{1}{4}$m. descent, steep descent, very steep descent, and descent to Angsi chhu, *le* on either side of the river, cross the 3 feet deep river to its right bank, the river is broadened into lakelets at several places, the valley is broad and grand, good pastures,

$\frac{1}{2}$m. Angsi valley,

$1\frac{1}{4}$m. mild and steep ascent,

$2\frac{1}{2}$m. very gentle up on a plateau to Shibla-ringmo la, the pass is very narrow like a lane, about 4 feet broad between two steep beautiful mountains on either side, *laptche*, very near the pass on the right hand side of the road a deep lake, (about $\frac{3}{4}$m. before reaching the pass there is another lake on the left side of the road), several herds of *goa* and *cho* are seen on the plateau,

$\frac{3}{4}$m. steep descent down a narrow gauge to a beautiful lake situated on the left side of the road,

$3\frac{1}{4}$m. ups and downs on beds of stones (midway is a beautiful semi-circular lake with an island in the middle), some more lakelets, cross a stream,

$\frac{1}{2}$m. ascent,

Chema-yungdung chhu ($9\frac{3}{4}$) ($89\frac{3}{4}$) $\frac{1}{2}$m. very steep descent to Chema-yungdu chhu, the whole bed of the river on the right bank is full of sand of white opaque quartz as if covered with snow, like the Angsi, this valley also is broad and the river broadens into a series of lakelets at several places,

CHEMA-YUNGDUNG-PU ($5\frac{1}{2}$) ($95\frac{1}{4}$) $5\frac{1}{2}$m. up along the Chema-yungdung, *le* everywhere on the way, just in front, on the other side of the river is Chema-yungdu-pu, the first glacier of the Tamchhok Khambab; huge debris and landslips are lodged at the tongue of the glacier; there are some lakelets on the debris and on the glacier proper, from here the path takes a westward turn,

6. **Tamchok Khambab**[1] ($\frac{3}{4}$) (96) $\frac{3}{4}$m. the **Source of the Brahmaputra,**

Tamchok Khambab Kangri (1) (97) 1m. the Tamchok Khambab Kangri, glacial source of the Brahmaputra,

$12\frac{3}{4}$m. Shibla-ringmo la,

7. Angsi chhu (17) (114) $4\frac{1}{4}$m. Angsi chhu, *le*,

1 Tamchok Khambab (*Tamchok* means the celestial horse, and *Khambab* means coming out of the mouth of) the Horse-Mouthed river has got its traditional source here. Here is a big boulder about 12 feet high on which there are two footprints, over which is built a loose stone-walled hut facing the east. On the top of the hut are placed two horns of a wild yak. Adjacent to the boulder there are one roofed and two unroofed *donkhangs* of loose stones, piled up crudely. All around are several cairns. There is a dry spring nearby which is said to contain water in summer and rainy seasons. The river Tamchok Khambab or Chema-yungdung as is called here, is 50 yards from this monument or *chhorten*. 1m. up this place is another glacier which the guide said was the main glacier of Tamchok Khambab, for the river Tamchok Khambab actually takes its rise here. Nyakoras who regularly come here every year to graze their cattle give the following derivation of the word Tamchok Khambab: *ta* means horse, *amchok* means ears, and *khambab* means coming out of the mouth of; so, the meaning of the word Tamchok Khambab is 'Horse-ears-mouthed-river'. The Tamchok Khambab glacier and the Chema-yungdung-pu glacier are considered to be the two ears of the Brahmaputra and go by the common name of Chema-yungdung-pu or simply Chema-yungdung; and the spring near the *chhorten* is the mouth. It is also pronounced as Chema-yuntung, Chema-yungdung, or Choma-yungtung. *Chema* means sand and *yungtung* or *yungdung* means *svastika* (卐). Opposite this monument is a broad-faced peak separating the two glaciers of Tamchok Khambab atleast for the appearance. It is just possible that these two glaciers are connected with each other on the back of this peak. From Chema-yungdung-pu glacier this broad-faced peak appears to be a sharp pointed conical peak.

To the west or north-west of the main glacier of the Tamchok Khambab there is another small glacier behind which is the Angsi glacier. The author visited the source of the Brahmaputra on June 17 and 18, 1937, when the whole bed of the river 15 to 60 feet broad was frozen *en block*, 6 to 7 feet thick, for 3m. beginning from the main glacier downwards. In the middle of the frozen bed of the river there was, as it were, a beautiful trench 3 to 6 feet broad and about 6 feet deep, between the perpendicular ice-walls of which the river was flowing with gurgling noises. Nyakora nomad shepherds go there in August for yak-hunting, for wild yak is found here in large numbers. Sven Hedin has wrongly placed the source of the Brahmaputra in the Kubi kangri glaciers, instead of in the Chema-yungdung glaciers, partly because he could not get transport to this real source. The subject has been fully discussed by the author in his book 'Exploration in Tibet' published by the Calcutta University, now running the second edition. There is plenty of grass in the Chema-yungdung valley and many shepherds came here to graze their cattle. The white quartz sands of the river are very conspicuous for about 10m. from the source downwards and they could be seen from long distances as if there had been a fresh snow fall.

13m. Tag la,

8. Tag-ramochhe (21) (135) 8m. Tag-ramochhe camp, *le*,

4½m. Chhumik-thungtol, sacred spring, *le*,

14½m. almost along the Tag, cross the 3½ feet deep and furious Tag to its left bank,

1¼m. further down Tomomopo, geysers, boiling hot springs, luke warm water springs, *kund*, *le*,

9. Nyomba-chhuten (16¼) (155) ¾m. Nyomba-chhuten (mad hot springs, *le*, (see p. 47),

'3½m. ascent and descent into the Nimapendi valley to Nonokur shepherd camp, (see Table III), cross the 2 feet deep river to its left bank,

3¼m. Yerngo Gompa, seventh monastery of the Lake,

10. **Thugolho** (9) (164) 2¼m. Thugolho Gompa, eighth monastery of the Holy Lake, the Headquarters of the author (see Table III),

9½m. Gurla la,

11. Baldak (18) (182) 8½m. to Baldak camp, *le*, (see p.p. 121 and 122),

12. **Taklakot** (16) (198).

TABLE XXIII

TAKLAKOT TO THE SOURCE OF THE KARNALI

AT MAPCHA CHUNGO—23 MILES.

Taklakot (0) (0) (see Table V),

1. Harkong (14¼) (14¼),

2. **Mapcha Chungo** (8¾) (23) spring, **Traditional Source of the Map chhu or Karnali.** The glacial and genetic source of the Karnali is in the Lampiya pass, which is at a distance of two short days' march from here.

TABLE XXIV

TARCHHEN TO THE SOURCE OF THE SUTLEJ

AT DULCHU GOMPA—21 MILES.

Tarchhen (0) (0) (see Table V),

2¼m. Lha chhu,

After the Angsi and the Rongak chhu join the Chema-yungdung, a little further down, the Chema-yungdung tsangpo—as it is called there—broadens enormously into two big lakes called Rapgyal-chhungo and Guru-kyok. The Bhotia merchants who go from Manasarovar beyond the Kubi or Kupi chhu for purchase of wool regard this broadened river to be the source of the Brahmaputra, and call it Brahma-kund. As such, they consider it sacred and bathe in it.

3m. Karleb chhu,
$7\frac{1}{4}$m. Changje-Changju camp, *le*,

1. **Dulchu Gompa** (21) (21) $8\frac{1}{2}$m. Dulchu Gompa, some black tents, *mani*-walls, about 250 yards from the gompa there are several fresh water springs welling out of the marshy ground, which the Tibetans assert to be the **Traditional Source of the Langchen Khambab or the Sutlej**; the Darma pass wherein lies the source of the Darma-yankti (Langchen Tsangpo) the biggest of the headstreams of the Sutlej, is at a distance of four days' march from here.

TABLE XXV

ALMORA TO PINDARI GLACIER—

74 MILES

Almora (0) (0) (see p.p. 90-92).

1. Takula (15) (0) P., D.B., S., shop,
2. BAGESHVAR (12) (27) confluence of the Saraju and the Gomati, P., H., D.B., S., *D.*, bazaar, temples etc. (see p. 95 & Table XI),
3. Kapkot (14) (41) D.B., *D.*, shops,
   Loharkhet (9) (50) D.B., shop,
4. Dhakuri (6) (56) D.B., shop,
   Khati (5) (61) D.B., shop,
   Dwali (7) (68) D.B.,
5. Phurkiya (3) (71) D.B.,

Pindari Glacier (3) (74) one of the most beautiful glaciers; 1m. before reaching the glacier there is a cave, believed to be the winter abode of the goddess Nanda Devi. To the east of the glacier is the peak Nandakot (22,510); to the west is Trisul (23,306); and to the north is Nanda Devi (25,645); From here one path goes over the snow range to the village Martoli on the third route to Kailas (see Table XI). This pass was first crossed by Trail in 1830. So it is called Trail's pass (17,700). There is a veteran guide by name Divan Singh in the village Martoli, who has guided several tourists over this difficult andyet interesting pass from the mountaineering point of view.

TABLE XXVI

SRINAGAR TO AMARNATH

VIA PAHALGAM 59×28¾=87¾ MILES

Srinagar (0) (0) [5,260] Capital of Jammu and Kashmir State,

9m. Pampur, saffron fields, from which saffron is collected, from *Ashvin Purnima* (October),

9½m. Avantipura, ruins of old temples,

7m. Sangam, confluence of Jhelum and Vishva rivers,

3½m. Bijbihara, town,

4m. Khanabal, Jammu-Srinagar road meets here, Jammu is 173m. from here,

1. ANANTA-NAG[1] (34) (34) [5,300] 1m. also called Islamabad, town,

2m. Gautam-nag, spring,

1¼m. Bavan, village,

1m. Mattan[2], *Pandas* of Amarnath live here,

¾m. Bunzu, situated in the mountain on the right side of the road, there is a cave 200 yards long, the cave is very dark and one shall have to take a torch to get in, at places one shall have to crawl on the belly,

8¼m. Aishmukam, there is a Mohammedan shrine here,

2½m. Ganeshpura, Head-Works of Martand canal,

3m. Batkut, one third of the offerings of Amarnath go to the Mohammedans of this village,

2. **Pahalgam**[3] (25) (59) [7,200] 6m. to Pahalgam camping ground,

[1] *Ananta* means many and *nag* means springs. So Anantanag means place of many springs. From the foot of a hill here several springs are swelling out forming into a big *kund* (tub or tank), 4 feet deep, which has been paved with slabs of stones on all sides. The water from this *kund* falls into another *kund* and thence a regular stream flows out. From here one road goes to Achhabal and one to Verinag.

[2] Here is also a big spring with two *kunds* which are each 12 feet deep. Two miles from here situated on a mountain are the ruins of the famous Martand (Sun) temple, which was constructed by the king Lalitaditya who ruled over Kashmir from 699 to 735. The foundation of the temple is 225 feet by 150 feet and 84 feet high.

[3] From Srinagar to Pahalgam for a distance of 59m. there is bus service. For going to Amarnath one can get coolies, *dandies*, and ponies from here. Every arrangement shall have to be made for the to and fro journey of Amarnath, which is 28¾m. from here. One can go there very comfortably in 3½ days and return in two days. For the *Shravana Purnima* grand arrangements are made by the Dharmarth Department of the Kashmir Government. The whole road is repaired and at every stage shops are opened and all foodstuffs are sold at graded rates fixed by the Kashmir Durbar. The wages of ponies, coolies, etc. are also fixed. Every arrangement is made for *sadhus* regarding food, clothing, tent etc. The Superintendent of the Dharmarth department with his staff, police, travelling dispensaries, accompanies the pilgrim parties; 20,000 to 30,000 rupees are spent by the Department to make arrangements for the comfort and convenience of pilgrims. Shree 108 Shankaracharya of Sharda Peetha starts with a silver *chhadi*, Shiva's standard, from Srinagar on foot and reaches Pahalgam by the tenth day of the bright half of the month of *Shravana*. From here the whole pilgrim party starts in the 12th. One can also visit Amarnath on *Ashadha Purnima, Bhadrapada Purnima*, or on any suitable date, but one shall have to make one's own arrangements.

shops, cold place, health resort, confluence of Liddar and Sesbnag rivers,

1m. Pahalgam, village,

1m. Pahalgam, pilgrim-sheds on the right bank of Seshnag stream,

2½m. Frishin, last village,

1. Chandanvadi[1] (8½) (8½) [9,500] 4m. cross the Asthan-marg stream to its left bank (a little before reaching this place is the confluence of Asthan-marg and Sesh-nag rivers), five Pilgrim-sheds, one Tourist-hut with two beds, hirable,

1½m. ascent to Pishu-ghati[2], forest ends here,

2¼m. Zozipal,

2¼m. Kutta (the first ¾m. steep ascent),

1m. [11,730] Seshnag lake[3],

2. Wavjan (8) (16½) [12,320] 1m. Waujan or Wavjan, 5 Pilgrim-sheds and one Tourist-hut with two beds, scarcity of fuel from here onwards, a sort of furze or juniper which burns even when green is used as fuel, place of severe winds (cross the ice bridge to its left bank and after 1m. recross to its right bank, from here begins the steep ascent up to Mahagunus),

1½m. Ashad-dhaki, C.,

1½m. [14,000?] Mahagunus pass, before reaching the pass and on the descent form the pass for a short distance one may have to go on ice, from the pass up to the Pancha-tarani it is one continuous steep descent but up to Kailnad it is very steep,

1m. Huksar,

¾m. Kailnad, stream, Asthau-marg route meets here, (from here Hatyara-talav is 2m. ascent where hundreds of pilgrims died once due to heavy snow fall ; hence the name Hatyara-talav—the murderous lake ; ½m. further

[1] From here one road goes to Amarnath via Asthan-marg and Hatyari-talav but it has now been abandoned by the Kashmir Government. The stage Chandanvadi is situated in the midst of a pine forest. A little beyond Chandanvadi huge avalanches are lodged on the Sheshnag river forming naturol ice bridges.

[2] From Chandanvadi to Pishu-ghati it is a very hard ascent but in 1937 or so, another road has been made to reduce the steepness of the ascent, but it is a little longer than the first.

[3] The Lake Sheshnag is 500 feet below the level of the road situated in the icy lap of the Kohenhar glacier [17,000]. The beautiful snow peaks and the Kohenhar glaciers are situated a few miles on the north of the lake and form a picturesque background to it, and the melted snow water of these glaciers feed the lake. The river Sheshnag flows out of the lake in beautiful cascades. One shall have to get down for nearly a mile from the road to reach the shore of the lake. Due to the presence of gypsum in the surrounding mountains the water in the lake is milky white. The scenery of the lake is very sublime and fascinating and the spiritual vibration of the lake is superior to that of Amarnath.

very steep ascent to Saskati [13,860]; from here 3m. very steep and headlong descent on scree to Asthanmarg [10,800]; 4m. steep descent to Chandanvadi; a total of 9½m. from Kailnad to Chandanvadi), from here up to Panchatarani one shall have to cross the stream thrice from one side to the other,

2m. Nagarpal, huge boulder,

3. Panchatarani[1] (8¼) (24¾) [12,015] 1½m. cross the river to its right bank, 5 Pilgrim-sheds, one Tourist-hut with two beds,

Amarnath Cave[2] (4) (28¾) [12,729] there is an ice image of *Shiva-*

[1] Before reaching this stage one shall have to cross the five branches of Panchatarani. Panchatarani is a tributary of the river Sindh, which in turn is a tributary of the river Jhelum. From here one path goes direct to Amarnath over a very steep mountain called Bhirav-ghati [14,350]. Amarnath is at a distance of 3m. by this route. One shall have to start from Panchatarani to Amarnath and then return back to this place or to Wavjan according to one's own capacity. After going for a mile from Panchatarani there is a steep ascent of ¾m. to a pass; from here the road takes a sharp turn to the right. Leaving a few places here and there from here upto Amarnath one shall have to go over a glacier or over several feet thick ice, that has been lodged in the bed of the Amaravati river. About 200 yards of ascent takes one to the cave of Amarnath.

[2] The cave of Amarnath is about 150 feet cubical. The whole cave leaks from the roof with the exception of a small space under the projection of a rock (as much as 3 persons could lie down side by side) on the left hand side at the entrance of the cave while going in; so the whole cave is damp. It seems that the walls of the cave are of gypsum. There are two holes in the northern wall of the cave, from which water trickles out and freezes into ice as soon as it comes out. One of the holes is bigger, below which a huge snow *linga* is formed which is the famous snow image of Amarnath. On the left side of the *linga* is formed another

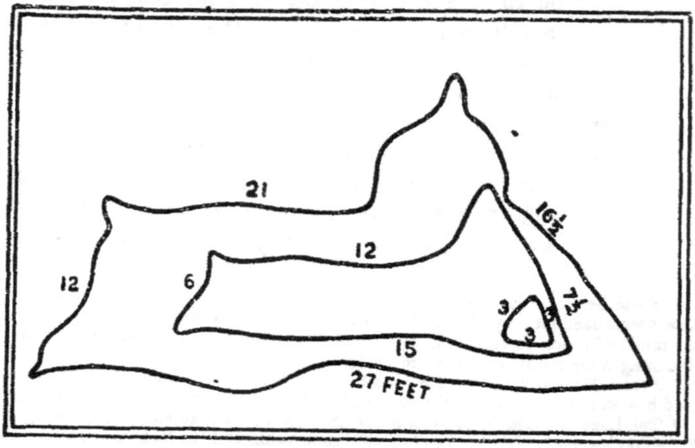

Comparative Sizes of the Snow Image of Amarnath in Different months.

Perpendicular height of the Image

on July 21, 1929	7½ feet
on August 20, 1929	4 feet
on September 18, 1929	1 foot

linga in the cave. In the inner roof of the Amarnath cave there is not one, as is wrongly described by many people, but there are several pairs of wild pigeons, raven, crow, yellow-billed chough, red-billed chough, sparrow, owl, *mina*, and some other birds. Besides these birds, kites are seen flying over the cave. Just below the cave and the surrounding regions there are marmots and wild rats.

ice formation called Ganesh and on its right Parvati and Bhairav, but by *Shravana Purnima* all these three melt away. So, *Pandas* bring some blocks of ice from down below and place them here and wrap some blankets round them. The cave is facing south and sun's rays do not fall directly on the image of Amarnath. So the snow image of Amarnath does not completely melt away in summer. The stories regarding the snow image of Amarnath that it grows gradually in the bright half of the lunar month up to full moon day and melts away in the dark fortnight of the month by the new moon day, are completely false and fabrications. The author stayed in the cave for a fortnight beginning from August 8, 1929, and closely studied the subject and also took measurements of the snow image on *Ashadha, Shravana*, and *Bhadrapada Purnimas* (full moon days). The perpendicular height of the image was 7½, 4 and 1 foot respectively. In July the shape of the *linga* was sharp and conspicuous, in August it was ordinary, and in September the form of the image has completely gone away and a triangular block of ice one foot thick was all that was left. So it is evident that the snow image in Amarnath cave forms in six months and melts in the succeeding six months like any other glaciers, or ice blocks.

Inside the cave of Amarnath there is a small cave on the left side of the image, from which a chalk-like substance is dug out and taken as *vibhuti* of Amarnath. On *Shravani* day the Mohammedans of Batkot sell this white substance and those who visit the cave at other times may take as much as they like. On chemical examination it is found to contain calcium chloride in large quantities and calcium sulphate in sufficient quantities. On the western side of the cave there is a small stream called Amar Ganga in which pilgrims take their bath. There are large quantities of this white substance in the bed of this stream also.

Beginning from Chandanvadi up to Amarnath and three miles further up and in by-valleys, *Gujjars* (grazers especially of buffaloes and goats) of Punjab and Chaupans (sheep grazers) of Kashmir come in rainy season with their buffaloes, goats, and sheep, and camp at various places. They are all Mohammedans. About 400 years back the Mohammedan shepherds of Batkot (a village 6m. before reaching Pahalgam), gave information to the Hindus of Kashmir about the existence of this cave. Thus began the worship of the snow image in this cave. All the offerings that are made to this image on *Shravani* day (money, fruits, clothes, etc.) are divided into three shares : of these one share goes to Shree Shankaracharya Math of Srinagar, one goes to the *Pandas*, and one to the Mohammedans of Batkot, whose ancestors showed the caves to the Hindus. In return the Mohammedans of Batkot undertake the duty of repairing the road every year from Pahalgam to Amarnath for *Shravani Purnima*.

There is no mention of Amarnath either in *Shiva Purana* or in any other *Purana*. There is a detailed description of all the *tirthas* of Kashmir in *Nilamat Purana*, one of the oldest *Puranas* of Kashmir, but in *sloka* 1535 there is a mere mention of the name Amarnath. In that very *Purana, Vitasta* or the Jhelum is described as the greatest and holiest of the *tirthas* of Kashmir, but nothing about Amarnath. Similarly in *Rajatarangini*, the famous history of Kashmir, in sloka 267 of the first part, there is only the mere mention of the word Amareshvara and no description of it. This clearly goes to prove that the present Amarnath is not the one that is mentioned in *Nilamat Purana* or *Rajatarangini*. But Dr. Stein, who has translated *Rajatarangini* into English, says that the simple mention of the name Amarnath, in *Rajatarangini*, it seems that it must have been a very ordinary place at that time. One old Kashmiri Pandit told the author that the names of all the *tirthas* of Kashmir are given in *Bhavani Sahasranama*, but no mention is made of Amarnath. It is also said that *Amar-katha* was written only about a century back by a Kashmiri Pandit and that no mention of it is made in any Sanskrit work or in any history. An old Kashmiri Pandit of Anantanag said that Pandit Haridas Trikku, a relative of Dewan Nandaram of Kabul, discovered the cave of Amarnath for the first time about 225 years back. Then the route was via Bhairav-ghati ; about a century later, Sant Singh, a relative of Raja Ranjit Singh, visited this cave by another route by which the *yatra* goes now-a-days ; as such, the route is up to day called Sant Singh's route.

There is no spring or lakelet just on the roof of Amarnath cave, for the mountain rises

TABLE XXVII

RAXAUL TO PASHUPATINATH—
77 MILES

Raxaul[1] (Indian) (0) (0) Railway Terminus of B. N. W. Ry.,
½m. Raxaul (Nepali), Light Railway,
3½m. Birganj, Railway station, Bazar, *dharmashala,*
1. Amlekhganj (24) (24) 20m. Railway Terminus, bazaar, hotels, during pilgrim-season goods lorries are used for carrying passengers between Amlekhganj and Bhimphedi,
6m. Chandi-mayi's temple, from here buses pass through two tunnels about a furlong long,
2. Bhimphedi[2] (27) (51) 21m. bazaar, *D.*, change of passport here, cross the river to its right bank,

abruptly from the cave upwards. Getting down from the cave, cross the Amravati to its left bank by an ice bridge. After proceeding for two or three furlongs, recross the Amravati by another ice bridge to its right bank and proceed up the Jnana Ganga northwards. On the way there are several caves, of which four still contain ice. One of them contains as much of ice as in Amarnath cave, with two or three *Shivalinga*-like protuberances on the mass of ice. All these caves are situated on the right side of the path while going up at a distance of a furlong. No shepherds pass by this way. The path is either on ice or over scree. After a steep and hard ascent one reaches the top of Amarnath mountain or Amarnath pass. Getting down a few yards to the other side of the mountain are two beautiful crystal clear blue watered lakelets situated amidst a snowfield or glacier. One is called **Jnana-sar** and is bow-like in shape and some icebergs are floating in it. The temperature of the water was 34°F. The outer lakelet is called **Soma-sar** and is eye-like in shape and is a little smaller but much deeper. These two lakes are separated by a huge mass of ice. There is a subterranean passage from the latter into the former, out of which a stream flows out into the Zozi la stream falling towards Drass. Getting down from the lake one path goes to Matayan on Zozi la-Ladakh road. The author visited this place on August 23, 1929 when he sojourned in the Amarnath cave.

Just opposite the cave of Amarnath, there is a mountain called Bhairav-ghati, crossing which one path goes direct to Panchatarani. Several years back it is said that some stray pilgrims use to fling themselves down this top and give up their lives in anticipation of salvation; so also from the top of the Amarnath cave. Hence on *Shravana Purnima* day police are posted on the way to Bhairav-ghati and to the top of the Amarnath cave to avoid any accident. The pilgrimage begins at 7 a.m. on that day and is over by 2 or 3 p.m. and nobody is allowed to stay after that. From Amarnath cave one path goes down the Amravati up to its confluence with Panchatarani. The combined river is called Sindh. Then get down the river to Baltal. Srinagar to Baltal is 50m. and Baltal to Amarnath cave it is 12m. One can visit Amarnath by this route in June and July (*Jyeshtha* and *Ashadha*) when the ice bridges on the river are still in tact.

[1] One can reach Raxaul via Ayodhya and Gorakhpur, or via Samastipur and Muzzaffarpur. From here Nepal-Raxaul is at a distance of ½m. wherefrom Light Railway Line of Nepal begins. For going to Kathmandu or Pashupathinath one shall have to secure the passport of Nepal Government, but on the occasion of *Shivaratri*, for seven days before, and ten days after that day, the gates of Nepal are as it were open to the outsider, and the passport slips are nominally given at the railway station at the time of issuing tickets, just to ascertain the exact number of pilgrims who have visited Nepal. From Nepal-Raxaul up to Amlekhganj there is train service for 24m. Only half fares are charged from the pilgrims during this period. Due to heavy rush of pilgrims at this time most of the third class passengers shall have to travel in goods wagons, closely packed up.

[2] One shall have to engage coolies, *dandies* etc. from here. From here up to Kathmandu there are *dharmashalas* in every *chatti* and temporary tents and free catering houses are set up by the Nepal Durbar for the service of *sadhus* and the needy pilgrims. In this pilgrimage one shall have to go on foot or *dandy* between Bhimpedi and Thankot, a distance of 16m. and the remaining distance could be done either by train or by bus. Of this distance of 16m.,

2½m. very steep ascent to Chisa-garhi, again change of passport, old fort, shops,
½m. ascent,
2½m. very steep descent to the village Kuli-khani,
½m. cross the river to the *Chatti* Kuli-khani, shops, *D.*, tents for pilgrims,

3. Markhu (8) (59) 2m. shop, *D.*,
2½m. ascent,
½m. descent to the village Chitlang,
2m. very steep ascent to Chandan-garhi, fine view of Nepal valley and the snow peaks,
2½m. very steep descent to Pani-ghat, *chatti*, shops,

Thankot (8) (67) ½m. descent, *langar* or free feeding house for *sadhus*, during pilgrim season buses run from here up to Kathmandu,
1½m. ropeway station,
5m. Pachali-ghat, Octroi Post,
½m. Thapthali, *Sadhus' Akhadas*,

4. **Katmandu**[1] (8) (55) 1m. also called Kathmandu, Kashthamandapa, or Kathmandav, capital of Nepal,

5. **Pashupatinath**[2] (2) (77) about 2m. east of Kathmandu is the

one shall have to do 4m. steep ascent and 5½m. steep descent. There is the Electric Ropeway Station at Dhorsung, (which is situated at a place 1½m. before reaching Bhimphedi) for a distance of 19m., from here up to 5½m. before reaching Katmandu. Big iron posts are set up at intervals and thick iron ropes are passed over them with transmitters at intervals. Cradles are hung over these ropes in which goods are carried day and night. Those who have got extra luggage can send it by Ropeway if they cannot secure adequate transport, but a lot of formalities shall have to be undergone in taking the luggage back at Kathmandu. About 12 as. per maund are charged as freight.

[1] Kathmandu is the capital of Nepal. There are palatial buildings of the members of the royal families, old Hindu and Buddhistic temples, and several temples of Gorakhnath. On *Shivaratri* day there is held a great military exhibition on the parade ground from 2-30 p.m. The King of Nepal (*Panch Circar*), the Prime Minister (*Teen Circar*), Supreme Commander-in-Chief, Assistant Commander-in-Chief, and other high officials assemble here on the occasion and about 4,000 to 5,000 Gurkha soldiers line the parade ground on all the four sides. As a mark of respect of salutation to the Lord Shree Pashupatinath, at about 3-30 or 4 p.m. continuously for ten minutes, there will be firing of guns and of big and small cannons. After that all the officials make a round of the temple of Bhadrakali that is situated on the eastern side of the parade ground and then disperse. From here one can have a fine view of the double peak of Gouri-Shankar (not Everest).

The King of Nepal is called Panch Circar, for five *shrees* (श्री) are written before his name and the Prime Minister is called Teen Circar, for three *shrees* are written before his name. In fact the Prime Minister is the virtual head of the state and the King himself a nominal figurehead. Nepal has got its own postage stamps and coinage. Nepali Rupee is equivalent to 12½ annas and Mohar 6¼ annas. There are other smaller silver and copper coins.

[2] The temple of Pashupatinath is situated on the right bank of the river Baghmati. The superstructure of the temple is like that of a Chinese Pagoda and is all wood and has fine specimens of carvings. Inside the temple there is a three-foot high *shivalinga* with four faces on the four sides. The *pujari* of the temple hails from South India. In front of the temple there is a huge brass image of sitting Nandi or bull. During the time of pilgrimage all *sadhus* are catered free by the Nepal Durbar and on the third and fourth day all *sadhus*

temple of Pashupatinath.

are given a send off by payment of cash ranging from 1 to 30 rupees. There is a great rush on *Shivaratri* day in the temple and there will be illumination during the whole night; and pilgrims keep awake all through the night spending their time in meditation in the surroundings of the temple. Just opposite the temple situated on the other side of the river are the rows of memorials of the departed Kings and Maharajas of Nepal. The river Baghmati flows here in a deep gorge with steep mountains on either side. During pilgrim season there is 1½ to 2 feet deep water in the river.

About ½m. north-east of Pashupatinath temple there is the temple of Guhyeshvari, which is said to be one of the eighteen *Peethas* of *Devi*. About ¾ or 1m. north of Guhyeshvari is the great *stupa* called Bodha, also called Mahabodhi. It is said that the Emperor Asoka had got this constructed. There are houses alround the stupa, most of the residents of which are Tibetans. 2½m. south of Kathmandu is the suburb called Pattan, also called Lalita-pattan or Asoka-pattan. Emperor Asoka got it inhabited. ½m. further from this place there is the famous Buddhist temple called Namo Buddhaya on which there are innumerable images of Buddha. About 2m. west of Kathmandu, situated on the top of a mountain is another great *stupa* called *Svayambhu*. Besides these there are several other *tirthas* in the surroundings of Kathmandu like Balaji, Budha-nilakanth, Vajra-yogini, Ugra-tara, Bhagavati, Dattatreya, Dakshina-kali, Godavari, Mano-kamanaand others (See Map No. 10). There are some trees of *rudraksha* in the neighbourhood of Kathmandu; but the *rudrakshas* used in India as rosary are mostly imported in bagfulls from Sumatra and Java. These are later sorted and stringed. At a distance of 12 days' march from Kathmandu is Muktinath; and two or three days' march further is Damodar-kund, the source of the river Gandaki, where *shalagrams* of marine fossils are found in large numbers. One road goes from Muktinath to Kailas and Manas via Khochar, and one via Mastang up the Brahmaputra valley; but these routes are long and tedious ones and as such, trekked only by *sadhus*.

The time of pilgrimage to Pashupatinath being winter, it is very cold, both at Kathmandu and on the way; besides this, sometimes there will be snowfall also; so pilgrims would do well to take sufficient warm clothing and blankets with them.

KAILAS - MANASAROVAR

FIFTH WAVE

GENERAL INFORMATION FOR TOURISTS.

CHAPTER I

GENERAL INFORMATION FOR TOURISTS

WHO CAN UNDERTAKE THE JOURNEY

Any person with strong lungs and sound heart and who is not suffering from high blood-pressure can undertake the journey to the Holy Kailas and Manasarovar. He should be able to bear hardships, difficulties, and inclemencies of weather. Every year 50 to 200 pilgrims, young and old, children and women, from India visit these Holy *Tirthas*; besides, hundreds of Indian borderland Bhotia merchants of both the sexes go there every year for trade.

PASSPORT

No passport is needed for Indians (whether they be pilgrims, tourists, or traders) for going to any part of Western Tibet. Passport from the Government of India is required by those who want to visit Lhasa, the Capital of Tibet, which is not a place of Hindu pilgrimage. Europeans and other foreigners who wish to visit any part of Tibet from India are required to possess a passport from the Government of India. Up to Dhauli Ganga, Mansyari, and Phurkiya in Almora District and from Suraitota to Kedarnath in Garhwal District it is called "Inner Line". Non-Indians shall have to get the permit of the Deputy Commissioner to cross it and go up to the Indian borderland.

ARTICLES NEEDED FOR THE JOURNEY

Clothes

(1) 2 or 3 good woollen blankets.
(2) *Chutka* (thick Tibetan blanket, to be hired or bought at Garbyang or at Taklakot).
(3) Bedding according to one's own requirements.
(4) 1 Woollen shirt.
(5) 2 Woollen pyjamas or trousers.
(6) 1 Woollen sweater.
(7) 2 Pairs of woollen stockings.
(8) 1 Woollen muffler.
(9) 1 Pair of woollen gloves.
(10) 1 Pair of *pattis* for legs.
(11) 1 Woollen balaclava cap (monkey-cap).
(12) 1 Woollen overcoat.
(13) 1 Light waterproof coat.
(14) 1 Waterproof covering for the hat when one is taking a hat.
(15) 2 or 3 pieces of oil-cloth or waterproof to cover the bedding and luggage.

(16) 4 Cotton shirts.
(17) 1 Pair of cotton pyjamas.
(18) 1 Pair of *dhoties*.
(19) 1 Pair of towels.
(20) 3 or 4 yards of spare cloth.
(21) 1 Pair of strong full-boots, preferably of canvas and one pair of ordinary shoes.
(22) 1 Umbrella.

Medicines

(1) Chlorodyne, Camphorodyne or Bismuth—for diarrhoea.
(2) Salphagannidine or Dover's powder—for dysentery.
(3) Soda bicarb } for indigestion.
(4) *Bhaskar-lavan* } for indigestion.
(5) Fruit salt—for indigestion and free motion.
(6) Mepacrine or Palludrine tablets—for malaria.
(7) Sticking plaster. } For dressing wounds, cuts, boils, etc.
(8) Potassium Permanganate
(9) Tincture of Iodine
(10) Acid Boric and Sulphanilamide powder
(11) Absorbent cotton
(12) Rolled bandages
(13) A. B. C. liniment—for pain in joints.
(14) Cafiaspirin or Aspro—for headaches, slight indispositions, aching limbs, etc.
(15) Influenza mixture.
(16) Purgative pills.
(17) Vaseline bottles—for applying to face, nose, and hands in cold places.
(18) Amritdhara and Amrutanjan—for all complaints.
(19) Smelling salt } for colds.
(20) Vapex } for colds.
(21) Ginger chips or some citrus article—for billiousness.
(22) J. J. Dechen's People's Medical Service Set.
(23) D. D. T. Powder—for bugs, flies, lice etc.
(24) Carbolic acid or some other toothache cure.
(25) Tooth-brush and tooth-powder.
(26) Enema can or syringe.
(27) Rubber catheter.
(28) Hot water bag.
(29) Clinical Thermometer.
(30) Cibazal tablets—for Pneumonia and Bronchitis.

Miscellaneous Articles

(1) Torch light with spare batteries.

(2) Candles.
(3) Hurricane lantern.
(4) Kashmiri *Kangri* (an earthen pot, for holding fire, encased in an indigenous willow-basket, generally carried under the long loose cloak, for keeping the body warm ; can be secured from some Kashmiri friend).
(5) Stove with accessories including methylated spirit.
(6) Kerosene oil (to be taken from Almora).
(7) Match boxes.
(8) Portable cooking vessels, ladle, dishes, plates, tea-kettle, cups, spoons, tiffin carrier, etc.
(9) Pressure, Ic-mic, Annapurna, or Rukmini Cooker (rice is not well cooked in ordinary vessels at altitudes above 10,000 ft.)
(10) Thermos flask.
(11) 2 Buckets or empty tins with handles—for fetching and heating water on the way.
(12) 1 or 2 Light package boxes for keeping vessels, kettle, cups, bottles, and such other breakables.
(13) 1 Tin with lock—for keeping sweets and other eatables (often pilgrims complain against servants for pilfering eatables)
(14) 2 Gunny bags—for putting the holdall and other boxes so as to be portable for carrying either by coolies or ponies.
(15) 2 Kit-bags with locking arrangement.
(16) 6 Small cloth bags for bringing Kailas-incense and other articles on the return journey.
(17) 2 Ropes, each 20 feet long.
(18) Knife.
(19) A pair of scissors.
(20) Hand axe.
(21) 2 Locks.
(22) Soaps for bathing and washing.
(23) Stick with an iron point (to be bought at Haldwani or Almora).
(24) A pair of green goggles to protect eyes from snow-glare and the effects of the severe cold winds.
(25) Binocular.
(26) One good portable camera with sufficient number of roll films or film packs.
(27) Kodak's magnesium ribbon holder, ordinary magnesium ribbon, or flash powder for taking photos in dark rooms, as at Khochar and for seeing clearly the caves, as at Dira-phuk, Zuthul-phuk, and other places.
(28) Maximum and Minimum Thermometer.
(29) Centigrade Thermometer for measuring temperatures of thermal springs.

(30) One portable aneroid barometer.
(31) Some toys, soaps, mirrors, cigarettes, and other petty presents to servants, horse-men, and to the monks of the monasteries.
(32) Dried vegetables.
(33) Spices, pickles, chutneys, tamarind, dried mango pieces etc.
(34) Dry fruits—grapes, *kismis*, dates, almonds etc.
(35) Tea, ovaltine, condensed milk, milk-powder, corn-flakes, the sweets of *bal*[1] and chocolates of Almora, biscuits, lemon-drops, lozenges, sweetto, sugar-cubes, sugar-candy, etc.
(36) Stationery, papers, pencils, pens, ink-bottles, postage-stamps, envelopes, cards, needles and thread, etc., a copy of the *Bhagvad-Gita* and copy of *Bhajans.*
(37) Spring-balance which can weigh up to 100 lbs.—for weighing luggage at different stages.
(38) 3 or 4 empty hydrogen peroxide bottles or some other strong bottles with good corks for bringing the Holy waters of Kailas, Manasarovar, Gouri-kund, and Tirthapuri hot springs.
(39) 1 Pair of double-panniers [2] for each person—for keeping eatables and other miscellaneous articles to be placed on the riding-pony.
(40) Camphor, *dhup*, *supari*, *agarbatti*, wicks soaked in ghee, vermilion, cardamom, and any other sundry articles which the pilgrim might choose to carry.

A list of all articles possibly needed is given ; but one can make a choice according to one's own requirements and position.

EXPENSES

The total expenses of the trip to the Holy Kailas and Manas from Almora and back would range from Rs. 250 to Rs. 600 per head according to the standard of living of the pilgrim. It is always advisable to go in batches to curtail unnecessary expenditure and to secure mutual help.

Haldwani to Almora, bus hire including toll at Almora.	Rs. 5.
Almora to Dharchula (90 miles, hire of a pony, either for luggage (two maunds) or for riding.	Rs. 40 to 45.
Dharchula to Garbyang (55 miles), coolie (coolie carries 40 seers of load) at Rs. 4 per day.	Rs. 20.
Garbyang to Taklakot (32 miles), hire of a *Jhabbu*, yak, pony, or mule of riding or of luggage (60 seers)[3].	Rs. 10.

1 *Bal* and chocolates are made purely out of evaporated milk (*khoa*) with a little sugar added to it. These could be preserved even for months.

2 Two small bags made of thick cloth (originally bread-baskets) and tied together either firmly or loosely for carrying light luggage. Tibetans and Bhotias use double-panniers made of leather or a thick woollen cloth.

3 One seer is equivalent to two pounds.

106. Embankments of smaller pieces of ice, resembling Glasspanes
[*See p.* 32

107. Manasarovar Frozen, with Fissures and regular Blocks of Ice piled up into Embankments due to Coastal Explosions
[*See p.* 32

108. Irregular Blocks of Ice
[*See p.* 32

109. Zebra-like Deposits of snow on the Southern shores of Rakshas Tal
[See p. 30

110. Lachato with Kailas in the background.
[See pp. 17 & 19

111. The Island Lachato [See p. 19

112. The Breeding ground of *Nagangba* on the Lachato, Mandhata in the background
[*See p.* 19

113. The Island Topserma
[*See p.* 20.

14 Rakhas Tal with Oceanic waves on one side, Mandhata in the background
[*See p.* 17

115. Rakshas Tal frozen into Ice on another side, Kailas Mirroring in it
[*See p.* 17

116. Sutlej flowing out of Rakshas Tal
[See p. 16 & 18

117. Ganga Chhu and Chiu Hill
[See p. 18

118. Dr. Sven Hedin, the Famous Swedish Explorer
[See p. 224

Taklakot to Tirthapuri, Kailas-*parikrama*, touching Manasarovar, Khocharnath to and fro journey, and back to Garbyang, *or* the same journey excluding Tirthapuri and including Manas-*parikrama*, for one yak, mule, or pony for riding or luggage (80 seers).	Rs. 30.
If Manas-*parikrama* or Tirthapuri trip is not included	Rs. 25.
Guide at Rs. 4 to 5 per day, for 25 days with or without food (as arranged).	Rs. 100 to 125.
For every four animals engaged from Garbyang to Taklakot, for one attendant[1] at Re. 1 per day.	Rs. 3.
Hire of a *chhauldari* (tent) from Garbyang and back.	Rs. 10.
Hire of a *chutka*.	Rs. 4.
Almora to Garbyang, *dandy* charges for 6 coolies at Rs. 4 per day, for 13 days.	Rs. 312.
Garbyang upwards and back, for 8 coolies at Rs. 5 per day, for 25 days.	Rs.1,000.
The hire of the *dandy* shall have to be paid for separately; but if it is to be taken for the whole journey it would be cheaper to buy one at Almora; it may cost about	Rs. 25.
Wages of the cook for two months at Rs. 1½ per day, plus food, a pair of shoes, one pyjama, one shirt and, one cap.	Rs. 150.
Servant, for bringing water, cleaning utensils, heating water, bringing fuel wherever available, spreading bedding, looking after other personal comforts, from Garbyang upwards and back, at Rs. 2 per day, for 25 days.	Rs. 50.
Presents to pony-men, servants and others.	Rs. 25.
Initial expenses for clothes etc.	Rs. 50 to 200.
Fooding expenses, per day, at Re. 1 to 2 per day for two months.	Rs. 60 to 120.

CONVEYANCE

Coolies, ponies, mules, or *dandies*, the only means of conveyance in the mountainous regions, can be arranged from Almora, Dharchula, Khela, Garbyang, and Taklakot. As far as possible coolies should not be engaged from Almora to Dharchula, for they take more time to do the journey than the ponies and often reach the staging place

1 Seeing the Bhotia pony-men charging for the attendant on horses the Tibetan yak-men also have begun demanding for some presents. So the author has arranged that the yak-men as a lot should be paid one rupee a day and that they should bring water and clean utensils by turns. But this service would be at their convenient time; so those who require regular service shall have to engage a full-time servant from Garbyang.

much later than the pilgrims, which is a source of inconvenience and annoyance. When coolies are engaged from Almora, Dotyals (Nepali coolies) should invariably be given preference, as they are the hardiest in mountain-journeys and more serviceable.

At Almora one can get ponies cheaper and more easily through Messrs Laxmilal Ananda Brothers of Shyam Nivas than other sources, firstly because they do it with a spirit of service to the pilgrims, secondly because two of their brothers had been to Kailas and so are aware of the difficulties and necessities of the pilgrims, and thirdly because they regularly send their own goods up to Dharchula, as such pony-men go to them on their own accord for goods.

Usually for ladies who cannot walk, ponies shall have to be engaged up to Dharchula. The pack-ponies go slowly and the rider would get used to riding very easily in a day. If a *dandy* is engaged from Almora up to Dharchula, there would be a difference of Rs. 100 for one side of the journey ; and if it is for the whole journey, it would cost Rs. 1,600 whereas the pony-cum-*dandy* journey (by *dandy* between Dharchula and Garbyang) would cost only Rs. 400. Up till now only three ladies went to Kailas on a *dandy*.

The road between Dharchula and Garbyang is bad and is not negotiable by riding or laden ponies, since the path becomes slippery during rainy season and at times stones from the slopes of mountains fall on the road. So pilgrims shall have to cover this distance either on foot or by a *dandy* and engage coolies for luggage. In case the required number of coolies could not be procured from Dharchula right up to Garbyang, they may be engaged for a day up to Khela, wherefrom fresh coolies could be arranged right up to Garbyang.

From Garbyang onwards ponies, mules, yaks, and *jhabbus* could be had and they move everywhere. So one should engage ponies up to Taklakot only. Generally ponies are supplied for riding and yaks or *jhabbus* for luggage. It is always advisable to engage ponies or mules whenever possible as yaks or *jhabbus* are furious and most uncontrolable. It is also advisable to engage ponies or yaks at Taklakot for the journey to Kailas and Manasarovar and back to Garbyang, since conveyance can be had much cheaper there than at Garbyang. It should be noted that it would be very difficult or even impossible to get separately one single pony or a yak either at Garbyang or at Taklakot, and that the fare is the same whether it is a riding or a luggage-animal and whether it is a pony, mule, yak, or *jhabbu*. Animals for conveyance are to be engaged in a batch, in which case the charges would be less. Usual rates of conveyance are given here for the general guidance of the pilgrim. But the charges may rise if the number of pilgrims is great or if there happens to be any epidemic amongst the animals.

From Garbyang onwards, ponies and yaks have got Tibetan type of wooden saddles to ride on. So heavy blankets and rugs should be placed on and under the saddles, which would reduce the weight of the luggage and at the same time gives comfort to the rider. Besides this, pilgrims would do well if they keep their eatables, bathing clothes, drinking vessels, and other articles of necessity, weighing about 15 seers, in double-panniers and place on the saddles of the riding ponies. In this way the weight of the luggage would be reduced, which will not be charged for and some of the necessities would always be within reach when one is on the move. A rider is allowed to carry the double-panniers weighing up to 15 seers.

At the time of engaging the ponies the pilgrims shall have to fix up with pony-men that they would halt for one full day at Kailas and another day on the Manas (preferably at Thugolho). By fixing up like this in the beginning, nothing is charged extra or else they will be charged. So also it is to be fixed up that they shall have to camp at the hot springs near Chiu Gompa for the night.

Between Almora and Garbyang coolies usually carry one maund of luggage and each load shall have to be covered with a waterproof sheet. Bhotia pony-men at Garbyang load only 1½ maunds of luggage on each of their ponies and charge at that rate if a small load is in excess. They weigh all luggage including blankets but not double panniers; whereas the Tibetan pony or yak-men carry two full maunds of load on each luggage-animal and do not weigh blankets and rugs, if they are put under or over the saddles of both the riding and luggage-animals, for they have to bring their own cushions for the saddles if the blankets are not used in their stead. In this way also much money would be saved by engaging Tibetan animals from Taklakot.

As far as possible, bedding and loads should not be made very bulky. Three suspension bridges near Bade-chhina, Thal, and Garjiya are narrow and hence bulky loads and boxes get very badly damaged by striking against the walls. So also, while getting down the Gouri-kund on the Kailas-*parikrama*, the path is narrow, steep, and lined with big boulders on either side. Before loading the luggage on animals, all articles liable to breakage should be carefully packed in boxes, for especially the yak is very turbulent and often throws down the luggage on ascents and descents, causing considerable damage; but the *jhabbu* is comparatively milder.

One gets very much tired during the journey in the mountains and will not generally be able to cook food one's self. So a cook shall have to be secured at Almora. As far as possible one should try to get a *Kshatriya* cook, since the *Brahmin* cook would worry very much with his *chauka*, which will be a cause of annoyance on the way; the second reason is that another *Brahmin* or *Kshatriya* servant shall have to be engaged for bringing water. The *Kshatriya* cook would bring water for himself up to Garbyang; and for cleaning utensils some arrangement could be made either with the pony-men or with the servant of the shopkeepers. From Garbyang a Bhotia or Huniya servant can be engaged for doing all this work.

A servant should be engaged from Garbyang for doing every other work except cooking since he would be able to serve better, being accustomed to the severe cold of the Manas Region. The guide would arrange for the servant. Servants taken from plains or from Almora would feel the cold of the upper regions as much as the pilgrim himself, so he would not be of much service as the one from Garbyang. The servant from the plains shall have to be fed and given other facilities like the riding-pony, clothes etc. Usually the servant from Garbyang would look to the bedding, bring water, clean vessels, get hot water ready by the time the pilgrim gets up from his bed, collect fuel, help in pitching the tents, help the cook, and above all would narrate local traditions. So, as far as possible, one should not take the servant from the plains unless one is prepared to give him equal facilities as one's self. Three or four people can jointly engage a cook from Almora and a servant from Garbyang.

While going in big batches or when one requires more personal comforts, a mate (cooly-head) has to be engaged from Dharchula up to Garbyang to look after the coolies. He is to be paid as much as other coolies. He would tie and untie the bedding, get all the loads tied in order and despatch in time, bring water in staging places, clean vessels, and would hold himself responsible for the coolies. He will not carry a big load but would accompany the pilgrim and carry his tiffin-carrier, thermos flask, umbrella, and waterproof coat to the extent of 10 to 12 seers, so that he might be able to keep company with the pilgrim and not left behind with other coolies.

There is a proverb in Tibetan that 'if a pony does not carry the rider during the ascent, the pony is no pony; and if a person does not get down and walk on the descent, the man is no man.' So one should get down the pony during very steep descents, for it would be advantageous to both. Also while moving through marshy regions one should get down the pony, if necessary, or else the animal would get stuck up or one might be thrown down in the mud very badly. While riding, always make sure that the belt (*lo*) of the pony is tied tightly.

There are many oaks on the roadside between Berinag and Askot, the leaves of which fall on the road, and rot during rainy season where innumerable leeches crop up. One shall have to put on full-boots and stockings to protect one's self from these pests. If perchance a leech catches the leg, a pinch of tobacco-powder or common salt would make it drop down.

HELP AND POPULAR PERSONS

At Almora pilgrims should not fail to be benefited by the vast experience of Shree Pandit Rudra Dutta Bhatt and his sons who had rendered great service to several parties, of foreign expeditions, explorers, and big parties of pilgrims. Pandit Bhatt evinces a great interest in the Himalayas and in those who intend to visit them. He has a fine collection of books on the Himalayas and is a veteran Congress worker of the place. For general information and help for conveyance, one can approach Messrs Laxmi Lal Ananda Brothers, General Merchants, who are very generous and religious minded, or the secretary of the Orphanage, Arya Samaj. The Chairman of the District Board, Deputy Commissioner, or the Tashildar could as well be approached with advantage for any special help.

Pandit Umapati, Pandit Jivanand, and Pandit Narottam have their own ponies and mules and a big shop at Ganai Gangoli (30 miles beyond Almora). By writing to them in advance, any number of ponies could be arranged ready from Almora to Dharchula or vice versa, on any appointed date.

At Dharchula Rai Sahib Pandit Prem Vallabh, Thakur Kundan Singh, cloth merchant, and Pandit Haridatt, shopkeeper are ever ready to help the pilgrims in every way. *At Khela*, Kunwar Pratap Singh Man Singh, Government shopkeepers, are very obliging. If the pilgrims were to write to Pratap Singh on the date of their departure from Almora as to how many coolies and *dandies* they would need, he would keep them ready by the time they reach Dharchula. One or two days before reaching or as soon as they reach Dharchula, they should send a reminder, and they would get their coolies at Dharchula on the appointed day.

At Garbyang the veteran guide Kich Khampa or Thakur Rukum Singh, would keep everything ready for the pilgrims if they are intimated in advance. If the definite date of their arrival at Garbyang is made known to any one of them, he would bring a few riding ponies up to Lamari (9 miles before reaching Garbyang) to give a lift to the foot-pilgrims on the steep and tiring ascent, for which a small amount is charged. In the absence of a guide, help may be taken from Thakur Sindal Singh Garbyal, the Post Master, the School Master, and the Patwari, who would gladly render all help to pilgrims. At the time of leaving Almora, if Thakur Mohan Singh Garbyal is intimated at his Garbyang address, he would make necessary arrangements for Tibetan ponies and yaks from Taklakot for further journey.

At Taklakot, some of the well-known Bhotia merchants like Thakur

Mohan Singh Garbyal, Thakur Jaman Singh Garbyal, Thakur Bhup Singh Guniyal, Thakur Prem Singh Chaudansi, and others would render great help to the pilgrims in arranging transport animals, securing foodstuffs etc., and in getting mails from Garbyang. *At Gapudosa* (one mile beyond Barkha) Thakur Mangal Singh Pangty, *at Thugolho* Thakur Ratan Singh Arya, Thakur Jaman Singh and Bishan Singh Garbyal, *at Gyanima Mandi* Thakur Bhagat Singh Pangty, Thakur Ratan Singh Pangty, Thakur Kundan Singh Jangpangi, or any other Johar merchant, and *at Nabra Mandi* Thakur Hayat Singh Nityal, would do the needful for the pilgrims.

HIGHWAY ROBBERS, FIREARMS, AND GUIDES

Up to a day's journey beyond Taklakot there is no fear of any robbers. Near the Gurla la, the shores of Manasarovar and Rakshas Tal, Kailas-*parikrama* route, between Kailas and Gyanima Mandi, between Gyanima and Tirthapuri, between Tirthapuri and Kailas, between Gyanima and Sibchilim, and between Tirthapuri and Gartok, and on the way to the sources of the Indus and the Brahmaputra it is often frequented by highway robbers and freebooters of nomad shepherd-tribes of Ngakora and of Kham from the month of May to October. They carry all sorts of arms including swords, daggers, old type of matchlock guns, latest types of Russian and German pistols, revolvers, and rifles. These freebooters of nomadic tribes come here from far Eastern Tibet on a pilgrimage to the Holy Kailas and Manas to sell their wool and sheep. When they come across any unarmed pilgrim or trader they loot him and run away on their horses with the booty, including luggage and ponies.

For reasons stated above, the intending pilgrims and tourists should go in batches and take a firearm with them. The guide Kich Khampa has got his own gun, or a gun or a rifle can be hired from some merchant at Taklakot on payment of a small amount. At halting places where robbers are usually apprehended, one or two hours after sunset, two or three blank shots may be fired into the air, so that any robber lurking in the neighbourhood might know that the party have fire-arms. As a matter of fact there would not arise any occasion for actually using it; its mere presence in the party would go a long way in frightening the robbers. The cost of the cartridges used shall have to be paid for.

Usually every pilgrim-party, whether big or small, shall have to engage a guide who will charge a minimum of Rs. 3 per day. As soon as the party reaches the camping place, the guide will get all the animals unloaded, make the pony-men, with the help of other servants, pitch the tents, get the luggages kept in tents in their proper places, dig trenches round the tents if rain is apprehended in the night, and secure milk, curd, butter, or any other article from the neighbouring shepherd-camp. In the morning he would get the tents struck, loads retied and animals loaded, and make the party move. He narrates the history of different places and persons ; he is the guard, the interpreter, and in one word he is held responsible for everything both in the camp and while on the move. All Bhotias know Tibetan and some Tibetans know Hindi. Invariably all guides know Hindi and Tibetan both. So a separate intrepreter is not needed.

At Garbyang there is one veteran guide by name Kich Khampa, a Tibetan domiciled in Garbyang. He had been up till now 58 times to Kailas and Manasarovar. He is a polite, calm, intelligent, enduring, smart, jolly, and very serviceable man and a good cook as well. Intending pilgrims should book his services by sending a few rupees in advance. He will make every arrangement to the minutest detail and to the entire satisfaction of the pilgrims. Thakur Rukum Singh Garbyal is another good guide who had been to Kailas a number of times. Besides being a guide he is a good cook as well, and entertains the pilgrims with his *bhajans*. There is one guide by the name of Thakur Mansingh in Soosa of Chaudans. He is a calm and good-natured man. There is one more guide at Garbyang by the name of Ringjen, but he is a hot-headed man. Pilgrims can procure some of their curios through their guide. It is to be noted here that the pilgrims shall have to carry at their own cost the luggage belonging to the cook, guide, and servant, not exceeding 25 seers each. In the absence of any guide or in the case of a single person the pony-man himself would do the whole service on extra payment. Pilgrims should send postage stamps for getting a prompt reply from the guides and merchants.

KAILAS TO BADRINATH

Those who want to go to Badrinath from Kailas should first return to Taklakot after visiting Kailas. The route via Niti is the shortest from here, but the road is very rocky, so one cannot get ponies for this journey ; only yaks and *jhabbus* can be had up to Niti which is 10 days' march from here. The fare per yak would be Rs. 25 and the yak-man also shall have to be paid for, as much as a yak, but he would do the work of a servant also to some extent. The village Niti is 147½ miles from Taklakot ; Joshimath is 43½ miles from Niti ; and Badrinath is 19 miles from Joshimath, i.e. 210 miles in all. From Niti one shall have to engage coolies up to Badrinath who may charge any amount.

LODGING AND TENTS

From Almora up to Garbyang there are small *dharmashalas* and shops, where one can rest for the night. Besides these, there are Dak Bungalows and Forest Rest Houses at important places and District Board or Local Primary School Buildings, which can be used by the pilgrims with the permission of the authorities concerned. A Dak Bungalow can be occupied without previous notice, provided it is vacant at the time; but in the case of Forest Rest Houses one has to apply and secure permission from the District Forest Officer much in advance and shall have to strictly follow the programme which may not always be possible for pilgrims, who are dependent upon the indefinite programme of their pony-men and coolies. There is a two-roomed *dharmashala* at Malpa, but one has to send a messenger in advance from Jipti to get it cleaned and reserved for them, for otherwise pilgrims would be put to a great inconvenience if it has already been occupied when they reach there late in the afternoon, in which case they shall have to proceed further for about 8 miles up to Budi to get shelter, and then there is every possibility that the coolies might not be able to go such a long distance. A few miles beyond Kalapani there are some cell-like Bhotia *dharmashalas*. On the other side of the Lipu Lekh pass there are two *dharmashalas* with four rooms each at Pala, but these are not fit for the stay of pilgrim-parties and can be used only by stray pilgrims and *sadhus*. For further journey one shall have to take tents which can be hired from Garbyang. If one wishes he can take a portable tent of one's own, the transportation charges would be as much as the cost of the tent itself. The *chhauldari* or bivouac-tent that could be had on hire at Garbyang would accommodate three to four persons and is not air-tight like the full-fledged tent; but by keeping one or two extra *chutkas*, one can get on very comfortably. A separate *chhauldari* shall have to be hired for the kitchen.

There are no *dharmashalas* or Rest Houses in general on the routes in Tibet. Places where there are water facilities, and good pasture for yaks and ponies, where there is fuel or good shelter from sever winds are generally selected for camping grounds. Pilgrims and traders stop at such places for the night. At such places people pile up some stones in semi-circular walls 3 to 4 feet high, just to protect themselves from the severe cold winds, which the author would call 'walled enclosures' or 'camping parapets'. They are called *le* in Tibetan. In a few places there are caves to halt.

CLIMATE AND WEATHER CONDITIONS

Sky is foggy or smoky from May to June and cloudy up to the end of August or middle of September. So one might miss the grand view of the snows from Almora and other places during these months, but the sky usually get cleared up after a heavy rainfall.

Almora, Dhaul-chhina, Berinag, and Khela are cool places and blankets may be needed for covering in the nights. Sera-ghat, Ganai, Thal, Balvakot, and Dharchula are hot places and the heat is oppressive. From Khela to Garbyang it is cold. From Garbyang upwards it is very cold. But Taklakot and Khochar are pretty warm in day-time. Beyond Kalapani there will be tempestuous and severe cold winds characteristic of Tibet. To guard one's self against the effects of the severe cold winds and the ultra-violet rays of the sun present in higher altitudes, one should apply vaseline to nose, face, hands, and feet early in the morning before starting for the day's march. Otherwise these limbs turn black, crack, peel off skin, and bleed.

Monsoon sets in at Almora by the end of June. So by the time the pilgrimage to Kailas begins, rainy season sets in; as such the journey becomes tedious during ascents and descents when the days are raining. Monsoon sets in late in Tibet and rains are comparatively less; but when it rains, it rains in torrents. Gyanima Mandi is so cold even during the market season (July and August) that the temperature at night would be below the freezing point. The mean temperature in Manasa Khanda during the pilgrim-season is between 50°-65° F. in shade. One may have to go on frozen ice for a furlong while reaching the Lipu Lekh pass and a furlong while getting down to the Tibetan side if one reaches the pass before the end of June; but in the month of July hardly there may be snow for a hundred yards, unless there has been an unusually heavy snowfall in the previous winter. Frequently there would be showers of snow on the Lipu Lekh pass and Dolma la. Mornings are a little misty; after midday severe winds begin to blow; so it is always advisable to cross the Lipu Lekh in the early hours of the day.

As we go higher and higher above the sea-level, air gets lighter and lighter and consequently oxygen gets lesser and lesser. This insufficiency of oxygen has a great effect upon mind and its functions; and the finer senses get blunted frequently. So while travelling at altitudes above 10,000 feet, one loses self-control and gets irritable and quarrelsome quickly. So it is often noted amongst pilgrim-parties that the members get highly irritated and quarrelsome over petty matters, to which they would not pay much attention or importance while on lower altitudes. When they get down to Almora they forget their quarrels and become friends again and sometimes they wonder as to how they could exchange such hot words. So pilgrims going in batches would do well to note from Garbyang onwards, that if any one in their party were to lose temper, others should keep cool for a while. In a short time he would also get calm. In doing so, when somebody else loses his temper, this person would remain calm himself. In this way pilgrims could avoid a good deal of unpleasantness on the way and make the journey smoother. Pilgrims would please note that they should not get excited when their pony-man or guide loses his temper when they call him to do some work while he is taking tea in the evening, after the day's rough journey. This is another factor which makes the journey smooth.

It is generally noted that people of billious temperament get all the more billious and get headache and nausea while going on higher altitudes and especially while getting up passes. Normal persons also sometimes get headache and nausea. Due to insufficiency of oxygen supply to the system, liver might be discharging more bile and spleen more contracted. Perhaps it is due to this hyper activity of liver and the consequent nauseating tendency that one has a craving for eating some citrus article. While travelling on mountains it has been observed that appetite of some people increases while it decreases in the case of others. Anyway many would like to take some tiffin and tea in the morning before starting for the day's march.

The boiling-point of water falls down by 1° F. for every 300 feet of ascent. So at the height of Manasarovar, the boiling-point of water falls down by about 50° F. Hence, all the articles that are cooked at higher temperature will not cook well in these regions.

BENEFITS OF A MOUNTAIN TRIP

Mountain-journey would certainly reduce the unnecessary fat of the bulky people and make them healthier and smarter and look better. One is cured of several minor ailments dormant in the body; there is an influx of new blood into the system; nervous system gets toned up and endocrine glands get more invigorated; heart and lungs are strengthened; brain is refreshed and mind tranquil, and one feels rejuvenated. By the time one returns from mountains one feels that a new life has come into the body and becomes fit to do one's work with double vigour and efficiency. So, young men in general and busy workers of all walks of life in particular should make it a point, in consideration of their health and even in consideration of better out-turn of work which they have been doing, to go on a holiday once in a year, for a month or more into mountains, forgetting time and space and leaving their watch and office-brain at home. When once you do this, you will realise how profitable it is even from a business point of view to go on a holiday for a trot into mountains and feel why you had not done it earlier.

WHEN TO START FOR THE JOURNEY

Lipu Lekh pass becomes passable from the month of May up to the end of November for pilgrims from the plains, though Tibetans cross the pass for full ten months. One can very conveniently start from Almora in the middle of June if one wants to avoid rains on the outward journey. For fear of cold and snow, pilgrims generally begin to start from the end of June. There is nothing to be feared from snow on the pass. As a matter of fact some adventurous youths leave Almora in the last week of May. The times of clearing of other passes will be given in the description of the routes concerned. But those who start before the setting in of the monsoon would feel the oppressive heat and scarcity of water on the way. They may not get tea at many places where they would get at other times. At Almora also there would be scarcity of water until heavy rains set in.

TIME TAKEN FOR THE JOURNEY

The journey from Almora to Manasarovar and to do the *parikrama* of Kailas including a hurried visit to the famous Khochar Monastery and back to Almora takes about 50 days including halting days at Dharchula, Garbyang, and Taklakot. If one wants to visit Gyanima Mandi and Tirthapuri, it will take 3 days more and if one wants to do the *parikrama* of the Manasarovar also, it will take 2 days more at the most. About 10 days can be saved in the journey if arrangements for transport are made beforehand at Almora, Dharchula, Garbyang, and Taklakot.

MAILS OR DAK

Garbyang is the last village and last Post Office in the Indian territory on the route to Kailas via Lipu Lekh pass. So before proceeding beyond Garbyang, pilgrims should give instructions to the Post Master to deposit their mails in the Post Office or make arrangements through Thakur Jaman Singh Bishan Singh Garbyal Brothers for delivery at Taklakot. They render great service to the pilgrims in this direction. If a Post Office could be opened at Taklakot with at least a tri-weekly delivery and despatch, it would be of great service both to merchants and pilgrims. The Post Office would be self-maintained.

PROVISIONS

All sorts of foodstuffs are available everywhere on the route from Almora to Garbyang excepting for a day at Malpa, which is between Jipti and Garbyang. Articles of special liking just as *basmati* rice, *suji* (semolina), *besan*, sage, tinned fruits, *bari*, *papar*, etc. may be taken from Almora. Berinag is the last place where one can get sweets on the way. From Berinag to Dharchula plantains can be had in abundance. Mangoes can be had at Bade-chhina, Sera-ghat, Thal, and Dharchula in season (July and August) while going to Kailas or on the return journey. Guavas can be had at Dharchula and apples and pears at Sirkha on the return journey. Oranges can be had at Dharchula, Balvakot, Jauljibi, Garjiya, Askot, Didihat, and Thal from the middle of October up to the end of November. Good cow-ghee can be had either from Dharchula or from Khela at the rate of 4 rupees per seer. Cabbage, radish, and a few other leafy vegetables are available at Garbyang on the return journey, and potatoes can be had throughout from Almora to Garbyang. Cucumber (*kakri*) is available from Almora upwards up to Sirkha. Occasionally green chillies, turnips, radish (fresh or dried), inferior variety of apricots (*chullu*), and potatoes are put up for sale in Taklakot Mandi. From Taklakot to Kardung, green peas can be obtained in plenty. Pilgrims will do well to take the necessary provisions from Garbyang for the outward journey to Kailas and back to Garbyang, i.e. for about 25 days. The following are the current rates of foodstuffs both at Garbyang and Taklakot.

Rice	1	seer	per	rupee
Wheat flour	1	,,	,,	,,
Musoor dal	1	,,	,,	,,
Mash dal	1	,,	,,	,,
Barley *sattu*	1	,,	,,	,,
Pea *sattu*	1	,,	,,	,,
Sugar or *misri*	$\frac{1}{3}$	,,	,,	,,
Raisins	$\frac{1}{4}$	,,	,,	,,
Butter	$\frac{1}{3}$	,,	,,	,,
Spices	$\frac{1}{4}$	,,	,,	,,

Gur (Jaggery) Rs. $1\frac{1}{2}$ to $3\frac{1}{2}$ per *bheli* (one lump) or 1 to $2\frac{1}{2}$ seers.

Candles, cigarettes, match boxes, utensils, stationery, piece-goods, etc. can also be had.

There is a mandi of the Bhotias of Johar and Darma Parganas at Tarchhen where foodstuffs and other articles are sold. Those who intend going to Gyanima Mandi direct from Taklakot can as well get all articles from Gyanima which is the biggest mandi in Western Tibet. Those who go on a *parikrama* of Manasarovar will come across the Thokar Mandi, situated on her southern shores. *Demo* (Tibetan cow), goat, or sheep-milk, butter, and *chhura* (Tibetan cheese) can be purchased from shepherds here and there beyond Taklakot.

Generally pilgrims prepare a sweet called *gur-papari* or *panjeera* for using it as a ready-made tiffin in the morning on the way, in the evening as soon as one reaches the staging place, or at any other time. Wheat-flour is fried in ghee; and *gur* or sugar, resins, and copra are added to it. It remains in good condition even for two or three months. This may be prepared at Khela, where one can get good ghee and flour cheaper; and preserve it in a tin. At the time of starting for the day's march one should take out a small quantity of it in a bag for use on the way. Pilgrims are expected to distribute this and other eatables to co-pilgrims and servants especially on the Lipu Lekh pass, Gurla la, Manasarovar, Gouri-kund, and other places.

FUEL

From Almora to Garbyang, fuel is available in all shops. From Garbyang up to Kalapani, the servant is expected to bring fuel from the jungle; and at Taklakot, one has to buy it from the Indian merchants at the rate of one anna per seer. In Tibet there is no good fuel excepting *dama* (a kind of juniper or furze which burns even when green but gives out so much of smoke that it makes one's eyes smart), dried yak-dung, the fallings of sheep and goat, and champa-estrella (*pang*). Tibetans always keep bellows for kindling and flint for making fire. When a servant is engaged he would bring green fuel or collect dry dung wherever available, for heating water. For cooking purposes, one shall have to carry a stove, kerosene oil, etc.

CURRENCY

All Indian coins and currency notes are passable up to Taklakot; but beyond that, Indian rupees and the Tibetan coins, *tongas* only are in vogue in money transactions. Up to 1942 the rate of exchange of the *tongas* was 8 per rupee. But the present rate of exchange is 4; even then they are not available. So, pilgrims should take sufficient Indian change with them which is freely exchangeable (see p. 78).

GENERAL AILMENTS ON THE WAY

Dysentery, diarrhoea, cold, cough, fatigue, and feverishness due to tiresome ascents and descents, and reeling sensation or headache during high ascents are the general ailments on the way. While getting up very steep ascents, not only very weak persons but very stout persons also may experience palpitation and suffocation; people of billious temperament may feel nausea or vomiting sensation, in which cases, some sour articles like tamarind, dried mango-pieces, citric acid, or cafiaspirin may conveniently be used with advantage; and the ascent should be done slowly.

One may take tea in the morning and in the evening since it would keep the body warm, and would remove the exhaustion of the day's journey. Hot water bath may be used during nights for chilblains (swelling of fingers in cold regions). When fingers, hands, or feet are very badly benumbed or frozen, they should never be basked on fire, for they ache much more. They should be warmed slowly by being placed in arm-pits or knee-pits. In the case of aching limbs, one may either take cafiaspirin or give a hot salt-water bath to the feet. Pilgrims should be careful about their diet during the journey.

While travelling on altitudes above 15,000 feet, some people bleed through nose and mouth due to high blood pressure and rarified air. They should not get worried over this. By sprinkling cold water on the nose and drinking a cup of cold water they will get the necessary relief. When one travels without goggles on ice, or with snows in the front, eyes may be affected and by night they may become red and swollen and pain very badly. In such cases boric compress may be applied or boric solution (one pinch of boric powder in one ounce of water) may be put in the eyes.

Many people believe that nausea, headache, deep breathing, etc. that one gets while crossing the passes is due to the inhaling of the air coming from poisonous flowers and drugs; this is a wrong notion; the rarified atmosphere at higher altitudes is the real cause.

While travelling in a bus from Haldwani or Kathgodam, people of billious temperament would begin to vomit during ascents and descents. Such people should occupy the front seat (by paying an extra amount of a rupee), for this would reduce the nauseating tendency. In such cases, one may walk the distance to Almora by the short cut.

CHAPTER II

PRASADS

KAILAS : (1) A variety of scented creeper called *Kang-po* or Kailas-*dhup* grows round Kailas in the midst of pebbles, at a height of 16,000 to 17,000 feet. It is dried and used as an incense. It is believed that this herbal incense grows only round about Kailas and nowhere else. The author too could not find this herb anywhere else excepting in the upper part of the Namreldi valley in small quantities. (2) A sort of white substance called *ku-sa* in Tibetan (see p. 50) brought from the northern foot of Kailas by the monks of Dira-phuk Gompa and is taken by the pilgrims as Kailas-*vibhuti*. This too can be bought from Dira-phuk and Zuthul-phuk Gompas. (3) Water from any side of the Kailas Peak. (4) Water from Gouri-kund. (5) Water from Tso Kapala or Kapali Sar. (6) Earth from Kapali Sar (*sa-nga*). (7) The white substance near the hot springs at Tirthapuri, taken as Bhasmasura's *bhasma*. (8) The yellow ochre from the Sindura hill at Tirthapuri is taken as *Devi's prasad*.

MANASAROVAR : (1) Water from Manasarovar. (2) Smooth pebbles of various shapes and colours are picked up from any shore, either for purposes of *puja* or for keeping them in amulets or talisman-caskets. (3) A sort of violet sand named *chema-nenga*, which consists of particles of five colours, red, black, yellow, white, and green is picked up from the east coast, where it is found in thin layers over the ordinary white sand for a distance of about three miles only. It is believed by Tibetans to contain particles of gold, silver, turquoise, coral, and iron. A few grains of it are eaten as *prasad*. This sand is much heavier than the ordinary sand and as such ordinary sand particles can be husked out of this very easily. This can be had only by those who do the round of the Manas. (4) A variety of scented artemesia (*davanam*) plant grows all round Manasarovar. It is called *Tso-po* (Lake-incense) and it grows everywhere up to an altitude of 10,000 feet. (5) *Pang-po* is another herbal root-incense which grows a little to the east of Manas and can be had in small quantities at Thugolho. It is called *masi* by Bhotias. (6) Small and big fishes abound in the Lake, which when beaten by high dashing waves, die and are drifted to the shores and stranded. These dead fish are picked up and dried in the sun and are taken by the pilgrims as *prasad* of the Holy Lake. They are preserved carefully, or are used as incense, which is said to have the efficacy of dispelling evil spirits, of effacing the evil influence of planets, and of curing various cattle diseases. Dried fish and herbal incense are sold by the monks in the monasteries, but nobody kills the fish in the Lake.

REACTIONS OF THE KAILAS-MANAS ON WESTERN MINDS

It will not be out of place if a few lines are quoted here from the "Trans-Himalaya" of Dr. Sven Hedin, giving the reactions of these two Holy places on his mind.

"The stranger also approaches Kang-rimpoche with a feeling of awe. It is incomparably the most famous mountain in the world. Mount Everest and Mount Blanc cannot vie with it.

"Manasarovar is the abode of sanctity and of peace......No language on earth contains words forcible enough to describe the view from it over the lake........I, too, was the victim of an illusion which almost made me catch at the parapet for support. I wondered whether it was a fit of giddiness......A dream-picture in the most ethereal transitory tones floats before us. We seem to stand on a promontory jetting out into space which yawns around us and in front......I should have liked to remain a while under its enchantment......I enjoy the voyage to the full, for nothing I remember in my long wanderings in Asia can compare with the overpowering beauty of this nocturnal sail......Two flocks of geese are swimming on the water producing diverging ripples. All is so indescribably quiet; so ethereal, transparent and transitory, so subtile and sensitive, that I scarcely dare breathe. Never has a church service, a wedding march, a hymn of victory, or a funeral made a more powerful impression on me......Wonderful, attractive, enchanting lake! Theme of story and legend, playground of storms and changes of colour, apple of the eye of gods and men, goal of weary, yearning pilgrims, holiest of the holiest of the lakes, are thou, Tso-mavang, lake of all lakes. Navel of old Asia, where four of the most famous rivers of the world, the Brahmaputra, the Indus, the Sutlej and the Ganges, rise among gigantic peaks......Manasarovar is the pearl of all the lakes of the world. Hoary with age when the books of the *Veda* were written......Oh! what a wonderful lake it was! I have no words to describe it. To my dying day I shall never forget it, and even now is in my mind as a legend, a poem and a song. Nothing that I can recall through all my wanderings can compare with the overwhelming beauty of this night journey. It was like listening to the silent and mighty throbs of the heart of Nature......It seemed as though the landscape, ever-changing as the hours creep slowly by, were unreal; as though it no longer belonged to this earth, but lay on the borders of the world beyond, nearer to Heaven, the region of dreams and phantasies, of hopes and longings, a mysterious fairy land, rather than to this earth of men and sinners, of worldliness and vanity......I threw a farewell glance at Tso-mavang, and experienced a feeling of bereavement at the thought that I must now leave its shores."

August Gansser writes, "The fundamental idea of Asiatic Religions is embodied in one of the most significant temples I had ever seen, a sun-lit rock and ice! Its remarkable structure and peculiar harmony of its shape, justify my speaking of Kailas as the most sacred mountain in the world......the holiest mountain in the world and the Sublime Throne of the Gods."[1]

"The unrivalled position of this unique mountain of the shape of Shiva's lingam has made it the holiest throne of the gods of the great Asiatic religions......The Kailas, not only is the holiest mountain for several hundred million Buddhists and Hindus, but is also geologically a unique feature. It seems to represent the highest tertiary conglomeratic series of our globe, still in the position of deposition."[2]

LET US TO THE DIVINE LAKE

Return journey should be done, taking proper rest wherever needed, following the route of the onward journey. As this pilgrimage cannot be undertaken easily, or often, one should spend some days leisurely in quiet meditation, either at Kailas or preferably on the shores of Manasarovar, wherefrom one can enjoy the view of the Holy Kailas and a sacred dip in the Manas. Whether one be a pilgrim or a tourist, one should not fail to derive full benefit from these holy and hallowed places by staying there atleast for a few days, and not run on in undue haste. Pilgrims should make it a point to devote sometime daily for peaceful meditation and contemplation by the side of the azure-blue surface of the charming Lake. Forgetting the idea of time and space for a while, just ponder over the questions—Whence this Boat of our Life-Journey has started sailing? Where It is now? Whither It is bound? What is the aim of this Journey? What is Its Goal? and, What is the relation between this Boat and its Projector?

1 Arnold Heim and A. Gansser, "The Throne of the Gods."
2 Arnold Heim and A. Gansser, "Central Himalaya, Geological observations of Swiss expeditim 1936."

EPILOGUE

One can spend days and nights together like so many minutes, watching the weird grandeur, splendour, and majesty of the sacred Peak of Kailas without being tired, or in peaceful meditation and contemplation, by the side of the turquoise-blue surface of the charming Lake Manasarovar, lulled by her awe-inspiring solemnity. One breathes more happily and with greater ease ; one feels real pleasure in life, and yearns to remain sailing indefinitely on the fascinating blue depths and the sacred waves. Discoveries in the domain of geology or geography of the Mount Kailas or study of the hydrographic relation of this unique Lake to lakes similarly situated in other parts of the world are no doubt extremely pleasant pastimes and many be attempted by a person of an average intellectual calibre ; but the inner joy which one feels when one is face to face with an object of supernatural beauty and eternal charm, such as is presented by this Summit under a cupola of perpetual snow, where, according to Hindu traditions, Shiva (the Universal Spirit) abides permanently with His Divine Consort Parvati (the personification of *Prakriti* or Nature) and where, in terms of the Tibetan scriptures, the Buddha resides with his hierarchy of 500 *Bodhisattvas*, and the tutelary deity Demchhog (Supreme Bliss) with His Divine Consort Dorje-Phangmo (the Absolute Void), may be better described by one, more gifted poetically and aesthetically disposed than the author. How could Kailas and Manasarovar be the objects of Divine honour from two religions so different as Hinduism and Buddhism, unless it be that their overpowering beauty and charm have not only so appealed to but made an indelible impression on the human mind, that they seemed to belong rather to heaven than to earth ! Even the first view from the Gurla pass or from the hills on the shore is simply marvellous and breath-taking and causes one to burst into tears of joy at the magnificent landscape ; a more intimate association undoubtedly throws one into mystic trances, when, one feels nearer the Divine Presence than at any other time. The author feels that if he has been able to stimulate interest in any of his readers to undertake this very educative and wholesome journey to this abode of Bliss (Kailas and Manasarovar) in the Region of Snows (Himalayas) and to feel that inner joy which is surely to be felt by every mortal, like himself, his labour will have been amply rewarded. Besides, if some devotee, having been inspired by the August Presence, himself can hand over the Torch of Illumination to his fellow-brothers, the gratifying reflection of having originated and perpetuated this chain of inspiration will fill the author with supreme satisfaction—a natural and legitimate result of the fulfilmemt of a noble and self-imposed mission of serving humanity.

OM !

APPENDICES

APPENDIX I

GLOSSARY OF TIBETAN AND OTHER WORDS

[H—Hindi; S—Sanskrit; K—Kumaon; Bh—Bhotia; and the rest are all Tibetan words.]

Bhot (H)—Indian Borderland of North Almora, North Garhwal, North Tehri, etc.
Bhotia (H)—An inhabitant of Bhot.
Bodhisattva (S)—One who is qualified to attain Buddhahood or *Nirvana*, but has delayed it and has remained in this world to help the striving human beings by preaching the Law.
Bot, Bod, or Bod-yul—Tibet.

Chakarma—Gull.
Chakta—Matchbox.
Chak-tak—Chain.
Cham—How many; madam.
Chamba or Champa—Maitreya.
Cham-kushok—Madam or *mem-sahiba*.
Champa—*Sattu* or parched barley powder.
Chatti (K)—A staging place on the pilgrim-route to Badrinath and Pashupatinath.
Chema—Sand.
Chema-kara—Sugar.
Chema-nenga—Five coloured sands of Manasarovar (see p. 199).
Chen-khang—A small image-hall where *pujas* are performed regularly, daily morning and evening.
Chenresig or Chenrezig—Avalokiteshvara.
Chhagna-dorje—Vajra-pani.
Chhak-chhal-gang or Changja-gang—A place, wherefrom prostration-salutation is made to any holy place.
Chham—Solitary confinement for a fixed period for doing meditation and *pujas*.
Chhang—A kind of light beer made by fermenting barley.
Chhang-rin—Present or *bakshish* (literally price of *chhang*).
Chhasu—Tax-collector.
Chheme—Butter lamp.
Chhen or Chhe—Big.
Chhen—Night.
Chherba—Rain.
Chhongra—Mart or *mandi*.
Chhopa—Images made of *sattu* and butter used in *tantrik* rites.

Chhorten—A sort of monument, *stupa*, or *chaitya*.
Chhu—Water, river, rivulet, or stream.
Chhu-mar—Ghee or clarified butter.
Chhura—Cheese.
Cho—Tibetan great antelope (Pantholops Antelope).
Chomo—Nun.
Chong—Onion ; any commodity for sale.
Cho-nga—Full moon day.
Chung—Small.

Daba—Ordinary *sadhu* or monk.
Dalai Lama—Ocean *Guru*, the Sovereign political head of Tibet, believed to be the incarnation of Bodhisattva Avalokiteshvara.
Dama—A sort of thorny juniper bush, which is used as fuel and which burns even when green, Tibetan furze.
Damaru (S)—A vibrant (double) hand-drum.
Dang—Yesterday.
Dazang—The managing body of a monastery.
De—Rice.
Demchhok or Demchhog—The presiding deity of Kailas.
Demo—Tibetan cow.
Dhak—Nepalese Rupee.
Dhara (H)—A water tap.
Dhura (H)—Pass.
Diring—Today.
Do—Stone.
Dok-pa—Dweller of a black tent or shepherd.
Dong—A black tent of a shepherd.
Donkhang—*Dharmashala* or a free rest house.
Dorje—*Vajra* or diamond.
Dorje-Phagmo—Vajra-Varahi.
Du—Barley.
Duk—Yes or there is.
Duk—Bhutan State.
Duk-pa—A person belonging to Bhutan State.
Dum—Chinese brick-tea.
Duvang—General image-hall.
Gad (K)—A hill stream or rivulet.
Gangri—Glacier or Kailas.
Gar-pon—Officer of Gar or Gartok, Viceroy of Western Tibet.
Go—Head.
Goa—Tibetan gazelle.
Gokpa—Garlic.
Gompa or Gonpa—Buddhist monastery or lamasery.

Gopa or Goba—Village headman.
Gormo—Indian Rupee.
Gur (H)—Jaggery.
Gutang—Nepalese *Mohar*.
Gya-gar—White plain or India.
Gya-nak—Black plain or China.
Gyalpo—Raja, chief, or king.

Havan (S)—Offerings to the fire.
Hun or Hundesh (Bh)—Tibet.
Huniya (Bh)—Tibetan.

Ja—Tea.
Jamb-yang—Manju-ghosh.
Ja-ril—A ball of chinese tea.
Jav—Half a *Tanga*.
Jhabbu—Crossbreed of a Tibetan bull and an Indian cow.
Jilab—*Prasad*, something taken as a memento either from a holy person or place.
Jinbu or Jimbu—Tibetan onion leaves.
Joo—Salutation or thanks.

Kang-ri—Snow-mountain, glacier, or Kailas.
Kangri Karchhak—*Kailas Purana*.
Kang Rinpochhe—Jewel of Snows or Holy Kailas.
Kanjur—Translation of Buddha's sayings and teachings in 108 volumes (see p. 59).
Kara—Sugar-candy.
Khamjam—Salutation.
Khampa—A Tibetan domiciled in India or a native of Kham (a province in Eastern Tibet).
Khar—Fort.
Khatak—Loosely woven gauze-like white linen used as a garland in Tibet, a ceremonial scarf.
Khangba—House.
Khi—Dog.
Khir—Bring.
Kiyang or Kyang—Wild horse or ass.
Kong—High, up, or senior ; rate.
Kora—Circumambulation.
Korlo—Prayer-cylinder or prayer-mill.
Kunchhok-sum—By God ; an oath.
Kund (H)—A trough, tub, or tank either artificial or natural.
Kur—Tent.

Kushok—Mister, *shreeman*, or *saheb*.

La—Pass.
Labrang—General Managing Body of a monastery, usually deputed by a bigger monastery in Central or Eastern Tibet to its branch in Western Tibet.
Labu—Turnip.
Lam—Path.
Lama—Buddhist monk of higher order, Guru or high priest, or spiritual teacher.
Langak Tso—Rakshas Tal.
Langchen Khambab—The river coming out of the mouth of an elephant—Sutlej.
Laptche—A heap of stones generally raised at the top of mountains, at the end of ascents, wherefrom some holy place is seen conspicuously, or at the top of passes, or on the way to any holy place representing the deity of that place, all amounting to clear the way of stones. Streamers are hung on them.
Lha—*Devata* or deity.
Lha-khang—Deity-house or image-hall.
Lham—Tibetan boots coming up to the knees.
Lharchi or Lharche—Musk.
Le—Camping ground with walled enclosures.
Lo—Belt of a horse.
Luk—Sheep.
Lung—Wind.
Lung, Lungba, Lungma, or Lungva—Valley.

Maidan (H)—Plain.
Mak-pon or Magpon—Military Officer or *Patwari*.
Mandal—Cairn or stones piled one over another like a pillar; a *yantra* (see footnote on p. 58).
Mandi (H)—Market or mart.
Mani—The *mantra Om ma ni pa dme hum*, or jewel.
Mani-cylinder—Cylinder in which slips of *mani-mantra* are kept.
Mani-stone—Stone on which *mani* is inscribed or embossed.
Mani-wall—Wall on which *mani*-stones are kept.
Mantra (S)—Mystic formula (see footnote on p. 61).
Mapcha Khambab—The river coming out of mouth of a peacock—Karnali.
Map chhu—Karnali.
Mapham—The Unconquerable Manasarovar.
Mar—Butter.
Marku—Oil.

Mathova—Manasarovar.
Mavang—Manasarovar.
Mayur—Crevasse or fissure.
Me—Fire; no.
Men—Medicine.
Mi—Man.
Mi-duk—No or there is not.

Namkang—New moon day.
Naning—Last year.
Naza—Disease.
Nechen—Place of pilgrimage or a *tirtha*.
Nerpa or Nerba—Steward or secretary.
Ngangba—Swan.
Ngari—Western Tibet.
Ngato—Tomorrow.
Ngima—Day or sun.
Ngyul—Silver or money.
Nirbishi (K)—A variety of aconite.
Nirvana (S)—Salvation.
Num-nak—Mustard oil.
Nya—Fish.
Nyakor—Pilgrim.
Nyan—Great Tibetan sheep (Ovis Ammon).
Nyima—Day, sun, or sunlight.

Odyar (K)—Cave.
Oma—Milk.

Pa—*Wala*.
Padav (H)—Staging-place.
Palden—*Shree*.
Pan-chakki (H)—Water-mill.
Panchhen Lama or Penchhen Lama—Spiritual head of Tibet, believed to be the incarnation of the Bodhisattva Amitabha Buddha.
Par—Photo.
Parikrama (S)—Circumambulation.
Phagbe—Wheat flour.
Phing—Tibetan vermicelli made of pea flour.
Phuk—Cave.
Phuldo—Crude Tibetan soda or baked *seru-tsa*.
Po—Incense.
Po or Poyul—Tibet.
Pombo—Officer.
Pomo—Woman; female; daughter.

Prasad (S)—Something taken from a Holy place or person, charge with spiritual vibrations as a sacred memento or remembranc
Puja (S)—Worship.
Purana (S)—A book of ancient Indian history and mythology.
Puram—*Gur* or jaggery.

Ra—Goat.
Re—Cotton cloth ; 'yes sir'.
Ri—Mountain.
Ring—Price.
Rinpochhe—Jewel ; holy ; holiness.

Sa or Za—Day of the week.
Sadhu (S)—A Hindu ascetic or holy man.
Sakya-Thubha—Sakya-Muni or Buddha.
Sangpo or Sampo—Brahmaputra.
Sapta—Map.
Sarai (H)—*Dharmashala.*
Sattu (H)—Parched barley powder.
Senge Khambab—The river coming out of the mouth of a lion—Indus.
Ser—Gold or yellow.
Seru-tsa—A kind of crude soda (unbaked).
Shapje—Footprint.
Shing—Tree ; fuel ; wood ; stick.
Shok—Come on.
Shung-chhong—Government Trader.
Shya—Meat.
Shyo—Curds.
Siddha (S)—One who has attained high psychic and supernatura powers.
Sola—Charcoal.
Sug—Pain.

Ta—Horse.
Ta-lo—Horse-year ; this year.
Tamchok Khambab—The river coming out of the mouth of a horse,—Brahmaputra.
Tamo—Cold.
Tanjur—Translation of all *shastras* (see p. 59).
Tanga or Tanka—Tibetan silver coin, equivalent to four annas.
Tantrik (S)—Mystic.
Tantrism (S)—Mystic cult.
Tara—Buttermilk.

Tara (S)—A female deity, common both to Hindus and Buddhists.
Tarchema—*Chook* or a sour fruit.
Tarchok—Flags and festoons especially of five colours : white, red, green, yellow, and blue.
Tasam or Tarzam—Transport or Post Stage Officer.
Tasam—High road.
Te—Mule.
Thanga—Plateau or *maidan*.
Thanka—A Tibetan banner painting especially of Buddhistic deities, saints, *yantras*, etc.
Thukpa—A semi-liquid dish made of *sattu*, cheese, and meat.
Thu—A preparation made of mixing cheese with *gur* and butter.
Thuma—An aphrodesiac or rejuvenating herbal root.
Ti (Bh)—Water.
Tima—Cream.
Tisi—Kailas.
To—Stone.
Trama—Pea.
Tsa—Salt.
Tsabo—Hot.
Tsampa or tsamba—*Sattu*.
Tsangpo—Big river; commonly used for the Brahmaputra in Central Tibet.
Tso—Lake.
Tuchhe-chhe—Thanks.
Tugu—Son; boy.
Tulku—*Avatar* or incarnation.
Tulku lama—Incarnation Lama.
Tumo—Heat.

Udyar (H)—Same as *odyar*, cave.
Urko Kong—Viceroy Senior.
Urko Yok—Viceroy Junior.

Vihara (S)—University or monastery.

Yak—Tibetan bull.
Yambu—Nepal.
Yankti (Bh)—River.
Yantra (S)—Mystic circle geometrically subdivided into circles and squares.
Yok—Lower or junior.

Yul—Village.
Yung-chhong—Government Trader or State Merchant.

Zaharmora (H)—Serpentine.
Zong or Zongpon—Governor ; Governor's residential building ; fort.

NUMERALS

1	2	3	4	5	6	7	8
Chik	Nyi	Sum	Shi	Nga	Tug	Dun	Gye

9	10	20	30	40
Gu	Chu	Nyi-shu	Sum-chu	Ship-chu
50	60	70	80	90
Map-chu	Tug-chu	Dun-chu	Gye-chu	Gup-chu

100	200	300	1,000
Gya-thamba	Nyi-gya	Sum-gya	Tong
10,000	1,00,000	10,00,000	1,00,00,000
Thi	Bum	Chhiva	Sayap

$\frac{1}{2}$	$1\frac{1}{2}$	$2\frac{1}{2}$
Pheka or chheka	Chhedang-nyi	Chhedang-sum
$3\frac{1}{2}$	$4\frac{1}{2}$	$\frac{1}{4}$
Chhedang-shi	Chhedang-nga	Shi-ja

APPENDIX II

SYMBOLISM IN TIBETAN BUDDHISM[1]

YIDAM (यिदम्) AND YAB-YUM POSE (यब्-युम् मुद्रा)

EVERY Buddhist Sect in Tibet, every gompa (monastery) and every lama (Tibetan high monk) has a *Yidam* (*Ishta-devata*), tutelary deity, or god-protector of its or his own. The *Yidam* of a lama and that of the sect or monastery to which he belongs need not necessarily be the same. It is only a monk that can prioptiate or worship the *Yidam* directly, the householder (*grihastha*) cannot do so but through a monk. *Dolma* (*Tara*) is the only *Yidam* of the higher order who can be worshipped by the layman.

The *Yidam* is almost invariably represented in *Yab-Yum Mudra* (lit. father-mother pose). The fundamental principle of the Yoga System, namely the union of the individual soul with the Universal Spirit or the union of the Spirit with matter is symbolically represented by the Tibetan mystics as *Yab-Yum* posture. *Yab* represents primeval male, *Purusha*, Divinity, *Shiva*, *Vajra-dhatu*, or the subject. *Yum* represents primordial female (or producing) principal, *Prakriti* (matter), *Shakti*, *Kali Garbha-dhatu*, or object. So the *Yab-Yum* pose represents divine ecstacy or the spiritual communion with the Most High. As a matter of fact *Yidam* is considered by Tibetans to be more efficacious if worshipped with his *Shakti* in *Yab-Yum* pose. This posture is also called *Vajra-mudra*.[2]

This *Yab-Yum mudra* is geometrically represented in *Mandalas* or *Yantras* by two triangles—one resting on its base and the other resting on its apex, mutually interlocked as shown below.

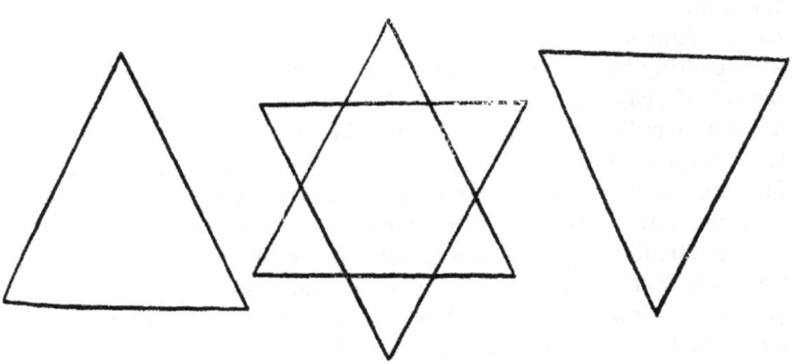

1 This was originally published in the 'Journal of the United Provinces Historical Society', Vol. XVIII (July-December 1945).

2 In the esoteric doctrine *Vajra* is the symbol of *Linga*.

The first represents *Yoni*, *Prakriti*, imperfection, the exoteric principle, or objectivity, and the second represents *Linga*, *Purusha*, perfection, the esoteric principle, or subjectivity. Subjectivity and objectivity, acting and reacting upon each other, produce this universe of diversity and many-ness. This is the underlaying principle for representing the *Brahmanda Charkra* or the Wheel of Universe by two interlocked triangles. Various forces of the *Mula-prakriti* or *Maha-Kali* have been represented as different *Yums* or *Matirkas* of different *Yabs*. Just as the Hindu, whether male or female, has not got even the least idea of sex or sensuous feeling while worshipping the *Linga* or phallus of Shiva, so a Tibetan, when he or she does the worship of the *Yidam*, in *Yab-Yum* pose.

CHHAM

Lamas of higher order usually retire to a solitary place, almost invariably to a cave for a month or two in a year for the worship of their *Yidam*. This kind of retirement either for a short time or for a long period is called *chham* in Tibetan. The author was in *chham* for a month in *Pushya* 1945, with the *tulku lama* (*avatari* or incarnation lama) Jayan Chhojur, popularly known as Nav-Kushok of the Simbiling Gompa, in a cave in Kailas-Manasa Region.

At the commencement of the *chham* the lama does *digbandhana* of the cave or the place where he intends staying for the purpose. *Digbandhana* (lit. restraining of the quarters) is a *tantrik* rite by which he restricts all evil spirits and evil influences coming from all quarters to throw obstacles in his *sadhana* (spiritual practices). During the period of *chham*, the lama would neither go out of the cave even for attending the calls of nature, nor would he speak with any outsider but for a servant or a monk-disciple, who would be putting up in a separate chamber of the same cave, for cooking his food and for rendering any other service, nor any outsider is allowed to enter the cave. Almost the whole of the day, from 4 a.m. to 9 p.m. is spent in repeating the *mantra* of the *Yidam* a number of times. During the period of *chham* the *mantra* of the *Yidam* is repeated 50,000 times, a lakh, a million times, or any number that he has fixed to do. At the completion of the fixed number or fixed time, *purnahuti* (or final fire-oblations) are offered with elaborate rites which may take four to five hours. As in other rites, *sattu* and butter images (छोपा) of a particular type are made for the occasion. The *chhopas* made for each *Yidam* vary in shape, size, and number, though some are common. Splinters of wood of a particular length, clarified butter, *durva* (a kind of grass), barley, wheat, rice, peas, *til* seeds, mustard seeds, cooked rice, etc. are used for *ahutis*.

Tibetans believe that if *chham* is well observed for a sufficiently long period, the *Yidam* would manifest himself to the devotee and would lead him to the Highest Blissful State. It may be noted here that according to Tibetan Buddhists, *Nirvana* or the highest state of perfection is not extinction of the Self, but blowing out the flame of selfishness and longings and the attainment of the Highest Blissful State. *Chham* is also observed, oftentimes, for the fulfilment of some desire of the observer himself or of his devotee.

MANDALA

Every *Yidam* has got a separate *mandala* which is used only in the worship of that particular deity. A *mandala* or *yantra* is a mystic circle geometrically subdivided into circles, squares, or chords in which are painted some symbols, deities and *bijaksharas*. When the *Yidams* are worshipped in the gompas, their respective *mandalas* are elaborately prepared with finely powdered stone dyed in various colours. They are drawn in relief with minute details, wonderful precision, execution, and great skill. The author witnessed four such *mandalas* or *yantras* in the Simbiling Monastery of Taklakot in Kailas-Manasarovar Region, where he stayed as an inmate for some time in 1936-37 and 1943-44. The diameter of the *yantras* was 4 to 5 feet. For the portable use of individuals during *chham*, the *mandalas* of different *Yidams* are painted on banners and planks of wood.

It is said that Tibetan lama-teachers took these *Yidams* from Bharatavarsha to Tibet; so the names of the lamas who had actually invoked or took them to Tibet are given both in paintings and in books written about the *Yidam*. There are a number of *Yidams* in Tibetan Buddhism like Demchhog, Sangdul (presiding deity of Gurla Mandhata), Jigje, Kunrig, etc. The author proposes to give from time to time the description of a number of these tutelary and other deities of Tibetan pantheon which may throw some light on the undeciphered iconography of India.

DEMCHHOG or DHARMAPALA[1]

Demchhok or Demchhog is the presiding deity of the Holy Mount Kailas according to Tibetan mythology and scriptures. He is also the presiding deity of two more mounts, (1) Lapchi on Nepal borders

1 "Shamvara was an *Asura* (demon) in Indian mythology, opposed to Indra, literally *sham* means bliss, and *vara* means screening. While translating the name in Tibetan, *shamvara* became 'Bliss Excellent' (Skt. *vara* also meaning excellent) and thus Shamvara in place of the demon that witholds bliss, became the deity of Supreme Bliss and was indentified with Shiva, presiding deity of Kailas". Dr. Vasudeva Saran Agrawala.

and (2) Chari, 200 miles east of Lhasa. The iconographic form of Demchhog is highly interesting as understood in the light of the explanation which Tibetan mystics [1] offer for the many attributes associated with him. According to them, Demchhog represents Supreme Bliss, as he is of the rank of the Buddha.

Demchhog has four faces—the middle one is blue, the right one is white, the left green, and the back one is red. They represent the four-fold sets of ideas like four elements—earth, water, fire, and air; four virtues—compassion, affection, love, and impartiality; and so on. Each face has three eyes which symbolizes that he knows the time past, present, and future, that the three worlds are under his vision, and so on.

Each of his heads is adorned with a crown of five skulls representing the five-fold wisdom. The faces frown and the teeth are set showing that all vices are overcome by him. On each head the hair is tied in a knot and each skull in the crown of head is adorned with a pearl or gem, showing that merit has been acquired to the fullest degree. The wheel of bone over the head is symbolic of meditation. The ear-rings symbolize fortitude; necklace charity; bracelets chastity; and girdle symbolizes energy. His blue body is the symbol of never changing form.

Demchhok has twelve hands which represent the knowledge of the twelve causes of the round of life (*avidya, samskara, vijnana, namarupa, shadayatana, sparsa, vedana, trishna, upadana, bhava, jati,* and *jara-marana*). The first pair of upper hands holds *dorje* (*vajra*) representing the knowledge and *tilbu* (bell) the method. To show that they are ever in union, the two hands clasp the *Shakti*. The second set of two hands holds a raw elephant-hide which they are tearing asunder. Elephant-hide is the symbol of nescience. The third right hand holds a *damaru* proclaiming joyous tidings; the fourth right hand brandishes a *tari* (battle axe) with which he cuts off the ties of births and deaths; the fifth right hand holds a *di* (dagger) to show that the six sins of pride etc. are cut off; and the sixth right hand grasps a *khatam* (*trishula*) showing that the root passions of *kama, krodha,* and *lobha* are controlled.

The third left hand holds a *khatvanga* (a staff surmounted by a *dorje* and *amrita-kalasha*), a sign of Supreme Bliss; the fourth left hand holds a blood-filled *kapala* (human skull) signifying that all ideas, material as well as non-material, are done away with; from the fifth left hand dangles a *thagpa* (noose) which denotes knowledge that grasps the nature of sentient beings; and in the sixth left hand is the

1 This is the exposition given to the author by the incarnation Lama Nava-Kushok of the Simbiling Gompa, taken from the book '*Yidam Demchhog*'.

head of four-faced *Chhangpa* (*Brahma*) showing that all delusions of the worldly cycle (*samsara*) have been shaken off.

He tramples an emaciated figure, symbolising time, under his right foot and his left leg spurns the form of a black demon. Both these bodies are four-armed, the former a male figure and the latter a female one.[1]

Round the waist, Demchhog is loosely draped in a tiger-skin as he is released from all distinction of matter and spirit. There is full symmetry and grace in his body, his countenance is heroic, stern and severe. He is full of energy ; he is awe-inspiring and yet he is compassionate, and his features are of a peaceful cast. This is the *ugra* (fierce) form of Demchhog. In the Tibetan mythology, most of the deities have three forms—the *ugra* or the fierce form, the *ranjaka* or the fascinating form, and the *saumya* or the peaceful form.

Dorje-Phangmo (lit. *Vajra-Varahi*) is the *Yum* or divine consort of Demchhog. The small snow-clad pyramidal peak called Tijung that is adjacent to the Mount Kailas on its western side, is the abode of Dorje-Phangmo. Dorje-Phangmo, Demchhog's *Yum*, sumbolic of Energy, clings to him in an inextricable embrace. She is red in colour which, in Tibetan art, is the symbol of affection for all beings. She has only one face since all things have one taste ; she possesses two hands, for she comprehends both aspects of truth—the apparent and the real ; her right hand holds a curved knife which is wisdom or consciousness that cuts away all qualifying thoughts and passions. She brandishes this weapon in all directions. With her left had she clasps her partener. To signify that she has united the knot which holds all things to be what they appear, her hair is loose and flowing. She is naked for she is free from the obscuring veil of passion (*kama*). She, like her partner, is three-eyed and wears the crown of five skulls of five wisdoms.

He is *Purusha* and she is *Prakriti*. They are inseparable, so they are shown mutually interlocked and touching at all points of contact.[2] The marriage is consummated in the midst of a halo of flames, the fire of Supreme Widom which burns up all obstacles and nescience.

In Tibetan paintings of gods and goddesses, bliss is represented by blue colour, and devotion to the service of beings by red colour. So most of the *Yidams* are painted in blue colour.

1 In the clay model of Guru-gem there are four female figures under the right foot and four male figures under the left foot of Demchhog.

2 The ten-foot high clay model in Guru-gem Gompa and the bronze image in Simbiling Gompa are of this type. In some paintings, the right leg of the *Yum* is thrown hanging over the left thigh of the *Yab* and this is the type of the pose in the banner collected by August Gansser from the Deserted Cave-City of Pangtha. Still in some other paintings both the legs of the *Yum* intertwine the *Yab* ; this is the type of representation which the author had seen in the banners of Simbiling Gompa. Those who are interested in the subject would do well to have a look into the bronze images of *Yidams* in *Yab-Yum* pose kept in the Museum and in the art gallery of R. B. Jalan at Patna.

APPENDIX III

DISTINGUISHED VISITORS TO MANASA KHANDA

There is a reference to Kailas (Mount Meru) in the *Vedas*, the oldest books in the world's library. It is written in the *Puranas*, that Lord Shiva and Brahma, gods of destruction and creation respectively, did penance in Manasa Khanda. Marichi, Vasishtha, and other sages did penance here for twelve years. Manasarovar is said to have been created by Brahma who, it is believed, floats in it in the form of a Royal Swan. Emperor Mandhata in *Krita-yuga* (Golden Age), Ravana, Bhasmasura, and others in *Treta-yuga* (Silver Age) did penance to propitiate Lord Shiva. There is a reference to Kailas and Manasarovar in the great epic *Ramayana*. Rishi Dattatreya did the pilgrimage to Kailas and Manasarovar.

There are several references to Kailas and Manasarovar in the great epic *Mahabharata*, according to which about 5,050 years ago at about the beginning of the *Kali Yuga* (Iron Age) Arjuna visited and conquered this Region, in consequence of which the vassal Kings of this Region sent black and white yak-tails, best steeds, gold, brilliant gems, and other things as presents to the Emperor Yudhishthira on the occasion of *Rajasuya-Yaga* or Horse-Sacrifice. After that, Rishi Vyasa and Bhima visited Kailas once and Sri Krishna and Arjuna on another occasion. Rishis, sages, and spiritual aspirants had been visiting and sojourning in this hallowed Region from time immemorial. According to some historians the great Emperor Asoka (269 B.C.) deputed the Katyuri Raja Nandi Deva of Kumaon who invaded Western Tibet through the Unta-dhura pass and annexed it to the Indian Empire. On his return journey he visited Kailas and Manasarovar. Nandi Deva visited this Region once again in the following year. According to the copper plate inscription in the temple of Pandukeshvar[1], the Katyuri Raja Lalita Sura Deva and Deshata Deva invaded and conquered Hun-desh (Manasa Khanda of Tibet). The famous Chinese pilgrim Hiuen Tsang (A.D. 635) says that the Katyuri Kings of Kumaon ruled over Tibet (western parts) in the sixth century. In the seventh century, I-Tsing and several other Chinese travellers (675-685) came to India through Manasa Khanda, to study Buddhism in the Nalanda University and to visit places of Buddhistic pilgrimage in India.

Some biographers of Jagad Guru Shree Adi Shankaracharya write that he had dropped down his body near Kailas. According to Eastern Pandits, Shankaracharya lived before the Christian era, and according to the Western scholars he lived in the 8th century A.D.

1 This village is midway between Joshinath and Badrinath. The copper plate dates the 25th year of Vikrama era, i.e., about 33 B. C.

In the *Kangri Karchhak* it is written that Geva Gozangba first discovered the *parikrama*-route to Kailas and Manasarovar. Once seven sages from India visited Manasa Khanda and desposited seven loads of silver with the King of Kardung, with which the image of Khochar were made. On another occasion seven maidens from India visited the Manas and had set up seven cairns, with stones taken from India, on the south-western corner of Manasarovar at Momo-dungu (see p. 134). The dates of these could not be ascertained.

Some Tibetans claim that Acharya Shanta Rakshita and Guru Padmasambhava visited Manasa Khanda, but authentic evidence could not be gathered of the visits of these two and those of Hiuen Tsang and I-Tsing. In the middle of the 9th century Chinese topographers and officers visited this Region and took some notes and drew maps of the Region later.

Adinath Vrishabhadeva, the first Tirthankara of Jainism, was said to have attained *Nirvana* at Kailas (*Ashtapada*). The Lochava (Tibetan translator) Rinchhen Zangbo (958-1058) visited Kailas and Manas and sojourned for 12 years at Khochar, preaching Lord Buddha's gospel. His *gaddi* is still preserved there.

In the year 1027 Pandit Somanath of Kashmir visited this Region and translated the *Kalachakra Jyotisha* into Tibetan (see p. 80). Pandit Lakshmikara and Danashree Chandra Rahula also accompanied him.

In the 11th century, the great Tibetan mystic and poet, *Siddha* Milarepa [2] sojourned in this Region for several years, doing his penance remaining completely naked. He wrote over a lakh of verses in Tibetan, which have all been printed along with his biography. *Kailas Purana* gives a good account of his miracles in connection with his contest with the heretic lama Naropenchhung. There are several places on Kailas-*parikrama*, associated with this saint. Lama Marpa—Milarepa's Guru, and Tilopa—Milarepa's great grand-guru visited Kailas and Manasarovar, and the latter sojourned for some time at Cherkip.

On the invitation of the King Chang-chhup-o of Guge (Western Tibet), the great Achrya Deepankara Shreejnana, popularly known as Atisha (982-1054), the Rector of the Vikramashila University, went to Thuling, in 1042 at the age of 61, for preaching Buddhism, stayed there for nine months, and wrote several books in Tibetan. It is said that he got the monastery of Chhabrang constructed in 7 days.

2 According to the Tibetans, *Tantrik* cult started from Dorje-chhang. Tilopa was the first *Tantrik* teacher and hails from Bengal. Naropa is his disciple (1040) and is a Kashmiri pandit. Lama Marpa is his Tibetan disciple and is a married monk. His disciple is the great *yogi*, *Siddha* Jechun Milarepa (1038-1112). He is a full-fledged monk and his disciples are Thakpo Lhanjir and Rechung. His followers are called *Kargyudpa*, which sect is still prevailing in Tibet.

In 1044 he visited Kailas-Manas and spent a week in a cave on the shores of the Lake below the present Gossul Gompa. There are his footprints and a spring at Gejin (see Table IV). He stayed for one rainy season in Khocharnath. One of his Tibetan disciples who was with him till his last days, wrote an elaborate biography of the great Acharya. He died at the age of 83 and his skeleton and drinking vessel are, to this day, preserved in the temple of Dolma in Nythang Gompa. Lama Jigden-gombo, the first abbot of Dekung Gompa, with 13,000 disciples visited Kailas in the year 2057 of Buddha Era (A.D. 1513 ?). He visited Kardung and Khochar also. At the time of his visit there were many scholars and *Bhikshus* in the Purang valley.

Ra Lochava was in this Region for 21 years and had got constructed 108 image-halls at Thuling, Purang, Khochar, Limi, Shar, Piti, and other places. He got the faces of the image of the Khochar Gompa gilded. Some of the frescos in Khochar Gompa are said to have been executed by him. His time could not be ascertained. In 1553, the Khan of Yarkand sent his general, Mirza Haidar, with a big army to raze to the ground the idol-temples in Lhasa. " The army made havoc in the country like plague but was itself decimated and did not attain its desired object ". On the return journey Haidar halted for the night on the shores of the Lake.

It is said that the Moghul Emperor Akbar the Great, had sent a party in the middle of the 16th century to discover the source of the Ganges. The party went round the Manas and prepared a map in which was shown Sutlej and Brahmaputra coming out of Manasarovar and Saraju coming out of Rakshas Tal.

In 1625-26 the Portugese Jesuit Father Antonio de Andrade went to Chhabrang by the Mana pass and laid the foundation of a Christian Church in April 1626. In 1627 four more Jesuits went here but there are no traces of the church now.

Some say that Gosain Tulsidas, the author of *Rama-Charitamanasa*, visited Kailas and Manasarovar, but it is very doubtful. He describes Lord Shiva and Parvati as sitting under a huge banyan tree near Kailas Peak.

Raja Bajbahadurchand of Chand Dynasty ruled over Kumaon (with Almora as capital) between 1638 and 1678. Having heard of the atrocities committed by the Huniyas (Tibetans) on the pilgrims to Kailas and Manasarovar invaded this Region. He entered Tibet by Untadhura pass and visited Kailas and Manasarovar. On the return journey he had besieged the fort at Taklakot, took control of all the passes leading to this Region, and stopped all the taxes which the Indian Bhotia traders used to pay to the Tibetans. Later, on an assurance being given by the Tibetans that they would not molest either the pilgrims or the traders in future, he ordered the taxes to be paid to the Tibetans as usual. On his return from Kailas the Raja had founded a *Sadvarta*, in 1673 to distribute food and clothing free to the pilgrims to Kailas and Manasarovar, for which he had set apart the revenue of five villages by a deed engraved on a copper plate.

The fifth Tashi Lama Penchhen Lobsang Chhoki Gyalchhen, came on a pilgrimage to Manasa Khanda in the 17th century. It is said of him that he threw a *khatak* from Thugolho to the Lake-god residing on the tree in the centre of the Lake. The *khatak* appeared to have remained suspended in air to ordinary persons, for it was actually hanging on the branches of the holy tree which could only be seen by the pious few. On his return he had gilded the top of a temple at Tashi Lhunpo with a handful of *chema-nenga* (see p. 199) taken from the shores of the Manas. Some say that the Lama visited the Manas in the 19th century.

In 1715, the Roman Catholic Father, Desideri and Freyre travelled from Leh to Lhasa in the company of a Tartar Princess and her big retinue. They reached Manasarovar on November 9, 1715. Desideri and Freyre are the first white men to visit Manasarovar. Desideri describes the Ganges as taking rise in Kailas and Manasarovar and confuses it with the Sutlej and further says that Kailas is the source of the Indus.

Between 1711 and 1717, the Chinese Emperor Kang Hi deputed some lama-topographers to survey and reconnoitre this Region. They had later prepared a map of Tibet including this Region. About the year 1758, Khembo Sonam Gelzin of Ngor or Ngyur Gompa visited Kailas-Manas Region and wrote the *Khochar Karchhak* or *Khochar Purana*.

Purangir, a Brahmin, employed by Lord Warren Hastings as an interpreter and a spy and who accompanied Bogle[1] and Turner to Tibet, visited Manasarovar about the year 1770 and stayed for a day at Thugolho. He reports that the Ganges has its source on Kailas and from there it flows into Manasarovar and from the Manas it flows out again. Between 1770-80 Puranpuri an *urdhva-bahu sanyasi* (a monk with hands upheld), visited Balkh, Bukhara, Samarkand, China, Lhasa, and other places and then did the *parikrama* of the Manas in six days. He says that the Ganges issues out of Kailas, Saraju from Rakshas Tal, and Brahmaputra from the Manas.

In 1812, William Moorcroft, a veterinary surgeon and Captain Hearsay, in the guise of *sadhus* entered Tibet by Niti pass. On August 6, they camped near Chiu Gompa. At the that time there was no flow of water in the Ganga Chhu. But Harballabh, who accompanied

1 Bogle is the first Englishman to enter Tibet.

him, visited the Manas previously in 1796, when there was so much of water in the Ganga Chhu that he could not wade through it but to cross it by bridge near the hot springs. It is said that Moorcroft was killed near Manasarovar in 1838. One Debu or Dev Singh of Johar who was a *Patwari* for 24 years, helped Moorcroft a good deal in his wanderings in Ngari. Moorcroft and Hearsay are the first Englishmen to visit Manasarovar. In the year 1841 General Zoravar Singh invaded Western Tibet and reached Taklakot where he was assasinated by Tibetans. His tomb still stands at Toyo (see p. 79).

In September and October 1846 Captain Henry Strachey visited this Region by Darma pass. He went down the Darma yankti, travelled to Rakshas Tal, then to Chiu Gompa, and returned by the Lipu Lekh pass. He saw three feet deep water rapidly flowing in the Ganga Chhu and suggested for the first time whether the Darma yankti might not be the main head-stream of the Sutlej, from the quantity of water it carried. In 1848 his brother Sir Richard Strachey along with J. E. Winterbottom, visited this Region via Milam and Gyanima Mandi and travelled on the southern shores of Rakshas Tal up to Chiu Gompa. He returned via Sibchilim and Milam. The Strachey brothers contributed a good deal toward the geography of Manasa Khanda.

The famous *Siddha* Tailanga Swami of Benares is said to have visited Kailas-Manas for a number of times about the middle of the 19th century. His original name is Ganesh Swami and hails from Vizagapatam. Being a Telugu brahmin he is popularly known as as Tailanga Swami. He died in the year 1887 at a ripe age of 150 but many believe that his age was 280 at the time of his death.

In 1845 the Nepalis invaded Manasa Khanda and destroyed the fort of Siddikhar. (see p. 81). In July 1855, Adolf and Robert Schlagintweit proceeded up to Daba via Milam but were turned back. Again in the month of September they went to Thuling by Mana pass and Chhabrang, but were again turned back; so they could not do any exploration work. Sherring writes in his 'Western Tibet' that in 1855 or 1860 one Drummond, Commissioner of Bareilly sailed on Manasarovar but it could not be confirmed either from Almora or from Manasarovar Region. In 1864, Robert Drummond, Henry Hodgson, Lt. Col. Smith, and Webber went to the southern flank of Gurla Mandhata and proceeded up to the source of the Brahmaputra for hunting the wild yak. Webber places the source of the Ganges on the southern flank of the Mandhata and that of the Indus on the northern flank.

In June 1865, Captain H. R. Smith, together with A. S. Harrison, went to Tarchhen via Lipu Lekh. They went along the northern shores of the Rakshas and Manas, stayed for a day near Cherkip Gompa, and then proceeded to Gartok. The same year in the month of August Adrian Bennett visited Daba by Chor-Hoti pass. He stayed there for a month and returned back by the Niti pass as he was not allowed to proceed further.

Deputed by the Survey of India Office in 1856 through Captain T. G. Montgomery one, Johari Bhotia Thakur Nain Singh, C.I.E. visited Manasarovar. From his records a map of Manasarovar and Rakshas Tal was prepared. Though he did not actually visit the source of the Brahmaputra, yet the information he had gathered from local Tibetans was quite right. He writes that "the source of the Brahmaputra is in the Tamchok Khambab Kangri glaciers at the head of the river Chema-yungdung". He is called 'Pundit A.' in the Survey of India Records.

Between 1867-68 Montgomery sent some more pundits for survey, of whom some were murdered before reaching the source of the Indus. Almost at the same time as Nain Singh, the survey of India had sent Man Singh, son of Dev Singh a Johari Bhotia, for exploring the regions north of Kailas, but Man Singh being very well known in Manasa Khanda, Tibetans did not allow him to go beyond Kailas.

Between 1879 and 1882 a Johari Bhotia, Rai Bahadur Kishen Singh was sent to Tibet by the Survey of India Office to do some survey work. Most of his exploration work was done in Mongolia. On his way back home he visited Manas Region also. His explorations and maps are published by the Survey of India Office and he is known as "A. K. Pundit".

In 1900-03 the Japanese Buddhist Monk, Ekai Kawaguchi, travelled in Tibet and visited Manas Khanda in the year 1900, crossed the Brahmaputra (Chema-yungdung), and "drank deep the water at the source of the Ganges from the spring Chhumik-Chungtol," about 20 miles east of Manasarovar. He passed by Thugolho on his way to Gyanima Mandi and them did the round of Kailas and went to Lhasa. He makes the Sutlej a tributary of the Ganges and says that he found Rakshas Tal to be at a higher level than the Manas, that every ten years water from Rakshas Tal flows into the Manas and that the circumference of Manasarovar is 200 miles!

At the end of November 1904, Major C. H. D. Ryder, and Captain Rawling, marched along the shores of both the lakes and found no water in Ganga Chhu. Though he did not actually visit the place, Major Ryder makes the Chema-yungdung the main river of Brahmaputra and Kubi a tributary, from the information he had gathered from the local Tibetans. In 1905, Charles Sherring, Deputy Commissioner of Almora, and Dr. T. G. Longstaff visited Kailas and Manasarovar by the Lipu Lekh pass, proceeded to Gartok, and returned by Unta-dhura pass. Dr. Longstaff attempted to climb the Gurla

Mandhata, when he was almost about to reach the summit, a dangerous avalanche came down ; and so he had to come back. However, it was a successful climb. In 1907 or 1908 Mr. Cassel visited Gyanima Mandi as a special officer or most probably in the capacity of British Trade Agent of Western Tibet.

In 1907-1908 the Swedish explorer Dr. Sven Hedin, had travelled for two long years and did a good deal of exploraton work. He started the journey from Srinagar-Kashmir, passed through Ladakh, went as far as Shigartse, the place of Tashi Lama, spent over two months on the Holy Manasarovar, sailed on the Lake in a canvas boat, took several soundings, prepared an isobatic map of Manasarovar, and sounded the Lake Rakshas Tal partly. He was the first white man who sounded the Lakes Manas and Rakshas and rounded the Manas, the Rakshas, and the Kailas. It is he who had fully enjoyed the beauty of the twin Lakes. The description of his voyages on the Manasarovar are most thrilling, fascinating, and romantic. He finally fixed the sources of the Brahmaputra, the Indus, and the Sutlej and claimed to be the 'first European and white man' who had discovered them. These findings were finally carried by the Survey of India Office, until they were seriously questioned and challenged by the author as being defective and full of discrepancies, the authenticity of which is for the future explorer and geographer to judge (see 'Exploration in Tibet' for details). But this is a minor affair. However, Sven Hedin can safely be said to have contributed the greatest share towards the geography of Tibet and filled up several blank spots on it. He is at once a born explorer, geographer, and an adventurer. His two monumental works are the popular 'Trans-Himalaya' in three volumes with hundreds of illustrations and several maps and the more scientific work the 'Southern Tibet' in twelve volumes including two volumes of maps. Besides these he had written some ten more books incorporating his explorations and discoveries in Central Asia and other lands.

In 1908 Sri Hansa Swami of Bombay went to Kailas by Lipu Lekh pass. He stayed for twelve days on the shores of the Manas and later wrote a book on Kailas in Marathi, which was rendered into English by his disciple Purohit Swami under the name 'Holy Mountain'. He narrates many interesting things in it—that he saw Dattatreya in physical form on Gouri-kund, that by his grace he could negotiate a distance in fifteen minutes on his return journey which he previously did in 15 hours on the onward journey, and so on. One *sadhu* by name Mayura-pankhi Baba visited Kailas several times and lived at Khochar in 1912-13. In 1913 he made arrangements to live for an year in Gengta Gompa but died in February 1914 due to severe cold. In 1915 Sri Swami Satyadeva Parivrajaka visited Kailas and Manas.

He went there via Milam and Unta-dhura pass and returned by Lipu Lekh pass. He wrote a book on Kailas which may be the first book in Hindi.

In 1924 the author's Master Shree 1108 Swami Jnananandaji Maharaj visited Kailas and Manasarovar by Mana pass and returned by Hoti pass. He did the whole journey wearing only a *kaupeen* (a loin-cloth).

In 1922, Rai Bahadur S. R. Kashyap of Lahore visited Kailas and Manas via Lipu Lekh pass and returned via Puling and Mana pass. Again in 1926 he visited these places by Lipu Lekh pass and returned via Milam. He did the round of Kailas but not of the Manas. He wrote an article 'Some Geographical observations in Western Tibet'. There was nothing fresh in it excepting that he says that the length of the Ganga Chhu is 3 miles, which in fact is nearly six miles.

In 1926 Hugh Rutledge, the Deputy Commissioner of Almora and Capt. Wilson visited Kailas by Lipu Lekh pass. He did the round of Kailas and found no water in the Ganga Chhu. In 1927 Shree Swami Jayendrapuriji Mandaleshvar, Benares, with a party of 25 *Mahatmas* visited Kailas and Manas by Mana pass and returned by Lipu Lekh pass. He is the first Mandaleshvar to visit this Region. A pandit of that party wrote a book in Hindi '*Shree Kailasa Marga Pradipika*' in which he says that there are blue lotuses in Manasarovar and that excepting on a few days there would be snowfall without clouds. In 1929 Shree Swami Tapovanji (Kerala), and Shree Swami Krishnashramji of Gangotri visited Kailas and Manasarovar from Gangotri.

In 1929 E. B. Wakefield, Assistant Political Agent, Gangtok (or the Acting B. T. A.) visited this Region and found the Ganga Chhu deep and fast flowing. In 1931 His Highness Krishna Raja Wadayar Bahadur Maharaja of Mysore, visited Kailas. Shree Swami Sivanandaji, Shree Swami Advaitanandaji and Shreemati Suratkumari Devi, Rani of Singhai, also visited Kailas the same year. The Ran was the first pilgrim to travel on a *dandy* to Kailas.

Shree Ansingh Baba of Almora visited Kailas twice or thrice before 1930. In 1930-31 he sojourned at Khochar and during the winter of 1931 he stayed partly at Gengta and partly at Tarchhen. He used to live on potatoes and buck-wheat. In 1932 he became very weak and mad and died in a very bad condition at Taklakot in the month of July. It is about this Baba that one Swami of Rikhikesh wrote that he lived on water and leaves only and yet he was stout and sturdy. It is such incorrect reports that create sensation and curiosity amongst credulous people.

In 1932, F. Williamson, Political Agent and F. Ludlow visited

Kailas and Manasarovar, went to Gartok and returned via Simla. In 1933 or 1934 Shree Swami Krishnamachari, while on his way to Kailas was murdered by dacoits, two days before reaching the destination, since he resisted in parting with the money in his possession.

In 1934 Shree Uma Prasad Mookerjee, M.A.,B.L., brother of Dr. Syama Prasad Mookerjee of Calcutta, visited Kailas and Manasarovar and took a cine-film of his trip, which would run for about half an hour, a copy of which was presented to the University of Calcutta for public use.

In 1925, the Italian Orientalist Prof. Giuseppe Tucci visited this Region by Lipu Lekh pass and returned via Gartok and Ladakh. He is the second white man who did the round of Kailas and Manasarovar both, after Sven Hedin. He has edited and published some rare Sanskrit works which had been missing from India.

In 1936 Arnold Heim and August Gansser, two Swiss Geologists visited several places in the Central Himalayas for doing some geological survey. On three occasions the latter entered Manasa Khanda without a passport and collected a good deal of geological data. On the first occasion he filtered into Siddhikar from Nepal. Later he entered Tibet by Mangshang pass, did the round of Kailas, and returned by the same pass with his geological collection carried on sheep, as the author did once in 1928. While at the north-western corner of Rakshas lake he writes "broad fathomless bogs compel a wide detour. Here must once have been the outlet of the great lakes. Now the rivers flow in the opposite direction"[1] and nothing more. Perhaps he was not much interested with the geographical aspect of the Sutlej-problem. On the third occasion he entered Tibet by Balcha-dhura, went as far as the Sutlej, and returned by the Kungri-bingri pass. They wrote a popular work by name 'The Throne of the Gods" in German, later translated into English In the same year a young Austrian Geologist Herbert Tischy smuggled himself into this Region in the guise of a *sadhu*. He wrote a book 'The Holiest Mountain' incorporating his experiences.

In 1936-37 Shree Brahmachari OmSatyam sojourned at Tirthapuri for an year. At the end of 1937 or early in January 1938, while trying to do the round of Manasarovar, he was drowned in Gugta,[2] the ice under his feet having given way.

In 1937 a batch of Gujrati ladies, devotees of Shree Narayana Swamiji of Khela, did a complete round of Kailas and Manas both. Barring the Bhotias, this is the first batch of Indian ladies who had done the round of both these *tirthas*. In 1938 Shreemati Anandamayiji visited this Region.

[1] Arnold Heim and August Gansser, 'The Throne of the Gods' p. 97.

[2] Gugta is the outlet of Ding tso into the Manas on its north-easteen corner.

In 1940 Shreemati Uma Dar and Shree M. B. L. Dar (now Secretary, Local Self Government, U.P.) and Shreemati Rukmini and Shree G. Dikshit (now Deputy Engineer-in-Chief, E. I. Ry.) did the round of Kailas and Manas both and returned to Taklakot in nine days. This is the second batch of ladies who did the round of Kailas and Manasarovar.

From 1935 to 1941 Shree Narayana Swamiji of Shree Narayana Ashrama of Khela visited Kailas and Manasarovar successively for seven years, with big batches of his followers and devotees. He is much interested in this Region and is having a 'Manasa Vishramashala' constructed on the shores of Manasarovar.

In 1941, Shree Swami Kaivalyanandaji of the S. P. League, Calcutta, and Mr. R. D. Balvally, now Deputy Accountant General, Central Revenue, Delhi, with some of their friends, visited the Region by Lipu Lekh pass and did the complete pilgrimage by visiting Khocharnath and Tirthapuri and by doing the complete rounds of Kailas and Manasarovar, which very people could do so far.

Between 1930-42 one Ladakhi Lama sojourned near Silung Gompa on the southern slopes of Kailas for spiritual practices. He died in 1942. In 1942 Capt. R. K. M. Sekar, B. T. A. of Gyantse, came on special duty to Western Tibet via Ladakh and Gartok, did the round of Kailas, and returned by Lipu Lekh pass. A a result of his visit the headquarters of the Trade Agency of Western Tibet have been transferred from Simla to Gangtok. In 1931 and 1942 an American Christian Missionary by name Mr. Steiner, visited Kailas and Manasarovar on mission propaganda work and did the round of both Kailas and Manasarovar.

During 1943 and 1944 Shree Kailas Sarana, a Lingayat from Karnatak, did 100 rounds of Kailas and 12 of Manas, a great feat indeed. There are some Tibetans who undertook such a hard task, but it is done spread over several years.

In 1944 Shree T. N. Krishnaswami of Dalal & Co., Madras, with his assistant Shree Kalyanasundaram, visited Kailas and Manasarovar and did the round of both. This is the first batch of pilgrims from Tamilnad who did the round of both Kailas and Manasarovar. In 1945 Mr. Salim Ali, the well-known Indian Ornithologist of Bombay, was on an ornithological pilgrimage to Kailas-Manasarovar Region, and published the report of his exploration in August 1946 (see Appendix VI). In 1945, Major T. S. Blackney of Coimbatore visited Kailas and Manas but could not do the rounds due to the limitations of passports. The same year Shreemati Lopamudra and another lady from Guntur visited Kailas and Manasarovar. This is the first batch of ladies from Andhra Desa to visit this Region.

In 1947 Shree Kanwal Krishan, the well-known Indian artist, visited this Region, collected good many banners and other curios and made several paintings both in water-colours and oils. He started from Simla, went to Gartok and returned by Lipu Lekh pass. From 1937 to 1948 Shree Brahmachari Bhaskarji of Ahmedabad had been a regular visitor to this Region and did a round of Manasarovar also. He intends settling down in an *Ashrama* which he proposes to construct near about Didihat on Almora-Kailas route. Shree Swami Vidyananda Saraswatiji of the Gita Satsang Ashram, Mansiyari, has been visiting this Region for the last five years.

The last consignment of the last mortal remains (ashes) of the Father of the Indian Nation—Mahatma Gandhi—was immersed in the sacred deep blues of the Celestial Lake Manasarovar, on August 8, 1948, by a party of his intimate associates headed by Shree Surendra. May peace be unto the departed soul! The Gandhi Memorial Committee propose to erect a fitting memorial at a suitable place on the shores of Manasarovar.

Shree Buddha Bose of Calcutta, the well-known Yoga-Asanist, visited Kailas and Manasarovar by Niti-Hoti pass in 1940 and returned by Lipu Lekh pass. He visited this Region a second time by the same route in July-August 1948 and took a very interesting technicolour cine-film which runs for about two hours. He again visited this region in October-November and took some more cine-film to supplement the first consignment.

The author visited Kailas for the first time from Srinagar and returned by Niti Pass. Again from 1935 onwards he had been regularly visiting this Region every year by various routes and staying on the shores of the Holy Lake Manas from two to six months In all he did 23 rounds of Kailas and 25 of Manasarovar ; sojourned at Thugolho, on the southern shores of the Lake, once for a twelve-month during 1936-37 and on another occasion for a sixteen-month during 1943-44. He discovered the sources of the Four Great Rivers of this Region from all points of view, namely tradition, quantity of water, length, and glacier. He negotiated four new passes—Topchhen la, Lhe la, Charok-phurdod la, and Khando-sanglam la—, reached the northern, southern, and eastern bases of the Kailas Peak ; ascertained the number of islands in the Rakshas lake ; discovered the Tso Kapala ; studied the Lakes cursorily when they were frozen in winter ; sounded Gouri-kund and Manasarovar ; collected some fossils ; and undertook some other minor expeditions to the 'Deserted Cave-City' and other places. The author visits this Region primarily for the prosecution of his spiritual practices but during his leisure hours or as a recreation after his serious work, he takes to some work of scientific interest like exploration ; and as such, the readers should not be surprised if his findings or writings fall short of this standard of a professional and fullfledged scientist, in view of the fact that he, had absolutely no regular training whatsoever in any of the branches of the subjects he touches, nor has he got any expeditional equipment or kit.

APPENDIX IV

VILLAGES IN MANASA KHANDA

It is proposed to give here those villages with permanent residences or houses, since it is a bit difficult now to give a complete list of all the shepherd camps or moving tent-villages. Most of the villages are situated in the Purag valley, a list of which would be given first with the approximate number of houses in each, put in brackets.

On the right bank of the river Karnali from down to up : 1. Shar[1] (7 houses), by the side of the village is Sharba chhu, before reaching Khochar two more streams of Chhulung chhu and Salungba chhu fall on the way, 2. Khochar (100), these two villages are under the jurisdiction of Tarchhen Labrang ; about ¾ mile from the village is Lalungba chhu ; 3. Lilo (gompa and 4), 4. Kangje (6), these two villages go by the common name of Kangje and are under the jurisdiction of Toyo Magpon ; nearby flows the Kangje chhu ; 5. Gejin (7), 6. Toja (5), these two villages are under the jurisdiction of Parkha Tasam ; Gejin chhu flows nearby ; 7. Thayap (7), 8. Suje (10), 9. Chhulung (10), here is the house of Kirong Magpon, 10. Maphuk (6), 11. Kungarto (6), 12. Dangechhen (20), these six villages are under the jurisdiction of Kirong Magpon ; nearby is Kungar-lungba or Dangechhen chhu, on the right bank of which is the place called Chhegang, where a mandi of the Nepalis is held in summer ; 13. Chhorten Chhemo (6), 14. Khele (2), 15. Topa (5), here is the house of Toyo Magpon and Zoravar Singh's *samadhi*, 16. Lagun (4), 17. Shulung (5), Garu chhu flows nearby, 18. Garu (3), 19. Theji-gomba (3), 20. Delaling (4), 21. Lee or Toyo-ling (7), these nine villages go by the common name of Toyo and are under the jurisdiction of Toyo Magpon ; 22. Ronam (3), beyond this village is Ringung chhu, 23. Ringung (4), beyond this is Phurbu chhu, 24. Phurbu or Burfu (1), 25. Dungmar (11), these four villages go by the name of Ringung and are under the jurisdiction of Purang Zong and Tarchhen Labrang both ; beyond there is Baldak chhu ; 26. Kardung (7), this is under the jurisdiction of Parkha Tasam.

On the right bank of the Karnali from up to down : 27. Harkong (1), it is under the jurisdiction of the Simbiling *Nyarchang* ; 28. Doh (9), this is under the jurisdiction of Tarchhen Labrang ; 29. Salung (4), this is under the Gengta Gompa ; then comes the Yangse chhu ; 30. Gukung or Kumphur (30), this is under Kirong Magpon ; all the houses are in caves ; there is also a gompa here which is a branch of

1 A little up the village shar, Situated on the right back of the river Karnali is the village Ki, with 3 houses and some cultivation on either side of Ki chhu. Both Tibetans and the Nepalese claim this village to be theirs.

Gengta Gompa and a government Rest House; 31. Taklakhar or Taklakot (3), Simbiling Gompa, Sakya Gompa, and the fort of the *Zongpon*, at the foot of which there is the mandi of the Bhotia merchants; 32. Pili-phuk (30), here also the houses are in caves and are under the jurisdiction of Thiti and Toyo Magpons; 33. Chhungur (10), 34. Yidig (2), these two villages are situated between Yidig and Tagla chhu, 35. Dulum (3), 36. Tashigong (2), 37. Chhilchung (3), 38. Magrum or Thiti (30), here is the house of the Thiti Magpon, 39. Nayi (7), 40. Gunam (4), 41. Relashar (3), 42. Chhumi-thang (6), these ten villages go by the general name of Thiti; of these Tashigong belongs to Tashigong Gompa that is beyond Gartok; and the remaining nine villages are under the jurisdiction of Kirong Magpon. The three *pattis* of Toyo, Kirong, and Thiti are jointly called Chho-sum, and there is a joint *Panchayat* of the same name, 43. Phulak (3), 44. Chhokro (3), here is Chokro chhu, 45. Togang (4), 46. Shiddi-khar (3), above the village is the gompa and the old fort, 47. Dorjegang or Mayul (1), beyond this is Lok chhu, 48. Lok or Lo (20), 49. Lukpu (4), all these eight villages are under the jurisdiction of Simbiling Gompa.

To these may be added: 50. Thugolho (8 houses), on the southern shores of the Manas, under the jurisdiction of Simbiling Gompa; 51. Tarchhen (4), belonging to Bhutan State; 52. Debring (1), belonging to Shungba Goba, under the jurisdiction of Barkha Tasam; 53. Khyunglung (5), 54. Missar (3), these two are under the jurisdiction of Dapa Zong; and 56. Gartok (9), capital of Western Tibet, directly under the Viceroys.

The following are some of the important settled but moving shepherd camps or tent-villages, on the southern side of the Kailas Range: 1. Nonokur (25 tents) in Nimapendi valley, 2. Harkong (20?), 3. Chhomokur (25?), 4. Hor-Toma (25?), near Thokchhen, 5. Kongyu tso (30?), 6. Hor-Toshar (30), 7. Toshar (30), east of Tamlung tso, 8. Hor-Pangriya (30?), near about Ponri Gompa, 9. Kangjak (30?), near about Kuglung, 10. Shungba (25?), of Rakshas Tal, 11. Korpon (20?), of Tarchhen, 12. Hor-Gyeva (20?), 13. Chhujuthol (20?), near Chhakra, 14. Khyunglung (25?), near Gombachen, and 15. Missar (30?). The following are on the northern side of Kailas: 16. Diji (25), 17. Shungba-Majin (30?), 18. Songkora (25), 19. Seli-phuk (25?), 20. Rundara (25), 21. Gerke (25), 22. Bongba (30), and 23. Yagra (25?).

Every monastery can be counted as a village in as much as it has got a *pucca* building and some houses attached to it. To this list may be supplemented 1. Dongpu, 2. Geng-yul, 3. Dapa, 4. Mangnang, 5. Thuling, and 6. Chhabrang, which are situated in the Greater Manasa Khanda.

APPENDIX V

MONASTERIES OF MANASA KHANDA

1. Simbiling Gompa of Taklakot (170 monks), branch of Depung Gompa, *Gelukpa* ; 2. Khochar Gompa (30 monks), branch of Nor or Nur Gompa, *Sakyapa* ; 3. Siddi-khar Gompa (5), branch of Simbiling, *Sakyapa* ; 4. Gomba-kong (10), branch of Sakya Gompa, situated adjacent to Simbiling ; 5. Gukung Gompa (3), branch of Gengta Gompa, *Dekungpa* ; 6. Kangje Gompa (7), branch of Sang-chang-chhup-ling Gompa, *Dukpa* ; 7. Kirong-trama, 8. Thiti-trama, 9. Toyo-trama, all these there belong to Simbiling and are meant only for seasonal stay and are not full-fledged gompas ; 10. Gossul Gompa (3), branch of Simbiling, 11. Chiu (5), branch of Dira-phuk, 12. Cherkip (1), belongs to Tarchhen Labrang, 13. Langpona (6), branch of Hemmis Gompa of Ladakh, *Sakyapa* (?), 14. Ponri (6), branch of Sera Gompa, *Dukpa*, 15. Seralung (20), branch of Dekung, *Dekungpa*, 16. Yerngo (6), branch of Sakya Gompa, *Sakyapa*, 17. Thugolho (8), branch of Simbiling, these eight are Manas monasteries ; 18. Nyanri Gompa (5), belongs to Tarchhen Labrang, *Ngingmapa* (?), 19. Dira-phuk (6), branch of Dadingbochhe Gompa, *Kadampa*, 20. Zuthul-phuk (3), belongs to Tarchhen Labrang, 21. Gengta (6), branch of Dekung Gompa, *Dekungpa*, 22. Silung (2), under Gengta, all these five are Kailas monasteries ; 23. Chepgye, at present branch of Mangshang Gompa, but the site of the monastery belongs to Gengta Gompa ; so Chepgye pays a nominal tribute to Gengta by way of rent, 24. Kardung, branch of Mangshang Gompa, 25. Mangshang Gompa, these three gompas belong to an independent group called *Jokchhin* Sect, much akin to *Ngingmapa* ; there are about 50 monks and as many nuns in all these three monasteries combined ; 26. Thunsa (3), branch of Simbiling Gompa, one day's march north of Thockchen ; 27. Seliphuk (15), branch of Depung, *Gelukpa* ; 28. Dulchu (24), branch of Sera Gompa ; 29. Tirthapuri (15), it was once a branch of Hemmis Gompa but since 1945 it is under Simbiling Gompa ; 30. Khyunglung (10), branch of Sera Gompa, *Dukpa* ; 31. Gurugem (20) independent, the founder-lama originally belonged to *Bon* Sect but now he professes *Gelukpa* sect ; 32. Gartok (10), probably branch of Depung Gompa ; 33. One Nunnery, adjacent to Purang Zong's fort, affiliated to Gombakong (15 nuns) ; 34. one Nunnery at Toyo affiliated to Simbiling Gompa (15 nuns) ; and 35. one Nunnery at Guru-gem, attached to the monastery (30). Besides these there are five more monasteries in the Greater Manas Khanda : 1. Dongpu (15 monks ?) ; 2. Dapa (15) ; 3. Mangnang (5), branch of Depung ; 4. Thuling (20), branch of Sera Gompa ; and 5. Chhabrang Gompa (15), branch of Sera Gompa.

APPENDIX VI

AVIFAUNA OF KAILAS-MANASA KHANDA[1]

1. Tibetan Raven (Corvus corax tibetanus Hodgs), 2. Yellow-billed Chough (Pyrrhocorax gratculus), 3. Red-billed Chough (Pyrrhocorax pyrrhocorax), 4. Hume's Ground Chough (Pseudopodoces humilis Hume), 5. Rock Nuthatch (Sitta neumayer), 6. Wall Creeper (Tichodroma muraria), 7. Brown Dipper (Cinclus pallasii), 8. White-breasted Dipper (Cinclus cinclus), 9. Collared Bush Chat (Saxicola torquata), 10. Tibetan Desert Chat (Œnanthe deserti), 11. Eastern Indian Redstart (Phoenicurus ochruros), 12. Rubythroat (Calliope pectoralis), 13. Blue Rock Thrush (Monticola solitaria), 14. Robin Hedge Sparrow (Prunella rubeculoides), 15. Garhwal Hedge-Sparrow (Laiscopus collaris whymperi), 16. Tickell's Willow Warbler (Phylloscopus affinis), 17. Rosy Pastor (Pastor roseus), 18. Great Rose-Finch (Carpodacus rubicilla), 19. Red-breasted Rose-Finch (Pyrrhospiza punicea), 20. Pink-browed Rose-Finch (Propasser rhodochrous), 21. Goldfinch (Carduelis caniceps), 22. Twite (Acanthis flavirostris), 23. Gold-fronted Finch (Metaponia pusilla), 24. House-Sparrow (Passer domesticus), 25. Tree Sparrow (Passer montanus), 26. Tibetan Mountain Finch (Fringillauda brandti haematopyga), 27. Tibet Snow-Finch (Montifringilla nivalis adamsi), 28. Red-necked Snow-Finch (Montifringilla ruficollis,) 29. Blanford's Snow-Finch (Montifringilla blanfordi), 30. House Martin (Martula dasypus), 31. Sand Martin (Riparia riparia), 32. Crag Martin (Riparia rupestris), 33. Hodgson's Pied Wagtail (Motacilla alba alboides), 34. Yellow-headed Wagtail (Motacilla citreola), 35. Elwes's Horned Lark (Eremophila alpestris elwesi), 36. Long-billed Calandra Lark (Melanocorypha maxima), 37. Tibetan Skylark (Alauda gulgula lhamarum), 38. Rufous Short-toed Lark (Calandrella brachydactyla dukhunensis), 39. Short-toed Lark (Calandrella Acutirostris), 40. Hoopoe (Upupa epops), 41. Swift (Micropus apus), 42. Horned Owl (Bubo bubo), 43. Little Owl (Athene noctua), 44. Himalayan Griffon Vulture (Gyps himalayensis), 45. Lammergeler or Bearded Vulture (Gypaetus barbatus), 46. Kestrel (Falco tinnunculus), 47. Cherrug Falcon (Falco cherrug), 48. Eagle (Aquilla rapax), 49. Tawny Eagle (Aquilla rapax), 50. Pallas's Fishing Eagle (Haliaetus leucoryphus), 51. Buzzard (Buteo), 52. Turkestan Hill Pigeon (Columba rupestris turkestanica), 53. Snow

1 The author is grateful to Mr. Salim Ali, the well-known Indian Ornithologist of Bombay, for having kindly allowed him to reproduce the list of birds of this Region, which he had observed between June 8 and July 8, 1945 when he was on an ornithological pilgrimage to this Region. Those who are interested in the subject may refer to the Journal of the Bombay Natural History Society', Vol. 46, No. 2, August 1946.

Pigeon (Columba leuconota 54. Tibetan Sandgrouse (Syrrhaptes tibetanus), 55. Chakor (Alectoris graeca chukar), 56. Snow Cock (Tetraogallus), 57. Black-necked Crane (Grus nigricollis), 58. Brown-headed Gull (Larus brunnicephalus), 59. Tibetan Tern (Sterna hirundo tibetana), 60. Oystercatcher (Haematopus ostralegus), 61. Pamirs Lesser Sand-Plover (Charadrius mongolus), 62. Curlew (Numenius arquata), 63. Green Sandpiper (Tringa ochropus), 64. Redshank (Tringa totanus), 65. Temminck's Stint (Erolia temminckii), 66. Bar-headed Goose (Anser indicus) 67. Gadwall (Anas acuta), 68. Pintail (Anas strepera), 69. Brahminy Duck (Casarca ferruginea), 70. Goosander (Mergus merganser), 71. Great Crested Grebe (Podiceps cristatus).

APPENDIX VII

REPORT ON FOSSILS

As the book is in the press, the author gave some of the fossils he had collected to Mr. P. N. Mukherjee, Palæontologist, Geological Survey of India, for identification. The following is the provisional identification of the specimens, since some of them have been misplaced while in the Geological Survey Office. The author is thankful to Mr. P. N. Mukherjee for the report.

No.	Name	Locality	Age
1.	Kellawaysites greppini (A septate fragment)	Mangshang (Tibetan side of Kuti)	Already recorded from the Jurassic of Kachh.
2.	Indet. Ammonite fragment	,,	(?) Jurassic
3.	Indet. Ammonite	,,	may be Jurassic
4.	Belemnites cf. gerardi	Anura (South of Manas)	Recorded from the Jurassic of spiti.
5.	Perisphinctes sp.	Tinker - Lipu Lekh	Jurassic
6.	Orthoceras sp. (fragments)	Kuti	,,
7.	Rhynchonella sp.	Bongza Range (Central Tibet)	,,
8.	Fragments of Indet. Amonities etc.	Sumnath (Tibetan side of Kungri-bingri pass)	,,
9.	(?) Orthoceras in a rolled nodule	Tso Kapala (Southern foot of Kailas Peak)	,,
10.	Fragmentary Ammonites	Puling (Tibetan side of Gangotri)	(?) ,,
11.	Indet. nodules	Damodar-Kund	Unknown
12.	Indet. Amonites in nodules and pebbles	,,	(?) Jurassic
13.	Bactrites sp.	,,	Devonian
14.	A doubtful Coral	Tso Kapala	Unknown
15.	Fossilised bone of a Bovid	Tsepgye (west coast of Rakshas Tal)	Pleistocene

The general faunal assemblage of fossils identified under items 1. to 12. indicates a Jurassic age approximating to 130 million years.

The fossil specimen under item 13. indicates a Devonian age approximating to about 300 million years.

The last specimen under item 15. indicates a Pleistocene age approximating to one million years.

APPENDIX VIII

REV. SWAMI PRANAVANANDA, F.R.G.S,

(Of the Holy Kailas and Manasarovar).

A SKETCH OF HIS LIFE AND WORK[1]

Rev. Swami Pranavananda hails from East Godavari District in Andhra Desa and was born in 1896. His household name was Kanakadandi Venkata Somayajulu. He graduated from the D. A. V. College, Lahore, in the year 1919. For a short period he served in the Railway Accountant's Office, Lahore, but resigned the post and joined the Non-co-operation movement. The spirit of love and service has been the heritage from his parents. From 1920-26, he was an active Congress worker in West Godavari District. Then he had a call from the heights of the Himalayas in consequence of an internal urge for search after Truth. Accordingly, he was initiated into the Holy Order by the great Acharya Shree 108 Swami Jnananandaji Maharaj.

Dr. Jnanananda, after attaining Realization, took to Scientific Research with the aid of his intuitional knowledge. He had conducted experimental research for wellnigh 15 years on the Continent in different Physical Laboratories at Dresden, Berlin, Prague, Liverpool, Ann Arbor (Michigan) and other places, in Spectroscopy of X-Radiations, β-rays, Magnetic Electron Lenses, Isotopes, Nuclear Physics, Higher Vacua, and allied subjects; and he is at present taking part in the National Physical Laboratory, Delhi, as the Senior Scientific Officer. It is from this great Swami-Scientist that our Revered Swami Pranavananda derived his inspiration for search after and Truth for things Scientific.

Shree Swamiji has extensively travelled in the Himalayas for wellnigh 23 years in connection with his Spiritual *Sadhana.* During this period he has had occasion to study the Geography and Topography of several regions therein. He lived in Gangotri for full one year (1934-35), even after the temple-gates were closed for winter and visited Gaumukh, the glacial source of the Ganges, several times.

The Swami visited Kailas and Manasarovar for the first time in the year 1928 via Kashmir-Srinagar, Ladakh, and Gartok. Since then he has been visiting Kailas-Manasarovar Region every year mainly for his Spiritual practices; and he usually lives there for about six months

1 Taken from the 'Indian Geographical Journal', but the information has been brought up-to-date by the Publishers.

in the year, but carries on research work also in different branches of science, such as Geography, Geology, Botany, Zoology, Archaeology, etc., as a hobby during his leisure hours. He visited this Region by various routes in different seasons of the year.

The Swami spent a whole year in 1936-37 and a full sixteen-month in 1943-44 as an inmate of the Thugolho Monastery, on the southern shores of the Holy Lake Manasarovar, a rare privilege, never before accorded to a non-Buddhist monk, as we learn from Mr. Paul Brunton's book 'A Hermit in the Himalayas'. The minimum temperature during his stay in winter was 50.5°F. below freezing-point. During his stay at Manasarovar the Swami recorded how the Manas and Rakshas lakes froze in the beginning of winter, what changes ensued after freezing, and how the lakes thawed in spring. Thus he made a comparative study of the characteristic features of the sister-lakes. When the Ravan Hrad was frozen in winter, he went over the lake on ice and made a rough survey of the two islands in it. He is the first non-Tibetan to land on these two islands. Rev. Swami Pranavananda's competency for the task is unique. He has the simplicity and bravery, the fortitude and endurance of the best of the *sanyasis*; he has the inquisitiveness and fidelity to truth of the scientist; he is not dogmatic; he is keenly observant; records his observations carefully; and gathers them up with a view to making them available to people at large; above all he has the tenacity of the bulldog to do the work he takes up in hand. Up till now the Swami has completed 23 circumambulations of the Mount Kailas and 25 of the pre-historic Lake Manas.

Our Swami is very well-known in the Kailas-Manasarovar Region and other parts of Western Tibet and is loved deeply by officials, monks, and people in general, since he carries a 'Free Travelling Dispensary' and renders medical aid to the rich and the poor alike. He is known there as '*Gyagar Lama Guru*' (Indian Lama Guru), '*Thugu Rinpochhe*' (His Holiness of Thugolho Monastery), and '*Gyagar Amji*' (Indian Doctor). With the aid of the Governor of Purang-Taklakot and the Viceroys of Gartok (Western Tibet), he visited the real sources of the four Great Rivers of the Holy Kailas and Manasarovar, namely the Brahmaputra, the Indus, the Sutlej, and the Karnali. As a result of his several explorations and Geographical researches, the Swami has exploded the findings of Dr. Sven Hedin, the Swedish explorer, regarding the sources of the four rivers of the Holy Kailas and Manasarovar and has fixed the sources of these rivers from different criteria, namely tradition, length, quantity of water, and glaciers, after actually visiting these places. This has evoked great sensation among the Himalayan Geographers all the world over, since this very valuable contribution of the Swami has reopened a question supposed to have been settled by Dr. Sven Hedin as far back as 1908. It will not be out of place here to make a mention that "the very valuable contribution which the Swami has made to the Geographical knowledge of the Kailas Region", has been very much appreciated by the Surveyor-General of India. The Swami's findings have been accepted by the Royal Geographical Society, London and the Survey of India Office which have incorporated them in their maps of 1941 and 1945.—Hind 5000 Sheet N.H—44 and 62 F.

Though he does not profess to have the technical knowledge of a trained Geographer, the results he has achieved and the spirit of minute observation and searching enquiry displayed in his work are really commendable. One cannot but be convinced by the remarkably logical and lucid arguments with which the findings of Dr. Sven Hedin are challenged and disproved. He has exhibited to the world how Indians do not lag behind others in the spirit of adventure and exploration. The Swami is the first of the living Indian explorers, and has vindicated by his researches Indians' claim to original work of the kind. We trust that his work would inspire many an Indian youth to undertake travels of adventure and exploration. 'The Daily Telegraph' of London writes of him as "the distinguished Indian Sanyasi-Explorer and Scientist".

Some of the papers of the Swami have been published in the Journal of the Royal Geographical Society, London, Calcutta Geographical Review, The Indian Geographical Journal, and several leading Newspapers of India. He contributes papers to the Indian Science Congress as well. Two of his lectures delivered at the University of Calcutta have been published by the University in a book-form entitled 'Exploration in Tibet', which elicited the appreciation of several eminent Geographers like Dr. Longstaff, Dr. Somerwell of the Everest Expedition, Mr. Wadia and others. A thoroughly revised and enlarged second edition of this book is being brought out by the University of Calcutta. This book has been prescribed as one of the text-books for the M. A. and M. Sc. Examinations in Geography, since the year 1942. He also wrote the book 'Pilgrim's Companion to the Holy Kailas and Manasarovar', a review of which was published in Vol. XVII, No. 1 of this Journal ; this has now been developed into the present Volume 'Kailas-Manasarovar'. Besides these two books, the Swami has written an exhaustive work in Hindi in four parts, *Kailas-Manasarovar'*, covering about 450 pages, the counterpart of which is awaiting publication in Gujrati, Bengali, Marathi, Telugu, Tamil, and Kanarese. The Swami has written an elaborate commentary of over 1000 pages on Srimad Bhagavad Gita in Telugu, which is awaiting publication. He has also written a few pamphlets on spiritual subjects.

In 1946, the Swami has taken a three-seater light rubber boat 'JANMA-BHOOMI' and sounded the Gouri-kund, the highest lake (18,400 feet above the sea-level) ever sounded so far, This is a unique feature in the annals of the Gouri-kund, for it was completely cleared of ice for the first time in its history. Before concluding his trips to Kailas Region the Swami wants to sink his lead in the Manas lakes and definitely locate the thermal springs situated in their bed and to reach the centre of the Lake which is considered inaccessible by Tibetans and which has not been reached by any one hitherto. To achieve this end he had bought, in1942, an up-to-date four-seater full length 18-gauge galvanized-steel sailing-dinghy 'JNAN NAUKA', weighing 440 lbs., with sailing equipment and airtight chambers fore and oft, to make it unsinkable. He had taken this 'JNAN NAUKA' to Manasarovar in August last and launched it in the Lake and took a few tentative soundings. He has taken an outboard motor during the summer of 1948 to complete his work. This will indeed be a unique incident in the history of the Sacred Lake. After the exploration work is completed the Swami has no intention of bringing the boat back to India, but wants to hand it over to the Darma Seva Sangha for the benefit of future pilgrims and tourists.

In October 1942, the Swami did a close and complete circumambulation of the Ravan Hrad (Rakshas Tal) for which he had been planning for a decade. He ascertained the actual circumference of the lake and the number of islands in it; traced the source of the Sutlej by examining the so-called 'Old Bed of the Sutlej', noted the flow of the water in the Ganga Chuu from July to October and collected a few geological specimens. He also reached the perpendicular wall of the northern and southern bases of the Kailas Peak for the third time and crossed all alone for the second time the Khando-sanglam la, a pass with deceptive crevasses, on the eastern side of the mount, which was neither known to nor crossed by any non-Tibetan up till now. He crossed the pass for the first time in July 1941. Besides the Khando-sanglam la, he had negotiated three more new passes, namely Charok-phurdod la (in 1937, 1942, and 1946), Topchhen la, and Lhe la, all above 18,000 feet high (in 1937).

In 1942, the Swami collected a fourteen-pound marine fossil-bed from the Tso Kapala, which is the first find of fossils from Kailas Range. It has been examined by the Geological Survey of India Office and was found to belong to the Mesozoic age (19 crore-year old). In 1945, the Swami reached the northern and southern perpendicular walls of the Kailas Peak and brought some specimens of the rock. He also brought some marine fossils from the Ganga Chhu and specimens of serpentine (*Zaharmora*) from the south-eastern side of Kailas. In 1946, he visited the deserted Cave-Colony of Pangtha and he now proposes to lead a small Archaeological Expedition to this Colony once again, to take some photos of the fresco paintings and collect from the caves all materials that may be of interest. In 1947, he collected 99 fossils from Bongza Range in Central Tibet, and some more marine fossils and bone fossils from different parts of the Manas Region. He also collected from this Region a few implements of the stone-age. He brought to the notice of the Geog aphers several hot springs which might, with great advantage, be tested for Radio-activity and radon content. He did a full round of the Mandhata Range in October 1948 and found that the boundary of Nepal adjoining the Manasa Khanda, as given in Survey Maps, is erroneous.

It may be mentioned that there is no lotus or lily in Manasarovar. So, far the last few years, the Swami has been making experiments to culture lotus, lily, *singhada* (water-chest nut), and *makhana*, in the Manas Lakes. It is yet to be seen how far he would be successful in his experiments, but all the same it is a novel idea worthy of praise and worth the trouble. The Swami, being an Ayurvedic Physician himself, has discovered a wonderful aphrodisiac drug in the Manas Region which, it is said, is not to be found in other parts of the Himalayas. We understand that the drug is being sent for analysis and confirmation of the properties attributed to it. A description of the drug is given in page 46 of this book.

The Swami has been carrying on research on 'Musk and Musk-deer' for over twelve years which he hopes to complete in a year after a systematic Histological and Cytological study of the animal by bringing a live animal to a laboratory in the plains. It may be remembered that the Swami has read a paper on 'Musk and Musk-deer' (though not concluded) in the Medical and Veterinary Section of the Science Congress held in Baroda, and in the Universities of Benares, Lucknow, Patna, and Calcutta and Lahore Ayurvedic Conference. Every year he does some exploration or research work in some branch of Science or other in his own humble way. It is really a matter of pity that none of our Universities utilize the experience and services of such a brilliant explorer and scientist like our Swami. Yet the Swami, unmindful of any help does his work for work's sake, in the spirit of a true *Karma Yogi*.

Our Swami is not only a full-fledged Spiritual *Sadhaka*, Explorer, and a Scientist but also a bit of a Historian. He has collected a good deal of material regarding the Kashmiri General Zoravar Singh, who was killed in an engagement with the Tibetans in Manasarovar Region in 1841 and whose death centenary was celebrated at Taklakot by the Darma Seva Sangha, in which the Swami gave a learned talk. We learn from one of his friends, Mr. Paul Brunton, that he is well up both in Hatha and Raja Yoga and that he carried on a systematic research in the famous *Khechari Mudra*.

The Swami has made a good collection of Tibetan curios for his 'Kailas-Manasarovar Museum', which we understand, the Provincial Museum, Lucknow, has acquired. The Swami has done a great service to the cause of Archæology by surveying and getting a full and first-hand detailed account and a plan of the 'Barari Caves' near Bhagalpur (Bihar) published in the 'Journal of the Bihar Research Society', Vol. XXXIV, Parts I & II, 1948. The Caves are considered to be of pre-Buddhistic period though they were later used by Buddhist monks. A mention of these caves was made by the Chinese pilgrim Huen Tsang (A.D. 635). He had also thrown some new light regarding the real site of the famous Buddhist Royal University of Vikramashila. It may be remembered in this connection that the site of Vikramashila has not been identified so far. The attention of the Government of Bihar is drawn to these new archæological finds.

The Swami has got constructed a YAJNA VEDI on the shore of the Manas at Thugolho, where the Birthday of Lord Shree Krishna is celebrated every year. Besides, he has been trying for the last several years to construct Rest Houses on the shores of the Holy Lake and at Kailas.

It is no small surprise that a Swami who repaired to the Himalayas chiefly for spiritual practices, besides being inspired by the mystic grandeur of the holy places, could still find leisure and inclination to study the Aesthetics, Geography, etc., of the same and also render a faithful and minute account of the whole, for the benefit of Humanity. We fully wish and hope that Shree Swamiji will continue to enlighten the outside world on the many other Himalayan Problems awaiting solution and combine scientific pursuit with Spiritual *Sadhana*, as in fact like our ancient *Rishis*, he has striven to do so far with such wonderful results. Mr. D. N. Wadia, formerly of the Geological Survey of India and President of the Indian Science Congress of Baroda, writes in 'Current Science' thus, "Sincere thanks and congratulations of all Geographers and of Indian Naturalists in particular are due to the Rev. Swami Pranavananda for publishing results of valuable explorations conducted by him during his pilgrimages in the Region of Mount Kailas and Manasarovar in Western Tibet".

"As a mark of appreciation and recognition of his excellent achievements, explorations, and other scientific researches," the Indian Geographical Society has elected the Revered Swami Pranavananda as an Honorary Life Member.

OM !